Contents

W9-CCD-202

Maps

How This Guide Will Save You Money

If you're one of the rock-bottom-budget travelers who sleep on park benches to save money and would never, ever dress up for duck à l'orange at Jean-Louis, then look to another guidebook for your travel information.

But if you're among those who budget some of the finer things into their traveling life, if you would stay home before spending a night in a hostel dormitory with strangers, and if you're willing to pay a little more for crisp sheets, a firm bed, a soft pillow, and a really superb dining experience every now and again, read on. It's for you that Fodor's team of savvy, budget-conscious writers and editors have prepared this book.

We share your traveling style and your champagne tastes, and we know that saving money is all about making choices. Some of us do it by sticking to public transportation and picnic lunches. Others spend more on a hotel with amenities but don't care about fancy meals. Still others take the hostel route in order to go on a shopping spree.

In this guide, we've tried to include enough options so that all of you spend time and money in the ways you most enjoy. The hotels we suggest are good values, and there are no dives, thank you—only clean, friendly places with an acceptable level of comfort, convenience, and charm. We also recommend a range of inexpensive and moderately priced restaurants where you can eat well in pleasant surroundings. You'll read about the best budget shopping and how to make the arts-and-nightlife scene without breaking the bank. And we'll tell you how to get around inexpensively by public transportation.

As for planning what to see and do, you'll find the same lively writing and authoritative background information available in Fodor's renowned Gold Guides.

Please Write to Us

Everyone who has contributed to *Affordable London* has worked hard to make the text accurate. All prices and opening times are based on material supplied to us at press time, and Fodor's cannot accept responsiblity for any errors that may have occurred. The passage of time always brings changes, so it's a good idea to call ahead to confirm information when it matters—particularly if you're making a detour to visit specific sights or attractions. When making reservations at a hotel or inn, be sure to mention if you have a disability or are traveling with children, if you prefer a private bath or a certain type of bed, or if you have specific dietary needs or any other concerns.

Do let us know about your trip. Did you enjoy the restaurants we recommended? Was your hotel comfortable and were the museums you visited worthwhile? Did you happen upon a treasure that we haven't included? We would love to have your feedback, positive and negative. If you have suggestions or complaints, we'll look into them and revise our entries when it's the right thing to do. So please send us a letter or postcard (we're at 201 East 50th Street, New York,

New York 10022). We look forward to hearing from you. In the meantime, have a wonderful trip!

Karen Cure
Editorial Director

Fodor's Choice for Budget Travelers

No two people will agree on what makes a perfect vacation, but it's fun and helpful to know what others think. We hope you'll have a chance to experience some of Fodor's Choices yourself while visiting London. For detailed information about each entry, refer to the appropriate chapters within this guidebook.

Views

From Waterloo Bridge at dusk, across to St. Paul's

The city seen from Parliament Hill Fields on a bright day

Down the Mall to Buckingham Palace, from underneath Admiralty Arch

The towers of Whitehall seen from St. James's Park, especially when lit up on a summer's night

Greenwich Royal Naval Hospital, viewed from Island Gardens, across the Thames

The floodlit Houses of Parliament, seen across the river from St. Thomas's Hospital

Tower Bridge, floodlit, which confronts you as you come out of the Design Museum on a winter's night

Walks

Across Kensington Gardens, Hyde Park, and St. James's Park—from Kensington Palace to the Horse Guards

Across Regent's Park at sunset, east (Cumberland Terrace) to west (the Mosque), pausing in summer to watch (or play) softball

Along the South Bank of the Thames, from Lambeth Palace to Blackfriars Bridge

Up-river from Chiswick Mall to Hammersmith Bridge

Across Hampstead Heath, from Hampstead Village to Kenwood

Gardens

Queen Mary's Rose Garden, Regent's Park, in early summer

The Little Cloisters of Westminster Abbey

The formal gardens of the Dutch House, at Kew

The Knot Garden at Hampton Court, and the spring tulips in the main gardens there

The Chelsea Physic Garden

Monuments

The Duke of Wellington's funeral car in St. Paul's

Physical Energy in Kensington Gardens

The Elgin Marbles in the British Museum

The monument to the Great Fire of London

The statue of Winston Churchill in Parliament Square

Free Museums and Galleries

The British Museum, Bloomsbury

The National Gallery, Trafalgar Square

Sir John Soane's Museum, Lincoln's Inn Fields

Serpentine Gallery, Kensington Gardens

The Tate Gallery, Millbank

Wallace Collection, Manchester Square

Free Activities

The buskers around Covent Garden

Foyer performances at the South Bank Arts Complex

Petticoat Lane, early Sunday morning

Softball in Regent's Park

Summer concerts at the lake, Kenwood House, Hampstead

Shopping

Saturday in the Portobello Road Market

The January sale at Harrods

Wandering round the Covent Garden area

Secondhand book trawling on Charing Cross Road

Hotels

Bulldog Club, Knightsbridge and elsewhere (*Moderate*)

Commodore, Bayswater (*Moderate*)

Fielding, Covent Garden (*Moderate*)

Hazlitt's, Soho (*Moderate*)

La Reserve, Fulham (*Moderate*)

London Elizabeth, Bayswater (*Moderate*)

Hotel 167, Knightsbridge (*Inexpensive*)

Swiss House Hotel, Knightsbridge (*Inexpensive*)

Vicarage, Kensington (*Inexpensive*)

Gate Hotel, Notting Hill Gate (*Budget*)

Restaurants

Bistrot Bruno, Soho (*Moderate;* French)

Criterion, Mayfair (*Moderate;* Modern British)

dell'Ugo, Soho (*Moderate;* Mediterranean)

St. John, City (*Moderate;* Modern British)

Wodka, Kensington (*Moderate;* Polish)

Melati, Soho (*Inexpensive;* Malaysian)

The Place Below, The City (*Inexpensive;* Vegetarian)

Wagamama, Bloomsbury (*Inexpensive;* Japanese)

Food for Thought, Covent Garden (*Budget;* Vegetarian)

Pubs

Black Friar

The Lamb

Lamb and Flag, Covent Garden

Prospect of Whitby (by the river)

Eating and People-watching

Quaglino's, St. James's (*Expensive;* Modern British)

L'Artiste Musclé, Mayfair (*Inexpensive;* French)

Bar Gansa, Camden Town (*Budget;* Spanish)

Bar Italia, Soho (*Budget;* Italian), after midnight

Lamb and Flag, Covent Garden (pub), lunchtime

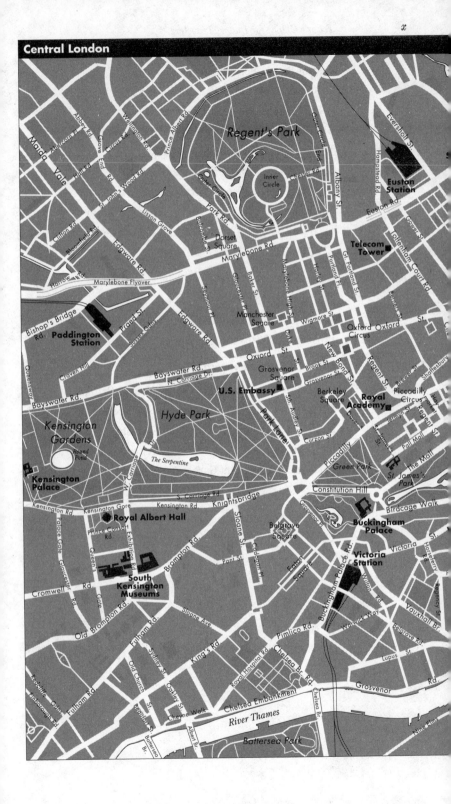

Central London

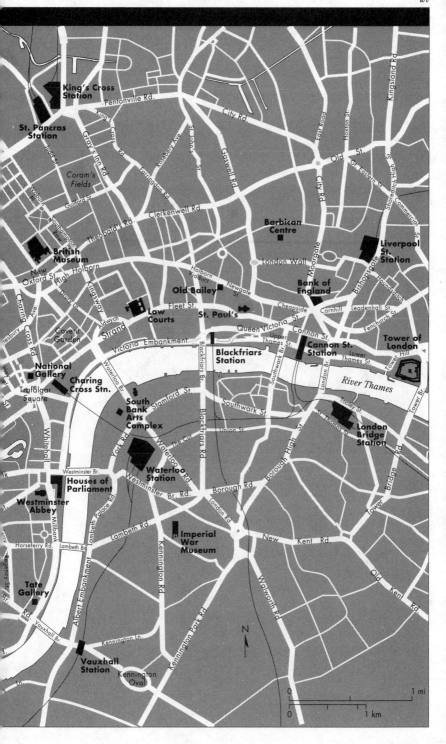

1 Affordable London: The Basics

IMPORTANT CONTACTS
A TO Z

No single travel resource can give you every detail about every topic that might interest or concern you at the various stages of your journey—when you're planning your trip, while you're on the road, and after you get back home. The following organizations, books, and brochures will supplement the information in *Fodor's Affordable London.* For related information, including both basic tips on visiting London and background information on many of the topics below, study Smart Budget Travel Tips A to Z, the section that follows Important Contacts A to Z.

A

Air Travel   The major gateways to London are Heathrow and Gatwick. Flying time is 6½ hours from New York, 7½ hours from Chicago, and 10 hours from Los Angeles.

Carriers   Carriers serving London include **American Airlines** (tel. 800/433–7300); **British Airways** (tel. 800/247–9297); **Continental** (tel. 800/231–0856); **Delta** (tel. 800/241–4141); **Northwest Airlines** (tel. 800/447–4747); **TWA** (tel. 800/892–4141); **United** (tel. 800/241–6522); **USAir** (tel. 800/428–4322); and **Virgin Atlantic** (tel. 800/862–8621).

Complaints   To register complaints about charter and scheduled airlines, contact the U.S. Department of Transportation's **Office of Consumer Affairs** (400 7th St. NW, Washington, DC 20590, tel. 202/366–2220 or 800/322–7873).

Consolidators   Established consolidators selling to the public include **BET World Travel** (841 Blossom Hill Rd., Suite 212-C, San Jose, CA 95123, tel. 800/747–1476); **Council Charter** (205 E. 42nd St., New York, NY 10017, tel. 212/661–0311 or 800/800–8222); **Euram Tours** (1522 K St. NW, Suite 430, Washington DC, 20005, tel. 800/848–6789); **TFI Tours International** (34 W. 32nd St., New York, NY 10001, tel. 212/736–1140 or 800/745–8000); **Travac Tours and Charter** (989 6th Ave., 16th Floor, New York, NY 10018, tel. 212/563–3303 or 800/872–8800; 2601 E. Jefferson, Orlando, FL 32803, tel. 407/896–0014 or 800/872–8800); and **UniTravel** (Box 12485, St. Louis, MO 63132, tel. 314/569–0900 or 800/325–2222).

Publications   For general information about charter carriers, ask for the Office of Consumer Affairs' brochure **"Plane Talk: Public Charter Flights."** The Department of Transportation also publishes a 58-page booklet, **"Fly Rights"** ($1.75; Consumer Information Center, Dept. 133B, Pueblo, CO 81009).

For other tips and hints, consult the Consumers Union's monthly **"Consumer Reports Travel Letter"** ($39 a year; Box 53629, Boulder, CO 80322, tel. 800/234–1970) and the newsletter **"Travel Smart"** ($37 a year; 40 Beechdale Rd., Dobbs Ferry, NY 10522, tel. 800/327–3633); *The Official Frequent Flyer Guidebook,* by Randy Petersen ($14.99 plus $3 shipping; 4715-C Town Center Dr., Colorado Springs, CO 80916, tel. 719/597–8899 or 800/487–8893); *Airfare Secrets Exposed,* by Sharon Tyler and Matthew Wonder (Universal Information Publishing; $16.95 plus $3.75 shipping from Sandcastle Publishing, Box 3070-A, South Pasadena, CA 91031, tel. 213/255–3616 or 800/655–0053); and *202 Tips Even the Best Business Travelers May Not Know,* by Christopher McGinnis ($10 plus $3 shipping; Irwin Professional Publishing, 1333 Burr Ridge Pkwy., Burr Ridge, IL 60521, tel. 800/634–3966).

B

Better Business Bureau	For local contacts in the home town of a tour operator you may be considering, consult the **Council of Better Business Bureaus** (4200 Wilson Blvd., Arlington, VA 22203, tel. 703/276–0100).
Bicycling	**Go By Cycle** (9 Templeton Pl., SW5 9NB, tel. 0171/373–3657) rents (mostly) brand-new mountain bikes for rates starting around £12 per day; less for longer periods, with a £150 deposit (on a credit card, preferably) required. Between March and October, it's a good idea to reserve; they have around 100 bikes, but demand is heavy.
Bus Travel *Information*	For information on all London bus and tube times, fares, etc., call 0171/222–1234; the line is operated 24 hours.
Discount Passes	Travelcards (*see* Underground Travel, *below*) are good for both tube and bus.

C

Car Rental	Major car-rental companies represented in London include **Alamo** (tel. 800/327–9633, 0800/272-2000 in the U.K.); **Avis** (tel. 800/331–1084, 800/879–2847 in Canada); **Budget** (tel. 800/527–0700, 0800/181–181 in the U.K.); **Dollar** (known as Eurodollar outside North America, tel. 800/800–4000, 0181/952–6565 in the U.K.); **Hertz** (tel. 800/654–3001, 800/263–0600 in Canada, 0181/679–1799 in the U.K.); and **National** (sometimes known as Europcar InterRent outside North America; tel. 800/227–3876, 0181/950–5050 in the U.K.). Rates in London begin at $21 a day and $126 a week for an economy car. This does not include tax, which in London is 17.5% on car rentals.
	Some less expensive local rental firms are **Budget** (tel. 0800/181181 toll-free in the U.K.); **Economy** (tel. 0181/521–0641); **Express** (tel. 0171/722–3763); and **Practical** (tel. 0171/284–0199).
Rental Wholesalers	Contact **Auto Europe** (Box 7006, Portland, ME 04112, tel. 207/828–2525 or 800/223–5555); **Europe by Car** in New York City (write 1 Rockefeller Plaza, 10020; visit 14 W. 49th St.; or call 212/581–3040, 212/245–1713, or 800/223–1516) or Los Angeles (9000 Sunset Blvd., 90069, tel. 800/252–9401 or 213/272–0424 in CA); **Foremost Euro-Car** (5658 Sepulveda Blvd., Suite 201, Van Nuys, CA 91411, tel. 818/786–1960 or 800/272–3299); or the **Kemwel Group** (106 Calvert St., Harrison, NY 10528, tel. 914/835–5555 or 800/678–0678).
The Channel Tunnel	For information, contact **Le Shuttle** (tel. 01345/353535 in the U.K., 800/388–3876 in the U.S.), which transports cars, or **Eurostar** (tel. 0171/922–4486 in the U.K., 800/942–4866 in the U.S.), the high-speed train service between London (Waterloo) and Paris (Gare du Nord). Eurostar tickets are available in the United Kingdom through **InterCity Europe,** the international wing of BritRail (London Victoria Station, tel. 0171/834–2345 or 0171/828–8092 for credit-card bookings), and in the United States through **Rail Europe** (tel. 800/942–4866) and **BritRail Travel** (1500 Broadway, New York, NY 10036, tel. 800/677–8585).
Children and Travel *Baby-sitting*	Local agencies include **Nanny Service** (9 Paddington St., London W1M 3LA, tel. 0171/935–3515), **The Nanny Co. Ltd.** (168 Sloane St., London SW1X 9QF, tel. 0171/581–5454), and **Universal Aunts** (19 The Chase, London SW4 ONP, tel. 0171/738–8937).
Flying	Look into **"Flying with Baby"** ($5.95 plus $1 shipping; Third Street Press, Box 261250, Littleton, CO 80126, tel. 303/595–5959), cowritten by a flight attendant. **"Kids and Teens in Flight,"** free from the U.S. Department of Transportation's Office of Consumer Affairs, offers tips for children flying alone. Every two years the February issue of *Family Travel Times* (*see* Know-How, *below*) details children's services on three dozen airlines.

Games The gamemeister, Milton Bradley, has games to help keep little (and not so little) children from getting fidgety while riding in planes, trains, and automobiles. Try packing the *Travel Battleship* sea battle game ($7); *Travel Connect Four,* a vertical strategy game ($8); the *Travel Yahtzee* dice game ($6); the *Travel Trouble* dice and board game ($7); and the *Travel Guess Who* mystery game ($8).

Know-How *Family Travel Times,* published four times a year by Travel With Your Children (TWYCH, 45 W. 18th St., New York, NY 10011, tel. 212/206–0688; annual subscription $40), covers destinations, types of vacations, and modes of travel.

The *Family Travel Guides* catalogue ($1 postage; tel. 510/527–5849) lists about 200 books and articles on family travel. *Traveling with Children—And Enjoying It,* by Arlene K. Butler ($11.95 plus $3 shipping; Globe Pequot Press, Box 833, 6 Business Park Rd., Old Saybrook, CT 06475, tel. 203/395–0440, 800/243–0495, or 800/962–0973 in CT) helps plan your trip with children, from toddlers to teens. Also check *Take Your Baby and Go! A Guide for Traveling with Babies, Toddlers and Young Children,* by Sheri Andrews, Judy Bordeaux, and Vivian Vasquez ($5.95 plus $1.50 shipping; Bear Creek Publications, 2507 Minor Ave., Seattle, WA 98102, tel. 206/322–7604 or 800/326–6566). *Innocents Abroad: Traveling with Kids in Europe,* by Valerie Wolf Deutsch and Laura Sutherland ($15.95 or $4.95 paperback; Penguin USA, 120 Woodbine St., Bergenfield, NJ 07621, tel. 201/387–0600 or 800/253–6476), covers child- and teen-friendly activities, food, and transportation.

Local Information For information and advice when in London, call **Kidsline** (tel. 0171/222–8070).

The *Children's Guide to London,* by Christopher Pick (Cadogan Books, 16 Lower Marsh, London SE1 7RJ; £3.50), and *Kids' London,* by Elizabeth Holt and Molly Perham (St. Martin's Press, 175 5th Ave., New York, NY 10010; $5.95), cover the subject. Up-to-date information is available in *Capital Radio's London for Kids* magazine, available at newsstands (£1.50).

The booklet "Children's London" (available free from the London Tourist Board, Tourist Information Centre, Victoria Station Forecourt, London SW1V 1JT, tel. 0171/730–3488) gives a complete story.

Lodging Hotels that are noticeably family- and child-friendly include **Basil Street Hotel** (Basil St., Knightsbridge, London SW3 1AH, tel. 0171/581–3311), **Edward Lear** (28 Seymour St., London W1H 5WD, tel. 0171/402–5401), and **Forte Hotels** (tel. 0171/837–1200).

Tour Operators Contact **Grandtravel** (6900 Wisconsin Ave., Suite 706, Chevy Chase, MD 20815, tel. 301/986–0790 or 800/247–7651), which has tours for people traveling with grandchildren ages 7 to 17; **Families Welcome!** (21 W. Colony Pl., Suite 140, Durham, NC 27705, tel. 919/489–2555 or 800/326–0724); or **Rascals in Paradise** (650 5th St., Suite 505, San Francisco, CA 94107, tel. 415/978–9800 or 800/872–7225).

Customs U.S. Citizens The **U.S. Customs Service** (Box 7407, Washington, DC 20044, tel. 202/927–6724) can answer questions on duty-free limits and publishes a helpful brochure, "Know Before You Go." For information on registering foreign-made articles, call 202/927–0540.

Canadians Contact **Revenue Canada** (2265 St. Laurent Blvd. S, Ottawa, Ontario K1G 4K3, tel. 613/993–0534) for a copy of the free brochure **"I Declare/Je Déclare"** and for details on duties that exceed the standard duty-free limit.

D

For Travelers with Disabilities Complaints To register complaints under the provisions of the Americans with Disabilities Act, contact the U.S. Department of Justice's **Public Access Section** (Box 66738, Washington, DC 20035, tel. 202/514–0301, fax 202/307–1198, TTY 202/514–0383).

Organizations **For Travelers with Hearing Impairments.** Contact the **American Academy of Otolaryngology** (1 Prince St., Alexandria, VA 22314, tel. 703/836–4444, fax 703/683–5100, TTY 703/519–1585).

For Travelers with Mobility Problems. Contact the **Information Center for Individuals with Disabilities** (Fort Point Pl., 27–43 Wormwood St., Boston, MA 02210, tel. 617/727–5540, 800/462–5015 in MA, TTY 617/345–9743); **Mobility International USA** (Box 10767, Eugene, OR 97440, tel. and TTY 503/343–1284, fax 503/343–6812), the U.S. branch of an international organization based in Belgium (*see below*) that has affiliates in 30 countries; **MossRehab Hospital Travel Information Service** (1200 W. Tabor Rd., Philadelphia, PA 19141, tel. 215/456–9603, TTY 215/456–9602); the **Society for the Advancement of Travel for the Handicapped** (347 5th Ave., Suite 610, New York, NY 10016, tel. 212/447–7284, fax 212/725–8253); the **Travel Industry and Disabled Exchange** (TIDE, 5435 Donna Ave., Tarzana, CA 91356, tel. 818/344–3640, fax 818/344–0078); and **Travelin' Talk** (Box 3534, Clarksville, TN 37043, tel. 615/552–6670, fax 615/552–1182).

For Travelers with Vision Impairments. Contact the **American Council of the Blind** (1155 15th St. NW, Suite 720, Washington, DC 20005, tel. 202/467–5081, fax 202/467–5085) or the **American Foundation for the Blind** (15 W. 16th St., New York, NY 10011, tel. 212/620–2000, TTY 212/620–2158).

In the U.K. Contact the **Royal Association for Disability and Rehabilitation** (RADAR, 12 City Forum, 250 City Rd., London EC1V 8AF, tel. 0171/250–3222) or **Mobility International** (Rue de Manchester 25, B–1070 Brussels, Belgium, tel. 00–322–410–6297), an international clearinghouse of travel information for people with disabilities.

Also contact **London Transport's Unit for Disabled Passengers** (55 Broadway, London SW1H 0BD, tel. 0171/222–5600, Minicom 0171/918–3051) for details on **Stationlink**, a wheelchair-accessible "midibus" service as well as other access information. **Artsline** (tel. 0171/388–2227) provides information on accessibility of arts events. **Holiday Care Service** (2 Old Bank Chambers, Station Rd., Horley, Surrey RH6 9HW, tel. 0293/774535) can tell you about accommodations.

Publications Several free publications are available from the U.S. Information Center (Box 100, Pueblo, CO 81009, tel. 719/948–3334): **"New Horizons for the Air Traveler with a Disability"** (address to Dept. 355A), describing legally mandated changes; the pocket-size **"Fly Smart"** (Dept. 575B), good on flight safety; and the Airport Operators Council's worldwide **"Access Travel: Airports"** (Dept. 575A).

The 500-page *Travelin' Talk Directory* ($35; Box 3534, Clarksville, TN 37043, tel. 615/552–6670) lists people and organizations who help travelers with disabilities. For specialist travel agents worldwide, consult the *Directory of Travel Agencies for the Disabled* ($19.95 plus $2 shipping; Twin Peaks Press, Box 129, Vancouver, WA 98666, tel. 206/694–2462 or 800/637–2256).

Travel Agencies and Tour Operators The Americans with Disabilities Act requires that travel firms serve the needs of all travelers. However, some agencies and operators specialize in making group and individual arrangements for travelers with disabilities, among them **Access Adventures** (206 Chestnut Ridge Rd., Rochester, NY 14624, tel. 716/889–9096), run by a former physical-rehab counselor. In addition, many general-interest operators and agencies (*see* Tour Operators, *below*) can also arrange vacations for travelers with disabilities.

For Travelers with Mobility Impairments. A number of operators specialize in working with travelers with mobility impairments: **Flying Wheels Travel** (143 W. Bridge St., Box 382, Owatonna, MN 55060, tel. 507/451–5005 or 800/535–6790), a travel agency that specializes in European cruises and tours; **Hinsdale Travel Service** (201 E. Ogden Ave., Suite 100, Hinsdale, IL 60521, tel. 708/325–1335 or 800/303–5521), a travel agency that will give you access to the services of wheelchair traveler Janice Perkins; **Nautilus Tours** (5435 Donna Ave., Tarzana, CA 91356, tel. 818/344–3640 or 800/345–4654); and **Wheelchair Journeys** (16979 Redmond Way, Redmond, WA 98052, tel. 206/885–2210), which can handle arrangements worldwide.

For Travelers with Developmental Disabilities. Contact the nonprofit **New Directions** (5276 Hollister Ave., Suite 207, Santa Barbara, CA 93111, tel. 805/967–2841), as well as the general-interest operators above.

Discount Clubs Options include **Entertainment Travel Editions** (fee $28–$53, depending on destination; Box 1068, Trumbull, CT 06611, tel. 800/445–4137); **Great American Traveler** ($49.95 annually; Box 27965, Salt Lake City, UT 84127, tel. 800/548–2812); **Moment's Notice Discount Travel Club** ($25 annually, single or family; 163 Amsterdam Ave., Suite 137, New York, NY 10023, tel. 212/486–0500); **Privilege Card** ($74.95 annually; 3391 Peachtree Rd. NE, Suite 110, Atlanta, GA 30326, tel. 404/262–0222 or 800/236–9732); **Travelers Advantage** ($49 annually, single or family; CUC Travel Service, 49 Music Sq. W, Nashville, TN 37203, tel. 800/548–1116 or 800/648–4037); and **Worldwide Discount Travel Club** ($50 annually for family, $40 single; 1674 Meridian Ave., Miami Beach, FL 33139, tel. 305/534–2082).

Passes *See* Rail Travel *and* Underground Travel, *below.*

E

Electricity Send a self-addressed, stamped envelope to the **Franzus Company** (Customer Service, Dept. B50, Murtha Industrial Park, Box 142, Beacon Falls, CT 06403, tel. 203/723–6664) for a copy of the free brochure "Foreign Electricity Is No Deep Dark Secret."

Embassies and Consulates **U.S. Embassy** (24 Grosvenor Sq., W1A 1AE, tel. 0171/499–9000). Located inside the embassy is the American Aid Society, a charity set up to help Americans in distress. Dial the embassy number and ask for extension 570 or 571.

Canadian High Commission (McDonald Ho., 1 Grosvenor Sq., W1, tel. 0171/258–6600).

Emergencies For police, fire department, or ambulance, dial 999.

Hospitals The following hospitals have 24-hour emergency wards: **Charing Cross** (Fulham Place Rd., Hammersmith W6, tel. 0181/846–1234), **Royal Free** (Pond St., Hampstead, NW3, tel. 0171/794–0500), and **St. Thomas's** (Lambeth Palace Rd., SE1, tel. 0171/928–9292).

Pharmacies Chemists (drug stores) with late opening hours include **Bliss Chemist** (50–56 Willesden La., NW6, tel. 0171/624–8000; 5 Marble Arch, W1, tel. 0171/723–6116), open daily 9 AM–midnight, and **Boots** (439 Oxford St., W1, tel. 0171/409–2857), open Thursday 8:30–7.

G

Gay and Lesbian Travel Organizations The **International Gay Travel Association** (Box 4974, Key West, FL 33041, tel. 800/448–8550), a consortium of 800 businesses, can supply names of travel agents and tour operators.

Publications The premier international travel magazine for gays and lesbians is *Our World* ($35 for 10 issues; 1104 N. Nova Rd., Suite 251, Daytona Beach, FL 32117, tel. 904/441–5367). The 16-page monthly **"Out & About"** ($49 for 10 issues; tel. 212/645–6922 or 800/929–2268) covers gay-friendly resorts, hotels, cruise lines, and airlines.

Tour Operators Cruises and resort vacations are handled by **Toto Tours** (1326 W. Albion, Suite 3W, Chicago, IL 60626, tel. 312/274–8686 or 800/565–1241), which has group tours worldwide.

Travel Agencies The largest agencies serving gay travelers are **Advance Travel** (10700 Northwest Freeway, Suite 160, Houston, TX 77092, tel. 713/682–2002 or 800/695–0880); **Islanders/Kennedy Travel** (183 W. 10th St., New York, NY 10014, tel. 212/242–3222 or 800/988–1181); **Now Voyager** (4406 18th St., San Francisco, CA 94114, tel. 415/626–1169 or 800/255–6951); and **Yellowbrick Road** (1500 W. Balmoral Ave., Chicago, IL 60640, tel. 312/561–1800 or 800/642–2488). **Skylink Women's Travel** (746 Ashland Ave., Santa Monica, CA 90405, tel. 310/452–0506 or 800/225-5759) works with lesbians.

H

Health Issues Contact **International SOS Assistance** (Box 11568, Philadelphia, PA
Medical- 19116, tel. 215/244–1500 or 800/523–8930; Box 466, Pl. Bonaventure,
Assistance Montréal, Québec, H5A 1C1, tel. 514/874–7674 or 800/363–0263);
Companies **Medex Assistance Corporation** (Box 10623, Baltimore, MD 21285, tel. 410/296–2530 or 800/573–2029); **Near Travel Services** (Box 1339, Calumet City, IL 60409, tel. 708/868–6700 or 800/654–6700); and **Travel Assistance International** (1133 15th St. NW, Suite 400, Washington, DC 20005, tel. 202/331–1609 or 800/821–2828). Because these companies also sell death-and-dismemberment, trip-cancellation, and other insurance coverage, there is some overlap with the travel-insurance policies sold by the companies listed under Insurance, *below.*

I

Insurance Travel insurance covering baggage, health, and trip cancellation or interruptions is available from **Access America** (Box 90315, Richmond, VA 23286, tel. 804/285–3300 or 800/284–8300); **Carefree Travel Insurance** (Box 9366, 100 Garden City Plaza, Garden City, NY 11530, tel. 516/294–0220 or 800/323–3149); **Near Services** (Box 1339, Calumet City, IL 60409, tel. 708/868–6700 or 800/654–6700); **Tele-Trip** (Mutual of Omaha Plaza, Box 31716, Omaha, NE 68131, tel. 800/228–9792); **Travel Insured International** (Box 280568, East Hartford, CT 06128-0568, tel. 203/528–7663 or 800/243–3174); **Travel Guard International** (1145 Clark St., Stevens Point, WI 54481, tel. 715/345–0505 or 800/826–1300); and **Wallach & Company** (107 W. Federal St., Box 480, Middleburg, VA 22117, tel. 703/687–3166 or 800/237–6615).

L

Lodging Among the companies to contact are **At Home Abroad** (405 E. 56th
Apartment St., Suite 6H, New York, NY 10022, tel. 212/421–9165); **Europa-Let**
Rentals (92 N. Main St., Ashland, OR 97520, tel. 503/482–5806 or 800/462–4486); **Hometours International** (Box 11503, Knoxville, TN 37939, tel. 615/588–8722 or 800/367–4668); **Interhome** (124 Little Falls Rd., Fairfield, NJ 07004, tel. 201/882–6864); **Property Rentals International** (1008 Mansfield Crossing Rd., Richmond, VA 23236, tel. 804/378–6054 or 800/220–3332); **Rental Directories International** (2044 Rittenhouse Sq., Philadelphia, PA 19103, tel. 215/985–4001); **Rent-a-Home International** (7200 34th Ave. NW, Seattle, WA 98117, tel. 206/789–9377 or 800/488–7368); **Vacation Home Rentals Worldwide** (235 Kensington Ave., Norwood, NJ 07648, tel. 201/767–9393 or 800/

633–3284); and **Villas and Apartments Abroad** (420 Madison Ave., Suite 1105, New York, NY 10017, tel. 212/759–1025 or 800/433–3020). Members of the travel club **Hideaways International** ($99 annually; 767 Islington St., Portsmouth, NH 03801, tel. 603/430–4433 or 800/843–4433) receive two annual guides, plus quarterly newsletters, and arrange rentals among themselves.

Home   Principal clearinghouses include **Intervac International** ($65 annual-
Exchange   ly; Box 590504, San Francisco, CA 94159, tel. 415/435–3497), which has three annual directories; and **Loan-a-Home** ($35–$45 annually; 2 Park La., Apt. 6E, Mount Vernon, NY 10552-3443, tel. 914/664–7640), which specializes in long-term exchanges. For London-based companies, *see* Chapter 2, Where to Stay on a Budget.

M

Mail   The **Trafalgar Square Post Office** (24–28 William IV St., WC2N 4DL, tel. 0171/930–9580), the main office, is open Monday–Saturday 8–8. Most other post offices are open weekdays 9–5:30, Saturday 9–12:30 or 1.

Receiving Mail   Have mail from home addressed to you c/o Poste Restante, **Trafalgar Square Post Office** (*see above*). Hours are Monday–Saturday 8–8. The service is free and may be used for three months. You'll need your passport or some other form of identification to claim your mail. You can also collect letters at **American Express** (6 Haymarket, SW1Y 4BS, tel. 0171/930–4411, or any other branch). The service is free to cardholders; all others pay a small fee.

Money   For specific foreign **Cirrus** locations, call 800/424–7787; for foreign
ATMs   **Plus** locations, consult the **Plus** directory at your local bank.

Currency   If your bank doesn't exchange currency, contact **Thomas Cook Cur-**
Exchange   **rency Services** (41 E. 42nd St., New York, NY 10017; 511 Madison Ave., New York, NY 10022, tel. 212/757–6915 or 800/223–7373 for locations) or **Ruesch International** (tel. 800/424–2923 for locations).

Wiring Funds   Funds can be wired via **American Express MoneyGram**^{SM} (tel. 800/926–9400 from the U.S. and Canada for locations and information) or **Western Union** (tel. 800/325–6000 for agent locations or to send using MasterCard or Visa, 800/321–2923 in Canada).

P

Passports   For fees, documentation requirements, and other information, call
U.S. Citizens   the **Office of Passport Services** information line (tel. 202/647–0518).

Canadians   For fees, documentation requirements, and other information, call the Ministry of Foreign Affairs and International Trade's **Passport Office** (tel. 819/994–3500 or 800/567–6868).

Photo Help   The **Kodak Information Center** (tel. 800/242–2424) answers consumer questions about film and photography. The ***Kodak Guide to Shooting Great Travel Pictures*** explains techniques for getting the best shots (Fodor's Travel Publications, tel. 800/533–6478; $16.50).

R

Rail Travel   If you plan to travel a lot in Britain, you might consider purchasing a
Passes   **BritRail Pass,** which gives unlimited travel over the entire British Rail network.

The adult first-class pass costs $315 for 8 days, $515 for 15 days, $645 for 22 days, and $750 for 1 month. The adult second-class pass costs $230 for 8 days, $355 for 15 days, $445 for 22 days, and $520 for 1 month. Senior citizens can obtain a **Senior Citizen Pass,** which entitles the bearer to unlimited first-class travel. It costs $295 for 8 days, $479 for 15 days, $585 for 22 days, and $675 for 1 month. The

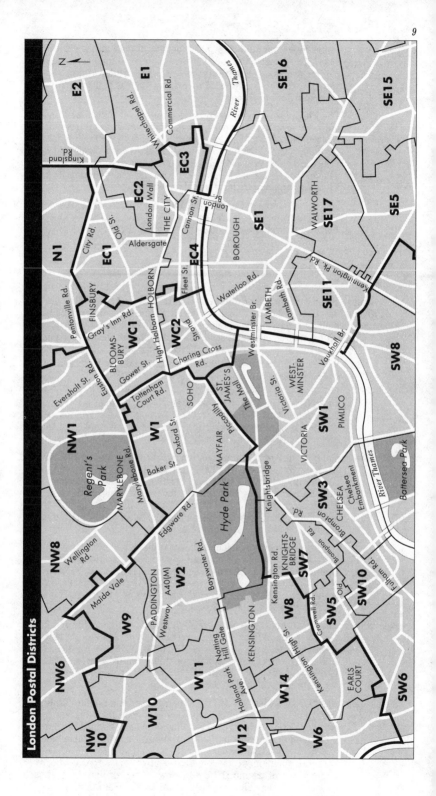

London Postal Districts

senior-citizen second-class pass costs $209 for 8 days, $320 for 15 days, $399 for 22 days, and $465 for 1 month. Young people (age 16–25) can purchase the **BritRail Youthpass,** which allows unlimited second-class travel. It costs $189 for 8 days, $280 for 15 days, $355 for 22 days, and $415 for 1 month.

The **Flexipass** offers a certain amount of travel within a one-month period; with a four-day pass, for example, you get four days' unlimited rail travel. The adult standard pass costs $195 for 4 days, $275 for 8 days, and $405 for 15 days. First-class costs $259 for 4 days, $399 for 8 days, and $540 for 15 days. Senior citizens and 16- to 25-year-olds get reduced rates. There's also a two-month Youth Flexipass offering 15 days' travel for $319.

You *must* purchase the **BritRail Pass** before you leave home. It is available from most travel agents throughout the world and from **BritRail Travel International** offices (1500 Broadway, New York, NY 10036, tel. 212/575–2667; 94 Cumberland St., Toronto, Ont. M5R 1A3, tel. 416/482–1777).

S

Senior Citizens Educational Travel
The nonprofit **Elderhostel** (75 Federal St., 3rd Floor, Boston, MA 02110, tel. 617/426–7788), for people 60 and older, has offered inexpensive study programs since 1975. The nearly 2,000 courses cover everything from marine science to Greek myths and cowboy poetry. Fees for two- to three-week international trips—including room, board, and transportation from the United States—range from $1,800 to $4,500.

For people 50 and over and their children and grandchildren, **Interhostel** (University of New Hampshire, 6 Garrison Ave., Durham, NH 03824, tel. 603/862–1147 or 800/733–9753) runs 10-day summer programs involving lectures, field trips, and sightseeing. Most last two weeks and cost $2,125–$3,100, including airfare.

Organizations Contact the **American Association of Retired Persons** (AARP, 601 E St. NW, Washington, DC 20049, tel. 202/434–2277; $8 per person or couple annually). Its Purchase Privilege Program gets members discounts on lodging, car rentals, and sightseeing, and the AARP Motoring Plan furnishes domestic trip-routing information and emergency road-service aid for an annual fee of $39.95 per person or couple ($59.95 for a premium version).

For other discounts on lodgings, car rentals, and other travel products, along with magazines and newsletters, contact the **National Council of Senior Citizens** (membership $12 annually; 1331 F St. NW, Washington, DC 20004, tel. 202/347–8800) and *Mature Outlook* (subscription $9.95 annually; 6001 N. Clark St., Chicago, IL 60660, tel. 312/465–6466 or 800/336–6330).

Publications ***The 50+ Traveler's Guidebook: Where to Go, Where to Stay, What to Do,*** by Anita Williams and Merrimac Dillon ($12.95; St. Martin's Press, 175 5th Ave., New York, NY 10010, tel. 212/674–5151 or 800/288–2131), offers many useful tips. "**The Mature Traveler**" ($29.95; Box 50400, Reno, NV 89513, tel. 702/786–7419), a monthly newsletter, covers travel deals.

Sightseeing By Bus
The "London Plus" guided sightseeing tour from **London Transport** (tel. 0171/828–7395) offers passengers a good introduction to the city from double-decker buses, which are open-topped in summer. Tours run daily every half-hour, 9:30–5:30 April–October, and on the hour 10–4 November–March, departing Haymarket, Baker Street, Embankment, Marble Arch, and Victoria. You may board or alight at any of around 21 stops to view the sights, and then get back on the next bus. Tickets (£10 adults, £5 children) may be bought

from the driver, LT Travel Information Centres, or tourist-information centers.

Other half- and full-day bus tours are available from **Evan Evans** (tel. 0171/930–2377), **Frames Rickards** (tel. 0171/837–3111), **Travellers Check-In** (tel. 0171/580–8284), and **The Big Bus Company** (tel. 0181/944–7810). These tours include stops at places such as St. Paul's Cathedral and Westminster Abbey. Prices and pickup points vary according to the sights visited, but many pickup points are at major hotels.

By Canal During summer, narrow boats and barges cruise London's two canals, the Grand Union and Regent's Canal; most vessels (they seat about 60) operate on the latter, which runs between Little Venice in the west (nearest tube: Warwick Avenue on the Bakerloo Line) and Camden Lock (about 200 yards north of Camden Town tube station). **Jason's Trip** (tel. 0171/286–3428) operates one-way and round-trip narrow-boat cruises on this route. During April, May, and September, there are two cruises per day; from June to August, there are four. Trips last 1½ hours and cost £3.75 for adults, £2.50 for children and senior citizens round-trip.

London Waterbus Co. (tel. 0171/482–2550) offers the Zoo Waterbus service daily from March to September, on weekends in winter. A round-trip canal cruise, London Zoo–Camden Lock, costs £3.20 adults, £1.90 children. Combined zoo entrance–waterbus tickets are also available.

Canal Cruises (tel. 0171/485–4433) offers cruises from March to October on the *Jenny Wren* (£3.90 adults, £1.80 children and senior citizens) and all year on the floating restaurant *My Fair Lady* (Tues.–Sat. dinner, £24.95; Sun. lunch, £16.95).

By River Boats cruise the Thames from April to October, offering a different view of the London skyline. Most leave from Westminster Pier (tel. 0171/930–4097), Charing Cross Pier (Victoria Embankment, tel. 0171/839–3312), and Tower Pier (tel. 0171/488–0344). Downstream routes go to the Tower of London, Greenwich, and the Thames Barrier; upstream destinations include Kew, Richmond, and Hampton Court. Most of the launches seat between 100 and 250 passengers, have a public-address system, and provide a running commentary on passing points of interest. Depending upon destination, river trips may last from one to four hours. For more information, call **Catamaran Cruisers** (tel. 0171/839–3572), **Tidal Cruises** (tel. 0171/928–9009), or **Westminster Passenger Services Association** (tel. 0171/930–4097).

Walking Tours One of the best ways to get to know London is on foot, and there are many guided walking tours to choose from. **The Original London Walks** (tel. 0171/624–3978) has a very wide selection and takes justifiable pride in the infectious enthusiasm of its guides. **Citisights** (tel. 0181/806–4325), **City Walks** (tel. 0171/700–6931), and **Streets of London** (tel. 0181/346–9255) are some of the other better-known firms, but you can investigate more tours at the London Tourist Information Centre at Victoria Station. The lengths of walks vary (usually 1–3 hours), and you can generally find one to suit even the most specific of interests—Shakespeare's London, say, or a Jack the Ripper tour. Prices range around £5 for adults.

For ideas on self-guided walking tours, you can get a book from the **British Travel Centre** (12 Regent St., W1) that lists a variety of London Regional Transport walks.

Excursions **LT, Evan Evans, Frames Rickards,** and **Travellers Check-In** (*see* Bus Tours, *above*) all offer day excursions to places of interest within easy reach of London, such as Windsor, Hampton Court, Oxford, Stratford-upon-Avon, and Bath. Prices vary and may include lunch and admission or admission only.

Sports For a recorded update on London's sports clubs and facilities, call **Sportsline** (tel. 0171/222–8000), weekdays 10–6.

Students Groups Major tour operators include **Contiki Holidays** (300 Plaza Alicante, Suite 900, Garden Grove, CA 92640, tel. 714/740–0808 or 800/466–0610) and **AESU Travel** (2 Hamill Rd., Suite 248, Baltimore, MD 21210-1807, tel. 410/323–4416 or 800/638–7640).

Hosteling Contact **Hostelling International–American Youth Hostels** (733 15th St. NW, Suite 840, Washington, DC 20005, tel. 202/783–6161) in the United States, **Hostelling International–Canada** (205 Catherine St., Suite 400, Ottawa, Ontario K2P 1C3, tel. 613/237–7884) in Canada, and the **Youth Hostel Association of England and Wales** (Trevelyan House, 8 St. Stephen's Hill, St. Albans, Hertfordshire AL1 2DY, tel. 01727/855215 or 01727/845047) in the United Kingdom. Membership ($25 in the U.S., C$26.75 in Canada, and £9 in the U.K.) gets you access to 5,000 hostels worldwide that charge $7–$20 nightly per person.

I.D. Cards To get discounts on transportation and admissions, get the **International Student Identity Card** (ISIC) if you're a bona fide student or the **International Youth Card** (IYC) if you're under 26. In the United States, the ISIC and IYC cards cost $16 each and include basic travel accident and illness coverage, plus a toll-free travel hot line. Apply through the Council on International Educational Exchange (*see* Organizations, *below*). Cards are available for $15 each in Canada from **Travel Cuts** (187 College St., Toronto, Ontario M5T 1P7, tel. 416/979–2406 or 800/667–2887) and in the United Kingdom for £5 each at student unions and student travel companies.

Organizations A major contact is the **Council on International Educational Exchange** (CIEE, 205 E. 42nd St., 16th Floor, New York, NY 10017, tel. 212/661–1450) with locations in Boston (729 Boylston St., Boston, MA 02116, tel. 617/266–1926), Miami (9100 S. Dadeland Blvd., Miami, FL 33156, tel. 305/670–9261), Los Angeles (1093 Broxton Ave., Los Angeles, CA 90024, tel. 310/208–3551), 43 college towns nationwide, and the United Kingdom (28A Poland St., London W1V 3DB, tel. 0171/437–7767). Twice a year, it publishes *Student Travels* magazine. The CIEE's Council Travel Service is the exclusive U.S. agent for several student-discount cards.

Campus Connections (325 Chestnut St., Suite 1101, Philadelphia, PA 19106, tel. 215/625–8585 or 800/428–3235) specializes in discounted accommodations and airfares for students. The **Educational Travel Centre** (438 N. Frances St., Madison, WI 53703, tel. 608/256–5551) offers rail passes and low-cost airline tickets, mostly for flights departing from Chicago. For air travel only, contact **TMI Student Travel** (100 W. 33rd St., Suite 813, New York, NY 10001, tel. 800/245–3672).

In Canada, also contact **Travel Cuts** (*see* above).

Publications See the *Berkeley Guide to London* ($13; Fodor's Travel Publications, tel. 800/533–6478 or from bookstores).

Subway Travel In London, the transportation system is known as the Underground or, more affectionately, the "Tube. For details, *see* Underground Travel, *below*.

T

Telephones The country code for the United Kingdom is 44. For local access numbers abroad, contact **AT&T** USADirect (tel. 800/874–4000), **MCI** Call USA (tel. 800/444–4444), or **Sprint** Express (tel. 800/793–1153).

Tour Operators Group tours and independent vacation packages can turn out to be a bargain depending on what they include (*see* Packages and Tours *in*

Smart Budget Travel Tips A to Z, *below*). Among the companies selling tours and packages to London, the following have a proven reputation, are nationally known, and offer plenty of options.

Group Tours   Look into **Brendan Tours** (15137 Califa St., Van Nuys, CA 91411, tel. 818/785–9696 or 800/421–8446); **British Airways** (tel. 800/247–9297); **Caravan Tours** (401 N. Michigan Ave., Chicago, IL 60611, tel. 312/321–9800 or 800/227–2826); **CIE Tours** (108 Ridgedale Ave., Morristown, NJ 07960, tel. 201/292–3438 or 800/243–8687); **Globus** (5301 S. Federal Circle, Littleton, CO 80123-2980, tel. 303/797–2800 or 800/221–0090); **Insight International** (745 Atlantic Ave., Boston MA 0211, tel. 617/482–2000 or 800/582–8380); and **Trafalgar Tours** (21 E. 26th St., New York, NY 10010, tel. 212/689–8977 or 800/854–0103), and. For budget tours, try Cosmos (*see* Globus, *above*) or **Trafalgar** (*see above*).

Packages   Just about every airline that flies to London sells packages that include round-trip airfare and hotel accommodations. Carriers to contact include **American Airlines Fly AAway Vacations** (tel. 800/321–2121); **British Airways** (*see above*); **Continental Airlines' Grand Destinations** (tel. 800/634–5555); **Delta Dream Vacations** (tel. 800/872–7786); and **United Airlines' Vacation Planning Center** (tel. 800/328–6877). Other packagers include **Certified Vacations** (Box 1525, Ft. Lauderdale, FL 33302, tel. 305/522–1414 or 800/233–7260); **CIE Tours** (108 Ridgedale Ave., Box 2355, Morristown, NJ 07962, tel. 201/292–3899 or 800/243–8687); **DER Tours** (11933 Wilshire Blvd., Los Angeles, CA 90025, tel. 310/479–4140 or 800/782–2424); and **Jet Vacations** (1775 Broadway, New York, NY 10019, tel. 212/474–8740 or 800/538–2762).

Theme Trips   Theme trips are, by their nature, more expensive than a general-interest tour or package, but they still may be a better deal than arranging everything on your own.

Travel Contacts (45 Idmiston Rd., London SE27 9HL, England, tel. 011/44–81766–7868, fax 011/44–81766–6123), with 135 member operators, can satisfy virtually any special interest in London. **Great British Vacations** (4800 Griffith Dr., Suite 125, Beaverton, OR 97005, tel. 503/643–8080 or 800/452–8434) creates custom-designed itineraries that include barging, walking, and visting stately homes.

Antiques. Travel Keys Tours (Box 162266, Sacramento, CA 95816, tel. 916/452–5200) specializes in tours to the antique fairs and flea markets of Europe.

Homes and Gardens. Coopersmith's England (Box 900, Inverness, CA 94937, tel. 415/669–1914, fax 510/339–7135) will wine and dine you with gourmet meals and book your accommodations in castles, historic country inns, and manor houses. **Expo Garden Tours** (145 4th Ave., Suite 4A, New York, NY 10003, tel. 212/677–6704 or 800/448–2685) visits the annual Chelsea Flower Show.

Music. Dailey-Thorp Travel (330 W. 58th St., New York, NY 10019, tel. 212/307–1555; book through travel agents) specializes in classical music and opera programs; its packages include tickets that are otherwise very hard to get.

Tennis. Championship Tennis Tours (9 Antigua, Dana Point, CA 92629, tel. 714/661–7331 or 800/545–7717) and **Sportstours** (6503 N. Military Trail, #207, Boca Raton, FL 33496, tel. 800/879–8647) have packages to Wimbledon, held each summer in London.

Organizations   The **National Tour Association** (546 E. Main St., Lexington, KY 40508, tel. 606/226–4444 or 800/755–8687) and **United States Tour Operators Association** (USTOA, 211 E. 51st St., Suite 12B, New York, NY 10022, tel. 212/750–7371) provide lists of member operators and information on booking tours.

Publications Consult the brochure **"On Tour"** and ask for a current list of member operators from the National Tour Association (*see* Organizations, *above*). Also get a copy of the **"Worldwide Tour & Vacation Package Finder"** from the USTOA (*see* Organizations, *above*) and the Better Business Bureau's **"Tips on Travel Packages"** (publication No. 24-195, $2; 4200 Wilson Blvd., Arlington, VA 22203).

Travel For names of reputable agencies in your area, contact the **American**
Agencies **Society of Travel Agents** (1101 King St., Suite 200, Alexandria, VA 22314, tel. 703/739–2782).

U

Underground For information on all London bus and tube times, fares, etc., call
Travel 0171/222–1234; the line is operated 24 hours.

Passes Several passes for tube and bus travel are available at tube and rail stations, as well as some newsstands. The One Day Travelcard allows unrestricted travel on both bus and tube; valid weekdays after 9:30 AM, weekends, and all national holidays (cost: £2.80–£3.80; children £1.50). The LT Card is the same as above, but without the time restrictions (cost: £3.90–£6.50, children £1.90–£2.70). There are also weekly and monthly Travelcards valid for bus and tube travel; the cost varies according to length and the number of zones covered. The Visitor's Travelcard may be bought in the United States and Canada for three, four, and seven days' travel; it is the same as the LT Card, but with a booklet of discount vouchers to London attractions. In the United States, they cost $25, $32, and $49 respectively ($11, $13, and $21 for children); in Canada, C$29, C$36, and C$55 respectively (C$13, C$15, and C$25 for children). Apply to travel agents or, in the United States, to **BritRail Travel International** (1500 Broadway, New York, NY 10036, tel. 212/382–3737).

V

Visitor Info Contact the **British Tourist Authority** (BTA) in the United States (551 5th Ave., Suite 701, New York, NY 10176, tel. 212/986–2200 or 800/462–2748), in Canada (111 Avenue Rd., 4th Floor, Toronto, Ont. MR5 3J8, tel. 416/925–6326), and in Britain (by mail, Thames Tower, Black's Rd., London W6 9EL).

In London, go in person to the **London Tourist Information Centre** at Victoria Station Forecourt for general information (Mon.–Sat. 8–7, Sun. 8–5) or to the **British Travel Centre** (12 Regent St., SW1Y 4PQ) for travel, hotel, and entertainment information (weekdays 9–6:30, Sat. 10–4). Other information centers are at **Heathrow Airport** (Terminals 1, 2, and 3) and **Gatwick Airport** (International Arrivals Concourse), and, open during store hours only, in **Harrods** (Brompton Rd., SW1 7XL) and **Selfridges** (Oxford St., W1A 2LR). The **London Travel Service** (Bridge House, Ware, Hertfordshire SG12 9DE, tel. 01992/456187) offers travel, hotel, and tour reservations (weekdays 9–5:30, Sat. 9–5).

The London Tourist Board's **Visitorcall** phone guide to London (tel. 01839/123456) gives information about events, theater, museums, transport, shopping, restaurants, and so forth. A three-month events calendar (tel. 01839/401279), or annual version (tel. 01839/401278), is available by fax (set fax machine to polling mode or press start/receive after the tone). Visitorcall charges a rate of 39p–49p per minute, depending on the time of day you call.

U.S. The U.S. Department of State's Overseas Citizens Emergency Cen-
Government ter (Room 4811, Washington, DC 20520; enclose SASE) issues **Con-**
Travel **sular Information Sheets**, which cover crime, security, political
Briefings climate, and health risks as well as embassy locations, entry requirements, currency regulations, and other routine matters. For

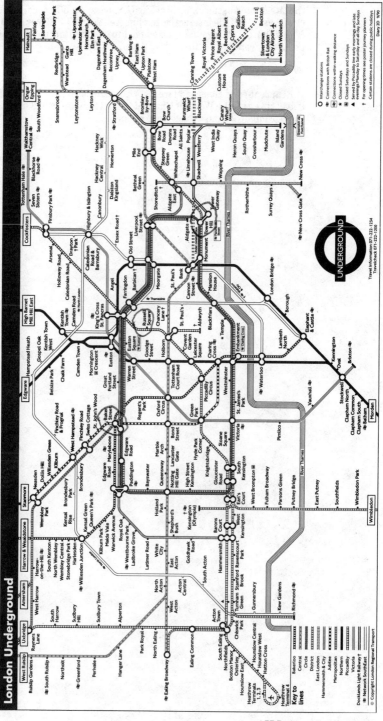

London Underground

15

Diary 20 9/90

Travel Information 071-222-1234
Travelcheck 071-222-1200

UNDERGROUND

○ Interchange stations
◉ Connections with British Rail
✦ Connections within walking distance
★ Closed Sundays
✱ Closed Saturdays and Sundays
▲ Served by Piccadilly line early mornings and late evenings; Monday to Saturday and all day Sundays
† For opening times see poster journey planners
Certain stations are closed during public holidays

Key to lines
Bakerloo
Central
Circle
District
East London
Hammersmith & City
Metropolitan
Northern
Piccadilly
Victoria
Docklands Light Railway
Network SouthEast
© Copyright London Regional Transport

LRT Registered User No. 96/2190

the latest information, stop in at any U.S. passport office, consulate, or embassy; call the interactive hot line (tel. 202/647–5225 or fax 202/647–3000); or, with your PC's modem, tap into the Bureau of Consular Affairs' computer bulletin board (tel. 202/647–9225).

W

Weather For current conditions and forecasts, plus the local time and helpful travel tips, call the **Weather Channel Connection** (tel. 900/932–8437; 95¢ per minute) from a touch-tone phone.

SMART BUDGET TRAVEL TIPS A TO Z

The more you travel, the more you know about how to make trips run like clockwork. To help you work within your budget and make your travels hassle-free, Fodor's editors have rounded up dozens of tips from our contributors and travel experts all over the world, as well as basic information on visiting London. For names of organizations to contact and publications that can give you more information, see Important Contacts A to Z, *above*.

A

Air Travel If time is an issue, **always look for nonstop flights,** which require no change of plane. If possible, **avoid connecting flights,** which stop at least once and can involve a change of plane, although the flight number remains the same; if the first leg is late, the second waits.

Cutting Costs The Sunday travel section of most newspapers is a good source of deals.

Major Airlines. The least-expensive airfares from the major airlines are priced for round-trip travel and are subject to restrictions. You must usually **book in advance and buy the ticket within 24 hours** to get cheaper fares, and you may have to **stay over a Saturday night.** The lowest fare is subject to availability, and only a small percentage of the plane's total seats are sold at that price. It's good to **call a number of airlines, and when you are quoted a good price, book it on the spot**—the same fare on the same flight may not be available the next day. Airlines generally allow you to change your return date for a $25–$50 fee, but most low-fare tickets are nonrefundable. However, if you don't use it, you can apply the cost toward the purchase price of a new ticket, again for a small charge.

Consolidators. Consolidators, who buy tickets at reduced rates from scheduled airlines, sell them at prices below the lowest available from the airlines directly—usually without advance restrictions. Sometimes you can even get your money back if you need to return the ticket. Carefully read the fine print detailing penalties for changes and cancellations. If you doubt the reliability of a consolidator, **confirm your reservation with the airline.**

Aloft **Airline Food.** If you hate airline food, **ask for special meals when booking.** These can be vegetarian, low-cholesterol, or kosher, for example; commonly prepared to order in smaller quantities than standard catered fare, they can be tastier.

Smoking. Smoking is banned on all flights within the United States of less than six hours' duration and on all Canadian flights; the ban also applies to domestic segments of international flights aboard U.S. and foreign carriers. Delta has banned smoking system-wide. On U.S. carriers flying to the United Kingdom and other destinations abroad, a seat in a no-smoking section must be provided for every passenger who requests one, and the section must be enlarged to accommodate such passengers if necessary as long as they have complied with the airline's deadline for check-in and seat assignment. If smoking bothers you, request a seat far from the smoking section.

Foreign airlines are exempt from these rules but do provide no-smoking sections. British Airways has banned smoking, as has Virgin Atlantic on most international flights; some nations have banned smoking on all domestic flights, and others may ban smoking on some flights. Talks continue on the feasibility of broadening no-smoking policies.

Jet Lag To avoid this syndrome, which occurs when travel disrupts your body's natural cycles, try to maintain a normal routine. At night, **get some sleep.** By day, move about the cabin to **stretch your legs, eat light meals, and drink water—not alcohol.**

Airport The cheapest connection with Heathrow is the Underground; the
Transfers Piccadilly Line connects with all terminals. Trains run every four to
Heathrow eight minutes; journey time is roughly 50 minutes; price is £3.10 one-way.

London Transport's *Airbus* service also runs to Heathrow; two routes stop at many central locations, including most major hotels. The A1 leaves every 30 minutes from Victoria Station, daily 6:40 AM–8:15 PM; travel time is about an hour. The A2 leaves Russell Square, near Euston Station, with the same frequency as the A1, daily 6 AM–8:25 PM; travel time is about an hour and 20 minutes. Price for each route is £6, one-way.

Another alternative is the 390 bus, which departs Stand 8, Buckingham Palace Road, weekdays at 7:35, 9:35, 11:05 AM and 1:05, 3:45, 5:20, 6:35, and 9:15 PM (times vary slightly on weekends), stopping at Hyde Park Corner and Kensington High Street. Journey time is about an hour, and the fare is £5 one-way.

By car, the most direct route from central London is via the M4. By taxi, the fare from downtown will be at least £25 plus tip; the journey time will depend on the traffic.

Gatwick Your least expensive option between Gatwick and London is aboard **Green Line Coaches** (tel. 081/668–7261), including the Flightline 777, which leaves Victoria Coach Station hourly, 5:30 AM–11:25 PM. A one-way ticket costs £6. Travel time: about 70 minutes.

A faster if slightly more expensive option is the nonstop trains connecting with Victoria Station. Trains leave every 15 minutes, 5:30 AM–10 PM; five times an hour, 10–midnight; and hourly, midnight–5 AM. Journey time varies from 30 to 39 minutes. Price is £8.90 one-way.

Thameslink trains depart King's Cross and Farringdon, Blackfriars, and London Bridge in the City twice hourly from 4 AM (7 AM Sun.) to 9 AM, and four times an hour between 9 AM and 8 PM, with the last train leaving around 11 PM. The fare is £9.50 (an increase was likely at press time). For information, call 01582/27612.

By car, take the A23 and then the M23 from central London. Taxis from the city to Gatwick are prohibitively expensive.

Stansted London's third airport serves mainly European destinations. The terminal is now linked to Liverpool Street via the Stansted Express. Trains run half-hourly and cost £9.80 one-way.

B

Bicycles Bikes are the most environmentally sound, diverting, healthy, convenient, and cheap way to get around London. It is probably the most dangerous, too, so **wear a helmet.**

Bus Travel "Bus" in Britain generally refers to local buses, "coach" to long-distance buses similar to Greyhound in the United States. Coach travel is far less expensive than rail, though you must offset the savings with the far greater (often double or more) time expenditure.

The **National Express** coach service has routes to more than 1,000 major towns and cities in Britain. There are several levels of fares, starting at Discount Economy (using a CoachCard) and going up to Standard (Fridays and other peak times). The discrepancy between these levels is typically less severe than for rail fares. National Express offers two useful discount cards for overseas visitors. The **BritExpress Card** costs £7 and gives a 30% discount on all fares in a 30-day period. The **Tourist Trail Pass** allows unlimited travel for 3, 5, 8, or 15 days, and starts at £49 (£39 with the BritExpress) for three days. These are available from Victoria Coach Station (Buckingham Palace Rd., SW1 9TP, tel. 0171/730–0202), which is also where all coaches depart.

In addition to National Express, **Green Line** operates bus services within a 30- to 40-mile radius of London. A Golden Rover ticket is available for either one or three days. For more information, call 0181/668–7261.

Within London London's bus system consists of bright red double- and single-deckers, plus other buses of various colors. Destinations are displayed on the front and back, with the bus number on the front, back, and side of the vehicle. Not all buses run the full length of their route at all times. Some buses still have a conductor whom you pay after finding a seat, but there are a lot of "one-man" buses on the road, in which you pay the driver upon boarding. One-way fares start at 90p in the central zone.

Buses stop only at clearly indicated stops. Main stops—at which the bus *should* stop automatically—have a plain white background with a red LT symbol on it. There are also request stops with red signs, a white symbol, and the word "Request" added; at these you must hail the bus to make it stop. Although you can see much of the town from a bus, *don't* take one if you want to get anywhere in a hurry; traffic often slows to a crawl, and during rush hour you may find yourself waiting 40 minutes for a bus and then not being able to get on it once it arrives. If you do go by bus, **ask for a free London Bus Map** at a Travel Information Centre.

Fares. One-way fares start at 90p in the central zone. If you plan to use public transportation a lot, **get a Travelcard** (*see* Underground Travel *in* Important Contacts A to Z, *above*), good for both the tube and bus.

Business Hours Banks are normally open weekdays 9:30–3:30, but some branches stay open later and provide services on Saturday. Banks at major airports and train stations also have extended hours.

Museums are usually open Monday–Saturday 10–5 or 10–6, Sunday 2–5 or 2–6, including most national holidays, but not Christmas Day, Boxing Day (Dec. 26), and New Year's Day. Check individual listings for definite opening hours.

Pubs are generally open Monday–Saturday 11 AM–11 PM, Sunday noon–3 and 7–10 or 10:30, though further relaxation of the blue laws were pending at press time, which would allow pubs to stay open all day on Sundays.

Stores typically stay open Monday–Saturday 9–5:30 or 9–6. Some have late opening hours on Wednesday or Thursday until 7 or 7:30 PM, and many more stay open seven days since the relaxation of the Sunday trading laws in late 1994.

C

Cameras, Camcorders, and Computers *Laptops* Before you depart, **check your portable computer's battery,** because you may be asked at security to turn on the computer to prove that it is what it appears to be. At the airport, you may prefer to **request a manual inspection,** although security X-rays do not harm hard-disk or floppy-disk storage. Also, **register your foreign-made laptop with U.S. Customs.** If your laptop is U.S.-made, call the consulate of the country you'll be visiting to find out whether or not it should be registered with local customs upon arrival. You may want to **find out about repair facilities at your destination** in case you need them.

Photography If your camera is new or if you haven't used it for a while, **shoot and develop a few rolls of film** before you leave. Always **store film in a cool, dry place**—never in the car's glove compartment or on the shelf under the rear window.

Every pass through an X-ray machine increases film's chance of clouding. To protect it, carry it in a clear plastic bag and **ask for hand inspection at security.** Such requests are virtually always honored at U.S. airports, and usually are accommodated abroad. Don't depend on a lead-lined bag to protect film in checked luggage—the airline may increase the radiation to see what's inside.

Video Before your trip, **test your camcorder, invest in a skylight filter to protect the lens, and charge the batteries.** (Airport security personnel may ask you to turn on the camcorder to prove that it's what it appears to be.) The batteries of most newer camcorders can be recharged with a universal or worldwide AC adapter charger (or multivoltage converter), usable whether the voltage is 110 or 220. All that's needed is the appropriate plug.

Videotape is not damaged by X-rays, but it may be harmed by the magnetic field of a walk-through metal detector, so **ask that videotapes be hand-checked.** Videotape sold in the United Kingdom is based on the PAL standard, which is different than the one used in the United States. You will not be able to view your tapes through the local TV set or view movies bought there in your home VCR. Blank tapes bought in London can be used for camcorder taping, but they are pricey. Some U.S. audiovisual shops convert foreign tapes to U.S. standards; contact an electronics dealer to find the nearest.

The Channel Tunnel The Channel Tunnel provides the fastest route across the Channel— 35 minutes from Folkestone to Calais, 60 minutes from motorway to motorway, or 3 hours from Waterloo, London to Paris, Gare du Nord. It consists of two large 50-kilometer- (31-mile-) long tunnels for trains, one in each direction, linked by a smaller service tunnel running between them.

Le Shuttle, a special car, bus, and truck train, operates a continuous loop, with trains departing every 15 minutes at peak times and at least once an hour through the night. No reservations are necessary, although tickets may be purchased in advance from travel agents. Most passengers travel in their own car, staying with the vehicle throughout the "crossing," with progress updates via radio and display screens. Motorcyclists park their bikes in a separate section with its own passenger compartment, while foot passengers must book passage by coach. At press time, prices for a one-day round-trip ticket began at £107–£154 for a car and its occupants. Prices for a five-day round-trip ticket began at £115.

Eurostar operates high-speed passenger-only trains, which whisk riders between new stations in Paris (Gare du Nord) and London (Waterloo) in three hours and between London and Brussels (Midi) in 3¼ hours. At press time, fares were $154 for a one-way, first-class ticket and $123 for an economy fare.

The tunnel is reached from Exit 11a of the M20/A20. Tickets for either tunnel service can be purchased in advance (*see* Important Contacts A to Z, *above*).

Children and Travel For recommended local sitters, **check with your hotel desk.**

If you are renting a car, **arrange for a car seat when you reserve.** Sometimes they're free.

Flying Always **ask about discounted children's fares.** On international flights, the fare for infants under age 2 not occupying a seat is generally either free or 10% of the accompanying adult's fare; children ages 2–11 usually pay half to two-thirds of the adult fare. On domestic flights, children under 2 not occupying a seat travel free, and older children currently travel on the lowest applicable adult fare.

Baggage. In general, the adult baggage allowance applies for children paying half or more of the adult fare. Before departure, **ask about carry-on allowances**, if you are traveling with an infant. In general, those paying 10% of the adult fare are allowed one carry-on bag, not to exceed 70 pounds or 45 inches (length + width + height) and a collapsible stroller; you may be allowed less if the flight is full.

Safety Seats. According to the Federal Aviation Administration (FAA), it's a good idea to **use safety seats aloft.** Airline policy varies. U.S. carriers allow FAA-approved models, but airlines usually require that you buy a ticket, even if your child would otherwise ride free, because the seats must be strapped into regular passenger seats. Foreign carriers may not allow infant seats, may charge the child's rather than the infant's fare for their use, or may require you to hold your baby during takeoff and landing, thus defeating the seat's purpose.

Facilities. When making your reservation, **ask for children's meals or freestanding bassinets** if you need them; the latter are available only to those with seats at the bulkhead, where there's enough legroom. If you don't need a bassinet, **think twice before requesting bulkhead seats**—the only storage for in-flight necessities is in the inconveniently distant overhead bins.

Lodging Most hotels allow children under a certain age to stay in their parents' room at no extra charge, while others charge them as extra adults; be sure to **ask about the cut-off age.** And keep in mind that in Great Britain, hotels will often allow only three people in a room.

Customs and Duties
In London There are two levels of duty-free allowance for travelers entering Great Britain: one for goods bought outside the EU, the other for goods bought in the EU (Belgium, Denmark, France, Germany, Greece, the Irish Republic, Italy, Luxembourg, the Netherlands, Portugal, or Spain).

Of the first category, you may import duty-free: 200 cigarettes or 100 cigarillos or 50 cigars or 250 grams of tobacco; two liters of table wine and, in addition, (a) one liter of alcohol over 22% by volume (most spirits), (b) two liters of alcohol under 22% by volume (fortified or sparkling wine), or (c) two more liters of table wine; 50 milliliters of perfume; ¼ liter of toilet water; and other goods up to a value of £36, but not more than 50 liters of beer or 25 cigarette lighters.

Of the second category, the EU has set guidelines for the import of certain goods. Following side trips entirely within the EU, you no longer need to go through Customs on your return to the United Kingdom; however, if you exceed the guideline amounts, you may be required to prove that the goods are for your personal use only ("personal use" includes gifts). The guideline levels are 800 cigarettes, 400 cigarillos, 200 cigars, and 1 kilogram of smoking tobacco, plus 10 liters of spirits, 20 liters of fortified wine, 90 liters of wine, and 110 liters of beer. No animals or pets of any kind can be brought into the United Kingdom without a lengthy quarantine. The penalties are severe and strictly enforced. Similarly, fresh meats, plants and vegetables, controlled drugs, and firearms and ammunition may not be brought into Great Britain.

You will face no customs formalities if you enter Scotland or Wales from any other part of the United Kingdom, though anyone coming from Northern Ireland should expect a security check.

Back Home **In the U.S.** You may bring home $400 worth of foreign goods duty-free if you've been out of the country for at least 48 hours and haven't already used the $400 exemption, or any part of it, in the past 30 days.

Travelers 21 or older may bring back 1 liter of alcohol duty-free, provided the beverage laws of the state through which they reenter the United States allow it. In addition, 100 non-Cuban cigars and 200 cigarettes are allowed, regardless of your age. Antiques and works of art more than 100 years old are duty-free.

Duty-free, travelers may mail packages valued at up to $200 to themselves and up to $100 to others, with a limit of one parcel per addressee per day (and no alcohol or tobacco products or perfume valued at more than $5); outside, identify the package as being for personal use or an unsolicited gift, specifying the contents and their retail value. Mailed items do not count as part of your exemption.

In Canada. Once per calendar year, when you've been out of Canada for at least seven days, you may bring in C$300 worth of goods duty-free. If you've been away less than seven days but more than 48 hours, the duty-free exemption drops to C$100 but can be claimed any number of times (as can a C$20 duty-free exemption for absences of 24 hours or more). You cannot combine the yearly and 48-hour exemptions, use the C$300 exemption only partially (to save the balance for a later trip), or pool exemptions with family members. Goods claimed under the C$300 exemption may follow you by mail; those claimed under the lesser exemptions must accompany you.

Alcohol and tobacco products may be included in the yearly and 48-hour exemptions but not in the 24-hour exemption. If you meet the age requirements of the province through which you reenter Canada, you may bring in, duty-free, 1.14 liters (40 imperial ounces) of wine or liquor *or* 24 12-ounce cans or bottles of beer or ale. If you are 16 or older, you may bring in, duty-free, 200 cigarettes, 50 cigars or cigarillos, and 400 tobacco sticks or 400 grams of manufactured tobacco. Alcohol and tobacco must accompany you on your return.

An unlimited number of gifts valued up to C$60 each may be mailed to Canada duty-free. These do not count as part of your exemption. Label the package "Unsolicited Gift—Value under $60." Alcohol and tobacco are excluded.

D

For Travelers with Disabilities When discussing accessibility with an operator or reservationist, **ask hard questions.** Are there any stairs, inside *or* out? Are there grab bars next to the toilet *and* in the shower/tub? How wide is the doorway to the room? To the bathroom? For the most extensive facilities, meeting the latest legal specifications, **opt for newer accommodations,** which more often have been designed with access in mind. Older properties or ships must usually be retrofitted and may offer more limited facilities as a result. Be sure to **discuss your needs before booking.**

Discount Clubs Travel clubs offer members unsold space on airplanes, cruise ships, and package tours at as much as 50% below regular prices. Membership may include a regular bulletin or access to a toll-free hot line giving details of available trips departing from three or four days to several months in the future. Most also offer 50% discounts off hotel rack rates. Before booking with a club, **make sure the hotel or other supplier isn't offering a better deal.**

Driving It's best to **avoid driving in London.** Because the capital grew up as a series of villages, there never was a central plan for London's streets, and the result is a winding mass of chaos, aggravated by a passion for one-way streets.

Speed Limits and Parking If you must risk life and limb, note that the speed limit is 30 mph in the royal parks, as well as (theoretically) in all streets—unless you see the large 40 mph signs (and small repeater signs attached to lampposts) found only in the suburbs.

Other basic rules: Pedestrians have right-of-way on "zebra" crossings (black-and-white stripes that stretch across the street between two Belisha beacons—orange-flashing globe lights on posts). The curb on each side of the zebra crossing has zigzag markings. It is illegal to park within the zigzag area, or to pass another vehicle at a zebra crossing. At other crossings pedestrians must yield to traffic, but they do have right-of-way over traffic turning left at controlled crossings—if they have the nerve.

Traffic lights sometimes have arrow-style lights directing left or right turns; it is therefore important not to get into the turn lane if you mean to go straight ahead, so try to catch a glimpse of the road markings in time. The use of horns is prohibited between 11:30 PM and 7 AM.

You can park at night in 30-mph zones, provided you are within 25 yards of a lit street lamp, but not within 15 yards of a road junction. To park on a bus route, you must show side (parking) lights, but you'll probably get a ticket anyway. On "Red Routes"—busy stretches with red lines painted in the gutter—you may not even stop to let out a passenger. During the day—and probably at all times—it is safest to believe that you can park nowhere except at a meter, in a garage, or where you are sure there are no lines or signs; otherwise, you run the risk of a tow-away cost of about £100, or a wheel clamp, which costs about the same, since you pay to have the clamp removed, plus the one or two tickets you'll have earned first. It is illegal to park on the sidewalk in London.

London Districts Greater London is divided into 32 boroughs—33, counting the City of London, which has all the powers of a London borough. More useful for finding your way around, however, are the subdivisions of London into various postal districts. Throughout the guide we've listed the full postal code for places you're likely to be contacting by mail, although you'll find the first half of the code more important. The first one or two letters give the location: N=north, NW=northwest, etc. Don't expect the numbering to be logical, however. You won't, for example, find W2 next to W3.

I

Insurance Travel insurance can protect your investment, replace your luggage and its contents, or provide for medical coverage should you fall ill during your trip. Most tour operators, travel agents, and insurance agents sell specialized health-and-accident, flight, trip-cancellation, and luggage insurance as well as comprehensive policies with some or all of these features. Before you make any purchase, **review your existing health and home-owner policies** to find out whether they cover expenses incurred while traveling.

Baggage Airline liability for your baggage is limited to $1,250 per person on domestic flights. On international flights, the airlines' liability is $9.07 per pound or $20 per kilogram for checked baggage (roughly $640 per 70-pound bag) and $400 per passenger for unchecked baggage. Insurance for losses exceeding the terms of your airline ticket can be bought directly from the airline at check-in for about $10 per $1,000 of coverage; note that it excludes a rather extensive list of items, shown on your airline ticket.

Flight You should **think twice before buying flight insurance.** Often purchased as a last-minute impulse at the airport, it pays a lump sum when a plane crashes, either to a beneficiary if the insured dies or sometimes to a surviving passenger who loses eyesight or a limb. Supplementing the airlines' coverage described in the limits-of-liability paragraphs on your ticket, it's expensive and basically unnecessary. Charging an airline ticket to a major credit card often automatically entitles you to coverage and may also embrace travel by bus, train, and ship.

Health If your own health-insurance policy does not cover you outside the United States, **consider buying supplemental medical coverage.** It can cover from $1,000 to $150,000 worth of medical and/or dental expenses incurred as a result of an accident or illness during a trip. These policies also may include a personal-accident, or death-and-dismemberment, provision, which pays a lump sum ranging from $15,000 to $500,000 to your beneficiaries if you die or to you if you lose one or more limbs or your eyesight, and a medical-assistance provision, which may either reimburse you for the cost of referrals, evacuation, or repatriation and other services, or may automatically enroll you as a member of a particular medical-assistance company.

Trip Without insurance, you will lose all or most of your money if you must cancel your trip because of illness or any other reason. Especially if your airline ticket, cruise, or package tour is nonrefundable and cannot be changed, it's essential that you **buy trip-cancellation-and-interruption insurance.** When considering how much coverage you need, look for a policy that covers the cost of your trip plus the nondiscounted price of a one-way airline ticket should you need to return home early. Read the fine print carefully, especially sections defining "family member" and "preexisting medical conditions." Also **consider default or bankruptcy insurance,** which protects you against a supplier's failure to deliver. However, such policies often do not cover default by a travel agency, tour operator, airline, or cruise line if you bought your tour and the coverage directly from the firm in question.

L

Lodging If you want a home base that's roomy enough for a family and comes
Apartment and with cooking facilities, **consider a furnished rental.** It's generally
Villa Rentals cost-wise, too, although not always—some rentals are luxury properties (economical only when your party is large). Home-exchange directories list rentals—often second homes owned by prospective house swappers—and some services search for a house or apartment for you (even a castle if that's your fancy) and handle the paperwork. Some send an illustrated catalogue and others send photographs of specific properties, sometimes at a charge; up-front registration fees may apply.

Home If you would like to find a house, an apartment, or other vacation
Exchange property to exchange for your own while on vacation, **become a member of a home-exchange organization,** which will send you its annual directories listing available exchanges and will include your own listing in at least one of them. Arrangements for the actual exchange are made by the two parties to it, not by the organization.

M

Mail Stamps may be bought from main or substation post offices (the latter are located in stores), from stamp machines outside post offices, and from many newsagents stores and newsstands. Mailboxes are known as post or letter boxes and are painted bright red; large tubular ones are set on the edge of sidewalks, while smaller boxes are set into post office walls.

Rates Postal rates are: airmail letters up to 10 grams to North America, 41p; postcards 35p, aerogrammes 36p. Letters within Britain are 25p for first class, 19p for second class. Always check rates in advance, however, as they are subject to change.

Receiving Mail If you're uncertain where you'll be staying, you can have mail sent to you at the Trafalgar Square Post Office or any American Express branch. For mailing addresses, *see* Mail in Important Contacts A to Z.

Money and The units of currency in Great Britain are pound sterling (£) and
Expenses pence (p): £50, £20, £10, and £5 bills; £1 (100p), 50p, 20p, 10p, 5p, 2p, and 1p coins. At press time, the exchange rate was about $1.62 U.S. dollars, or $1.96 Canadian dollars, to the British pound.

ATMs Cirrus, Plus and many other networks connecting automated-teller machines operate internationally. Chances are that you can **use your bank card at ATMs** to withdraw money from an account and get cash advances on a credit-card account if your card has been programmed with a personal identification number, or PIN. Before leaving home, **check in on frequency limits** for withdrawals and cash advances. Also **ask whether your card's PIN must be reprogrammed** for use in London. Four digits are commonly used overseas. Note that Discover is accepted only in the United States.

On cash advances you are charged interest from the day you receive the money from ATMs as well as from tellers. Although transaction fees for ATM withdrawals abroad may be higher than fees for withdrawals at home, Cirrus and Plus exchange rates are excellent because they are based on wholesale rates only offered by major banks.

Costs Hotel room, double or twin, per person, per night: £35 (Swiss House).

B&B/budget hotel room, as above: £20 (Windsor House).

A fine dinner, three courses, coffee, VAT, no wine, per person: £30 (Quaglinos).

An everyday dinner, as above: £15 (L'Artiste Musclé).

A budget dinner, as above: £10 (Stockpot).

Fish-and-chips, take-out: £4.

Pizza, small, 2 toppings: £4.50 (Pizza Hut); £6 (posh).

Coffee: 80p–£2. (Anything more is a ripoff.)

Glass of house wine: £2.75 (Quaglino's), £1.80 (L'Artiste Musclé), £1.25 (Stockpot).

Taxi, 1 mile, including tip: £3.50.

Minicab, ditto: £2.50.

Tube ride, short: £1.30, longer £2.30.

Movie, West End: £7–9 (Odeon, Leicester Sq.); "Off-West End": £5.50 (Screen on the Hill); Local/Rep: £4.50 (Riverside).

Newspaper: 60p.

Exchanging For the most favorable rates, **change money at banks.** You won't do
Currency as well at exchange booths in airports, rail, and bus stations, or in hotels, restaurants, and stores, although you may find their hours more convenient. To avoid lines at airport exchange booths, **get a small amount of currency before you leave home.**

Traveler's Whether or not to buy traveler's checks depends on where you are
Checks headed; **take cash to rural areas and small towns, traveler's checks to cities.** The most widely recognized are American Express, Citicorp, Thomas Cook, and Visa, which are sold by major commercial banks for 1%–3% of the checks' face value—it pays to **shop around.** Both American Express and Thomas Cook issue checks that can be countersigned and used by you or your traveling companion, and they both provide checks, at no extra charge, denominated in pounds. You can cash them in banks without paying a fee (which can be as much as 20%) and use them as readily as cash in many hotels, restaurants, and shops. So you won't be left with excess foreign currency,

buy a few checks in small denominations to cash toward the end of your trip. Record the numbers of the checks, cross them off as you spend them, and keep this information separate from your checks.

Wiring Money You don't have to be a cardholder to send or receive funds through MoneyGram^{SM} from American Express. Just go to a MoneyGram agent, located in retail and convenience stores and in American Express Travel Offices. Pay up to $1,000 with cash or a credit card, anything over that in cash. The money can be picked up within 10 minutes in the form of U.S. dollar traveler's checks or local currency at the nearest MoneyGram agent, or, abroad, the main American Express Travel Office (6 Haymarket, London SW1Y 4BS, tel. 0171/930–4411). There are many other brances; check for the one nearest you or call 0800/521–313. There's no limit, and the recipient need only present photo identification. The cost runs from 3% to 10%, depending on the amount sent, the destination, and how you pay.

You can also send money using Western Union. Money sent from the United States or Canada will be available for pickup at agent locations in 100 countries within 15 minutes. Once the money is in the system, it can be picked up at any one of 25,000 locations. Fees range from 4% to 10%, depending on the amount you send.

P

Packages and Tours A package or tour to London can make your vacation less expensive and more convenient. Firms that sell tours and packages purchase airline seats, hotel rooms, and rental cars in bulk and pass some of the savings on to you. In addition, the best operators have local representatives to help you out at your destination.

A Good Deal? The more your package or tour includes, the better you can predict the ultimate cost of your vacation. Make sure you know exactly what is included, and **beware of hidden costs.** Are taxes, tips, and service charges included? Transfers and baggage handling? Entertainment and excursions? These can add up.

Most packages and tours are rated deluxe, first-class superior, first class, tourist, and budget. The key difference is usually accommodations. If the package or tour you are considering is priced lower than in your wildest dreams, **be skeptical.** Also, **make sure your travel agent knows the hotels** and other services. Ask about location, room size, beds, and whether the facility has a pool, room service, or programs for children, if you care about these. Has your agent been there or sent others you can contact?

Buyer Beware Each year consumers are stranded or lose their money when operators go out of business—even very large ones with excellent reputations. If you can't afford a loss, take the time to **check out the operator**—find out how long the company has been in business, and ask several agents about its reputation. Next, **don't book unless the firm has a consumer-protection program.** Members of the United States Tour Operators Association and the National Tour Association are required to set aside funds exclusively to cover your payments and travel arrangements in case of default. Nonmember operators may instead carry insurance; look for the details in the operator's brochure—and the name of an underwriter with a solid reputation. Note: When it comes to tour operators, **don't trust escrow accounts.** Although there are laws governing those of charter-flight operators, no governmental body prevents tour operators from raiding the till. Next, **contact your local Better Business Bureau and the attorney general's office** in both your own state and the operator's; have any complaints been filed? Last, **pay with a major credit card.** Then you can cancel payment, provided that you can document your complaint. Always **consider trip-cancellation insurance** (*see* Insurance, *above*).

Big vs. Small. An operator that handles several hundred thousand travelers annually can use its purchasing power to give you a good price. Its high volume may also indicate financial stability. But some small companies provide more personalized service; because they tend to specialize, they may also be experts on an area.

Using an Agent Travel agents are an excellent resource. In fact, large operators accept bookings only through travel agents. But it's good to **collect brochures from several agencies,** because some agents' suggestions may be skewed by promotional relationships with tour and package firms that reward them for volume sales. If you have a special interest, **find an agent with expertise in that area**; the American Society of Travel Agents can give you leads in the United States. (Don't rely solely on your agent, though; agents may be unaware of small-niche operators, and some special-interest travel companies only sell direct.)

Single Prices are usually quoted per person, based on two sharing a room.
Travelers If you are traveling solo, you may be required to pay the full double-occupancy rate. Some operators eliminate this surcharge if you agree to be matched up with a roommate of the same sex, even if one is not found by departure time.

Packing for You'll need an overcoat for winter and a light coat or warm jacket for
London summer; always **bring a raincoat or an umbrella.** As in any American city, jackets and ties are appropriate for expensive restaurants and nightspots; casual clothes are fine elsewhere. Jeans are as popular in Great Britain as they are at home and are perfectly acceptable for sightseeing and informal dining. Tweeds and nonmatching jackets are popular here with men. For women, ordinary street dress is acceptable everywhere.

Bring an extra pair of eyeglasses or contact lenses in your carry-on luggage, and if you have a health problem, **pack enough medication** to last the trip or have your doctor write a prescription using the drug's generic name, because brand names vary from country to country (you'll then need a prescription from a doctor in the country you're visiting). **Don't put prescription drugs or valuables in luggage to be checked,** for it could go astray. To avoid problems with customs officials, carry medications in original packaging. Also don't forget the addresses of offices that handle refunds of lost traveler's checks.

Electricity To use your U.S.-purchased electric-powered equipment, **bring a converter and an adapter.** The electrical current in London is 220 volts, 50 cycles alternating current (AC); wall outlets take plugs with three prongs.

If your appliances are dual voltage, you'll need only an adapter. Hotels sometimes have 110-volt outlets for low-wattage appliances marked "For Shavers Only" near the sink; don't use them for high-wattage appliances like blow-dryers. If your laptop computer is older, carry a converter; new laptops operate equally well on 110 and 220 volts, so you need only an adapter.

Luggage Free airline baggage allowances depend on the airline, the route, and the class of your ticket; ask in advance. In general, on domestic flights and on international flights between the United States and foreign destinations, you are entitled to check two bags—neither exceeding 62 inches, or 158 centimeters (length + width + height), or weighing more than 70 pounds (32 kilograms). A third piece may be brought aboard; its total dimensions are generally limited to less than 45 inches (114 centimeters), so it will fit easily under the seat in front of you or in the overhead compartment. In the United States, the FAA gives airlines broad latitude to limit carry-on allowances and tailor them to different aircraft and operational conditions. Charges for excess, oversize, or overweight pieces vary.

If you are flying between two foreign destinations, note that baggage allowances may be determined not by piece but by weight— generally 88 pounds (40 kilograms) in first class, 66 pounds (30 kilograms) in business class, and 44 pounds (20 kilograms) in economy. If your flight between two cities abroad *connects* with your transatlantic or transpacific flight, the piece method still applies.

Safeguarding Your Luggage. Before leaving home, **itemize your bags' contents** and their worth, and label them with your name, address, and phone number. (If you use your home address, cover it so potential thieves can't see it.) Inside your bag, **pack a copy of your itinerary.** At check-in, **make sure that your bag is correctly tagged** with the airport's three-letter destination code. If your bags arrive damaged or not at all, file a written report with the airline before leaving the airport.

Passports and Visas If you don't already have one, **get a passport.** While traveling, **keep one photocopy of the data page** separate from your wallet and leave another copy with someone at home. If you lose your passport, promptly call the nearest embassy or consulate and the local police; having the data page can speed replacement.

U.S. Citizens All U.S. citizens, even infants, need a valid passport to enter Great Britain for stays of up to three months. New and renewal application forms are available at any of the 13 U.S. Passport Agency offices and at some post offices and courthouses. Passports are usually mailed within four weeks; allow five weeks or more in spring and summer.

Canadians You need a valid passport to enter Great Britain for stays of up to three months days. Application forms are available at 28 regional passport offices as well as post offices and travel agencies. Whether for a first or a renewal passport, you must apply in person. Children under 16 may be included on a parent's passport but must have their own to travel alone. Passports are valid for five years and are usually mailed within two to three weeks of application.

R

Rail Travel London is served by no fewer than 15 railroad stations, so **be absolutely certain of the station for your departure or arrival.** All have Underground (subway) stations either in the train station or within a few minutes' walk, and most are served by several bus routes.

British Rail still controls all major railroad services, though it is in the process of splitting into seven divisions that are due to be sold to private operators. Little about this operation was certain at press time. The principal routes that connect London to other major towns and cities are on an InterCity network; unlike its European counterparts, British Rail makes no extra charge for the use of this express-service network.

Seat Reservations Seats cannot be reserved by phone. You should **apply in person to make a seat reservation** any British Rail Travel Centre or directly to the station from which you depart. Seat reservations cost £1.

Major Stations **Charing Cross** serves southeast England, including Canterbury, Margate, and Dover/Folkestone.

Euston/St. Pancras serves East Anglia, Essex, the northeast, the northwest, and northern Wales, including Coventry, Stratford-upon-Avon, Birmingham, Manchester, Liverpool, Windermere, Glasgow, and Inverness.

King's Cross serves the east Midlands, the northeast including York, Leeds, Newcastle, and north and east Scotland including Edinburgh and Aberdeen.

Liverpool Street serves Essex and East Anglia.

Paddington serves the south Midlands, west and south Wales, and the west country, including Reading, Bath, Bristol, Oxford, Cardiff, Swansea, Exeter, Plymouth, and Penzance.

Victoria serves southern England, including Gatwick Airport, Brighton, Dover/Folkestone, and the south coast.

Waterloo serves the southwest, including Salisbury, Bournemouth, Portsmouth, Southampton, and the isles of Wight, Jersey, and Guernsey.

Fares   Generally speaking, it is less expensive to buy a return (round-trip) ticket, especially for day trips not far from London; **always ask about discounted fares** for your route. Buying a ticket on the train is the most expensive way to go, since you must pay the full one-way fare. You can hear a recorded summary of timetable and fare information to many InterCity destinations by dialing the appropriate "dial and listen" numbers listed under British Rail in the telephone book.

Passes   To save money, **look into rail passes** (*see* Important Contacts A to Z, *above*). But be aware that if you don't plan to cover many miles, you may come out ahead by buying individual tickets.

Many travelers assume that rail passes guarantee them seats on the trains they wish to ride. Not so. You need to **book seats ahead even if you are using a rail pass**; seat reservations are required on some European trains, particularly high-speed trains, and are a good idea on trains that may be crowded—particularly in summer on popular routes. You will also need a reservation if you purchase overnight sleeping accommodations.

Renting a Car   When considering a rental car, it's worth noting that unless you are going to be traveling a lot outside London, a car in the city will often be more of a liability than an asset. If you do choose to rent a car, **remember that Britain drives on the left,** and the rest of Europe on the right. If you're planning to cross the Channel, you may want to leave your rented car in Britain and pick up a left-side drive on the mainland. *See also* Driving, *above*.

Cutting Costs   To get the best deal, **book through a travel agent and shop around.** When pricing cars, **ask where the rental lot is located.** Some off-airport locations offer lower rates—even though their lots are only minutes away from the terminal via complimentary shuttle. You may also want to **price local car-rental companies,** whose rates may be lower still, although service and maintenance standards may not be up to those of a national firm. Also **ask your travel agent about a company's customer-service record.** How has it responded to late plane arrivals and vehicle mishaps? Are there often lines at the rental counter, and, if you're traveling during a holiday period, does a confirmed reservation guarantee you a car?

Always **find out what equipment is standard** at your destination before specifying what you want; **do without automatic transmission or air-conditioning** if they're optional. In Europe, manual transmissions are standard and air-conditioning is rare and often unnecessary.

Also in Europe, **look into wholesalers**—companies that do not own their own fleets but rent in bulk from those that do and often offer better rates than traditional car-rental operations. Prices are best during low travel periods, and rentals booked through wholesalers must be paid for before you leave the United States. If you use a wholesaler, **know whether the prices are guaranteed** in U.S. dollars or foreign currency, and if unlimited mileage is available; find out about required deposits, cancellation penalties, and drop-off charges; and confirm the cost of any required insurance coverage.

Insurance   When you drive a rented car, you are generally responsible for any damage or personal injury that you cause as well as damage to the vehicle. Before you rent, **see what coverage you already have** by means of your personal auto-insurance policy and credit cards. For about $14 a day, rental companies sell insurance, known as a collision damage waiver (CDW), that eliminates your liability for damage to the car; it's always optional and should never be automatically added to your bill.

Requirements In London your own driver's license is acceptable. An International Driver's Permit, available from the American or Canadian Automobile Association, is a good idea.

Surcharges Before picking up the car in one city and leaving it in another, **ask about drop-off charges or one-way service fees,** which can be substantial. Note, too, that some rental agencies charge extra if you return the car before the time specified on your contract. To avoid a hefty refueling fee, **fill the tank just before you turn in the car.**

S

Senior-Citizen Discounts To qualify for age-related discounts, **mention your senior-citizen status up front** when booking hotel reservations, not when checking out, and before you're seated in restaurants, not when paying your bill. Note that discounts may be limited to certain menus, days, or hours. When renting a car, **ask about promotional car-rental discounts**—they can net lower costs than your senior-citizen discount.

Students on the Road To save money, **look into deals available through student-oriented travel agencies.** To qualify, you'll need to have a bona fide student I.D. card. Members of international student groups also are eligible. *See* Students *in* Important Contacts A to Z, *above.*

Subway Travel *See* Undergroud Travel, *below.*

T

Taxis Big, black taxicabs are as much a part of the London streetscape as the red double-decker buses. But taxis now come in a variety of colors, and some carry advertising on their sides. Hotels and main tourist areas have cab stands (just take the first in line), but you can also **flag down a taxi from the roadside.** If the yellow "fcr hire" sign on the top is lit, then the taxi is available. Many cab drivers often cruise at night with their "for hire" signs unlit; this is to enable them to choose their passengers and avoid those they think might cause trouble. If you see an unlit, passengerless cab, hail it: You might be lucky.

Fares Fares start at £1 for the first 582 yards and increase by units of 20p per 291 yards or 60 seconds. A 40p surcharge is added on weekday nights 8–midnight and Saturday up to 8 PM. The surcharge rises to 60p on Saturday nights, Sundays, and national holidays—except over Christmas and New Year's Eve when it rises to £2. Fares are usually raised in June of each year.

Telephones There are three types of phones: Those that accept (a) only coins, (b) only BT (British Telecom) phonecards, or (c) BT phonecards and credit cards.

The coin-operated phones are of the push-button variety; most take all but 1p coins. Insert the coins *before* dialing (minimum charge is 10p). If you hear a repeated single tone after dialing, the line is busy; a continuous tone means the number is unobtainable (or that you have dialed the wrong—or no—prefix). The indicator panel shows you how much money is left; add more whenever you like. If there is no answer, replace the receiver and your money will be returned.

Card phones operate with special cards that you can buy from post offices or newsstands displaying the green and white phone card sign. They are ideal for longer calls, are composed of units of 10p, and come in values of £2, £4, £10, and more. To use, lift the receiver, insert your card, and dial the number. An indicator panel shows the number of units used. At the end of your call the card will be returned.

For long-distance calls within Britain, dial the area code (which begins with a zero–one), followed by the number.

London numbers are prefixed by 0171 for inner London or 0181 for outer London. You do not need to dial either if you are calling from inside the same zone, but you will have to dial 0181 from an 0171 number and 0171 from an 0181 number. Drop the zero from the prefix and dial only 171 or 181 when calling London from overseas.

All calls are charged according to the time of day. Standard rate is in effect weekdays 8 AM–6 PM; cheap rate is charged weekdays 6 PM–8 PM and all day on weekends.

Long-Distance The long-distance services of AT&T, MCI, and Sprint make calling home relatively convenient and let you avoid hotel surcharges; typically, you dial a local number. Before you go, **find out the local access codes** for your destinations.

Long-distance and international calls are usually cheaper when made weekdays between 8 PM and 8 AM and at any time on weekends. For direct dialing, dial 00, then the country code, area code, and number. For the international operator, credit card, or collect calls, dial 155. For directory inquiries (information) in most countries, dial 153. Bear in mind that hotels usually levy a hefty surcharge on calls made from hotel rooms; it's better to use the pay phones located in most hotel foyers.

Operators and To call the operator, dial 100; directory inquiries (information), 192;
Information international directory inquiries, 153. A charge is made for directory inquiries.

Tipping Many restaurants and large hotels (particularly those belonging to chains) will automatically add a 10%–15% service charge to your bill, so always check in advance before you hand out any extra money. You are, of course, welcome to tip on top of that for exceptional service. If you are dissatisfied with the service, however, refuse to pay the service charge, stating your reasons for doing so; you will be within your rights legally. In a budget hotel or B&B, try to be sensitive to tipping protocol, about which there are no hard-and-fast rules. If the owner's husband is helping you with your bags, for instance, a tip may offend. The British can be funny about money.

Do not tip movie or theater ushers, elevator operators, or bar staff in pubs—although you may buy them a drink if you're feeling generous. Washroom attendants may display a saucer, in which it's reasonable to leave 10p–50p or so.

Here's a guide for other situations:

Restaurants: 10%–15% of the check for full meals if service is not already included; a small token if you're just having coffee or tea.

Taxis: 10%–15%, or perhaps a little more for a short ride.

Porters: 50p–£1 per bag.

Doormen: £1 for hailing taxis or for carrying bags to in desk.

Bellhops: £1 per bag for carrying bags to rooms, £1 for room service.

Hairdressers: 10%–15% of the bill, plus £1–£2 for the hair-washer.

U

Underground Known colloquially as "the tube," London's extensive Underground
Travel system is by far the most widely used form of city transportation.

Trains run both beneath and above ground into the suburbs; to find a station, **look for the London Underground circular symbol.** (In Britain, the word "subway" means "pedestrian underpass.")

There are 10 basic lines—all named—plus the East London line, which runs from Shoreditch and Whitechapel across the Thames and south to New Cross, and the Docklands Light Railway, which runs from Stratford in east London to Greenwich, with an extension to the Royal Docks that should be completed by the time you read this.

The not-yet-built Metro Express, which will run from Haringey to Wimbledon underneath Soho and Fulham, may start appearing on maps too—it's the light green line. The Central, District, Northern, Metropolitan, and Piccadilly lines all have branches, so be sure to **note which branch is needed for your particular destination.** Electronic platform signs tell you the final stop and route of the next train, and some signs also indicate how many minutes you'll have to wait for the train to arrive.

Hours   From Monday to Saturday, trains begin running just after 5 AM; the last services leave central London between midnight and 12:30 AM. On Sundays, trains start two hours later and finish about an hour earlier. Frequency of trains depends on the route and the time of day, but normally you should not have to wait more than 10 minutes in central areas.

Fares   For both buses and tube fares, London is divided into six concentric zones; the fare goes up the farther out you travel. For details on the fare system, **ask for a London Transport booklet describing various ticket options**; it's available at most Underground ticket counter. Traveling without a valid ticket makes you liable for an on-the-spot fine (£10 at press time), so always pay your fare before you travel.

For one trip between any two stations, you can buy an ordinary single (one-way ticket) for travel anytime on the day of issue; if you're coming back on the same route the same day, then an ordinary return (round-trip ticket) costs twice the single fare. Singles vary in price from £1 to £3.10—expensive if you're making several journeys in a day. There are several passes good for both the tube and the bus; *see* Important Contacts A to Z, *above*.

Information   To help you find your way around, **get a free pocket map,** also available from most Underground ticket counters. There is a large map on the wall of each platform.

There are LT (London Transport) Travel Information Centres at the following tube stations: Heathrow (daily, varying times at each terminal); Victoria (daily 8:15 AM–9:30 PM); Piccadilly Circus (daily 8:15–6); Oxford Circus (Mon.–Sat. 8:15–6); Euston (Mon.–Thurs. and Sat. 7:15–6, Fri. 7:15 AM–7:30 PM, Sun. 8:15–6); and King's Cross (Mon.–Thurs. 8:15–6, Fri. 7:15 AM–7:30 PM, Sat. 7:15–6).

W

Walking   London is a walker's city, sort of. The parks, if you can incorporate them into your route, are lovely, but wherever you go there is plenty to look at. Still, London is big and often damp, its layout complicated and not necessarily logical, and the things you want to see are invariably miles apart. The best approach is to **mix foot travel with public transportation:** Take the tube to the general vicinity, and then, as you may hear somebody say, "ride Shanks's pony."

Many guided walking tours are available (*see* Important Contacts A to Z), but for those who would rather explore on their own, the City of London Corporation has laid out a Heritage Walk leading through Bank, Leadenhall, and Monument streets; **follow the trail of the Heritage Walk** by the directional stars set into the sidewalks. A map of this walk may be found in *A Visitor's Guide to the City of London*, available from the City Information Centre across from St. Paul's Cathedral.

Another option is to **follow the Silver Jubilee Walkway,** created in 1977 in honor of the 25th anniversary of the accession of the present queen. The entire route covers 10 miles and is marked by a series of silver crowns set into the sidewalks; Parliament Square makes a good starting point.

When to Go The heaviest tourist season in Britain runs from mid-April to mid-October, with a small peak around Christmas—though the tide never really ebbs away. The spring is the time to see the countryside and the London gardens at their freshest; early summer to catch the roses and full garden splendor; the fall for near-ideal exploring conditions. The British take their vacations mainly in July and August, and the resorts are crowded. London in summer, however, though full of visitors, is also full of interesting things to see and do. But be warned: Air-conditioning is *very* rare in London, and in a hot summer you'll swelter. The winter can be rather dismal and is frequently wet and usually cold, but all the theaters, concerts, and exhibitions are going full speed. January and February are the cheapest months, full of special deals from hotels desperate for bodies in beds, and peppered with promotional menus in restaurants. Beware Christmas and New Year's: London empties completely; the only places you can get a meal are hotel dining rooms; and every museum, gallery, theater, and movie house goes home for turkey.

Climate London's weather has always been contrary, and in recent years it has become positively erratic, with hot summers and mild winters owing, apparently, to the greenhouse effect. It is virtually impossible to forecast what the pattern might be, but you can be fairly certain that it will not be what you expect! The main feature of the British weather is that it is generally mild—with some savage exceptions, especially in summer. It is also fairly damp—though even that has been changing in recent years with recurring periods of drought.

What follows are the average daily maximum and minimum temperatures for London.

Jan.	43F	6C	May	62F	17C	Sept.	65F	19C
	36	2		47	8		52	11
Feb.	44F	7C	June	69F	20C	Oct.	58F	14C
	36	2		53	12		46	8
Mar.	50F	10C	July	71F	22C	Nov.	50F	10C
	38	3		56	14		42	5
Apr.	56F	13C	Aug.	71F	21C	Dec.	45F	7C
	42	6		56	13		38	4

Festivals and Seasonal Events **Early Jan.: London International Boat Show,** the largest boat show in Europe. Earl's Court Exhibition Centre, Warwick Rd., London SW5 9TA, tel. 01784/473–377.

Feb.–Mar.: London Arts Season showcases the city's extensive arts scene, with bargain-priced tickets and special events.

During Mar.: Camden Jazz Festival is 10 days of concerts sponsored by the Borough of Camden. For information, call 0171/860–5866.

Mid-Apr.: London Marathon, a New York–style marathon through London's streets. Information from Box 262, Richmond, Surrey TW10 5JB, tel. 0181/948–7935.

Late May: The Chelsea Flower Show, Britain's major flower show, covers 22 acres. Royal Hospital Rd., Chelsea SW3, tel. 0171/630–7422.

Early June: Beating Retreat by the Guards Massed Bands, when more than 500 musicians parade at Horse Guards, Whitehall. Tickets from Household Division Fund, Block 8, Wellington Barracks, Birdcage Walk, London SW1E 6HQ, tel. 0171/414–3253.

June 4: Trooping the Colour. Queen Elizabeth's colorful official birthday parade, is held at Horse Guards, Whitehall. Write for tickets *only* between January 1 and February 28, enclosing a self-addressed stamped envelope: Ticket Office, Headquarters, Household Division, Chelsea Barracks, London SW1H 8RF, tel. 0171/414–2497.

Late June–Early July: Wimbledon Lawn Tennis Championships, held at the All England Lawn Tennis and Croquet Club in Wimbledon. Write early to enter the lottery for tickets for Center and Number One Courts; tickets for outside courts available daily at the gate. Church Rd., Wimbledon, London SW19 5AE, tel. 0181/946–2244.

Mid-July–mid-Sept.: Henry Wood Promenade Concerts, a marvelous series of concerts at the Royal Albert Hall. Box Office, Royal Albert Hall, Kensington Gore SW7 2AP, tel. 0171/589–8212.

Late July: The Royal Tournament features military displays and pageantry by the Royal navy, the Royal marines, the Army, and the Royal Air Force. Earl's Court Exhibition Centre, Warwick Rd., London SW5 9TA, tel. 0171/370–8226.

Early Oct.: The Horse of the Year Show has the world's top show jumpers at the Wembley Arena. Show Box Office, 4 Grove parade, Buxton, Derbyshire SK17 6AJ, tel. 0298/72272.

First Sun. in Nov.: London to Brighton Veteran Car Run, a run from Hyde park in London to Brighton in East Sussex. No tickets required. For information, call 0753/681–736.

Mid-Nov.: Lord Mayor's Procession and Show. At the lord mayor's inauguration, a procession takes place from the Guildhall in the City to the Royal Courts of Justice. No tickets are required. For information, call 0171/606–3030.

Early Dec.: Christmas festivities. London prepares for the holiday season with the lighting of a Christmas tree and carolling in Trafalgar Square.

2 Where to Stay on a Budget

Unless you're lucky enough to be staying in the guest bedroom of a London friend, the most expensive part of your trip is going to be your accommodations. The price of a hotel bed in London is, notoriously, just about the highest in Europe, although a welcome trend in recent years has been the increase in what's often dubbed "boutique hotels," which have far fewer rooms and consequently offer more personal attention and lower rates. Along with the clutch of megabucks hotels that opened during the early '90s (the Lanesborough, the restored Dorchester, the Regent, the little Halkin), which are no use at all to the budget traveler, a number of these little places appeared also. Some are still beyond a restrictive budget, but we list a few that, although not exactly priced at rock bottom, provide excellent value, lovely surroundings, and a human-scale experience of London. Another way to get fine decor at cut rates is to haggle for an expensive room off-season. This is a perfectly legitimate strategem, and it can yield spectacular results. Hotels don't advertise it, but they'd almost invariably rather fill a £250 room for £50 than have it empty, and the more expensive the hotel, the more likely this is to be true. Just ask—but be diplomatic and dress smart.

For the longer term, you'll need less risky options. We offer plenty of suggestions below for lower-cost roofs. But there are two ways to get even cheaper rates, and they're as different from each other as—well, are canvas and the family home.

Camping near London is generally best left to masochists, although in summer—if you despise the conventional and like tasting life as it's lived in *real* suburbs and outer boroughs—the experience can turn out wonderfully. A few sites to try (all accessible but well outside the center): **Hackney Camping** (Millfields Rd., E5, tel. 0181/985–7656) in the East End, open June–August only; **Abbey Wood** (Federation Rd., SE2 0LS, tel. 0181/310–2233) near Greenwich; **Lea Valley Campsite** (Sewardstone Rd., Chingford, E4, tel. 0181/529–5689) in a "green belt" area; **Tent City** (Old Oak Common La., W3,

London Lodging *(Boxes Refer to Detail Maps)*

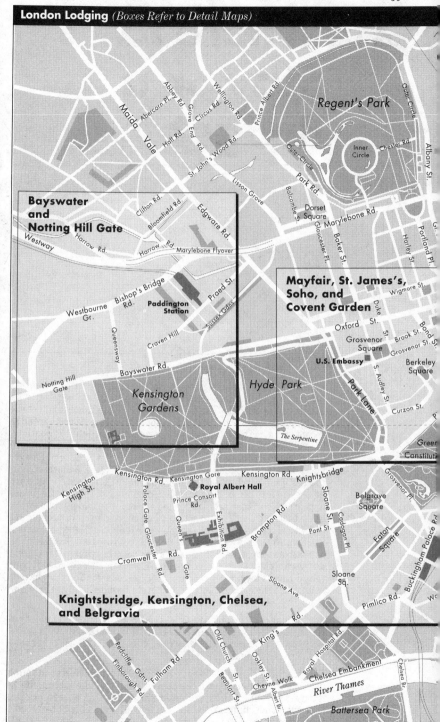

Bayswater and Notting Hill Gate

Mayfair, St. James's, Soho, and Covent Garden

Knightsbridge, Kensington, Chelsea, and Belgravia

Regent's Park

Inner Circle

Outer Circle

Maida Vale

Abbey Rd.

Abercorn Pl.

Grove End Rd.

Hall Rd.

Circus Rd.

Wellington Rd.

Prince Albert Rd.

St. John's Wood Rd.

Lisson Grove

Park Rd.

Balcombe S.

Dorset Square

Marylebone Rd.

Gloucester Pl.

Baker St.

Chester Rd.

Albany St.

Portland Pl.

Harley St.

Clifton Rd.

Bloomfield Rd.

Edgware Rd.

Westway

Harrow Rd.

Harrow Rd.

Marylebone Flyover

Westbourne Gr.

Bishop's Bridge Rd.

Paddington Station

Praed St.

Sussex Gdns.

Queensway

Craven Hill

Bayswater Rd.

Notting Hill Gate

Kensington Gardens

Oxford St.

Wigmore St.

Duke

Grosvenor Square

Brook St.

Grosvenor St.

Bond St.

U.S. Embassy

S. Audley St.

Berkeley Square

Park Lane

Curzon St.

Hyde Park

The Serpentine

Green

Constitut

Kensington Rd.

Kensington Gore

Kensington Rd.

Knightsbridge

Grosvenor Pl.

Kensington High St.

Palace Gate

Gloucester

Prince Consort Rd.

Queen's Gate

Exhibition Rd.

Royal Albert Hall

Brompton Rd.

Sloane St.

Pont St.

Cadogan Pl.

Belgrave Square

Eaton Square

Cromwell Rd.

Queen's Gate

Sloane Ave.

Sloane Sq.

Pimlico Rd.

Buckingham Palace Rd.

Redcliffe Gdns.

Finborough Rd.

Fulham Rd.

Old Church St.

King's

Oakley St.

Beaufort St.

Cheyne Walk

Albert Br.

Royal Hospital Rd.

Chelsea Embankment

Chelsea Br.

River Thames

Battersea Park

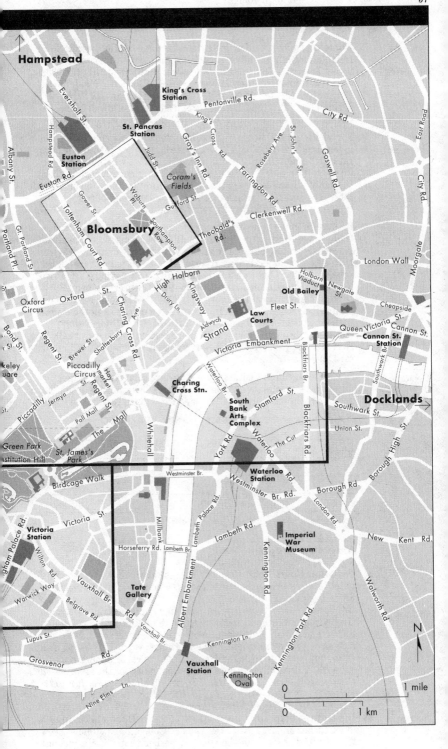

Hampstead

King's Cross
Station

Pentonville Rd.

City Rd.

East Road

St. Pancras
Station

King's Cross Rd.

Gray's Inn Rd.

Rosebery Ave.

St. John's

Goswell Rd.

City Rd.

Eversholt St.

Euston
Station

Hampstead Rd.

Albany St.

Coram's
Fields

Farringdon Rd.

Clerkenwell Rd.

Gr. Portland St.

Portland Pl.

Euston Rd.

Gower St.

Woburn

Southampton Row

Guilford St.

Judd St.

Bloomsbury

Tottenham Court Rd.

Theobald's Rd.

London Wall

Moorgate

High Holborn

Holborn Viaduct

Newgate St.

Cheapside

Oxford
Circus

Oxford
St.

Charing Cross Ave.

Drury Ln.

Kingsway

Aldwych

Old Bailey

Fleet St.

Law
Courts

Queen Victoria St.

Cannon St.

Cannon St.
Station

Bond St.

Regent St.

Brewer St.

Shaftesbury Ave.

Strand

Victoria Embankment

Blackfriars Br.

Southwark Br.

keley
uare

Piccadilly
Circus

Market

Regent St.

Haymarket

St. James's

Charing
Cross Stn.

Waterloo Br.

Stamford St.

Blackfriars Rd.

Docklands

Piccadilly

Jermyn

Pall Mall

South
Bank
Arts
Complex

Southwark St.

Southwark St.

St.

The Mall

Whitehall

Waterloo

The Cut

Union St.

Borough High St.

Green Park

stitution Hill

St. James's
Park

Birdcage Walk

York Rd.

Waterloo
Station

Borough Rd.

Westminster Br.

Westminster Br. Rd.

London Rd.

Borough Rd.

Victoria St.

Millbank

Lambeth Palace Rd.

Lambeth Rd.

Imperial
War
Museum

New Kent Rd.

ham Palace Rd.

Victoria
Station

Wilton Rd.

Horseferry Rd.

Lambeth Br.

Kennington Rd.

Walworth Rd.

Warwick Way

Vauxhall Br.

Belgrave Rd.

Tate
Gallery

Albert Embankment

Kennington Rd.

Kennington Park Rd.

N

Lupus St.

Rd.

Vauxhall Br.

Rd.

Kennington Ln.

Grosvenor

Nine Elms Ln.

Vauxhall
Station

Kennington
Oval

0   1 mile

0   1 km

tel. 0181/749–9074; open June–Aug.) in Acton, west London. Bring your own tent.

Home swapping provides the cheapest accommodations of all. Some reliable and longstanding agencies with plenty of Brits on their books: **Intervac** (6 Siddals La., Allestree, Derby DE3 2DY, tel. 0332/ 558931); **Homelink International** (84 Lees Gardens, Maidenhead, Berks SL6 4NT, tel. 0628/31951); **Home Base Holidays** (7 Park Ave., London N13 5PG, tel. 0181/886–8752); and the **Worldwide Home Exchange Club** (45 Hans Pl., London SW1X 0JZ, tel. 0171/589–6055).

For visitors who choose more conventional hotels and B&Bs, the general custom these days in all but the bottom end of the scale is for rates to be quoted for the room alone; breakfast, whether Continental or "full English," comes as an extra. VAT is usually included. All the hotels listed here are graded according to their spring 1995 rates, so check for the latest figures, remembering, of course, that there can be a significant difference off-season.

Be sure to make reservations well in advance, as seasonal events, trade shows, or royal occasions can fill hotel rooms for sudden brief periods. Planning ahead also allows you to investigate the various U.S.-based membership programs that offer discount travel in Europe, including London hotel rooms at up to 50% savings. Try **Privilege Card International** (tel. 800/236–9732), Entertainment Publications' **Europe Hotel Directory** (tel. 800/445–4137), or **RMC Travel Centre** (tel. 800/782–2674). However, if you do arrive in the capital without a room, the **London Tourist Board (LTB) Information Centres** at Heathrow and Victoria Station Forecourt can help, or call the **LTB Hotline** (tel. 0171/824–8844, weekdays 9:30–5:30) for credit card bookings (MC, V).

A word of warning: Visitors to London have complained of the exorbitant rates exacted by certain accommodations agencies (although, not LTB) for their "services." So try to deal directly with the hotel.

Highly recommended hotels are indicated by a star ★.

Category	Cost*
$$	£70–£120
$	£40–£70
¢	under £40

*cost of a double room; VAT included

Mayfair to Regent's Park

$$ **Bryanston Court.** Three Georgian houses have been converted into a
★   hotel in a historic conservation area, a couple of blocks north of Hyde Park and Park Lane. The style is traditional English—open fireplaces, comfortable leather armchairs, oil portraits—though the bedrooms are small and modern, with pink furnishings, creaky floors, and minute bathrooms. Rooms at the back are quieter and face east, so they're bright in the mornings; room 77 is as big as a suite, but being on the lower ground floor typical of London houses, it's dark. This family-run hotel is excellent value for the area. *56–60 Great Cumberland Pl., W1H 7FD, tel. 0171/262–3141, fax 0171/ 262–7248. 56 rooms with bath. Facilities: bar, lounge, restaurant. AE, DC, MC, V. Tube: Marble Arch.*

$$ **Durrants.** A hotel since the late 18th century, Durrants occupies a quiet corner almost next to the Wallace Collection, a stone's throw from Oxford Street and the smaller, posher shops of Marylebone High Street. Once a great bargain, the rates have been creeping up, and it's now at the top end of moderate and a little shabby round the

39

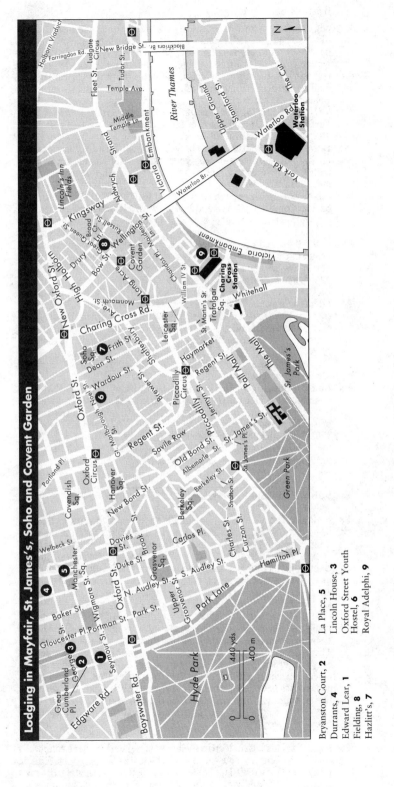

Lodging in Mayfair, St. James's, Soho, and Covent Garden

Bryanston Court, **2**
Durrants, **4**
Edward Lear, **1**
Fielding, **8**
Hazlitt's, **7**

La Place, **5**
Lincoln House, **3**
Oxford Street Youth
Hostel, **6**
Royal Adelphi, **9**

edges to boot. However, it's still good value for the area, and if you like Ye wood-paneled, leather-armchaired, dark-red-patterned-carpeted style of olde Englishness, this will suit you. Bedrooms, by way of contrast, are wan and motel-like but perfectly adequate—a few have no bathroom, which is reflected in the lower rate. Each landing harbors a communal minibar (a maxibar?) and ice machine. Best give the baron of beef–type restaurant a miss. *George St., W1H 6BH, tel. 0171/935–8131, fax 0171/487–3510. 96 rooms, 85 with bath. Facilities: restaurant, bar, private dining rooms, lounges. AE, MC, V. Tube: Bond Street.*

$$ Edward Lear. Onetime home of writer/artist Edward Lear (famous for his nonsense verse), this good-value hotel has an inviting entranceway leading to a black-and-white tiled hall. Rooms vary enormously in size, with some family rooms very spacious indeed and others barely big enough to get out of bed (avoid #14); rooms at the back are quieter. It's a friendly place with a lot of repeat customers, but there are no hotel-type facilities (although if you want a jacket pressed you're welcome to borrow the iron), and the only public area is the light and pleasant breakfast room. The management is very proud of the English breakfasts—they use the same butcher as the queen. *28–30 Seymour St., W1H 5WD, tel. 0171/402–5401, fax 0171/706–3766. 30 rooms, 15 with bath. V. Tube: Marble Arch.*

$ La Place. Near Madame Tussaud's and Regent's Park, this small hotel has a Continental feel, thanks to the predominantly French staff that the Swiss owner employs. Rooms offer ensuite bathrooms, color TV, direct-dial telephone, hair dryer, pants press, minibar, and tea/coffee facilities, and an English breakfast is included in the rate. *17 Nottingham Pl., W1M 3FB, tel. 0171/486–2323, fax 0171/486–4335. 20 rooms with bath/shower. Facilities: 24-hr wine bar. DC, MC, V. Tube: Baker Street.*

$ Lincoln House. One of the several Georgian row houses that have been converted into modest bed-and-breakfast hotels on a wide road off Oxford Street, this one is well kept, with good facilities for the price. Most rooms have ensuite shower and WC, and all have color TV, direct-dial phone, hair dryer, pants press, and tea/coffee facilities. *33 Gloucester Pl., W1H 3PD, tel. 0171/486–7630, fax 0171/486–0160. 22 rooms, 17 with shower. Facilities: lounge/breakfast room. AE, DC, MC, V. Tube: Marble Arch.*

Soho and Covent Garden

$$ Fielding. Tucked away in a quiet alley by the world's first police station (now Bow St. Magistrates' Court), and feeling far from the madding crowds of Covent Garden, this very small and pretty hotel is so adored by its regulars that you'd be wise to book well ahead. Cameron Mackintosh, the Broadway musical producer (who could no doubt afford Claridges), stays here—presumably for the homey atmosphere; the old London Town character; the continuity of a loyal, friendly staff who maintain the place as the two founders, now retired, have kept it for over two decades; and of course for the convenience of having the Royal Opera House, every theater, and half of London's restaurants within spitting distance. It is not uneccentric. The bedrooms are all different, shabby-homey rather than chic, and cozy rather than spacious, though you can have a suite here for the price of a chain-hotel double. There's no elevator; only one room comes with bath (most have showers); and only breakfast is served in the restaurant. Cute. *4 Broad Ct., Bow St., WC2B 5QZ, tel. 0171/836–8305, fax 0171/497–0064. 26 rooms, 1 with bath, 23 with shower. Facilities: bar, breakfast room. AE, DC, MC, V. Tube: Covent Garden.*

$$ Hazlitt's. This hotel, deep in the heart of Soho, is in three connected early 18th-century houses, one of which was the essayist William Hazlitt's (1778–1830) last home. It's an open secret that Hazlitt's is a disarmingly friendly place, full of personality. Robust antiques are everywhere, assorted prints crowd every wall, plants and stone sculptures (by one of the owners' father-in-law) appear in odd corners, and every room has a Victorian claw-foot bath in its bathroom. There are a tiny sitting room, wooden staircases, and more restaurants within strolling distance than you could patronize in a year. Book way ahead—this is the London address of media people and antique dealers everywhere. *6 Frith St., W1V 5TZ, tel. 0171/434–1771, fax 0171/439–1524. 23 rooms with bath. AE, DC, MC, V. Tube: Leicester Square.*

$ **Royal Adelphi.** This functional place—well kept and with an excellent location near theaterland, Covent Garden, Trafalgar Square, and the Thames Embankment—won't excite anybody, but it's fine if you're out a lot. Rooms have direct-dial phone, TV, tea/coffee facilities, safe, and (usually) hair dryers, and a Continental breakfast is included. Note that access is via a fairly steep staircase, and there's no elevator. *21 Villiers St., WC2N 6ND, tel. 0171/930–8764, fax 0171/930–8735. 55 rooms, 27 with bath/shower. Facilities: bar. AE, DC, MC, V. Tube: Embankment.*

¢ **Oxford Street Youth Hostel.** As always, this basic-style accommodation is not restricted to under-18s, though they might feel more comfortable sharing dorms and bathrooms than their parents would. However, this modern hostel has more small rooms than most, with 13 two-person bunk-bedded ones. There is 24-hour access, and the location can't be beat: It's right in Soho. You must join the International Youth Hostel Federation to stay here or at the other six YHA London hostels. *14–18 Noel St., London W1V 3PD, tel. 0171/734–1618, fax 0171/734–1657. 33 rooms, 17 shared bathrooms. Facilities: small kitchen, TV lounge, bureau de change. Tube: Oxford Circus.*

Kensington

$$ **Kensington Close.** This large, fairly utilitarian hotel feels like a smaller one and boasts a few extras you wouldn't expect for the reasonable rate and convenient location (in a quiet lane off Kensington High Street). The main attraction is the health club, with an 18-meter pool, two squash courts, and a beauty salon; there's also a secluded little water garden. Standard rooms are on the small side, with plain chain-hotel built-in furniture. Some Executive rooms are twice the size. Good value. *Wrights La., W8 5SP, tel. 0171/937–8170, fax 0171/937–8289. 530 rooms with bath. Facilities: 2 restaurants, 2 bars, lounge, garden, health club with indoor pool, satellite TV, baby-sitting. AE, DC, MC, V. Tube: Kensington High Street.*

$ **Eight Knaresborough Place.** Serviced apartments tend to come with minimum-stay requirements and a hefty tab, but these, which include daily maid service, a private phone line, color TV, and a tiny but complete kitchen (in the living room), start at around £80 for a suite that sleeps four (two on a sofabed), and you can book (and prepay) for just two nights. Decor features glass tables, brass lamps, and vinyl-cushioned chairs, but this—the long-haul traveler's neighborhood of Earl's Court—is no Park Avenue. *8 Knaresborough Pl., SW5 0TG, tel. 0171/244–8409, fax 0171/373–6455. 35 apartments with bath. Facilities: laundry room. AE, MC, V. Tube: Earl's Court.*

$ ★ **Vicarage.** Family-owned for over 30 years, the Vicarage feels like a real home. It's beautifully decorated, in a quiet location overlooking a magnificent garden square and close to the Kensington shops. *10 Vicarage Gate, W8 4AG, tel. 0171/229–4030. 19 rooms without bath. Facilities: lounge. No credit cards. Tube: Kensington High Street.*

¢ **Windsor House.** Earl's Court, the backpacker's mecca, has its advantages: There are plenty of places to eat cheap, and it's nothing if not lively. The huge Exhibition Hall is here, too. This hotel is typical of the area's budget establishments but has the distinction of cleanliness and *very* low rates. Guests can use the kitchen and garden. *12 Penywern Rd., SW5, tel. 0171/373–9087, fax 0181/960–7273. 15*

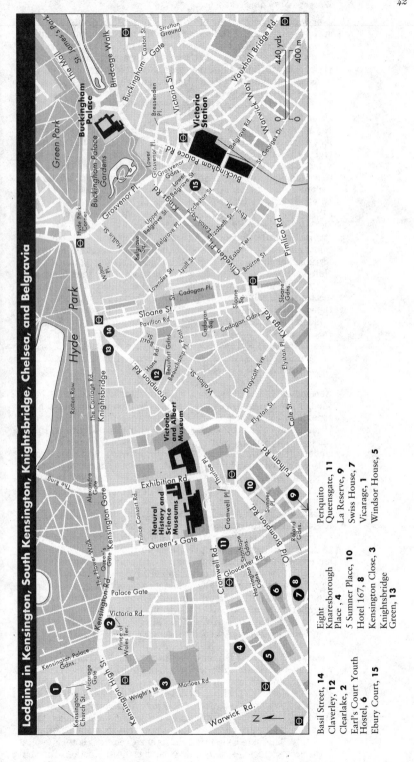

Lodging in Kensington, South Kensington, Knightsbridge, Chelsea, and Belgravia

42

440 yds
400 m

Basil Street, 14
Claverlake, 12
Clearlake, 2
Earl's Court Youth Hostel, 6
Ebury Court, 15

Eight
Knaresborough Place, 4
5 Sumner Place, 10
Hotel 167, 8
Kensington Close, 3
Knightsbridge Green, 13

Periquito Queensgate, 11
La Reserve, 9
Swiss House, 7
Vicarage, 1
Windsor House, 5

rooms, 1 with bath, 11 with shower. Facilities: garden, kitchen. AE, DC, MC, V. Tube: Earl's Court.

¢ **Earl's Court Youth Hostel.** The quintessential backpacker's bunk-house, with no frills, in one of the vast double-fronted town houses typical of the area. Every bed comes with a security locker, but there's no privacy—four-person rooms are the smallest, and there are only two of those. The hostel was last refurbished in 1991. Rates (around £16 per night) include breakfast and bed linens. *38 Bolton Gardens, SW5 0AQ, tel. 0171/373-7083, fax 0171/835-2034. 14 dormitories (123 beds), 20 public bathrooms. Facilities: common room, laundromat, cafeteria. Tube: Earl's Court.*

Knightsbridge, South Kensington, Chelsea, and Belgravia

$$ **Bulldog Club.** You must join Amanda St. George's *very* exclusive
★ B&B club before being eligible to book a stay with some of London's grandest families. Many have converted their now-grown-up-children's rooms; others have built guest annexes. All offer total comfort, with breakfast included and TV and tea/coffee facilities in your room. Not all the houses are in this neighborhood. *Further details from 35 The Chase, SW4 0NP, tel. 0171/622-6935, fax 0171/491-1328. Facilities vary. Most rooms have private bath/shower. AE, MC, V.*

$$ **Claverley.** This boutique hotel is on a quiet street a moment from Harrods. The less expensive rooms have either bath or shower (not both); as you go up the scale, rooms get larger, decor (homey florals, either Victorian- or Edwardian-style) newer, and bathrooms better equipped; some top-rate rooms have four-poster beds. The service is friendly, everything's spotless, and an enormous British breakfast is included. *13–14 Beaufort Gdns., SW3 1PS, tel. 0171/589-8541, fax 0171/584-3410. 36 rooms with bath. AE, V. Tube: Knights-bridge.*

$$ **Ebury Court.** Here five 19th-century houses have been converted into an old-fashioned, family-run hotel close to Victoria Station. The rooms are smallish, with antique furniture to give them extra character—one of them has a grandfather clock and a Hepplewhite four-poster bed. The reception area, lounge, and restaurant are all fresh-ly renovated, as are many of the bedrooms; some new ones were added recently, but some of them still have no bathroom. Be warned: Since the rates went up, these are the only "moderate" rooms. *26 Ebury St., SW1W 0LU, tel. 0171/730-8147, fax 0171/823-5966. 45 rooms, 36 with bath. Facilities: bar, restaurant. MC, V. Tube: Victoria.*

$$ **Five Sumner Place.** On a peaceful street near the big museums, this family-run small hotel has a pretty glass-roof Victorian-style con-servatory for breakfast, which is included in the rates. Rooms have TV and direct dial phones, and all are served by elevator. *5 Sumner Pl., SW7 3EE, tel. 0171/584-7586, fax 0171/823-9962. 13 rooms with bath. Facilities: breakfast room. AE, DC, MC, V. Tube: South Kensington.*

$$ **Knightsbridge Green.** There are more suites than bedrooms at this Georgian hotel two minutes' walk from Harrods. One floor is French-style with white furniture; another English, in beech. Being only just above moderate, the suites are not overpriced, and all the rooms have trouser presses and tea- and coffee-making facilities added. There's no restaurant, but there are plenty in the area; or if you ask they'll send the porter out to find you a sandwich. There's also coffee and cake left out in the lounge—a detail that exemplifies the friendliness of this place. *159 Knightsbridge, SW1X 7PD, tel. 0171/584-6274, fax 0171/225-1635. 24 rooms/suites with bath. Facil-ities: lounge. AE, MC, V. Closed 5 days over Christmas. Tube: Knightsbridge.*

$$ **La Reserve.** You'll find this unique small hotel in the lively, classy
★ residential neighborhood of Fulham. The varnished floorboards,
black Venetian blinds, works of art (for sale), and primary-colored
upholstery in the public areas are contemporary and sophisticated.
Bedrooms are cluttered only with the minibars, hairdryers, trouser
presses, and tea/coffee makers of more expensive places. It's a two-
minute walk from Fulham Broadway tube, near Chelsea Football
(soccer) Grounds and plenty of restaurants; there's also a brasserie
in-house. *422–428 Fulham Rd., SW6 1DU, tel. 0171/385–8561, fax
0171/385–7662. 37 rooms with bath. Facilities: restaurant, bar,
lounge, satellite TV. AE, DC, MC, V. Tube: Fulham Broadway.*

$ **Hotel 167.** A small, private hotel in a grand Victorian corner house,
★ this place is immediately cheering, with round marble tables,
wrought-iron chairs and palms in the reception/breakfast room, and
well-kept bedrooms with Venetian blinds over double-glazed win-
dows, antiques, large beds, tea/coffee facilities, direct-dial phone,
TV and VCR, hair dryer, minibar, and safe. A friendly staff com-
pletes the picture. *167 Old Brompton Rd., SW5 0AN, tel. 0171/373–
0672, fax 0171/373–3360. 19 rooms with bath/shower. Facilities:
lounge/breakfast area. MC, V. Tube: Gloucester Road.*

$ **Periquito Queensgate.** When a hotel calls its own rooms "compact,"
you should imagine a double bed, then add a foot all round—there
you have the measure of a room here. However, like a cruise ship
stateroom, all you need is creatively secreted—there's a closet, mir-
ror, satellite TV, tea/coffee maker, and a hairdryer. If you want a
divorce, the kids can share free, or else they get their own room half
price. The Natural History Museum is across the street. *68–69
Queensgate, SW7 5JT, tel. 0171/370–6111, fax 0171/370–0932. 61
rooms with bath. Facilities: bar, lounge. AE, MC, V. Tube: Glouces-
ter Road.*

$ **Swiss House.** The rates at this homey B&B undercut those of the ad-
★ jacent Hotel 167 by £10–£20. You sacrifice some fanciness of decor
for that, though it is not shabby here. Windows are double-glazed,
phones and TVs are standard, and many rooms feature canopied
beds. There is a welcoming ivy-clad entrance, a Continental buffet
breakfast, and—amazingly— modest room service from midday till
9 PM. *171 Old Brompton Rd., SW5 0AN, tel. 0171/373–2769, fax
0171/373–4983. 16 rooms, 10 with bath/shower. Facilities: breakfast
room, room service. MC, V. Tube: Gloucester Road.*

Bayswater and Notting Hill Gate

$$ **Camelot.** Top marks go to this affordable hotel, with its freshly deco-
★ rated bedrooms (featuring utility pine furniture, TVs, and tea/cof-
fee makers) and attractive bathrooms. A full English breakfast is
included in the room rate, which you eat in a very pretty breakfast
room complete with exposed brick wall, large open fireplace, wood-
en farmhouse tables and floorboards, and a gallery of child guests'
works of art. Everyone here is friendly beyond the call of duty. The
few bathless single rooms are great bargains, and there are occasional discounts on longer stays when you pay in advance. *45–47
Norfolk Sq., W2 1RX, tel. 0171/723–9118, fax 0171/402–3412. 34
rooms, 28 with bath. Facilities: free in-house videos, lounge. MC, V.
Tube: Paddington.*

$$ **Commodore.** This peaceful hotel of three converted Victorians has
★ some amazing rooms—as superior to the regular ones (which usual-
ly go to package tour groups) as Harrods is to Woolworths, but
priced the same. Twenty are split levels, with sleeping gallery, and
all have the full deck of tea/coffee makers, hairdryers, and TV with
pay movies. One (no. 11) is a duplex, entered through a secret mir-
rored door, with a thick-carpeted very quiet bedroom upstairs and a
bathroom below. It's getting very popular here, so book ahead. *50
Lancaster Gate, W2 3NA, tel. 0171/402–5291, fax 0171/262–1088. 90*

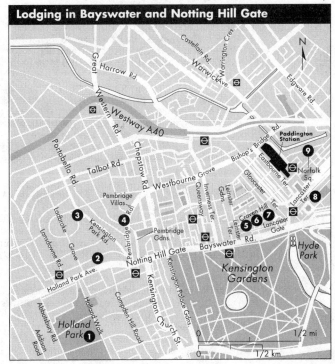

Lodging in Bayswater and Notting Hill Gate

rooms with bath. Facilities: bar, lounge, business center. AE, MC, V. Tube: Lancaster Gate.

$$ **London Elizabeth.** Steps from Hyde Park, Lancaster Gate tube, and ★ rows of depressing cheap hotels, is this family-owned gem. The foyer and lounge are crammed with coffee tables and chintz drapery, lace antimacassars, and little chandeliers, and this country sensibility persists throughout the freshly decorated bedrooms. Some rooms lack a full-length mirror, but they do have TV, direct dial phone, and hairdryer, and they're serviced by an exceptionally charming Anglo-Irish staff. *Lancaster Terrace, W2 3PF, tel. 0171/402–6641, fax 0171/224–8900. 55 rooms. Facilities: restaurant, bar, lounge, 24-hr room service. AE, DC, MC, V. Tube: Lancaster Gate.*

$$ **Portobello.** This small, eccentric hotel consists of two adjoining Vic- ★ torian houses that (as is common around here) back onto a beautiful large garden that is shared with the neighbors. It has long been the favorite of the arty end of the music biz and other media types. Some rooms are minute, others huge, and the smallest—aptly called "cab- ins"—are bargains. Big mirrors, palms, and ferns are everywhere, as befits the fantasy Victorian decor. The naughty round-bedded suite is popular. The basement bar/restaurant is one of many hang- outs for locals in this very happening area. *22 Stanley Gdns., W11 2NG, tel. 0171/727–2777, fax 0171/792–9641. 25 rooms with bath. Facilities: bar, restaurant. AE, DC, MC, V. Closed 10 days over Christmas. Tube: Notting Hill Gate.*

$ **Columbia.** The public rooms in these five joined-up Victorians are as ★ big as museum halls, painted in icy hues of powder blue and butter- milk or paneled in dark wood. The rooms are clean, have high ceil- ings, and are sometimes very large (especially those with three or four beds), boasting Hyde Park views and balconies; all have hairdryers, tea/coffee makers, TVs, and direct dial phones. It's just a shame that teak veneer, khaki-beige-brown color schemes, and av- ocado bathroom suites haven't made it back into the style bible yet. *95–99 Lancaster Gate, W2 3NS, tel. 0171/402–0021, fax 0171/706–*

4691. 103 rooms with bath. Facilities: restaurant, bar, lounge, conference rooms. AE, MC, V. Tube: Lancaster Gate.

$ **Holland Park Hotel.** A quiet town house, beautifully restored and decorated, with more antiques than you'd expect for the price, and even a four-poster bed or two (in Room 11, for example). There's a TV, hair dryer, tea/coffee facilities, and direct-dial phone in every room, and a gorgeous lounge with open fire and massive windows overlooking the leafy garden. Continental breakfast, brought to your room, is included. *6 Ladbroke Terr., W11 3PG, tel. 0171/727– 5815, fax 0171/792–0858. 23 rooms, 14 with bath/shower. Facilities: lounge, garden. AE, DC, MC, V. Tube: Notting Hill Gate.*

$ **Lancaster Hall Hotel.** This modest hotel is owned by the German YMCA, which guarantees efficiency and spotlessness. There's a bargain 20-room "youth annex" offering basic rooms with shared baths. *35 Craven Terr., W2, tel. 0171/723–9276, fax 0171/224–8343. 100 rooms, 80 with bath or shower. Facilities: restaurant, bar. MC, V. Tube: Lancaster Gate.*

¢ **Gate Hotel.** This tiny B&B, at the top of the famous Portobello Road,
★ is friendly and clean; its reasonably sized rooms boast modern furnishings and facilities that include minibar, TV, phone, tea/coffee maker, and safe. *6 Portobello Rd., W11 3DG, tel. 0171/221–2403. 8 rooms, 5 with bath/shower. Facilities: washer/dryer. MC, V. Tube: Notting Hill Gate.*

¢ **Holland House Youth Hostel.** This part Jacobean mansion, part modern extension in the middle of one of London's prettiest parks provides the usual dormitory accommodations (8–20 bunks per dorm, with one two-person room). In 1992, the whole place was refurbished, central heating and better showers installed, and the 11 PM curfew jettisoned. *Holland House, Holland Walk, W8 7QU, tel. 0171/937–0748, fax 0171/376–0667. 187 beds, 39 bathrooms. Facilities: common room, quiet room, cafeteria, kitchen, laundromat, bureau de change. Tube: Kensington High Street.*

Bloomsbury

$$ **Whitehall.** An imposing entrance promises good things, which the interior more than lives up to. There's an elegant lobby with arched windows, and a garden bar leading onto a patio and not-too-manicured garden. A fine dining room offers both Continental and English breakfast, which is included in the (very moderate) rate. *2–5 Montague St., WC1B 5BU, tel. 0171/580–5871, fax 0171/323–0409. 80 rooms, 20 with bath. Facilities: restaurant, bar. AE, DC, MC, V. Tube: Tottenham Court Road.*

$ **Morgan.** A Georgian row-house hotel, family-run with charm and
★ panache. Rooms are small and functionally furnished, yet friendly and cheerful overall, with those in the four newish apartments, complete with eat-in kitchens and private phone lines, particularly pleasing. The tiny, paneled breakfast room is straight out of a doll's house. The back rooms overlook the British Museum. *24 Bloomsbury St., WC1B 3QJ, tel. 0171/636–3735. 14 rooms with bath or shower, 4 apartments. No credit cards. Tube: Tottenham Court Road.*

$ **Ruskin.** Immediately opposite the British Museum, the family-owned Ruskin is both pleasant and quiet—all front windows are double-glazed. The bedrooms are clean, though nondescript; the back ones overlook a pretty garden. Note the bucolic mural (c. 1808) in the lounge. Well-run and very popular. *23–24 Montague St., WC1B 5BN, tel. 0171/636–7388, fax 0171/323–1662. 35 rooms, 7 with shower. Facilities: lounge. AE, DC, MC, V. Tube: Tottenham Court Road.*

$ **St. Margaret's.** This guest house on a tree-lined Georgian street has been run for many years by a friendly Italian family. You'll find spacious rooms and towering ceilings, and a wonderful location close to Russell Square. The back rooms have a garden view. *24 Bedford Pl.,*

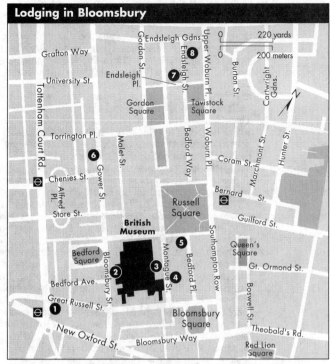

Lodging in Bloomsbury

WC1B 5JL, tel. 0171/636–4277. 64 rooms, 10 with bath. Facilities: 2 lounges. No credit cards. Tube: Russell Square.

¢ ★ **Central Club.** When this YMCA was refurbished in 1992, the rates were raised, but it's still good value considering its facilities, which include an excellent health club with a large pool, and its central location near Oxford Street, theaterland, and the British Museum. Unlike the YHA youth hostels, where under-18s get a reduced rate, the Central Club accepts only over-18s. *16–22 Great Russell St., WC1B 3LR, tel. 0171/636–7512 (ask for Reservations Manager). 104 rooms, 25 shared bathrooms. Tube: Tottenham Court Road.*

¢ **John Adams Hall.** A group of Georgian houses has been converted into student accommodations that are available at bargain rates during school vacations. There's nothing luxurious about the place, but it's a short walk to the British Museum, and Euston Station is across the street. *15–23 Endsleigh St., WC1H 0DH, tel. 0171/387–4086, fax 0171/383–0164 (ask for Ms. S. Waller). 148 rooms (of which 126 are single), 28 shared bathrooms. Closed Feb., May–June, Oct.–Nov. Tube: Euston.*

¢ **Passfield Hall.** A Georgian conversion round the corner from John Adams Hall (*see above*) and similar in all respects: The rooms are simple, the location is convenient, and it's open only during student breaks. *1 Endsleigh Pl., WC1H 0PW, tel. 0171/387–7743 (ask for Ms. J. Martin). 144 rooms (of which 100 are single), 36 shared bathrooms. Closed Oct.–Feb., May–June. Tube: Euston.*

¢ ★ **Ridgemount.** The kindly owners, Mr. and Mrs. Rees, make you feel at home. The public areas, especially the family-style breakfast room, have a friendly, cluttered Victorian feel. Some rooms overlook a leafy garden. *65 Gower St., WC1E 6HJ, tel. 0171/636–1141. 15 rooms, none with bath. Facilities: lounge. No credit cards. Tube: Goodge Street.*

Docklands

$$ **Scandic Crown.** This Swedish-owned place is Scandic by name and by nature, with efficiency and blond wood everywhere. It has its peculiarities, since it's split in two. Block 2 comprises a modern apartment building, while Block 1, containing all the bars and fun stuff, is a converted warehouse. Bedrooms in the latter (prefixed by a "1") are ten times nicer than the new ones, with rich exposed-brick walls, recessed spotlights, and big windows, some overlooking the Thames. All have the "Most Comfortable Beds in Town," on which you're offered a free night if you fail to sleep soundly (improbably, nobody's taken them up on it). A separate building houses a fine health club with pool, and the dining options (you need them out here—the courtesy bus into town stops early) include the lower deck of a dry-docked three-masted bark, a smörgåsbord buffet, and summertime terrace barbecues. *265 Rotherhithe St., SE16 1EJ, tel. 0171/231–1001, fax 0171/231–0599. 386 rooms with bath. Facilities: 2 restaurants, 2 bars, riverside terrace, lounges, health club with pool, in-room movies. AE, DC, MC, V. Tube: Rotherhithe, then taxi or a long walk. Courtesy bus from Charing Cross or Riverbus.*

$ **Lawrence Wharf.** They call this "London's first residential resort"; stay here for the fabulous river views and the compact self-catering apartments gleaming with the first flush of youth. Minimum stay is four days, but the daily rates are no great bargain; better to cram your whole family in and stay at least one week, when a two-bedroom flat works out to about £70 per day in peak season. Everything is provided, from towels and linens to TV, washing machine, and dishwasher, and there's access to the Scandic facilities next door for an extra fee. Use of the tennis court is free. You could feel isolated, though, without a car (there's free parking). *273–301 Rotherhithe St., SE16 1EJ, tel. 0171/815–0815, fax 0171/815–0818. Facilities: tennis court, health club with pool (fee payable). AE, MC, V. Tube: Rotherhithe, then taxi or a long walk; Riverbus.*

Hampstead and North London

$$ **Holiday Inn Kings Cross.** The newest London Holiday Inn is in a peculiar, deserted, not unseedy bit of north London, but it is accessible and safer than it looks. The decor is standard chain hotel, but the facilities are great, with in-room TV (plus movie channel), phone, hair dryer, pants press, tea/coffee maker, and minibar, and a health club complete with pool, sauna, steam room, solarium, gym, and even a squash court. The King's Cross/St. Pancras British Rail station is nearby, but a more pleasant walk in the other direction brings you to Bloomsbury and the British Museum. *1 Kings Cross Rd., WC1X 9HX, tel. 0171/833–3900, fax 0171/917–6163. 405 rooms with bath. Facilities: restaurant, bar/lounge, health club with pool, air-conditioning. AE, DC, MC, V. Tube: King's Cross.*

$$ **Swiss Cottage Hotel.** This charming, family-run hotel in a former retirement home is on a peaceful street behind Swiss Cottage tube stop. The lounge, bar, and reception area are stuffed with antiques and reproductions, cheerfully lit, and smilingly staffed. French windows open from the bar and restaurant—which serves an old-fashioned Anglo-French menu—onto the garden. Bedrooms off the creaky, labyrinthine corridors are freshly decorated in Victorian style, and most are good-sized. (Note that the elevator doesn't reach the 4th floor.) Executive rooms have bathrooms with pretty painted ceramic sinks and brass fittings. *4 Adamson Rd., NW3 3HP, tel. 0171/722–2281, fax 0171/483–4588. 80 rooms with bath. Facilities: lounge, bar, restaurant. AE, DC, MC, V. Tube: Swiss Cottage.*

$ **La Gaffe.** Another find, a short walk from the Hampstead tube stop. Italian Bernardo Stella has been welcoming the same guests back to these early 18th-century shepherds' cottages for over a decade. Rooms are tiny, and the predominantly pink and beige decor isn't luxurious, but the popular wine bar and restaurant, which (naturally) serve Italian food, are yours to lounge around in at all hours—there's a shelf of books to borrow. Between the two "wings" is a raised patio for summer, and each room has TV and phone. You'll love the place if you're a fan of quaint. *107–111 Heath St., NW3 6SS, tel. 0171/435–8965, fax 0171/794–7592. 14 rooms with shower. Facilities: restaurant, wine bar/café. AE, MC, V. Tube: Hampstead.*

¢ **Primrose Hill B&B.** Amazing—a small, friendly bed-and-breakfast agency that's genuinely "committed to the idea that traveling shouldn't be a rip-off." Expatriate American Gail O'Farrell has around 15 properties on her books, all family homes in or near villagey Hampstead, to which guests get their own latchkeys. All are comfortable or more than comfortable; "a pair of 19th-century cottages in a profusion of gardens with cats lazing around"—Gail's description of one of her favorites—is typical of the style to expect. So far this has been one of those word-of-mouth secrets, but now that everyone knows, book well ahead. *14 Edis St., NW1 8LG, tel. 0171/722–6869. 15 rooms with varying facilities. No credit cards.*

¢ **Regents College.** The nicest thing about this converted Regency mansion is that it's bang in the middle of Regent's Park, which at least half the rooms overlook. Again, this is an off-duty student accommodation, so it's somewhat communal, with bunk beds in many rooms and eight showers per bathroom. On the plus side, the college has its own café, bar, cafeteria, tennis courts, and weight room. *Inner Circle, Regent's Park, NW1 4NS, tel. 0171/487–7483 (ask for Mr. J. Barnes). 93 rooms, 9 shared bathrooms. Closed Feb.–Apr., Sept.–Nov. Tube: Baker Street.*

Londonwide

¢ **Central London Accommodations.** From their personally inspected pool of private-home B&Bs all over London, Peter and Vera Forrest will select one within your budget, in the area you prefer, and handle the booking. Calling to discuss your requirements is a good idea. Their own B&B, Forrest House, is perennially full of repeat guests who have become virtual family. *83 Addison Gardens, W14 0DT, tel. 0171/602–9668, fax 0171/602–5609. Facilities vary. AE, MC, V.*

¢ **London Homestead Services.** A family-run business offering B&B accommodation in private homes. Most of the more than 500 addresses are in quiet residential areas and offer second-floor bedrooms with shared bathrooms. Rates run around £30–£50 a night, for which you get a room in central London and a latchkey. (There are also a few self-catering apartments in the West End from £40 per person.) Naturally they vary in decor and ambience, but they've all been evaluated by LHS staff. The minimum stay is three nights; there's a 25% discount for under-12s. *Coombe Wood Rd., Kingston-Upon-Thames, Surrey, KT2 7JY, tel. 0181/949–4455, fax 0181/549–5492. 500-plus rooms, some with private bath. MC, V.*

¢ **Stayaway Abroad.** Julia Stebbing's B&B agency divides accommodations into A, B, and C categories, depending on location, facilities, and decor. Those on the A list are mostly around Victoria, Baker Street, Kensington, and more accessible or attractive bits of North London. Rates run from £15 per person per night. *71 Fellows Rd., NW3 3JY, tel. 0171/586–2768, fax 0171/586–6567. AE, DC, MC, V.*

3 Where to Eat on a Budget

Once upon a time, eating in London was an experience to be endured rather than enjoyed. Not anymore. There are restaurants offering cuisine from all over the world—and even from Britain itself. There have always been Italian and French restaurants, some dating back three-quarters of a century, solid reliable places with solid reliable menus. But now there are literally hundreds of possibilities offering exciting, adventurous cooking.

So here you are, sitting in your charming room watching the rain streaming down the Georgian sash windowpane, surrounded by history, and hungry as a horse. What do you do? A Londoner with nouse (British for savvy), when starving and not rich and in an unfamiliar neighborhood, goes to the local Indian **Tandoori house** for chicken *tikka*, rice, *dal*, and *nan* (chicken breast marinated in spices and yogurt and cooked in a clay oven called a tandoor; fragrant Basmati rice; soupy, spicy lentils; and tandoor-baked warm unleavened bread): about £12 for the meal. This north Indian food goes beyond a cliché into national-dish territory, which doesn't mar its deliciousness for those new to it. We haven't listed many curry places; discover your own and be guided by your budget. Expense is no measure of quality, and the cheapest (especially in Asian areas like Brick Lane and Southall) can be the best.

Judging by the rate at which they're opening, inexpensive **Thai** restaurants are next in line for the High Street Fixture award. (Many Brits vacation in Thailand.) Indeed, the general rule is: Eat anything, but eat ethnic.

Fish-and-chips—or egg-and-chips, sausage-and-chips, chip butties (Wonder Bread with margarine and fries), or chips and ketchup from the caff (the British diner)—are the indigenous options in British budgetland. Actually, that's finally changing, as health consciousness replaces the Church of England; by now good **sandwich bars**—often Italian-run—are more ubiquitous in central London than the old greasy spoons. In fact, quite a few former greasy spoons have taken to opening evenings, wearing tablecloths, and serving, say, the owners' native Thai food.

Many London restaurants have set-lunch menus that are half the price of their à la carte ones. This makes dining in some of the very fanciest eating places within the budget of almost any visitor. The one thing to be careful of is that you don't hike up the cost with the bar check.

A serious problem in dining in London is that it is difficult to do so on Sunday or late at night, and all but impossible over Christmas and New Year's. You should always check if a restaurant is open on Sunday; it could save you a wasted journey.

A law obliges all British restaurants to display their prices, including VAT (sales tax), outside their establishments, and if you are on a tight budget, it's wise to read carefully. Look for the hidden extras, such as service, cover, extra charge for vegetables, and minimum charge, that are usually at the bottom in fine print. Also beware of paying twice for service, sometimes figured into the check (the "tips" and "total" sections of the credit card slip are left open).

Except where otherwise noted, dress is casual. Where reservations and credit cards are not mentioned, none is taken. Highly recommended restaurants are indicated by a star ★.

Category	Cost*
$$	£15–£30
$	£8–£15
¢	under £8

per person without VAT, service, or drinks

Mayfair

$$
American
Smollensky's Balloon. This American-style bar-restaurant is a favorite spot for family dining. There are a few weekly specials, but your best bet is one of the different types of steak, which come with various sauces and fries and include a salmon steak for non–red meat eaters. There's also a vegetarian selection. Sunday lunch is "A Family Affair"—bring the kids along and be entertained by a clown, a magician, video cartoons, and a Punch-and-Judy show. *1 Dover St., W1, tel. 0171/491–1199. Reservations advised Fri.–Sun. AE, DC, MC, V. Closed Dec. 24–26 and Jan. 1. Tube: Green Park.*

$$
Mediterranean
Zoe. Handy for West End shopping, this two-level place serves two-level food—proper dinners downstairs in a sunlit basement of jazzy colors and posh cocktails, coffee, and sandwiches ("hot spicy pork with prunes and crispy bacon" is typical) upstairs. It's an Antony Worrall Thompson place (*see* Bistrot 190 in South Kensington, *below*) and so features the trademark heartiness. The schizophrenic restaurant menu is half smart "City" dishes (corn crab cakes, poached eggs, hollandaise, and wilted greens), half huge "Country" ensembles (poached ham, parsley sauce, pease pudding, and hot potato salad), most offered in two sizes, rendering decisions impossible. *St. Christopher's Pl., W1, tel. 0171/224–1122. Reservations advised. AE, DC, MC, V. Closed Sat. lunch, Sun. (bar open 7 days). Tube: Bond Street.*

$$
Modern British
★
Criterion. This palatial neo-Byzantine mirrored marble hall, which first opened in 1874, is now back on the map, with an unpretentious "nouveau Brit" menu—grilled squid on spinach with lemon vinaigrette, cod and crab cakes, sticky toffee pudding—and a generous attitude toward set-priced dining: About half the dishes on the main menu are offered at £10 for two courses, any time. This is a very wel-

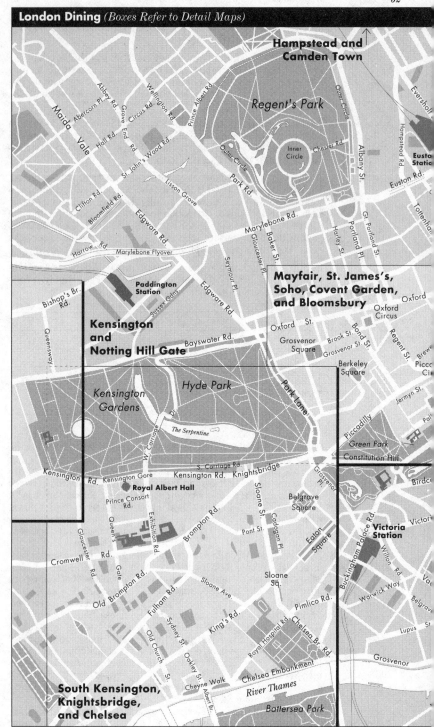

London Dining *(Boxes Refer to Detail Maps)*

Hampstead and Camden Town

Regent's Park

Mayfair, St. James's, Soho, Covent Garden, and Bloomsbury

Kensington and Notting Hill Gate

Hyde Park

Kensington Gardens

The Serpentine

Royal Albert Hall

Victoria Station

South Kensington, Knightsbridge, and Chelsea

River Thames

Battersea Park

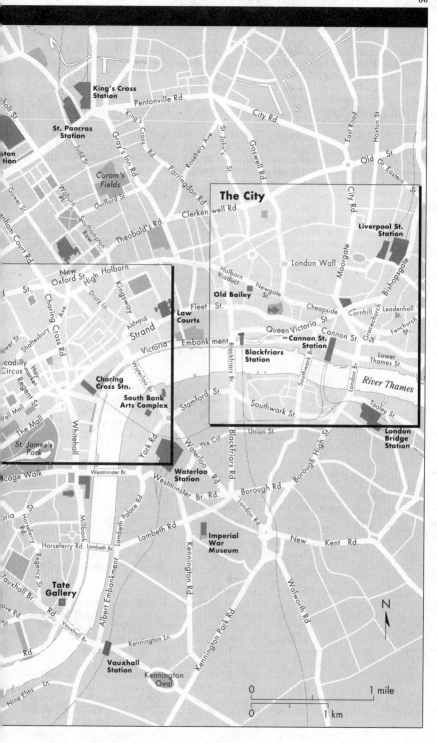

King's Cross Station

St. Pancras Station

Pentonville Rd.

City Rd.

Gray's Inn Rd.

Coram's Fields

Guilford St.

Woburn

Southampton Row

Judd St.

King's Cross Rd.

Rosebery Ave.

St. John's St.

Farringdon Rd.

Goswell Rd.

Old St.

Gt. Eastern St.

Hoxton St.

East Road

City Rd.

Theobald's Rd.

Clerkenwell Rd.

The City

London Wall

Liverpool St. Station

Moorgate

Bishopsgate

New Oxford St.

High Holborn

Kingsway

Drury Ln.

Aldwych

Charing Cross Rd.

Shaftesbury Ave.

Holborn Viaduct

Newgate St.

Old Bailey

Cheapside

Cornhill

Leadenhall St.

Fenchurch St.

Gracechurch St.

Law Courts

Fleet St.

Strand

Victoria

Embankment

Queen Victoria St.

Cannon St.

Cannon St. Station

Lower Thames St.

Piccadilly Circus

Haymarket

Regent St.

Pall Mall

Blackfriars Br.

Blackfriars Station

Southwark Br.

London Br.

River Thames

Charing Cross Stn.

South Bank Arts Complex

Stamford St.

Southwark St.

Tooley St.

The Mall

Whitehall

York Rd.

Waterloo Br.

St. James's Park

Union St.

London Bridge Station

Birdcage Walk

Westminster Br.

Waterloo Station

The Cut

Waterloo Rd.

Blackfriars Rd.

Westminster Br. Rd.

Borough Rd.

Borough High St.

London Rd.

Victoria

Horseferry Rd.

Lambeth Br.

Lambeth Palace Rd.

Lambeth Rd.

Kennington Rd.

Imperial War Museum

New Kent Rd.

Regency St.

Millbank

Tate Gallery

Albert Embankment

Kennington Rd.

Walworth Rd.

Vauxhall Br. Rd.

Kennington Park Rd.

N

Vauxhall Br.

Kennington Ln.

Vauxhall Station

Kennington Oval

Nine Elms Ln.

0		1 mile

0		1 km

come oasis in the Piccadilly desert. *Piccadilly Circus, W1, tel. 0171/925–0909. Reservations advised. AE, DC, MC, V. Tube: Piccadilly Circus.*

$ **The Hard Rock Café.** People (especially tourists) stand in line for
American   hours to get into this huge, split-level room with ceiling fans, pool lamps, long tables, and ear-splitting rock music. Favorites include BLT sandwiches, ice-cream sodas, and calorific desserts. The hamburgers and steaks are as good as at any theme restaurant. *150 Old Park La., W1, tel. 0171/629–0382. V. Closed Dec. 24–26. Tube: Hyde Park Corner.*

$ **L'Artiste Musclé.** This crowded, wooden-floor wine bar in pictur-
French   esque Shepherd Market serves exactly what you'd find in a small-
★   town brasserie in France (*boeuf Bourgignon*, smoked chicken salad, steak) and is wonderful on a sunny day when you can fight for the few outside tables. *1 Shepherd Market, W1, tel. 0171/493–6150. Reservations accepted for 5 or more. AE, DC, V. Closed Sun. lunch. Tube: Green Park.*

$ **Down Mexico Way.** Many of London's proliferating Mexican joints
Mexican   serve horrid food, but this one's good and serves a few adventurous numbers, such as fish in almond-chili sauce, with sides of cheese and jalapeño muffins or spiced spinach. Look for the beautiful Spanish ceramic tiles and avoid evenings if you want a quiet night out. *25 Swallow St., W1, tel. 0171/437–9895. Reservations advised. AE, MC, V. Closed Dec. 25–26. Tube: Piccadilly Circus.*

¢   **The Chicago Pizza Pie Factory.** An inexpensive, Chicago-style place
American   serves enormous deep-dish pies with the usual toppings, in a wooden-floor basement, loud with the sounds of WJMK, the Windy City's oldies station. The rest rooms are labeled "Elton John" and "Olivia Newton John." *17 Hanover Sq., W1, tel. 0171/629–2669. Reservations advised for lunch. No credit cards. Closed Dec. 25–26. Tube: Oxford Circus.*

¢   **The Granary.** A useful place for lunch, this superior self-service café
English   has well-spoken young men explaining the specials as you stand in line. Lemon chicken, moussaka, salads, quiches, and raspberry cobbler are typical dishes; portions are huge. The place is packed from 1 to 2. *39 Albermarle St., W1, tel. 0171/493–2979. Closed Sat., dinner Sun. Tube: Green Park.*

St. James's

Splurge   **Quaglino's.** Glamour, taste (in every sense), and a check that just
Modern British   squeezes into an "Affordable" guide. This famous pre–World War II
★   restaurant was resurrected in '93, bigger and better than ever, by Sir Terence Conran of Habitat, Bibendum, and Pont de la Tour fame. Eat fashionable Pan-European food (rabbit with prosciutto and herbs, *plateau de fruits de mer*); stare, be stared at, enjoy. *16 Bury St., SW1, tel. 0171/930–6767. Reservations necessary. AE, DC, MC, V. Tube: Green Park.*

$$ **Café Fish.** Just to the east of St. James's proper, this cheerful, bus-
French   tling restaurant has a wonderful selection of fish (shark and turbot join the trout, halibut, salmon, and monkfish, some brought daily from Normandy), arranged on the menu according to cooking method: chargrilled, steamed, meunière. There are also several plats du jour, some classics of fish cuisine like bouillabaisse and *moules marinières*, and a *plateau de fruits de mer* straight out of a Paris brasserie. A delicious little quenelle of smoked fish paté is served with crusty bread to help you order. Downstairs is an informal wine bar with a smaller selection of dishes. *39 Panton St., SW1, tel. 0171/930–3999. Reservations advised. AE, DC, MC, V. Closed Sat. lunch, Sun., Dec. 25–26, Jan. 1. Tube: Picadilly Circus.*

$ **The Fountain.** At the back of Fortnum and Mason is this old-fash-
Traditional   ioned restaurant, frumpy and popular as a boarding school matron,
English   serving delicious light meals, toasted snacks, sandwiches, and ice-cream sodas. During the day, go for the Welsh rarebit or cold game

pie; in the evening, a no-frills fillet steak is a typical option. Just the place for afternoon tea and ice cream sundaes after the Royal Academy or Bond Street shopping, or for pretheater meals. *181 Piccadilly, W1, tel. 0171/734–4938. Reservations accepted for dinner only. AE, DC, MC, V. Closed Sun., national holidays. Tube: Green Park.*

$ **Woodlands.** This place next door to Café Fish serves south Indian
Indian   vegetarian food, which features lentils and chickpeas, light yogurt sauces, tamarind and coconut chutneys, paper-thin rice-flour pancakes (*dosas*), and spicy vegetable stews. The prices are not the lowest, but anything good and ethnic is hard to find in fast-food Piccadilly. *37 Panton St., W1, tel. 0171/839–7258. Reservations advised for weekend dinner. AE, DC, MC, V. Tube: Piccadilly Circus.*

¢   **Stockpot.** Another Panton Street favorite, this bustling café has
International   been serving plentiful stews, roasts, fry-ups, soups, and omelets for just about forever. It's popular with theater workers as well as West End theatergoers who have spent every cent on their tickets. *40 Panton St., W1, tel. 0171/839–5142. Tube: Piccadilly Circus.*

¢   **The Wren at St. James's.** The perfect place for lunch, tea, or early dinner after a visit to the Royal Academy—especially when the sun is shining, since there are plenty of tables in the church courtyard. Inside it's almost as bright. The self-service counter holds vegetarian specials, tea and coffee, and especially good desserts and cakes. *35 Jermyn St., SW1, tel. 0171/437–9419. Closes 7 PM (5 PM Sun.). Tube: Picadilly Circus.*

Soho

$$ **L'Escargot.** This ever-popular media haunt serves Anglo-French
Anglo-French   food in its ground floor brasserie and its more formal upstairs restaurant. A comprehensive, reasonably priced wine list sets off a robust ragout of spiced lamb or a simple, fresh poached or grilled fish. This place is reliable and relaxed. *48 Greek St., W1, tel. 0171/437–2679. Reservations advised upstairs, not taken downstairs. AE, DC, MC, V. Closed Sun., public holidays. Tube: Leicester Square.*

$$ **Fung Shing.** This comfortable, cool green restaurant is a cut above
Chinese   the Lisle/Wardour Street crowd in both service and ambience, as well as in food. The usual Chinatown options are supplemented by some exciting dishes. Salt-baked chicken, served on or off the bone with an accompanying bowl of intense broth, is essential, and the adventurous might try intestines—deep-fried cigarette-shape morsels, far more delicious than you'd think. *15 Lisle St., WC2, tel. 0171/437–1539. Reservations suggested. AE, DC, MC, V. Tube: Leicester Square.*

$$ **Bistrot Bruno.** Bruno is Bruno Loubet, who earned three Michelin
French   stars at the astronomically expensive Four Seasons Restaurant in
★   Mayfair and may be the most dedicated and original chef in London. Here he does everything but cook (especially since he opened L'Odeon on Regent Street in summer '95), but the menu is unmistakably his work, dotted with bits of animals you wouldn't want in your freezer, which in his hands become balanced, beautiful Cuisine du Terroir dishes. Order *fromage de tête*, or brawn (a pâté from the Lorraine made from pig's head in aspic), or tripes niçoise (cow's stomach, frankly), or be a coward and go for scallops on puff pastry or duck leg confit with crushed potato and cèpe sauce, then an iced meringue and cherry slice. Coffee arrives with minisorbets encased in chocolate. Next door is the cheaper, more casual Café Bruno. *63 Frith St., W1, tel. 0171/734–4545. Dress: smart casual. Reservations required. MC, V. Closed Sat. lunch, Sun. Tube: Leicester Square.*

$$ **Soho Soho.** The ground floor is a lively café bar with a rotisserie, while upstairs is a more formal and expensive restaurant. Inspiration comes from Provence, both in the vivid and flavorful food and the decor with its murals, primary colors, and pale ocher terra-cotta floor tiles. The Rotisserie serves omelets, salads, charcuterie, and

56

Dining in Mayfair, St. James's, Soho, Covent Garden, and Bloomsbury

Arts Theatre Café, **54**
Bahn Thai, **30**
Bar Italia, **31**
Bertorelli's, **52**
Bistrot Bruno, **29**
Café Casbar, **55**
Café des Amis du Vin, **51**
Café Fish, **42**
Café Flo, **45**
Café Pelican, **44**

Centrale, **34**
Chez Gerard, **14**
Chicago Pizza Pie Factory, **10**
Crank's, **13**
Criterion, **40**
dell'Ugo, **28**
Deals West, **11**
Diana's Diner **54**
Down Mexico Way, **8**
Ed's Easy Diner, **36**

Fatboy's Diner, **48**
Food for Thought, **56**
Fountain, **6**
French House Dining Room, **27**
Fung Shing, **39**
Govinda's, **20**
Granary, **4**
Hard Rock Café, **1**
Joe Allen's, **47**
L'Artiste Musclé, **2**

L'Escargot, **35**
Le Tire Bouchon, **12**
Lorelei, **23**
Maison Bertaux, **37**
Mandeer, **15**
Maxwell's, **49**
Melati, **25**
Minang, **21**
Museum Street Café, **18**
Neal's Yard Dining Rooms, **58**

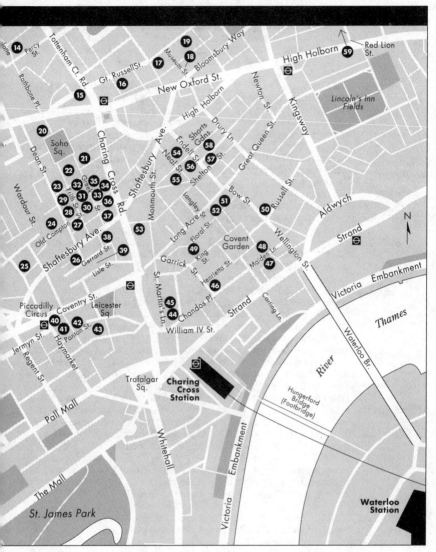

New World, **38**

North Sea Fish
Restaurant, **59**

Old Orleans, **50**

Patisserie Valerie, **24**

Pizza Express, **17**

Pollo, **33**

Porter's, **46**

Quaglino's, **5**

Rasa Sayang, **22**

Rock & Sole
Plaice, **57**

Smollensky's
Balloon, **3**

Soho Soho, **32**

Stockpot, **43**

Tai Wing Wa, **26**

Truckles of Pied Bull
Yard, **19**

Wagamama, **16**

Woodlands, **41**

Wren at
St. James's, **7**

Zoe, **9**

cheeses, plus a handful of such bistro dishes as Toulouse sausages with fries; herbed, grilled poussin; and tarte tatin. Or you can stay in the café-bar and have just a kir or a beer. *11–13 Frith St., W1, tel. 0171/494–3491. Reservations advised upstairs. AE, DC, MC, V. Closed Sun., Sat. lunch upstairs, Dec. 25–26, Jan. 1. Tube: Leicester Square.*

$$
Mediterranean
dell'Ugo. A three-floor Mediterranean café-restaurant from the stable of Antony Worrall Thompson (*see* Bistrot 190 in South Kensington, *below*). You can choose light fare—bruschetta loaded with marinated vegetables, mozzarella, parmesan, etc., Tuscan soups, and country bread—or feast on wintry, warming one-pot ensembles and large platefuls of sunny dishes like spicy sausages and white bean casserole with onion confit. Fortunately, trendiness doesn't interfere with pleasure here. *56 Frith St., W1, tel. 0171/734–8300. Reservations advised. AE, MC, V. Closed Sun. Tube: Leicester Square.*

$$
Modern British
French House Dining Room. One of London's trendier haunts, this table-hopping Bohemia above the eponymous pub has a difficult menu to categorize. Perhaps the truffled pâté, herring in oatmeal, grilled guinea fowl, figs with shortbread, and Welsh rarebit are Scottish nursery food that has traveled a lot in France. It's owned by the St. John people (*see below*). *49 Dean St., W1, tel. 0171/437–2477. Reservations advised. AE, DC, MC, V. Tube: Leicester Square.*

$$
Thai
Bahn Thai. Many people find this the best of London's many Thai restaurants (you can see at least four others from the door). An immensely long menu features little chili symbols for the nervous of palate, plus easy options like chargrilled poussin marinated in honey and spices with a plum dipping sauce. Other Thai dishes are well explained. Wine, by the way, is not a great accompaniment to this food; beer is better. *21A Frith St., W1, tel. 0171/437–8504. Reservations advised for dinner. AE, MC, V. Closed Dec. 25–26. Tube: Leicester Square.*

$$
Thai/American
Deals West. Viscount Linley and his two partners have hit on a winning formula here (and in the original **Deals** at Chelsea Harbour, tel. 0171/376–3232): an unlikely-sounding merger between America and Thailand. Off Carnaby Street in a relaxed, barnlike diner with exposed brick walls, wood floors and beams, loudish music accompanies ribs, salads, and burgers—as well as Thai curries. Cocktails, extended hours, and live jazz on weekends make this popular with a young, after-work crowd. *14–16 Fouberts Pl., W1, tel. 0171/287–1050. Reservations advised for dinner. AE, DC, MC, V. Closed Sun. dinner, public holidays. Tube: Leicester Square.*

$
Malaysian
★
Melati. The fact that every pine table on both floors is full by 8 PM testifies to the reliability and style of this place, which Londoners discover as students and never desert. From the huge menu, *tahu telor* (bean curd omelet) is a favorite, as are the usual *gado-gado* (salad with peanut sauce), *mee goreng* (fried noodles with bits), and *saté*. Beware the occasional syrupy glaze on chicken. Portions are enormous. *21 Great Windmill St., W1, tel. 0171/437–2745. Reservations necessary for dinner. AE, DC, MC, V. Tube: Piccadilly Circus.*

$
Minang. The much younger sibling of Melati (*see above*) is a little classier and quieter and, consequently, pricier. But the midday Indonesian Buffet Lunch, at around £6.50, is actually a full-blown rijsttafel—a succession of small dishes served with rice—that will render dinner obsolete. *11 Greek St., W1, tel. 0171/287–1408. AE, DC, MC, V. Tube: Leicester Square.*

$
Rasa Sayang. A venerable Soho resident, this restaurant holds no surprises, but it's useful for quiet posttheater pigouts. The menu is similar to Melati's, though dishes here tend to resemble each other more than their descriptions suggest. *10 Frith St., W1, tel. 0171/734–8720. AE, DC, MC, V. Closed Sat. lunch. Tube: Leicester Square.*

¢ **Ed's Easy Diner.** A faux-'50s diner with wraparound windows, Ed's
American holds the hamburger laurels in many people's eyes. This one and
three branches have extroverted counter staff (who sing along to
Eddie Cochran on the jukebox), long-neck Bud, cheese fries, and
low prices. *12 Moor St., W1, tel. 0171/439–1955. Tube: Leicester
Square.*

¢ **New World.** A cavernous dim sum palace—probably the best-known
Chinese one in London's small Chinatown—serving from trollies between 11
and 6 daily. Demanding gourmets might not enjoy. *1 Gerrard Pl.,
W1, tel. 0171/734–0677. Reservations not necessary (700 seats).
AE, DC, MC, V. Tube: Leicester Square.*

¢ **Tai Wing Wa.** This newcomer does good dim sum for beginners—
there's a menu in English, and the waiters are friendly. *7–9 Newport Pl., WC2, tel. 0171/287–2702. Reservations advised. AE, DC,
MC, V. Closed Sat. Tube: Leicester Square.*

¢ **Le Tire Bouchon.** Tucked away near Carnaby Street in "West Soho"
French is this wine bar, French from its baguettes to its checkered tablecloths. You can snack on a plate of smoked fish, charcuterie, or *fro-
mage*, or order something like cassoulet from the short, protein-
packed menu. You may also want to take advantage of the bargain
set menu, chalked on the blackboard. *6 Upper James St., W1, tel.
0171/437–5348. AE, MC, V. Closed weekends, public holidays.
Tube: Piccadilly Circus.*

¢ **Bar Italia.** To the horror of Soho-ites, the Formica counter, round
Italian stools, and boxing posters of this late-night institution were recently faced with extinction when an architect was appointed to reno-
vate. Luckily he had the good sense to make the cramped stand-up
Italian expats' coffee bar look exactly the same as before. Eat sandwiches and panettone. Shoot espresso. Look cool. *22 Frith St., W1,
tel. 0171/437–4520. Closed almost never. Tube: Leicester Square.*

¢ **Centrale.** Around the corner from the Pollo, this café is very basic to
look at but serves excellent pasta at rock-bottom prices. There's no
bathroom—diners use the "Superloo" outside—and no alcohol li-
cence. BYOB; corkage is 50p. *16 Moor St., W1, tel. 0171/437–5513.
Closes 9:45 PM. Tube: Leicester Square.*

¢ **Pollo.** This family-run café gets buried under young club animals,
art students, and fashion victims Thursday–Saturday nights; otherwise it's a reliable purveyor of pasta, risotto, and other Italian home
cooking. *20 Old Compton St., W1, tel. 0171/734–5917. Closed Sun.
Tube: Leicester Square.*

¢ **Maison Bertaux.** As the world is divided into dog or cat people, so
Patisserie London is divided into Bertaux or Valerie people, though both are
quite wonderful in their special ways. Bertaux's Gallic pastries (the
mille feuilles, coffee eclair, and *coeur de palmier* are winners) are
displayed in the window. You point, mount the stairs to the tiny salon, and have them brought up, with coffee (not cappuccino) or tea.
*28 Greek St., W1, tel. 0171/437–6007. Closes 8 PM, 1–3 PM Sun., pub-
lic holidays. Tube: Leicester Square.*

¢ **Patisserie Valerie.** You will normally see somebody wearing dark
glasses in Valerie's back room, despite the lack of light, and dipping
what may be London's best croissant into cappuccino, or tackling
the white chocolate truffle cake, fruit tartes, or cheesecake. *44 Old
Compton St., W1, tel. 0171/437–3466. Closes 8 PM(6 PM Sun.). Tube:
Leicester Square.*

¢ **Lorelei.** A tiny unlicensed café, tucked unobtrusively in a back
Pizza street, that manages to undercut the price of the cheapest London
pizza parlor without sacrificing quality. There are a few other Ital-
ian dishes on the menu, too, and service is very friendly. *21
Bateman St., W1, tel. 0171/734–0954. Closed Sun. Tube: Leicester
Square.*

¢ **Pizza Express.** Any branch of London's best pizza chain is equally
reliable, serving thin-crusted Italian-style pies, plus ham and eggs
and a missable salade niçoise. Choose the *Veneziana* (onions, pine
nuts, and sultanas) and you help prevent Venice from sinking, be-

cause they contribute to the Venice in Peril fund. Check the phone book for other branches. *30 Coptic St., W1, tel. 0171/636–3232. AE, DC, MC, V. Tube: Holborn.*

¢   **Crank's.** This is a popular vegetarian chain (there are other
Vegetarian branches at Covent Garden, Great Newport Street, Adelaide Street, Tottenham Street, and Barrett Street), bought out by the management in 1992, and now serving more up-to-date meatless meals than the 60s menu that made their name. They remain always crowded, and irritatingly, insist on closing at 8. *8 Marshall St., W1, tel. 0171/437–9431. AE, DC, MC, V. Closed Sun., national holidays. Tube: Oxford Circus.*

¢   **Govinda's.** Run by Buddhists in a nondenominational kind of way, this bright café serves Indian vegetarian dishes in large quantity at small prices. The *thali*—a sampling of several dishes with rice—is, at about £8.50, the most expensive item, and most dishes cost only £2–£3. *9 Soho St., W1, tel. 0171/437–3662. Closes 7 PM; closed Sun. Tube: Tottenham Court Road.*

Covent Garden

$$ **Joe Allen's.** This New York–clone basement restaurant, behind the
American Strand Palace Hotel, is a great place to spot stage and screen per-
★   sonalities. The ribs these days come with trendy wilted greens and black-eyed peas, but you can still get burgers and fries and brownies and ice cream, and if you eat after 9, you'll be entertained by a pianist—if you can hear through the din. *13 Exeter St., WC2, tel. 0171/ 836–0651. Reservations required. Closed Easter, Dec. 25–26. Tube: Covent Garden.*

$$ **Old Orleans.** This Cajun place is an exact replica of a U.S.-style chain, with indifferent food (blackened things, beer-batter shrimp, mud pie, etc.), but you can order any drink from the huge cocktail menu, including those hard-to-locate slushy, sugary frozen ones, and they do a jazz brunch on Sunday for around £8. Avoid the latter half of happy hour (3–7 except Sunday) unless you like drunken office workers. *29–31 Wellington St., WC2, tel. 0171/497–2433. AE, DC, MC, V. Tube: Covent Garden or Aldwych.*

$$ **Porter's.** Good British food (really), an Olde Worlde public house in-
British terior, a nob owner (the earl of Bradford), and a reasonable check— no wonder Americans invariably like this place. Pies star on the menu—lamb-and-apricot or chicken-and-chili—alongside the traditional fish or steak-and-kidney, with steamed sponges and custard for afters. *17 Henrietta St., WC2, tel. 0171/836–6466. Reservations required for weekend dinner. AE, MC, V. Tube: Covent Garden.*

$$ **Café des Amis du Vin.** In a lane beside the Royal Opera House, this
French place is split into three: a wine bar in the basement, the Café on the ground floor, and the Salon restaurant on the second floor. Seating in the Café is rather cramped, but the genuine French atmosphere and wine compensate. The menu offers regional dishes, salads, and wines: calf's liver, croque monsieur, leek tart, Toulouse sausages, and the like. The Salon restaurant upstairs is considerably more expensive. There are a few tables outside for summer eating. *11–14 Hanover Pl., WC2, tel. 0171/379–3444. Reservations advised. AE, DC, MC, V. Closed Sun. Tube: Covent Garden.*

$$ **Café Pelican.** A full meal at this much-frequented brasserie by the National Gallery fits this category, but you can easily eat for less— *moules marinière*, bread, a glass of wine, for around a tenner; croque monsieur and coffee for half that. The front section is for snacking and, like the outside tables, fills fast at prime times. *45 St. Martin's La., WC2, tel. 0171/379–0309. Reservations advised weekends. AE, MC, V. Closed Sun. lunch. Tube: Charing Cross.*

$$ **Arts Theatre Café.** You don't need a show ticket to eat at this tiny
Italian basement rustic-Italian restaurant, as quantities of Londoners have come to realize. At just over £10, the three-course set menu is great value. Spinach polenta "lasagna," carpaccio, and marinated red

peppers with salt cod fritters are typical dishes. *6 Great Newport St., W1, tel. 0171/497–8014. Reservations advised. Closed weekends. Tube: Leicester Square.*

$$ **Bertorelli's.** Right across from the stage door of the Royal Opera
★ House, Bertorelli's is quietly chic, the food better than ever now that Maddalena Bonnino (formerly of 192) is in charge. Poached cotechino sausage with lentils; monkfish ragout with fennel, tomato, and olives; and *garganelli* with French beans, cob nuts, and parmesan are typical dishes. Downstairs is a very relaxed inexpensive wine bar serving a simpler menu of pizza, pasta, salads, and a few big dishes and daily specials. *44A Floral St., WC2, tel. 0171/836–3969. Dress: smart casual. Reservations required for restaurant; advised downstairs for dinner. AE, DC, MC, V. Tube: Covent Garden.*

$ **Maxwell's.** London's first-ever burger joint cloned itself and then
American grew up. Here's the result, a happy place under the Opera House serving the kind of food you're homesick for: quesadillas and nachos, Buffalo chicken wings, BBQ ribs, Cajun chicken, chef's salad, and a real NYC Reuben. *8–9 James St., WC2, tel. 0171/836–0303. Reservations advised weekends. AE, DC, V. Tube: Covent Garden.*

$ **Café Flo.** This useful brasserie serves the bargain "Idée Flo"—soup
French or salad, *steak-frites* or *poisson-frites*, and coffee—a wide range of French café food, breakfast, wines, *tartes*, espresso, fresh orange juice, simple set-price weekend menus . . . everything for the francophile on a budget. There are branches everywhere. *51 St. Martin's La., WC2, tel. 0171/836–8289. Reservations advised. MC, V. Closed Dec. 25, Jan. 1. Tube: Charing Cross.*

¢ **Fatboy's Diner.** One for the kids, this is a 1941 chrome trailer trans-
American planted from the banks of the Susquehanna in Pennsylvania and now secreted, unexpectedly, in a backstreet, complete with Astroturf "garden." A '50s jukebox accompanies the dogs, burgers, and fries. *21 Maiden La., WC2, tel. 0171/240–1902. Tube: Covent Garden or Aldwych.*

¢ **Diana's Diner.** Not a diner as Americans know it, but a British "caff"
English with the usual Italian accent. Although the original Diana has moved on, the quality—and quantity—of the food is as impressive as it ever was, with pasta dishes, liver and onions, fry-ups, stews, and casseroles always on the menu. *39 Endell St., WC2, tel. 0171/240–0272. Closes 8:30 PM (5 PM Sun.). Tube: Covent Garden.*

¢ **Rock & Sole Plaice.** Fresh fish-and-chips from a counter, with tables outside and inside, posters and flyers on the walls, a cheerful attitude, and low prices. *47 Endell St., WC2, tel. 0171/836–3785. Closed Sun. Tube: Covent Garden.*

¢ **Café Casbar.** A no-frills place with better food than you might ex-
Modern British pect for the price. Warm goat cheese salads; interesting sandwiches on granary, rye, ciabatta, and pita breads; hot daily specials; breakfasts; cakes; and wine are available. Evenings here feature readings or performances, and there's art on the walls. *52 Earlham St., WC2, tel. 0171/379–7768. Tube: Covent Garden.*

¢ **Food for Thought.** This simple basement restaurant (no liquor li-
Vegetarian cense) seats only 50 and is extremely popular, so you'll almost al-
★ ways find a line of people down the stairs. The menu—stir-fries, casseroles, salads, and desserts—changes every day, and each dish is freshly made; there's no microwave. *31 Neal St., WC2, tel. 0171/836–0239. Closed after 8 PM, 2 weeks at Christmas, national holidays. Tube: Covent Garden.*

¢ **Neal's Yard Dining Rooms.** You'd think the cooks here handle the PR for the Vegetarian Society, such is the variety of flavors they produce. Choose platefuls from different nations (Turkish *meze* includes baba gannooj, hoummous, carrot purée; Indonesian *sambal* has a coconut and lemongrass sauce; Indian *thali* is several curries), or soup and salad. You can eat outside in the pretty cobbled yard. *14 Neal's Yard (upstairs), WC2, tel. 0171/379–0298. Closes 8 PM (5 Mon., 6 Sat.), all day Sun., public holidays. Tube: Covent Garden.*

Bloomsbury

$$ **Chez Gerard.** One of a small chain of superior steak-frites restau-
French   rants. All the Chez Gerards offer old-fashioned Gallic staples like vi-
chyssoise (chilled leek and potato soup), salad with garlic croutons,
and charcoal-grilled meat, with a good-value prix fixe menu also
available. *8 Charlotte St., W1, tel. 0171/636–4975. Reservations ad-
vised. AE, DC, MC, V. Tube: Tottenham Court Road.*

$$ **The Museum Street Café.** This place near the British Museum serves
Modern British   a limited selection of impeccably fresh dishes, intelligently and
plainly cooked by the two young owners. The evening menu might
feature grilled, maize-fed chicken with pesto, followed with a rich
chocolate cake; at lunchtime you might choose a sandwich of Stilton
on walnut bread and a big bowl of soup. *47 Museum St., WC1, tel.
0171/405–3211. Reservations required for dinner. Closed weekends,
public holidays. Tube: Holborn.*

$ **Truckles of Pied Bull Yard.** This wine bar (of the venerable Davy's
English   chain) with its paneled basement restaurant is worth patronizing
only for its large, sunny courtyard, which gets packed with office
people during summer lunchtimes. Stick to simple food like ham or
roast beef salad, plates of English cheeses or sausages, or something
chargrilled when it's available. *Off Bury Pl., WC1, tel. 0171/404–
5334. Dress: jacket and tie in basement restaurant. AE, DC, MC, V.
Closed 3–5:30 and after 9; after 3 Sat.; all day Sun. Tube: Tottenham Court Road or Holborn.*

¢   **Mandeer.** Buried in a basement, with tile floors, brick walls, and
Indian   real temple lamps, Mandeer features tofu curry and stuffed egg-
plant. Lunch is self-service and cheap. *21 Hanway Pl., W1, tel.
0171/580–3470. Reservations advised for Fri. and Sat. dinner. AE,
DC, MC, V. Closed Sun., national holidays, 2 weeks over New Year.
Tube: Tottenham Court Road.*

¢   **Wagamama.** London's gone wild for Japanese noodles in this big
Japanese   basement. It's high-tech (your order is taken on a handheld comput-
★   er) and high-volume—there are always crowds, with which you
share wooden refectory tables, so the noise level is inevitably high.
You can choose ramen in or out of soup, topped with sliced meats or
tempura, or "raw energy" dishes—rice, curries, tofu, and so on. *4
Streatham St., WC1, tel. 0171/323–9223. Tube: Holborn.*

¢   **The North Sea Fish Restaurant.** This is the place for the British na-
Seafood   tional dish of fish-and-chips—battered and deep-fried whitefish
★   with thick fries shaken with salt and vinegar. It's a bit tricky to
find—three blocks south of St. Pancras station, down Judd Street.
Only freshly caught fish is served, and you can order it grilled—
though that would defeat the object. You can take out or eat in. *7–8
Leigh St., WC1, tel. 0171/387–5892. Reservations advised. AE, DC,
MC, V. Closed Sun., national holidays. Tube: Russell Square.*

South Kensington

$$ **Lou Pescadou.** Walking into this little restaurant is like stepping
French   into the south of France. The staff is emphatically French and, al-
★   though fish is the specialty—*petite bouillabaisse* (fish soup) or red
mullet poached in tarragon sauce—there are meat dishes, too,
sometimes very unusual ones, such as delicate and delicious braised
cervelles—brains. *241 Old Brompton Rd., SW5, tel. 0171/370–1057.
AE, DC, MC, V. Closed Aug. Tube: South Kensington.*

$$ **Bistrot 190.** Chef-restaurateur and popular guy Antony Worrall
Mediterranean   Thompson dominates this town's medium-priced eating scene with
his happy, hearty food from southern Europe (country bread with
olives and tapenade; liver and wild mushroom terrine; chargrilled
squid with red and green salsa; lemon tart) in raucous hardwood-
floor-and-art settings. This place, the first opened in '91 and is
handy to museum or Albert Hall excursions. The others listed here
are the next-door Downstairs at 190 (*see below*), dell'Ugo in Soho

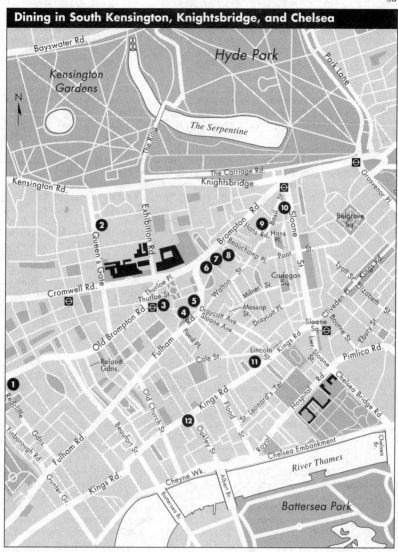

Dining in South Kensington, Knightsbridge, and Chelsea

Bistrot 190, **2**

Caravela, **7**

Chelsea
Kitchen, **11**

Daquise, **3**

Downstairs at 190, **2**

Henry J.
Bean's, **12**

La Brasserie, **5**

Le Metro, **9**

Lou Pescadou, **1**

Luba's Bistro, **8**

Patisserie Valerie, **7**

PJ's Bar and Grill, **4**

St. Quentin, **6**

Stockpot, **10**

(*see above*), and Zoe on St. Christopher's Place, off Oxford Street (*see* Mayfair, *above*). *190 Queen's Gate, SW7, tel. 0171/581–5666. Dress: smart casual. AE, DC, MC, V. Closed Sat. lunch, Sun., Dec. 25–26, Jan. 1. Tube: South Kensington.*

$$ **Downstairs at 190.** Worrall Thompson's good-value fish restaurant (*see* Bistrot 190, *above*) offers "Snacking Food," or appetizers, such as grilled mussels and clams with garlic crumbs or smoked haddock and salmon carpaccio with anchovy ice cream, and such entrées as lobster ravioli or a cassoulet of fishes. Then try whisky fudge cake with caramelized oranges. *190 Queen's Gate, SW7, tel. 0171/581–5666. Reservations advised. AE, DC, MC, V. Closed Sun. Tube: South Kensington.*

$ **La Brasserie.** This big, sunlit brasserie is where local bond traders
French and trust funders hang out in droves, especially Sunday morning over the papers. Classic French dishes are on offer, and since it's a true brasserie, nobody minds if you just sip a coffee for an hour. *272 Brompton Rd., SW3, tel. 0171/584–1668. AE, DC, MC, V. Tube: South Kensington.*

¢ **Daquise.** This venerable and well-loved Polish café by the tube sta-
Polish tion is incongruous in this neighborhood, since it's neither style-conscious nor expensive. Fill your stomach without emptying your pocketbook (or, it must be said, overstimulating your taste buds) on *bigos* (sauerkraut with garlic sausage and mushrooms), stuffed cabbage and cucumber salad, or just coffee and cakes. *20 Thurloe St., SW7, tel. 0171/589–6117. Reservations advised weekend dinner. Tube: South Kensington.*

Knightsbridge

$$ **St. Quentin.** A very popular slice of Paris, frequented by French ex-
French patriates and locals alike. The cuisine is meaty, Gallic, and plain, with some more modern dishes—lime and honey marinated duck breast, for instance, or sweetbreads with a hazelnut sauce. Tartes for dessert come from St. Quentin's gourmet food shop, Les Specialités, as do the cheeses. It can become a lot more expensive if you dine à la carte. *243 Brompton Rd., SW3, tel. 0171/589–8005. Dress: casual but neat. Reservations advised. AE, DC, MC, V. Tube: Knightsbridge.*

$$ **Caravela.** This narrow lower-ground-floor place is one of London's
Portuguese few Portuguese restaurants. You can get *caldo verde* (cabbage soup), *bacalhau* (salt-cured cod), and other typical dishes while listening (on Friday or Saturday) to the national music, fado—desperately sad songs belted out at thrash-metal volume. *39 Beauchamp Pl., SW3, tel. 0171/581–2366. Reservations advised weekend dinner. AE, DC, MC, V. Closed Sun. lunch, Christmas, Easter. Tube: Knightsbridge.*

$ **Stockpot.** You'll find speedy service in this large, jolly restaurant,
International often packed to the brim with young people and shoppers. The food is filling and wholesome: Try the Lancashire hot pot, for example, and the apple crumble. *6 Basil St., SW3, tel. 0171/589–8627. Reservations accepted. Closed national holidays. Other branches at 40 Panton St., off Leicester Sq. (tel. 0171/839–5142); 18 Old Compton St., Soho (tel. 0171/287–1066); and 273 King's Rd., Chelsea (tel. 0171/823–3175). Tube: Knightsbridge.*

$ **Patisserie Valerie.** This is the Soho Valerie's sister, with the same ir-
Patisserie resistible pastries, plus light entrées (salade niçoise, salmon mousse), but minus the bohemian patrons. Instead there are lunching ladies sipping wine, because there's an alcohol licence. *215 Brompton Rd., SW3, tel. 0171/823–9971. AE, MC, V. Closes 7:30 PM (7 Sat., 6 Sun.). Tube: Knightsbridge.*

$ **Luba's Bistro.** Popular for decades: long wooden tables, plain decor,
Russian and authentic Russian cooking—chicken Kiev, beef Stroganoff, etc. Bring your own wine. *6 Yeoman's Row, SW3, tel. 0171/589–2950.*

Reservations required. MC, V. Closed Sun., national holidays.
Tube: Knightsbridge.

Chelsea

$$ **PJ's Bar and Grill.** The decor here evokes the Bulldog Drummond
American lifestyle, with wooden floors and stained glass, a vast, slowly revolving propeller from a 1940s Curtis flying boat, and polo memorabilia.
A menu of all-American staples (soft shell crab, chowder, gumbo,
steaks, smoked ribs), and big salads, then lemon tart, brownies, and
Häagen-Dazs should please all but vegetarians, and portions are big
(especially the local bankers' favorite "Confusion Solution"—half
the menu with fries). This place is more remarkable for ambience
than for food—it's open late; it's relaxed, friendly, and efficient; and
it has bartenders who can mix anything. Both this and the PJ's in
Covent Garden (30 Wellington St., tel. 0171/240–7529) do a very
Stateside Sunday brunch; the other one also has an excellent weekend "Fun Club" for kids. *52 Fulham Rd., SW3, tel. 0171/581–0025.*
Dress: smart casual. AE, DC, MC, V. Closed Dec. 25–26, Jan. 1.
Tube: South Kensington.

¢ **Henry J. Bean's (but his friends all call him Hank) Bar and Grill.** This
American popular place (related to The Chicago Pizza Pie Factory in Mayfair,
above) is a cheap and cheerful, useful dive for any homesick American prepared to endure a menu (on napkins; you order from the bar)
that calls salad "a bit on the side" or "let's go gardening." It's worth
it to sit in the big, lovely patio garden. Nachos, burgers, hot dogs,
fried chicken, potato skins, and mud or pecan pie complete the
menu, along with a score of cocktails. Loud fun. *195–197 King's Rd.,*
SW3, tel. 0171/352–9255. Closed Dec. 25–26, 31. Tube: Sloane
Square, then walk.

¢ **Chelsea Kitchen.** This café has been crowded since the '60s with hun-
International gry people after hot, filling, and inexpensive food. Expect nothing
more fancy than pasta, omelets, salads, stews, and casseroles. The
menu changes every day. *98 King's Rd., SW3, tel. 0171/589–1330.*
Tube: Sloane Square.

Kensington and Notting Hill Gate

Splurge **First Floor.** A place for well-off but arty locals who know and watch
Modern British each other, popular both for its inventive food and its ambience—it
looks like a bombed church inhabited by distressed nobility. There
might be Thai fishcakes or Tuscan lamb stew in the evening, when
you'll need to keep an eye on the check. Lunch, at about half the
price, consists of such lighter dishes as focaccia with grilled vegetables. *186 Portobello Rd., W11, tel. 0171/243–0072. Reservations required. AE, MC, V. Tube: Ladbroke Grove or Notting Hill Gate.*

$$ **L'Artiste Assoiffé.** Stanley and Sally the parrots will scold you in the
French bar of this eccentric Victorian house before you proceed to the Can-
can room or the Carousel room to eat. The music is usually operatic.
Pop stars, actors, and royals come here not for the awful food (fillet
steak with dijon mustard; spinach pancakes with nuts and cheese),
but more for the unique atmosphere. *122 Kensington Park Rd.,*
W11, tel. 0171/727–4714. Dress: casual but neat. Reservations required. AE, DC, MC, V. Closed Sun., national holidays. Tube:
Notting Hill Gate.

$$ **Kalamaras.** Here are two small, friendly, authentic Greek restau-
Greek rants, one "micro" and one "mega," nearly next door to each other.
The micro, which doesn't have a liquor license, is cheaper but more
cramped than the mega. Try a plate of *mezze* for starters, and go on
to, say, kebabs and salads. *76–78 Inverness Mews, W2, tel. 0171/*
727–9122. Reservations advised. AE, DC, MC, V. Dinner only.
Closed Sun., national holidays. Tube: Queensway.

$$ **The Belvedere.** There can be no finer setting for a summer supper or
Mediterranean a sunny Sunday brunch than a window table—or a balcony one if you

All Saints, **7**
Belvedere, **1**
Ben's Thai, **8**
Costa's Grill, **11**
First Floor, **4**
Geales, **12**
Julie's, **3**
Kalamaras, **9**
L'Artiste
Assoiffé, **6**
192, **5**
Tootsies, **2**
Wodka, **10**

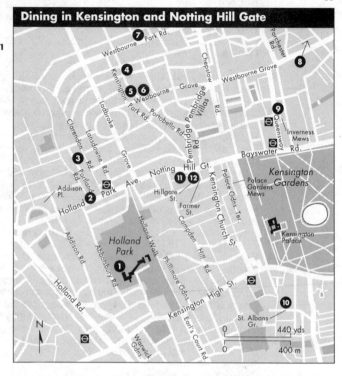

Dining in Kensington and Notting Hill Gate

luck out—at this stunning restaurant in the middle of Holland Park. The menu is big on shaved parmesan, sun-dried tomatoes, and arugula, which suits the conservatory-like room, but both food and service do occasionally miss the target. Still, with a view like this, who cares about water glasses or bland chicken? *Holland Park, off Abbotsbury Rd., W8, tel. 0171/602–1238. Dress: smart casual. Reservations required weekends. AE, DC, MC, V. Closed Sun. dinner. Tube: Holland Park.*

$$ **Wodka.** This smart, modern Polish restaurant is the only one in the
Polish   world, as far as we know, to serve smart, modern Polish food. It is
★   popular with elegant locals plus a sprinkling of celebs and often has the atmosphere of a dinner party. Alongside the smoked salmon, herring, caviar, and eggplant *blinis*, you might also find venison-and-wild-boar sausages or roast duck with honey sauce. Try the flavored vodkas brewed by the owner—an *echt* Polish prince. *12 St. Albans Grove, W8, tel. 0171/937–6513. Dress: casual but neat. Reservations required for dinner. AE, DC, MC, V. Closed weekend lunch, public holidays. Tube: Kensington High Street, then walk.*

$$ **192.** Upstairs is a noisy wine bar where the local trendies actually
Modern British   live; downstairs is a perennially popular, relaxed restaurant serving
★   modern, flavorsome cooking. On a menu that changes twice a day, there are always inventive salads (like romanesco, broccoli, anchovy, and gremolata), plus at least one fish (sea bass with fennel, lemon, and rosemary), and something unexpected (scallop, chickpea, chorizo, and clam casserole). Since first courses are often more exciting, many people order two of them instead of an entrée, and this practice keeps the check in check, too. *192 Kensington Park Rd., W11, tel. 0171/229–0482. Dress: smart casual. Reservations advised. AE, MC, V. Closed Mon., lunch, public holidays. Tube: Ladbroke Grove, then walk.*

$$ **Julie's.** This restaurant has two parts; an upstairs wine bar and a
Traditional   more expensive basement restaurant, both decorated with Victori-
British   an ecclesiastical furniture. The cooking is sound, old-fashioned En-

glish (salmon-and-halibut terrine, roast pheasant with chestnut stuffing and wild rowan jelly). The traditional Sunday lunches are very popular, and in summer there's a garden for outside eating. *135 Portland Rd., W11, tel. 0171/229–8331. Jacket and tie suggested. Reservations advised for dinner and on weekends. MC, V. Closed Sat. lunch, Dec. 25 and 31, Easter. Tube: Holland Park.*

$ **Tootsies.** A superior burger place, dark but cheerful, decorated with
American   vintage advertisements and playing vintage rock. Alternatives to the burgers, which come with thick, crinkly fries, are big salads, steak, BLTs, and chili in a bottomless pan—they'll give you as much as you can take. The usual ices and pies do for dessert. There are branches in Fulham, Chiswick, Notting Hill, and Hampstead. *120 Holland Park Ave., W11, tel. 0171/229–8567. MC, V. Tube: Holland Park.*

$ **Costa's Grill.** Come for good value and such down-to-earth Greek
Greek   food as grilled fish and *kleftiko* (roast lamb on the bone). The atmosphere is lively and great fun. *14 Hillgate St., W8, tel. 0171/229–3794. Reservations advised for groups of more than 4. No credit cards. Closed Sun., national holidays, 3 weeks in summer. Tube: Notting Hill Gate.*

$ **Khan's.** An institution, this spacious north Indian restaurant is al-
Indian   ways packed. Upmarket decor of trompe l'oeil skies and palms and downmarket prices ensure its popularity. The rich butter chicken is a favorite among countless standard Bangladeshi dishes. *13–15 Westbourne Grove, tel. 0171/727–5420. Reservations advised. AE, DC, MC, V. Closed Christmas. Tube: Bayswater.*

$ **All Saints.** Still trendy after all these years and still a useful stop on a
International   Portobello market jaunt. During the day there are croissants, waffles, and danish in the morning, salads, pastas, and sandwiches for lunch. Come the evening it turns into a pan-European place with vast portions of dinner party food. The decor is spartan. *12–14 All Saint's Rd., W11, tel. 0171/243–2808. Reservations required for dinner. MC, DC, V. Closed Sun. dinner. Tube: Westbourne Park.*

¢   **Geales.** This is a cut above your typical fish-and-chips joint. The de-
Seafood   cor is stark but the fish will have been swimming in the sea just a few
★   hours beforehand, even the ones from the Caribbean (fried swordfish is a specialty). Geales is popular with the rich and famous, not just loyal locals. *2 Farmer St., W8, tel. 0171/727–7969. MC. Closed Sun., Mon., 2 weeks at Christmas, 3 weeks in Aug., national holidays. Tube: Notting Hill Gate.*

¢   **Ben's Thai.** Although this giant pub is off our map, it's a very pleas-
Thai   ant place on a balmy evening, when flocks spill out on the steps, the tables, and the grass-covered traffic island that serves as a garden. Improbably, you can order *kaeng kiew wan* (red or green Thai curry), *kwaitiew pad thai* (rice noodles), *tom yam goong* (prawn soup), or other Thai favorites at the full-scale restaurant upstairs, at minimal cost. *The Warrington, 93 Warrington Cres., W9, tel. 0171/266–3134. Reservations advised weekends. MC, V. No lunch; closes 9:30 PM Sun. Tube: Warwick Avenue or Maida Vale.*

The City

Splurge   **Le Pont de la Tour.** Sir Terence Conran's previous pièce de résistance
French   (before Quaglino's and Cantina del Ponte, that is) lies across the river, overlooking the bridge that gives it its name, and so comes into its own in summer, when the outside tables are a little bit of heaven. Inside the "Gastrodrome" (his word) there's a vintner and baker and deli, a seafood bar, and a brasserie, where an impeccable salade niçoise is about £8. Other bistro dishes are similarly well priced, but be careful how you order, and watch the drinks check. The place is no bargain, but it's worth it for the view, and the buzz. *36D Shad Thames, Butler's Wharf, SE1, tel. 0171/403–8403. Dress: smart. Reservations required for lunch, weekend dinner. MC, V. Tube: Tower Hill, then walk across the bridge.*

Bill Bentley's, **5**

Eagle, **1**

East/West, **4**

Le Pont de la Tour, **7**

Place Below, **6**

Quality Chop House, **2**

St. John, **3**

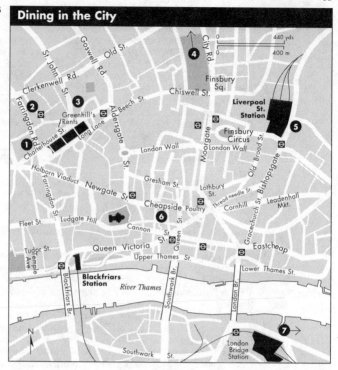

Dining in the City

$$ St. John.
Modern British
★

This former smokehouse (ham, not cigars) with soaring white walls, stone floors, and plain wooden chairs would be bleak, but for the nattering crowds. They're here for the buzz and the achingly trendy food—roast bone marrow and parsley salad; smoked eel, beetroot, and horseradish; and deviled crab, which is practically a parody of Britishness and often looks shockingly nude and lumpen, but tastes great. An all-French wine list has plenty cf affordable bottles, service is efficiently matey, and the pastry chef's chocolate slice belongs in the brownie hall of fame. *26 St. John St., EC1, tel. 0171/251–0848. Reservations required. AE, MC, V. Closed Sun. dinner, Christmas. Tube: Clerkenwell.*

$$ Quality Chop House.
Traditional British

This was converted from one of the most gorgeous "greasy spoon" caffs in town, retaining the solid Victorian fittings (including pewlike seats, which you often have to share). It is not luxurious, but the food is wonderful. It's almost a parody of caff food—bangers and mash turns out to be home-made herbed veal sausage with rich gravy, light, fluffy potato, and vegetables *à point;* egg and chips (fries) are not remotely greasy. There are also posh things like salmon fishcakes and steak, and desserts that change with the seasons. *94 Farringdon Rd., EC1, tel. 0171/837–5093. Reservations required. Closed Sat. lunch, Sun. dinner, public holidays. Tube: Farringdon.*

$$ Bill Bentley's.
Seafood

You can see from the bare walls and the arched ceiling that this was once a wine merchant's vaults. There are four other branches in London, all equally old-fashioned in feel, and all serving Bill Bentley's special oysters and seafood platters. *Swedeland Ct., 202 Bishopsgate, EC2, tel. 0171/283–1763. Jacket and tie required. Reservations required. MC, V. Lunch only. Closed weekends, national holidays. Tube: Moorgate.*

$ The Place Below.
Vegetarian
★

Below what, you may ask? This is the crypt of St. Mary-le-Bow church, and native gourmets, omnivores among them, duly call a Thursday or Friday night meal here a religious experience. At press time the full two- or three-course menu (roquefort terrine, hazelnut filo boat, chocolate truffle cake; BYOB) was only served twice a week, with a superior (budget) lunch on other days, but such is the success of the place that this state of affairs may have changed. *St. Mary-le-Bow, Cheapside, EC2, tel. 0171/329-0789. Reservations essential for dinner. Closed Mon.-Wed. dinner, weekends. Tube: St. Paul's.*

¢   **The Eagle.** If the name makes it sound like a pub, that's because it is
Italian a pub, albeit a superior one, with wooden floors, a few sofas, and art
★   on the walls. It does, however, belong in the "Dining" section by virtue of the amazingly good-value nouveau Tuscan food, which you choose from the blackboard menu (or by pointing) at the bar. There are about half a dozen dishes, a pasta and/or risotto always among them. There are currently quite a few places in London charging four times the price for remarkably similar—and no better—food. *159 Farringdon Rd., EC1, tel. 0171/837-1353. No food served Sat., Sun. evenings. Tube: Farringdon.*

¢   **East/West.** This self-service restaurant in a building of holistic
Vegetarian health practitioners, an organic food shop, and a New Age bookstore provides London's healthiest food. Get the macrobiotic set meal, balanced perfectly in two sizes, or build your own ensemble from the hoummous, salads, whole-meal breads, miso soup, tofu cheesecake, cashew cream, herbal teas, and fresh juices. You can even order a bottle of wine. *188 Old St., EC1, tel. 0171/608-0300. MC, V. Closes 7 PM (3 PM weekends), public holidays. Tube: Old Street.*

Camden Town and Hampstead

$$ **Camden Brasserie.** The perfect neighborhood restaurant (unless
Anglo-French you're vegetarian), this mellow, brick-walled, wood-floor haven makes its charcoal grill work hard (barbecued corn-fed chicken, salmon fillet, steak, etc., come with piles of matchstick fries) and offers a daily fish, pasta, soup, and salad, too. Convenient for market, Canal, and Zoo excursions. *216 Camden High St., NW1, tel. 0171/482-2114. Reservations advised weekends. MC, V. Tube: Camden Town.*

$$ **Belgo.** To enter what must be London's least normal restaurant, you
Belgian pass the wavy concrete facade and cross the spotlit "drawbridge" over the brushed-steel open kitchen. Inside, waitstaff in maroon monks' habits sweep over to your refectory-like table to take your order of *moules-frites* (steamed mussels in various sauces with fries), *waterzooi* (a whitefish stew), wild boar sausages, and other authentic Belgian dishes. Try the Kriek, cherry beer brewed by Trappist monks. Improbably, it's enormous fun—and the food's great. You can easily undercut the regular check by ordering set meals, which makes this a budget place. Look out for Belgo Central in Covent Garden, too. *72 Chalk Farm Rd., tel. 0171/267-0718. Reservations required, same day only. AE, MC, V. Tube: Chalk Farm.*

$$ **Café des Arts.** A welcome addition to the Hampstead scene, this
French brasserie is housed in a 17th-century cottage on the main street. Every wood-paneled wall is hung with work for sale—hence the name—and the patrons are just the sort to buy it, too. About half the beautifully presented dishes—tuna tataki (just-seared fillets) with five-spice lentils; provençale fish stew with rouille; chicken breast with lemon-herb dumplings—come in two sizes, so you can control the check. Don't miss the wicked warm chocolate soufflé. *82 Hampstead High St., NW3, tel. 0171/435-3608. Dress: smart casual. Reservations advised weekends. AE, DC, MC, V. Tube: Hampstead.*

$$ **Underground Café.** Next door to the Camden Brasserie, and a close
Italian relation, this pastel-walled, terra-cotta-floored basement place
★   serves big platefuls of irresistible Italianesque dishes (pappardelle with wild mushrooms; roast stuffed suckling pig; seafood risotto) to loyal locals. *214 Camden High St., NW1, tel. 0171/482-0010. Reser-*

vations advised weekends. MC, V. Closed Mon.–Sat. lunch, Sun. dinner. Tube: Camden Town.

$ **Lemonia.** On a very pleasant street near Regent's Park is this well-
Greek done version of London Greek—large and light, friendly, and packed every evening. Besides the usual *mezedes* (appetizers), *souvlakia* (kebabs), *stifado* (beef stewed in wine), and so on, there are interesting specials: quail, perhaps, or *gemista* (stuffed vegetables). *89 Regent's Park Rd., NW1, tel. 0171/586–7454. Reservations required for dinner. Closed Sat. lunch, Sun. dinner. Tube: Chalk Farm.*

$ **Nontas.** Chunky pine '70s decor, low lighting, alfresco dining in back, and a separate *Ouzerie* serving the aniseed-flavored aperitif and *mezedes* (appetizers) distinguish this long-serving Camden favorite from the competition. The Nontas Special—a taste of several meat dishes served with *pourgouri* (cracked wheat)—is reliable; so are the daily specials. *14–16 Camden High St., NW1, tel. 0171/387–4579. Reservations advised for weekend dinner. AE, DC, MC, V. Closed Sun., two weeks in August. Tube: Mornington Crescent.*

¢   **The Coffee Cup.** A Hampstead landmark for just about as long as
English anyone can remember, this smoky, dingy, uncomfortable café is lovable, very cheap, and therefore always packed. You can get anything (beans, eggs, kippers, mushrooms) on toast, grills, sandwiches, cakes, fry-ups, etc.—nothing healthy or fashionable whatsoever. There are tables outside in the summer, but no liquor license. *74 Hampstead High St., NW3, tel. 0171/435–7565. Tube: Hampstead.*

¢   **Crown & Goose.** A pub run by the Bar Gansa people (*see below*), and similarly good value, with steak in baguette, smoked chicken salad with honey-Dijon dressing, garlic mushrooms, and grilled herbed salmon typical of the short menu. There are wrought-iron tables on the sidewalk in summer, sofas around the open fire in winter, and a crowd always. *100 Arlington Rd., NW1, tel. 0171/485–2342. Tube: Camden Town.*

¢   **Lauderdale House Café.** This is simply the Waterlow Park café, but it transcends its humble status by offering home-cooked meals (lasagna, steak-and-kidney pie, ratatouille) alongside the sandwiches, cakes, ice cream, and styrofoam cups of tea. The 18th-century house itself, and the gorgeous view from the terrace, add further value. Nearby is Highgate Cemetary, where Karl Marx is buried. *Highgate Hill, N6, tel. 0181/341–4807. Closes 6 PM, all day Sat. and Mon. (except bank holiday Mons.). Tube: Highgate.*

¢   **Marine Ices.** Although ice cream is the main course here—in more
Italian than 15 flavors, plus fruit sorbets, and in various bombes, cassate, and sundaes—a full menu, biased toward pasta, is available, too, and the restaurant is licensed. There's a takeout window for gelati, with long lines of Camden Lock market shoppers in summer. *8 Haverstock Hill, NW3, tel. 0171/485–3132. Closes 8 PM Sun., public holidays. Tube: Chalk Farm.*

¢   **Primrose Brasserie.** The elegant tile floor and solid wooden arm-
Russian chairs belie the low prices at this neighborhood favorite. Salmon *kulebiak*, stuffed cabbage, or the peculiar chicken and carrot *tsimmes* (in sweet and sour sauce with apricots) might follow chopped liver, marinated herring, or borscht. Desserts, like *malakof* (whipped cream with marsala and sponge fingers), are rich and filling. Service is charmingly Slavic. BYOB, and look out for "Russian music evenings." *101 Regent's Park Rd., NW1, tel. 0171/483–3765. Reservations advised for dinner. Closed public holidays. Tube: Chalk Farm.*

¢   **Bar Gansa.** The continuing success of this tapas bar in central Cam-
Spanish den is a mixed blessing, since the noise of the crowd drowns conversation, especially on end-of-week evenings. But the tapas—from the classic tortilla and chorizo, *boquerones* (fresh, marinated anchovies) and *calamares* to grilled vegetable salad, leek and nutmeg tartlet, and excellent, fat fries—come in generous portions, three or four of which make a bargain meal for two. Decor and staff are suitably

Iberian. *2 Inverness St., NW1, tel. 0171/267–8909. Reservations advised for dinner. MC, V. Closed public holidays. Tube: Camden Town.*

Pubs

Black Friar. You can't miss it—it's the only wedge-shape, ornate building with a statue of a friar on the front as you step out of Blackfriars tube station! It was built in 1875 and is a triumph of Victorian extravagance, with inlaid mother-of-pearl, delicate woodcarving, stained glass, and bronze bas-reliefs of friars. In the "side chapel" you'll see red marble pillars and a magnificent mosaic ceiling, plus more friars, and devils, *and* fairies—all very art nouveau. There are six kinds of beer on tap. *174 Queen Victoria St., EC4, tel. 0171/236–5650. Tube: Blackfriars.*

Bunch of Grapes. This popular Victorian (1882) pub in the heart of Shepherd Market, the village-within-Mayfair, just off Piccadilly, attracts a colorful crowd. *16 Shepherd Market, W1, tel. 0171/629–4989. Tube: Green Park.*

Freemason's Arms. This place is supposed to have the largest pub garden in London, with two terraces, a summerhouse, country-style furniture, and roses everywhere. It's a favorite Hampstead pub, and popular with local young people. *32 Downshire Hill, NW3, tel. 0171/435–2127. Tube: Hampstead, then walk, or Southend Green British Rail.*

George Inn. The inn sits in a courtyard where Shakespeare's plays were once performed. The present building dates from the late 17th century and is London's last remaining galleried inn. Dickens was a regular—the inn is featured in *Little Dorrit*. Entertainments include Shakespeare performances, medieval jousts, and morris dancing. There's a choice between a real ale bar, a wine bar, and a regular restaurant. *77 Borough High St., SE1, tel. 0171/407–2056. Tube: Borough.*

Jack Straw's Castle. Straw was one of the leaders of the Peasant's Revolt of 1381, and was hanged nearby. In Tudor times it was a favorite hangout for highwaymen, but by the 19th century it had become picturesque and respectable; artists painted charming views from it, and Dickens (inevitably) stayed here. Sadly, it was blitzed during World War II, and rebuilt in the 1960s. *North End Way, NW3, tel. 0171/435–8885. Tube: Hampstead, then walk.*

The Lamb. Dickens lived close by and, yes, he was a regular here, too. It's a jolly, cozy pub, with the original cut-glass Victorian screens. The food is home-cooked, and you can eat or drink outside on the patio. It's crowded in summer. *94 Lamb's Conduit St., WC1, tel. 0171/405–0713. Tube: Holborn.*

Lamb and Flag. This 17th-century pub was once known as "The Bucket of Blood," because the upstairs room was used as a ring for bare-knuckle boxing. Now, it's a trendy, friendly, and entirely bloodless pub, serving food (at lunchtime only) and real ale. It's on the edge of Covent Garden, off Garrick Street. *33 Rose St., WC2, tel. 0171/836–4108. Tube: Covent Garden.*

Mayflower. An atmospheric 17th-century riverside inn with exposed beams and a terrace, this is practically the very place from which the Pilgrims set sail for Plymouth Rock. The inn is licenced to sell American postage stamps alongside its superior pub food. *117 Rotherhithe St., SE16, tel. 0171/237–4088. Tube: Rotherhithe.*

Prospect of Whitby. Named after a ship, this historic riverside tavern dates back to 1520. Once upon a time it was called "The Devil's Tavern," because of the numbers of low-life criminals—thieves and smugglers—who congregated here. It's ornamented with pewter ware and nautical memorabilia. There's an excellent à la carte menu, as well as good pub food. *57 Wapping Wall, E1, tel. 0171/481–1095. Tube: Wapping.*

Spaniards Inn. This is another historic pub on Hampstead Heath,

with superb views of the city. It's so called because the Spanish ambassador lived here in the early 1600s. Dick Turpin, the highwayman, used to frequent the inn; you can see his pistols on display.
Romantic poets—Shelley, Keats, Byron—hung out here, and so, of
course, did Dickens. It's extremely popular, especially on Sunday
when Londoners take to the Heath in search of fresh air. *Spaniards
Rd., NW3, tel. 0171/455–3276. Tube: Hampstead, then walk.*

4 Exploring London

Westminster and Royal London

Numbers in the margin correspond to points of interest on the Westminster and Royal London map.

This tour is London for Beginners. If you go no farther than these few acres, you will see many of the famous sights, from the Houses of Parliament, Big Ben, Westminster Abbey, and Buckingham Palace to two of the world's greatest art collections, the National and the Tate galleries—while spending very little money, since most of these major sights charge no entrance fee. It may be possible to do it all in a day, but picking a highlight or two is a better idea. The galleries alone deserve a day apiece, and if you're going to Westminster Abbey in summer, queuing up will consume most of your stamina. This is concentrated sightseeing, so pace yourself.

Westminster is by far the younger of the capital's two centers, postdating the City by some 1,000 years. Edward the Confessor put it on the map when he packed up his court from its cramped City quarters and went west a couple of miles, founding the abbey church of Westminster—the minster west of the City—in 1050. Subsequent kings continued to hold court there until Henry VIII decamped to Whitehall Palace in 1512, leaving Westminster to the politicians. And there they still are, not in the palace, which was burned almost to the ground in 1834, but in the Victorian mock-Gothic Houses of Parliament, whose 320-foot Clock Tower is as much a symbol of London as the Eiffel Tower is of Paris.

Trafalgar Square and the National Gallery

Trafalgar Square is the obvious place to start for several reasons. It is the center of London, by dint of a plaque on the corner of the Strand and Charing Cross Road from which distances on U.K. sign-

Central London Exploring *(Boxes Refer to Detail Maps)*

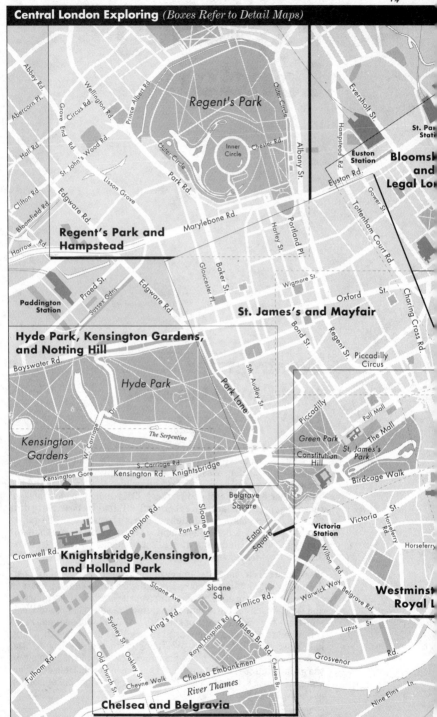

Regent's Park

Abbey Rd.
Abercorn Pl.
Hall Rd.
Wellington Rd.
Grove End Rd.
Circus Rd.
Prince Albert Rd.
Clifton Rd.
Bloomfield Rd.
St. John's Wood Rd.
Lisson Grove
Edgware Rd.
Harrow Rd.
Outer Circle
Inner Circle
Chester Rd.
Albany St.
Park Rd.

Eversholt St.
St. Pa
Stati
Euston Station
Hampstead Rd.
Euston Rd.
Gower St.
**Bloomsk
and
Legal Lo**

Marylebone Rd.

**Regent's Park and
Hampstead**

Paddington Station
Praed St.
Sussex Gdns.
Edgware Rd.
Gloucester Pl.
Baker St.
Portland Pl.
Harley St.
Wigmore St.
Tottenham Court Rd.
Oxford   St.
Charing Cross Rd.

St. James's and Mayfair

Bond St.
Regent St.

**Hyde Park, Kensington Gardens,
and Notting Hill**

Bayswater Rd.
Piccadilly
Circus

Hyde Park

Park Lane
Sth. Audley St.

The Serpentine

*Kensington
Gardens*
W. Carriage Dr.
Kensington Gore
S. Carriage Rd.
Kensington Rd.   Knightsbridge

Piccadilly
Pall Mall
Green Park
The Mall
Constitution Hill
*St. James's
Park*
Birdcage Walk

Belgrave
Square

Victoria   St.
Horseferry
Victoria
Station

Brompton Rd.
Sloane St.
Pont St.
Cromwell Rd.
Eaton
Square
**Knightsbridge,Kensington,
and Holland Park**

Wilton Rd.
Warwick Way
Belgrave Rd.
Horseferry

**Westminst
Royal L**

Sloane Ave.
Sloane
Sq.
Pimlico Rd.
Lupus   St.
Sydney St.
King's Rd.
Old Church St.
Odley St.
Royal Hospital Rd.
Chelsea Br. Rd.
Grosvenor
Rd.

Fulham Rd.
Cheyne Walk
Chelsea Embankment
Chelsea Br.
River Thames
Nine Elms Ln.

Chelsea and Belgravia

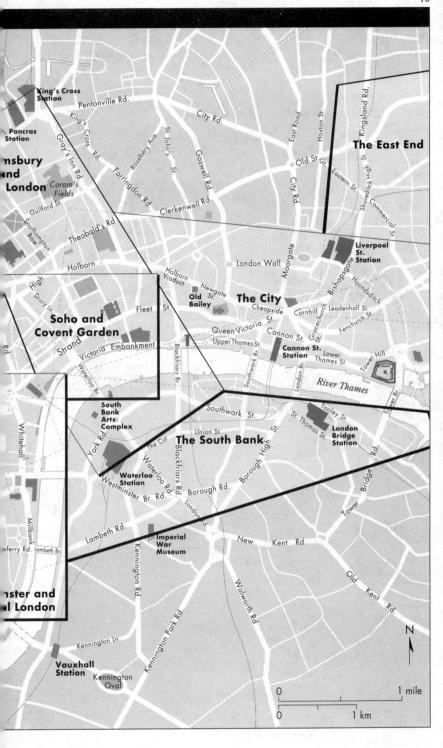

King's Cross Station

. Pancras Station

Pentonville Rd.

City Rd.

Kingsland Rd.

nsbury nd London

King's Cross Rd.

Gray's Inn Rd.

Rosebery Ave.

St. John's

Goswell Rd.

East Road

Hoxton St.

Old St.

Gt. Eastern St.

Shoreditch High St.

Commercial St.

The East End

Coram's Fields

Guilford St.

Farringdon Rd.

Clerkenwell Rd.

City Rd.

Moorgate

Bishopsgate

Houndsditch

Liverpool St. Station

Southampton Row

Theobald's Rd.

London Wall

Holborn

Holborn Viaduct

Newgate St.

Old Bailey

The City

Cheapside

Cornhill

Leadenhall St.

Fenchurch St.

High

Drury Ln.

Fleet St.

Soho and Covent Garden

Queen Victoria St.

Cannon St.

Gracechurch St.

Tower Hill

Strand

Victoria Embankment

Blackfriars Br.

Upper Thames St.

Cannon St. Station

Lower Thames St.

Waterloo Br.

Southwark Br.

London Br.

River Thames

Tower Br.

Whitehall

South Bank Arts Complex

Southwark St.

Tooley St.

St. Thomas St.

London Bridge Station

York Rd.

The Cut

Union St.

The South Bank

Borough High St.

Bridge Rd.

Waterloo Station

Waterloo Rd.

Blackfriars Rd.

Westminster Br. Rd.

Borough Rd.

London Rd.

Tower Bridge Rd.

Millbank

eferry Rd. Lambeth Br.

Lambeth Rd.

Kennington Rd.

Imperial War Museum

New Kent Rd.

Walworth Rd.

Old Kent Rd.

nster and l London

Kennington Ln.

Kennington Park Rd.

Vauxhall Station

Kennington Oval

N

0   1 mile

0   1 km

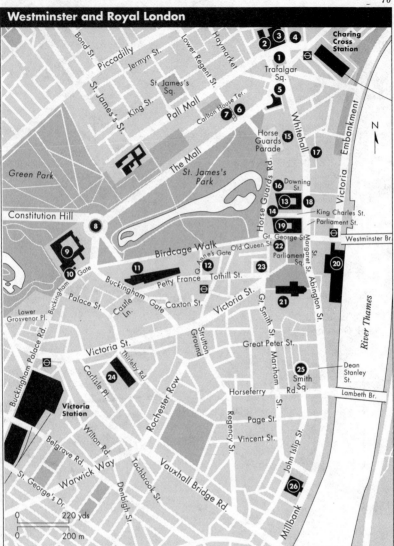

Westminster and Royal London

Admiralty Arch, **5**

Banqueting House, **17**

Buckingham Palace, **9**

Cabinet War Rooms, **14**

Cenotaph, **18**

Central Hall, **23**

Duke of York Steps, **7**

Foreign Office, **13**

Home Office, **19**

Horse Guards Parade, **15**

Houses of Parliament, **20**

Institute of Contemporary Arts (ICA), **6**

National Gallery, **2**

National Portrait Gallery, **3**

Nelson's Column, **1**

Queen Anne's Gate, **12**

Queen Victoria Memorial, **8**

Queen's Gallery, **10**

St. John's, Smith Square, **25**

St. Margaret's, **22**

St. Martin-in-the-Fields, **4**

Tate Gallery, **26**

10 Downing Street, **16**

Wellington Barracks, **11**

Westminster Abbey, **21**

Westminster Cathedral, **24**

posts are measured. It is the home of the National Gallery and of one of London's most distinctive landmarks, Nelson's Column, and the site of many political demonstrations, a raucous New Year's Eve party, and the highest concentration of bus stops and pigeons in the capital. In short, it is London's most famous square.

Long ago the site housed the Royal Mews, where Edward I (1239–1307) kept his royal hawks and lodged his falconers. (Not the numberless Edward the Confessor of Westminster Abbey fame, who died in 1066, this one was known as "Longshanks" and died of dysentery in 1307.) Later, all the kings' horses were stabled here, in increasingly smart quarters, until 1830, when John Nash had the buildings torn down as part of his Charing Cross Improvement Scheme—which he did not live to complete. The baton was passed to Sir Charles Barry, architect of the Houses of Parliament, and in 1840 the square was paved, with the fountains added five years later. (Sir Edwin Lutyens remodeled them in 1939, and they were further enhanced with cavorting sea creatures after World War II.)

Keeping watch from his 145-foot granite perch is E. H. Baily's 1843 statue of Admiral Lord Horatio Nelson, one of England's favorite heroes. Around the foot of **Nelson's Column,** three bas-reliefs depict his victories at Cape St. Vincent, the Battle of the Nile, and Copenhagen and the fourth, his death at Trafalgar itself in 1805; all four were cast from cannons he captured. The four majestic lions, designed by the Victorian painter Sir Edwin Landseer, were added in 1867. The calling cards of generations of picturesque pigeons have been a corrosive problem for the statue, but it may have been finally solved by a 150th-birthday present of a pigeon-proof gel coating. You can read about the area on a plaque marking the anniversary. Street performers were licensed for the first time last year, and they now enhance the square's intermittent atmosphere of celebration. This atmosphere is the strongest in December, first, when the lights on the gigantic Christmas tree (an annual gift from Norway to thank the British for harboring its royal family during World War II) are turned on, and then, when thousands see in the New Year.

The north side of the square is filled by the low, gray, colonnaded neoclassical facade of the **National Gallery.** The institution was founded in 1824, when George IV and a connoisseur named Sir George Beaumont persuaded a reluctant government to spend £57,000 on part of the collection of the recently deceased philanthropist John Julius Angerstein. These 38 paintings, including works by Raphael, Rembrandt, Titian, and Rubens, were augmented by 16 of Sir George's and were exhibited in Angerstein's Pall Mall residence until 1838, when William Wilkins's building was completed. By the end of the century, enthusiastic directors and generous patrons had turned the National Gallery into one of the world's foremost collections, with works from painters of the Italian Renaissance and earlier; the Flemish and Dutch masters; the Spanish school; and, of course, the English tradition, including Hogarth, Gainsborough, Stubbs, and Constable.

In 1991, following years of wrangling and the rehanging of the entire collection, the Sainsbury Wing was opened. It was financed by the eponymous British grocery dynasty to house the early Renaissance collection and designed—eventually—by the American architect Robert Venturi after previous plans were abandoned. (Prince Charles hadn't liked the other plans. "A monstrous carbuncle on the face of a much-loved friend" was his infamous comment.)

The collection is really too overwhelming to absorb in a single viewing. Therefore, it is wise to acquaint yourself with the layout—easy to negotiate compared with other European galleries—and plot a route in advance. The **Micro Gallery,** a computer information center in the Sainsbury Wing, may be the place to start. You can access in-depth information on any work here, choose your favorites, and print out a free personal tour map that marks the paintings you most want to see. Careful, though—you could spend hours in here scrolling through the colorful potted history of art.

Among the 2,200-odd paintings, most of them on permanent display, many are instantly recognizable; among the familiar ones are **van Eyck**'s *The Arnolfini Marriage;* **Leonardo da Vinci**'s haunting cartoon, *The Virgin and Child;* **Caravaggio**'s *The Supper at Emmaus;* and the works of two of the many great British painters: **Constable**'s *The Hay Wain* and **Turner**'s *The Fighting Téméraire.* You'll also see works by Titian, Holbein, Bosch, Brueghel, Rembrandt, Vermeer, Rubens, Canaletto, Claude, Tiepolo, Gainsborough, Ingres, Monet, Renoir, Van Gogh . . . you get the picture. *Trafalgar Sq., tel. 0171/ 839–3321; 0171/839–3526 (recorded general information); 0171/ 389–1773 (recorded exhibition information). Admission free; admission charge for special exhibitions. Free 1-hr guided tours start at the Sainsbury Wing weekdays at 11:30 and 2:30, Sat. 2 and 3:30. Open Mon.–Sat. 10–6, Sun. 2–6; June–Aug., also Wed. until 8; closed Good Friday, May Day, Dec. 24–26, Jan. 1. Tube: Charing Cross.*

Once you're done exploring the gallery's contents, stop a moment on the steps in front and admire the view over Trafalgar Square toward Admiralty Arch, with the former Canada House on the west side and the former South Africa House on the east. On the sloping lawn in front is Grinling Gibbons's statue of James II, who failed to return Britain to Catholicism during his short reign (1685–88). Gibbons, "Master Carver in Wood to the Crown," was much in vogue at the end of the 17th century (see his choir-stall carvings at St. Paul's). At the other end of the lawn is a bronze of George Washington, presented to the British by the Commonwealth of Virginia in 1921.

❸ The **National Portrait Gallery,** just around the corner, is a much smaller affair, an idiosyncratic collection that presents a condensed history of Britain through its residents, past and present. As an art collection it is eccentric, since the subject, not the artist, is the point, and there are notable works (a Holbein portrait of Henry VIII and Stubbs and Hockney self-portraits) mixed in with photographs, busts, caricatures, and amateur paintings. (The miniature of Jane Austen by her sister Cassandra, for instance, is the only likeness in existence of the great novelist.) Many of the faces are obscure and will be just as unknown to English visitors, since the portraits outlasted their sitters' fame. But the annotation is comprehensive, and there is a new, separate research center for those who get hooked on particular personages—part of an expansion that fixed up the layout (still chronological, with the oldest at the top) and added a photography gallery. *St. Martin's Pl., WC2, tel. 0171/306–0055. Admission free. Open weekdays 10–5, Sat. 10–6, Sun. 2–6. Closed public holidays. Tube: Charing Cross, Leicester Square.*

❹ Across the street, east of the National Gallery, is the much-loved church of **St. Martin-in-the-Fields,** completed in 1726. James Gibbs's classical-temple-with-spire design, unusual at the time, became a familiar pattern for churches in early Colonial America. Though it seems dwarfed by the surrounding structures, the spire is actually slightly taller than Nelson's Column. It is a welcome sight for the homeless, who have sought soup and shelter here since 1914. The church is also a haven for music lovers, since the internationally known Academy of St. Martin-in-the-Fields was founded here, and a popular program of lunchtime (free) and evening concerts continues today. St. Martin's is often called the royal parish church, partly because Charles II was christened here—not because his mistress, Nell Gwyn, lies under the stones, alongside William Hogarth, Thomas Chippendale (the cabinetmaker), and Jack Sheppard, the notorious highwayman. Also in the crypt is the **London Brass-Rub-**

bing Centre, where you can make your own souvenir knights from replica tomb brasses, with metallic waxes, paper, and instructions provided, and the **St. Martin's Gallery** showing contemporary work. There is also a crafts market in the courtyard behind the church. *St. Martin-in-the-Fields, Trafalgar Sq., tel. 0171/930–0089. Credit-card bookings for evening concerts, tel. 0171/839–8362. Brass rub-bing fee from £1. Church open daily 8–8; crypt open Mon.–Sat. 10–8, Sun. noon–6. Tube: Charing Cross, Leicester Square.*

There's a pathetic history attached to the **equestrian statue of Charles I** that stands near Whitehall on the southern slope of Trafal-gar Square (on a pedestal *possibly* designed by Sir Christopher Wren and *possibly* carved by Grinling Gibbons). After Charles's high treasurer ordered it (from Hubert le Sueur), the Puritan Oliver Cromwell tumbled Charles from the throne and commissioned a scrap dealer with the appropriate name of Rivett to melt the statue of the king down. Rivett made a fortune peddling knickknacks wrought, he claimed, from its metal, only to produce the statue mi-raculously unscathed after the restoration of the monarchy—and to make more money reselling it to the authorities. In 1767 Charles II had it placed where it stands today, near the spot where his father was executed in 1649.

St. James's Park and the Mall

Leave Trafalgar Square from its southwest corner through **⑤ Admiralty Arch,** designed in 1910 by Sir Aston Webb as part of a cer-emonial route to Buckingham Palace and named after the adjacent Royal Navy headquarters. As you pass under the enormous triple archway—though not through the central arch, opened only for state occasions—the atmosphere changes along with the color of the road, for you are exiting frenetic Trafalgar Square and entering **The Mall** (rhymes with "shall"), which has nothing to do with shopping.

The original Mall was laid out around 1660 for the game that gave Pall Mall (*see* St. James's and Mayfair, *below*) its name and quickly became the place to be seen. Samuel Pepys, Jonathan Swift, and Al-exander Pope all wrote about it, and it continued as the beau monde's social playground into the early 19th century, long after the game of pall mall had gone out of vogue. Something of the former style survives on those summer days when the queen holds a Buck-ingham Palace garden party: The Mall is thronged with hundreds of her subjects, from the grand and titled to the humble and hardwork-ing, all of whom have donned hats, frocks, and morning suits to take afternoon tea with her—or somewhere near her—on the lawns of Buck House. The old Mall still runs alongside the graceful, pink 115-foot-wide avenue that replaced it in 1904 for just such occasions.

St. James's Park, along the south side of the Mall, is London's small-est, most ornamental park, and the oldest of its royal ones. Henry VIII drained a marsh that festered here next to the lepers' hospital that St. James's Palace replaced and bred his deer on the newly dry land. Later kings tinkered with it further, James I installing an avi-ary and zoo (complete with crocodiles); Charles I laying formal gar-dens, which he then had to cross to his execution in 1649; and Charles II employing André Le Nôtre, Louis XIV's Versailles landscaper, to remodel it completely with avenues, fruit orchards, and a canal. Its present shape more or less reflects what John Nash designed under George IV, when he turned the canal into a graceful lake (which was cemented in at a depth of 4 feet in 1855, so don't even think of swim-ming) and generally naturalized the gardens.

More than 30 species of birds—including flamingos, pelicans, geese, ducks, and swans (which belong to the queen)—now congregate on Duck Island at the east end of the lake, attracting ornithologists at dawn. Later on summer days the deck chairs (which you must pay for) are crammed with office lunchers who are serenaded by music from the bandstands. The best time to stroll the leafy walkways, though, is after dark, with Westminster Abbey and the Houses of Parliament rising above the floodlit lake and peace reigning.

Back on the Mall, look to the other (north) side for a more solid example of John Nash's genius: **Carlton House Terrace.** Between 1812 and 1830, under the patronage of George IV (Prince Regent until George III's death in 1820), Nash was responsible for a series of West End developments, of which these white-stucco facades and massive Corinthian columns may be the most imposing. It was a smart address, needless to say, and one that prime ministers William Gladstone (1856) and Henry Palmerston (1857–75) enjoyed. Today Carlton House Terrace is home to the Royal College of Pathologists; the Royal Society; the Turf Club; and, at No. 12, the **⑥ Institute of Contemporary Arts,** better known as the **ICA.** Behind its incongruous facade, the ICA has provided a stage for the avant-garde in performance art, theater, dance, visual art, and music since it was established in 1947. There are two cinemas, an underused library of video artists' works, a bookshop, a café, a bar, and a team of adventurous curators. *The Mall, tel. 0171/930–3647. 1-day membership: £1.50 adults, children under 14 free. An additional charge is made for entry to specific events. Open daily noon–9:30, later for some events; closed Dec. 24–27, Jan. 1. Tube: Charing Cross.*

⑦ Bisecting Carlton House Terrace are the **Duke of York Steps,** surmounted by the 124-foot Duke of York's Column, from which an 1834 bronze of George III's second son, Frederick, gazes toward the Whitehall War Office. Frederick, the duke, was popular among his troops until each man in the army had one day's pay extracted to fund this £25,000 tribute, which was perched this high, said the wits, to keep him away from his creditors. He owed £2 million at his death.

Buckingham Palace to Parliament Square

⑧ Facing the palace from the traffic island at the west end of the Mall is the white marble **Queen Victoria Memorial.** The monument was conceived by Sir Aston Webb as the nucleus of his ceremonial Mall route and executed by the sculptor Thomas Brock, who was knighted on the spot when it was revealed to the world in 1911. Many wonder why Brock was knighted, since the monument is Victoriana incarnate: The frumpy queen glares down the Mall, with golden-winged Victory overhead and her siblings Truth, Justice, and Charity, plus Manufacture, Progress-and-Peace, War-and-Shipbuilding, and so on—in Osbert Sitwell's words, "tons of allegorical females . . . with whole litters of their cretinous children"—surrounding her. Climbing it is not encouraged, even though it's the best vantage point for viewing the daily **Changing of the Guard,** which, with all the pomp and ceremony monarchists and children adore, remains one of London's best free shows. *Guard leaves Wellington Barracks 11 AM, arrives Buckingham Palace 11:30. Daily Apr.–July; alternate days Aug.–March. Tube: St James's Park, Victoria.*

⑨ Buckingham Palace tops the must-see lists, although the building itself is no masterpiece and has housed the monarch only since Victoria moved here from Kensington Palace at her accession in 1837. At that time the place was a mess. George IV, at *his* accession in 1820, fancied the idea of moving to Buckingham House, his parents' former home, and employed John Nash, as usual, to remodel it. The government authorized only "repair and improvement"; Nash, who had other ideas, overspent his budget by about half a million pounds. George died, Nash was dismissed, and Edward Blore finished the building, adding the now-familiar east front (facing the Mall). Victoria arrived to faulty drains and sticky doors and windows nevertheless, but they did not mar her affection for the place, nor that of her son, Edward VII. The Portland stone facade dates only from 1913 (it, too, was part of the Aston Webb scheme), and the interior was renovated and redecorated only after it was damaged by bombs during World War II.

The palace contains some 600 rooms, including the State Ballroom and, of course, the Throne Room. The royal apartments are in the north wing; when the queen is in, the royal standard flies at the masthead. Until recently all the rooms were off-limits to the public, but a 1992 fire at Windsor Castle created an urgent need for cash. And so the state rooms are now on show—on something of an experimental basis through 1997—for eight weeks in August and September, when the royal family is away. Without an invitation to one of the queen's garden parties, however, you won't see much of the magnificent 45-acre grounds and, since the admission charge has come under much criticism for being somewhat greedy, you may prefer to restrict your visit to the external views. *Buckingham Palace Rd., tel. 0171/799–2331. Admission: £8 adults, £5.50 senior citizens, £4 children under 17. Call for hours, which had not been set at press time. Tube: St James's Park, Victoria.*

🔟 The former chapel at the south side, on the other hand, has been open to visitors since 1962 as the **Queen's Gallery.** On display here are paintings from her majesty's collection—the country's largest—including works by Vermeer, Leonardo, Rubens, Rembrandt, Canaletto . . . , and Queen Victoria. Sign-of-the-times note: Now that the queen is a taxpayer, her artworks, along with all her other possessions (for example, Buckingham Palace), are officially part of a business known as "Royal Collection Enterprises." *Buckingham Palace Rd., tel. 0171/799–2331. Admission: £3 adults, £2 senior citizens, £1.50 children. Open Tues.–Sat. 10–5, Sun. 2–5; closed Dec. 24–Mar. 4, Good Friday. Tube: St James's Park, Victoria.*

Nearly next door stand the Nash-designed **Royal Mews.** Mews were originally falcons' quarters (the name comes from the falcons' "mewing," or feather shedding), but horses gradually eclipsed birds of prey. Now some of the magnificent royal beasts live here alongside the fabulous bejeweled, glass, and golden coaches they draw on state occasions. The place is unmissable children's entertainment. *Buckingham Palace Rd., tel. 0171/799–2331. Admission: £3 adults, £2 senior citizens, £1.50 children. Combined ticket for Queen's Gallery and Royal Mews: £5 adults, £3.50 senior citizens, £2.20 children. Open Oct.–Mar., Wed. noon–4; Apr.–Oct., Tues.–Thurs. noon–4; closed Mar. 25–29, Oct. 1–5, Dec. 23–Jan. 5. Tube: St James's Park, Victoria.*

⓫ Turn back along Buckingham Palace Road, continue down Birdcage Walk, and on the right you'll soon see the **Wellington Barracks,** the headquarters of the Guards Division. Five regiments of elite foot guards (Grenadier, Coldstream, Scots, Irish, and Welsh) protect the sovereign and patrol the palace dressed in tunics of gold-purled scarlet and tall, fur "busby" helmets of Canadian brown bearskin. (The two items cost more than £4,000 for the set.) If you want to learn more about the guards, you can visit the **Guards Museum;** the entrance is next to the Guards Chapel. *Wellington Barracks, Birdcage Walk, tel. 0171/930–4466, ext. 3430. Admission: £2 adults, £1 children under 16 and senior citizens. Open Sat.–Thurs. 10–4; closed national holidays. Tube: St James's Park.*

⓬ Past the barracks on the right is the entrance to **Queen Anne's Gate,** two pretty 18th-century closes, once separate but now linked by a statue of the last Stuart monarch. (Another statue of Anne, beside St. Paul's, inspired the doggerel "Brandy Nan, Brandy Nan, you're left in the lurch/Your face to the gin shop, your back to the church"—

proving that her attempts to disguise her habitual tipple in a teapot fooled nobody.)

Have a look at the Henry Moore bronze *Mother and Child;* then follow Dartmouth Street out of Queen Anne's Gate. Great George Street, at the end, leads into Parliament Square. But turn left at Storey's Gate for a detour down Horse Guard's Road past the ⓭ **Foreign Office,** built in the 1860s by Sir Giles Gilbert Scott, who was better known for such fantastic Gothic Revival buildings as the House of Commons (*see below*).

Make a right before the Foreign Office into King Charles Street to ⓮ find the **Cabinet War Rooms**—an essential visit for World War II buffs. During air raids the War Cabinet met in this warren of 17 bomb-proof chambers. The Cabinet Room is still arranged as if a meeting were about to convene; in the Map Room, the Allied campaign is charted; the Prime Minister's Room holds the desk from which Churchill made his morale-boosting broadcasts; and the Telephone Room has his hot line to President Franklin D. Roosevelt. *Clive Steps, King Charles St., tel. 0171/930–6961. Admission: £3.90 adults, £3 senior citizens, £1.90 children under 16. Open daily 10–5:15; closed Good Friday, May Day, Dec. 24–26, Jan. 1. Tube: Westminster.*

Farther along Horse Guards Road, opposite St. James's Park, ⓯ stands **Horse Guards Parade.** Once the tilt-yard of Whitehall Palace, where jousting tournaments were held, it is now notable mainly for the annual Trooping the Colour ceremony, in which the queen takes the Royal Salute, her official birthday gift, on the second Saturday in June. (Like Paddington Bear, the queen has two birthdays; her real one is on April 21.) There is pageantry galore, with marching bands and the occasional guardsman fainting clean away in his busby, and throngs of people. The ceremony is televised and broadcast on Radio 4. You can also attend the queenless rehearsals on the preceding two Saturdays.

The quiet street barred by iron gates that you passed on your right before coming to Horse Guards Parade is **Downing Street,** which con- ⓰ tains London's modest version of the White House at **10 Downing Street.** Only three houses remain of the terrace built circa 1680 by Sir George Downing, who spent enough of his youth in America to graduate from Harvard—the second man ever to do so. No. 11 is the residence of the chancellor of the exchequer (secretary of the treasury), and No. 12, the party whip's office. No. 10 has officially housed the prime minister since 1732. (The gates were Margaret Thatcher's brainwave.)

At the other end of Downing Street (though, of course, you can't walk through it—you have to go all the way around via King Charles Street) is the wide street called Whitehall. Bang in the middle is the other facade of Horse Guards, where two mounted sentries, known as the Queen's Life Guard, provide what may be London's most frequently taken-up photo opportunity. The Life Guards change, quietly, at 11 AM Monday–Saturday, 10 AM on Sunday. On a site reaching from here to the Thames and from Trafalgar Square to Parliament Square once stood Whitehall Palace, established by Henry VIII, who married two of his six wives (Anne Boleyn and Jane Seymour) and breathed his last there. The sheer scale of this 2,000-room labyrinth in red Tudor brick must have been breathtaking, but we won't dwell on it, since it burned to the ground in 1698, thanks to a fire started by a Dutch laundress whose name has not made it to posterity.

⓱ All that remains today is the **Banqueting House,** but if the rest was like this, we should weep for its loss. Actually, we know that it was quite different. (One foreign visitor accused the palace of being "ill-built, and nothing but a heap of houses.") James I commissioned Inigo Jones to do a grand remodeling of the palace, but Banqueting

House is the only part that was completed. Jones (1573–1652), one of England's great architects, had been influenced by Andrea Palladio's work during a sojourn in Tuscany and brought that sophistication and purity back with him to London. The graceful and disciplined classical style of Banqueting House must have stunned its early occupants. James I's son, Charles I, enhanced the interior by employing the Flemish painter Peter Paul Rubens to glorify his father all over the ceiling. As it turned out, these allegorical paintings, depicting a wise monarch being received into heaven, were the last thing Charles saw before he was beheaded by Cromwell's Parliamentarians on a scaffold outside in 1649. But his son, Charles II, was able to celebrate the restoration of the monarchy here 20 years later. *Whitehall, tel. 0171/930–4179. Admission: £2.90 adults, £2.20 senior citizens, £1.90 children under 16. Open Mon.–Sat. 10–5; closed Good Friday, Dec. 24–26, Jan. 1, and at short notice for banquets, so call first. Tube: Westminster.*

18 Walk south on Whitehall toward Parliament Square, and in the middle of the street you'll see the **Cenotaph,** a stark white monolith designed in 1920 by Edward Lutyens to commemorate the 1918 armistice. On Remembrance Day (the Sunday nearest November 11) it is strewn with blood-red poppies to honor the dead of both world wars, with the first wreath laid by the queen. (Wherever you are on that day, you'll be inveigled to drop pennies for veterans' charities into tins for your own plastic poppy.)

The Houses of Parliament

19
★ 20 Continue down Whitehall (which becomes Parliament Street beside Gilbert Scott's Foreign Office), pass the **Home Office** on the right, bear left, and you will soon be confronted with London's most famous and photogenic sight: the **Houses of Parliament,** with the Clock Tower, which everyone mistakenly calls Big Ben, looming the largest, and Westminster Abbey ahead of you across Parliament Square.

The Palace of Westminster, as the complex is still properly called, was established by Edward the Confessor during the 11th century, when he moved his court from the City; it has been the seat of English administrative power ever since. In 1512, Henry VIII abandoned it for Whitehall (*see above*). It ceased to be an official royal residence after 1547: During the Reformation, the Royal Chapel was secularized and became the first meeting place of the Commons. The Lords settled in the White Chamber.

This, along with everything but the **Jewel Tower** and **Westminster Hall,** were destroyed in 1834 when "the sticks"—the arcane abacus beneath the Lords' Chamber on which the court had kept its accounts until 1826—were incinerated and the fire got out of hand. The same cellar had seen an earlier attempt to raze the palace: the infamous Gunpowder Plot of November 5, 1605, perpetrated by the Catholic convert Guy Fawkes and his fellow conspirators. If you are in London in late October or early November, you may see children with dressed-up teddy bears demanding a "penny for the guy!" They do it because, to this day, November 5 is Guy Fawkes Day (a.k.a. Bonfire Night), when fireworks bought with the pennies accompany pyres of these makeshift effigies of Guy Fawkes, and anyone who still knows it recites: "Remember, remember/The 5th of November,/The Gunpowder Treason and plot./There isn't a reason/Why gunpowder treason/Should ever be forgot."

After the 1834 fire, architects were invited to submit plans for new Houses of Parliament in the grandiose "Gothic or Elizabethan style." Charles Barry's were selected from among 97 entries, partly because Barry had invited the architect and designer Augustus Pugin to add the requisite neo-Gothic curlicues to his own Renaissance-influenced style. As you can see, it was a happy collaboration, with Barry's classical proportions offset by Pugin's ornamental flourishes—although the latter were toned down by Gilbert Scott when he rebuilt the bomb-damaged House of Commons after World War II.

The two towers were Pugin's work. The **Clock Tower,** now virtually the symbol of London, was completed in 1858 after long delays caused by bickering over the clock's design. (Barry designed the faces himself in the end.) It contains the 13-ton bell, known as Big Ben, that chimes the hour (and the quarter hour). Some say Ben was "Big Ben" Caunt, heavyweight champion; others, Sir Benjamin Hall, the far-from-slim commissioner of the Westminster building works. At the other end is the 336-foot-high **Victoria Tower,** which contains the 3-million-document parliamentary archives and now gleams from its recent restoration and cleaning. The rest of the complex was scrubbed down some years ago; the revelation of the honey stone under the dowdy, smog-blackened facades, which seemed almost symbolic at the time, cheered London up no end.

There are two Houses: the Lords and the Commons. The former (the Upper House) consists of over 1,000 peers (nowadays there are more "life peers," with recently bestowed titles, than aristocrats; there are also 26 Anglican bishops who are "spiritual peers"), the latter (the Lower House), of 650 elected members of Parliament (MPs). The party with the most MPs forms the government, its leader becoming prime minister; other parties form the Opposition. Since 1642, when Charles I tried to have five MPs arrested, no monarch has been allowed into the House of Commons. The State Opening of Parliament in November consequently takes place in the House of Lords, after a ritual inspection of the cellars in case a modern Guy Fawkes lurks.

Visitors aren't allowed many places in the Houses of Parliament, though the Visitors' Galleries of the House of Commons afford a fine view of the surprisingly cramped debating chambers. The opposing banks of green leather benches seat only 346 MPs—not that this is much of a problem, since absentees far outnumber the diligent. When MPs vote, they exit by the "Aye" or the "No" corridor, counted by the party "whips" (yes, it is a foxhunting term); when they speak, it is not directly to each other but through the Speaker, who also decides who will get the floor each day. Elaborate procedures notwithstanding, debate is often drowned out by the amazingly immature jeers and insults familiar to TV viewers since 1989, when cameras were first allowed into the House of Commons.

The House of Lords was televised first, perhaps because its procedures are more palatably dignified, with the Lord Chancellor, or Chief Justice, presiding from his official seat, the Woolsack (England's economy was once dependent on this commodity) over a few gently slumbering peers. Or perhaps the House of Lords was first because of its telegenic gold and scarlet chamber, Pugin's masterpiece. The Upper House remains the highest court of appeal in the land, though its parliamentary powers are restricted to delaying or suspending passage of a bill. It is separated from the Lower House by the octagonal **Central Lobby,** which is where constituents wait for their MPs and where the press is received—hence the term "lobby correspondent" for a domestic political reporter. Other public areas of the 1,100-room labyrinth are magnificently decorated in high neo-Gothic style and punctuated with stirring frescoes commissioned by Prince Albert. You pass these frescoes en route to the Visitors' Galleries—if, that is, you are patient enough to wait in line for hours (the Lords line is shorter) or have applied in advance through your embassy. *St. Stephen's Entrance, St. Margaret St., SW1, tel. 0171/219–3000. Admission free. Commons open Mon.– Thurs. 2:30–10, Fri. 9:30–3; Lords open Mon.–Thurs. 2:30–10.*

Closed Easter wk, May bank holiday, July–Oct., 3 wks at Christmas. Tube: Westminster.

As you cross Parliament Square, look at the statues dotted around: Lord Palmerston and Benjamin Disraeli, prime ministers under Queen Victoria; Sir Robert Peel, who formed the first Metropolitan Police Force (hence the nickname "bobbies"); a hulking, hunched Churchill in a 1973 bronze; Richard the Lionheart; Oliver Cromwell; and, on the far side (as if over the pond), Abraham Lincoln.

Westminster Abbey

★ ㉑ Off the south side of Parliament Square, announced by the teeming human contents of herds of tour buses, stands **Westminster Abbey.** Nearly all England's monarchs were crowned here, amid vast pomp and circumstance, and most are buried here, too. The place is crammed with spectacular medieval architecture and impressive and moving monuments. It is worth pointing out, though, that the abbey is still a place of worship, and while attending a service is not something to undertake purely for sightseeing reasons, it provides a glimpse of the abbey in its full majesty, accompanied by music from the Westminster choristers and the organ that Henry Purcell once played. Some parts are closed on Sunday except to worshipers.

The origins of Westminster Abbey are uncertain. The first church on the site may have been built as early as the 7th century by the Saxon King Sebert (who may be buried here, alongside his queen and sister); a Benedictine abbey was established during the 10th century. There were certainly preexisting foundations when Edward the Confessor was crowned in 1040, moved his palace to Westminster, and began building a church. Only traces have been found of that incarnation, which was consecrated eight days before Edward's death in 1065. (It appears in the Bayeaux Tapestry.) Edward's canonization in 1139 gave a succession of kings added incentive to shower the abbey with attention and improvements. Henry III, full of ideas from his travels in France, pulled it down and started again with Amiens and Rheims in mind. In fact, it was the master mason Henry de Reyns ("of Rheims") who, between 1245 and 1254, put up the transepts, north front, and rose windows, as well as part of the cloisters and Chapter House, and it was his master plan that, funded by Richard II, was resumed 100 years later. Henry V (reigned 1413–22) and Henry VII (1485–1509) were the chief succeeding benefactors. The abbey was eventually completed in 1532. After that, Sir Christopher Wren had a hand in shaping the place; his West Towers were completed in 1745, 22 years after his death. The most riotous elements of the interior were, similarly, much later affairs.

The **Nave** is your first sight on entering; you need to look up to gain a perspective on the awe-inspiring scale of the church, since the eye-level view is obscured by the 19th- (and part 13th-) century choir screen, past which point admission is charged. Before you pay, look at the poignant **Tomb of the Unknown Warrior,** an anonymous World War I martyr who lies buried here in memory of the soldiers fallen in both world wars. Nearby is one of the few tributes to a foreigner, a plaque to Franklin D. Roosevelt.

There is only one way around the abbey, and since there will almost certainly be a crocodile of shuffling visitors at your heels, you'll need to be alert to catch the highlights. Pass through the **Choir,** with its mid-19th-century choir stalls, into the **North Transept.** Look up to your right to see the painted-glass **Rose Window,** the largest of its kind, and to your left, for the first of the extravagant 18th-century monuments in the North Transept chapels. Then proceed into the **Henry VII Chapel,** passing the huge white marble tomb of Elizabeth I, buried with her half sister, "Bloody" Mary I, and the tomb of Hen-

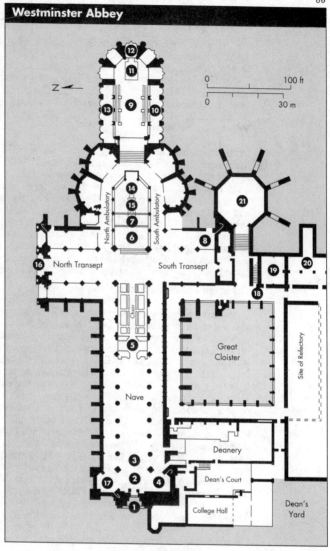

Westminster Abbey

ry VII with his queen, Elizabeth of York, by the Renaissance master Torrigiano (otherwise known for having been banished from Florence after breaking Michelangelo's nose). All around are magnificent sculptures of saints, philosophers, and kings, with wild mermaids and monsters carved on the choir stall misericords (undersides), and exquisite fan vaulting above—one of the miracles of Western architecture.

Next you enter the **Chapel of Edward the Confessor,** where beside the royal saint's shrine stands the **Coronation Chair,** which has been briefly graced by nearly every regal posterior. Edward I ordered it around 1300, and it shelters the Stone of Scone (pronounced *skoon*), a brown sandstone block on which Scottish kings had been crowned since time began and which Edward I symbolically stole in 1296. Scottish nationalists borrowed it back for about six months in 1950; otherwise, only Oliver Cromwell (who took it to Westminster Hall to "crown" himself Lord Protector) and wartime caution have removed it from here.

The tombs and monuments for which Westminster Abbey is probably best loved appeared at an accelerated rate starting during the 18th century. One earlier occupant, though, was Geoffrey Chaucer, who in 1400 became the first poet to be buried in **Poets' Corner.** Most of the other honored writers have only their memorials here, not their bones: William Shakespeare and William Blake (who both had a long wait before the dean deemed them holy enough to be here at all), John Milton, Jane Austen, Samuel Taylor Coleridge, William Wordsworth, and Charles Dickens. All of Ben Jonson is here, though—buried upright in accord with his modest demand for a two-foot-by-two-foot grave. ("O rare Ben Jonson," reads his epitaph, in a modest pun on the Latin *orare,* "to pray for.") Sir Isaac Newton, James Watt, and Michael Faraday are among the scientists with memorials. There is only one painter: Godfrey Kneller, whose dying words were "By God, I will not be buried in Westminster."

After the elbow battle you are guaranteed in Poets' Corner, you exit the abbey by a door from the South Transept. *Broad Sanctuary, tel. 0171/222–5152. Admission to nave free, to Royal Chapels and Poets' Corner £4 adults, £2 students and senior citizens, £1 children under 15. Open Mon., Tues., Thurs., and Fri. 9–4; Wed. 9–7:45; Sat. 9–2 and 3:45–5; Sun. all day for services only; closed weekdays to visitors during services. Tube: Westminster.*

Outside the west front is an archway into the quiet green **Dean's Yard** and the entrance to the **Cloisters,** where the monks strolled in contemplation. You may do the same and catch a fine view of the massive flying buttresses above in the process. You may also, for a modest fee, take an impression from one of the tomb brasses in the **Brass-Rubbing Centre** (tel. 0171/222–2085). Also here is the entrance to **Westminster School,** formerly a monastic college, now one of Britain's finest public (which means private) schools; Christopher Wren and Ben Jonson number among the old boys.

Also here are the Chapter House and the Norman Undercroft below. The **Chapter House,** a stunning octagonal room supported by a central column and adorned with 14th-century frescoes, is where the King's Council and, after that, an early version of the Commons met between 1257 and 1547. (The monks complained about the noise.) In the **Undercroft,** which survives from Edward the Confessor's original church, note the deliciously macabre effigies made from the death masks and actual clothing of Elizabeth I, Charles II, and Admiral Lord Nelson (complete with eye patch), among others. Finally, the **Pyx Chamber,** next door, contains the abbey's treasure, just as it used to when it became the royal strongroom during the 13th century. *Undercroft, Pyx Chamber, Chapter House, and Treasury, tel. 0171/222–5152. Joint admission: £2.10 adults, £1.65 senior citizens, £1.05 children under 15. Open daily 10:30–4; closed Good Friday, Dec. 24–26. Tube: Westminster.*

㉒ Dwarfed by the abbey is its northern neighbor, the church of **St. Margaret's,** founded during the 12th century and rebuilt between 1486 and 1523. It is the parish church of the Houses of Parliament and much sought after for weddings; Samuel Pepys married here in 1655, Winston Churchill in 1908. The east Crucifixion window celebrates another union, the marriage of Prince Arthur and Catherine of Aragon. Unfortunately, it arrived so late that Arthur was dead and Catherine had married his brother, Henry VIII. Sir Walter Raleigh is among the notables buried here, only without his head, which was removed at Old Palace Yard, Westminster, and kept by his wife, who would ask visitors, "Have you met Sir Walter?" and then would produce it from a velvet bag.

㉓ Across the road from the abbey's west front is **Central Hall,** headquarters of the Methodist Church in Britain. The building, now used mostly for concerts and meetings, was the site of the first General

Assembly of the United Nations in 1948. Next door is the 1986 **Queen Elizabeth Conference Centre,** which hosts both official and commercial functions.

Westminster Cathedral and the Tate Gallery

From Parliament Square, you have a choice between more religion or modern art, with Westminster Cathedral to the southwest and the Tate Gallery along the Thames to the south.

Taking the shorter—and, frankly, less interesting—route to the church first, turn your back on the abbey and exit Parliament Square down **Victoria Street,** the unlovely road to Victoria Station. Though it dates from the early 1860s, most of its Victorian and Edwardian buildings have been replaced by depressing concrete. On the right, note the three-sided steel sign that announces **New Scotland Yard,** which in 1967 replaced the granite-faced, turreted 1890 Thameside edifice (now called the Norman Shaw Building) that Sherlock Holmes knew so well.

㉔ You can't miss **Westminster Cathedral**—once you are almost upon it, that is. It's set back from the left side of the street in a 21-year-old paved square that has fallen on hard times. Westminster Council, the local authority, would like to turn it into the Piazza San Marco of London, but until funding is found, it remains the windy haunt of homeless people and pigeons.

The cathedral is the seat of the cardinal of Westminster, head of the Roman Catholic Church in Britain; consequently, it is London's principal Roman Catholic church. The asymmetrical redbrick Byzantine hulk, dating only from 1903, is banded with stripes of Portland stone and abutted by a 273-foot campanile at the northwest corner, which you can scale by elevator. Faced with the daunting proximity of the heavenly Westminster Abbey, the architect, John Francis Bentley, flew in the face of fashion by rejecting the neo-Gothic style in favor of the Byzantine idiom, which still provides maximum contrast today—not only with the great church, but with just about all of London.

The interior is partly unfinished but worth seeing for its atmosphere of broody mystery; for its walls, covered in mosaic of a hundred different marbles from all over the world; and for a majestic nave—the widest in England—distinguished by a series of Eric Gill reliefs depicting the Stations of the Cross. *Ashley Pl., tel. 0171/834–7452. Admission to tower: £2 adults, £1 senior citizens and children. Cathedral open daily, tower open daily Apr.–Sept.*

Retracing your steps east along Victoria Street, take a right in front of Westminster Abbey into Great Smith Street, then the second left into Great Peter Street, and a right off there for a detour into **Smith Square.** This elegant enclave of perfectly preserved early 18th-century town houses still looks like the London of Dr. Johnson. The address is much sought after by MPs, especially of the Tory persuasion, since No. 32 is the Conservative party headquarters. **㉕** The Baroque church of **St. John's, Smith Square,** completed around 1720, dominates charmingly. It is well known to Londoners as a chamber-music venue; its popular lunchtime concerts are often broadcast on the radio, and tickets are inexpensive.

Leave Smith Square by Dean Stanley Street, which brings you to traffic-laden Millbank along the river; turn right for a 10-minute **㉖** walk to London's *other* world-class art museum, the **Tate Gallery.** The Tate Gallery of Modern British Art, to give it its full title, opened in 1897, funded by the sugar magnate Sir Henry Tate. "Modern" is slightly misleading, since one of the three collections here consists of British art from 1545 to the present, including works by William Hogarth, Thomas Gainsborough, Sir Joshua Reynolds, and

George Stubbs from the 18th century and by John Constable, William Blake (a mind-blowing collection of his visionary works), and the pre-Raphaelite painters from the 19th. Also from the 19th century is the second of the Tate's collections, the Turner Bequest, consisting of J. M. W. Turner's personal collection. Turner left it to the nation on condition that the works be displayed together. The James Stirling–designed **Clore Gallery** (to the right of the main gallery) has fulfilled his wish since 1987 and should not be missed.

The Tate's modern collection is international and so vast that it's never all on display at once. The current director, Nicholas Serota, instituted the strategy of annual rehanging, which goes some way toward solving the dilemma of the gallery's embarrassment of riches but also means that a favorite work may not be on view, although the most famous and popular works are on permanent display. In the year 2000, the Tate's space dilemma will be solved with the opening of the new gallery, opposite St. Paul's, in the former Bankside Power Station (*see* The South Bank, *below*), currently undergoing a £100 million transformation to the plans of Swiss architects, Herzog & de Meuron. Even now, though, you can see works by an abundance of late 19th- and 20th-century artists and a good deal more besides. Your tour will deal you multiple shocks of recognition (such as Rodin's *The Kiss* and Lichtenstein's *Whaam!*), and you can rent a "Tateinform" handheld audio guide, with commentaries by curators, experts, and some of the artists themselves, to enhance the pictures. Here's a short list of names: Matisse, Picasso, Braque, Léger, Kandinsky, Mondrian, Dalí, Bacon, de Kooning, Pollock, Rothko, Moore, Hepworth, Warhol, Freud, and Hockney. *Millbank, tel. 0171/821–1313 or 0171/821–7128 (recorded information). Admission free; personal audio-guide rental, £2; admission charged for special exhibitions. Open Mon.–Sat. 10–5:50, Sun. 2–5:50; closed Good Friday, May Day, Dec. 24–26, Jan. 1.*

St. James's and Mayfair

Numbers in the margin correspond to points of interest on the St. James's and Mayfair map.

These neighboring areas (together with part of the following section, Soho and Covent Garden) make up the West End, which is the real center of London nowadays. Here is the highest concentration of grand hotels, department stores, exclusive shops, glamorous restaurants, commercial art galleries, auction houses, swanky offices—all the accoutrements of a capital city.

The western boundaries of St. James's have already been grazed in the previous section, and you may have gotten the picture: This has been a fashionable part of town from the first, largely by dint of the eponymous palace, St. James's, which was a royal residence—if not *the* palace—from the time of Henry VIII until the beginning of the Victorian era. Mayfair, though it is younger than St. James's, is just as expensively patrician, from leafy squares on the grand scale to the jewels on display at Asprey's. Our jumping-off point is the familiar landmark, Trafalgar Square.

St. James's

A late-17th-century ghost in the streets of contemporary St. James's would not need to bother walking through walls, since practically none has moved since he knew the buildings. Its boundaries, clockwise from the north, are Piccadilly, Haymarket, The Mall, and Green Park: a neat rectangle, with a protruding spur satisfyingly located at Cockspur Street. The rectangle used to describe "gentlemen's London," where "Sir" was outfitted head and foot (but not in between, since the tailors were, and still are, north of Piccadilly in Savile Row) before repairing to his club.

❶ Starting in **Trafalgar Square,** you'll find Cockspur Street on the left of former Canada House; follow it into St. James's. At the foot of
❷ **Haymarket**—which got its name from the horse fodder sold there until the 1830s—you'll find yourself facing streams of oncoming traffic. At the top is Piccadilly Circus; in between are two stray (from theaterland) theaters, the Haymarket and Her Majesty's, where Lloyd-Webber's *Phantom* has taken up residence. The **Design Centre,** at No. 28, is a showcase for British design, from interior to industrial, complete with a research library, gift shop, and café. The American Express office is also here, as are a couple of movie theaters—one that is mall-like and hawks every known Yankee snack. Back at the foot of Haymarket, turn right into Pall Mall. Immediately on your right, after the high-rise New Zealand House, is London's
❸ earliest shopping arcade, the splendid Regency **Royal Opera Arcade,** which John Nash finished in 1818.

Pall Mall, like its near-namesake, *the* Mall, rhymes with "shall" and derives its name from the cross between croquet and golf that the Italians, who invented it, called *pallo a maglio,* and the French, who made it chic, called *palle-maille.* In England it was taken up with enthusiasm by James I, who called it "pell mell" and passed it down the royal line, until Charles II had a new road laid out for it in 1661. Needless to say, Catherine Street, as Pall Mall was officially named (after Charles's queen, Catherine of Braganza), was *very* fashionable. No. 79 must have been one of its livelier addresses, since Charles's gregarious mistress, Nell Gwyn, lived there. The king gave her the house when she complained about being a mere leaseholder, protesting that she had "always conveyed free under the Crown" (as it were); it remains, to this day, the only privately owned bit of Pall Mall's south side.

Stroll slowly down Pall Mall, the better to appreciate the creamy facades and perfect proportions along this showcase of 18th- and 19th-
❹ century British architecture. You'll soon hit **Waterloo Place** on your left, a long rectangle punctuated by the **Duke of York memorial column** over the **Duke of York Steps,** which you may have seen from the other (Mall) side on the previous exploring tour. Waterloo Place is littered with statues, among them Florence Nightingale, the "Lady with the Lamp" nurse-heroine of the Crimean War; Captain R. F. Scott, who led a disastrous Antarctic expedition in 1911–12 and is here frozen in a bronze by his wife; Edward VII, mounted; George VI; and, as usual, Queen Victoria, here in terra-cotta.

Flanking Waterloo Place and looking onto Pall Mall are two of the gentlemen's clubs for which St. James's came to be known as
❺ Clubland: the **Athenaeum** and the former United Service Club, now the **Institute of Directors.** The latter was built by John Nash in 1827–28 but was given a face-lift by Decimus Burton 30 years later to match it with the Athenaeum, which he had designed across the way. It's fitting that you gaze on the Athenaeum first, since it was—and is—the most elite of all the societies. (It called itself "The Society" until 1830 just to rub it in.) Most prime ministers and cabinet ministers, archbishops, and bishops have belonged; the founder, John Wilson Croker (the first to call the British right-wingers "Conservatives"), decreed it the club for artists and writers, and so literary types have graced its lists, too (Sir Arthur Conan Doyle, Rudyard Kipling, J. M. Barrie—the posh ones). Women are barred. Most clubs will tolerate female guests these days, but few admit women members, and anyway, even if your anatomy is correct, it's almost impossible to become a member unless you have the connections—which, of course, is the whole point.

91

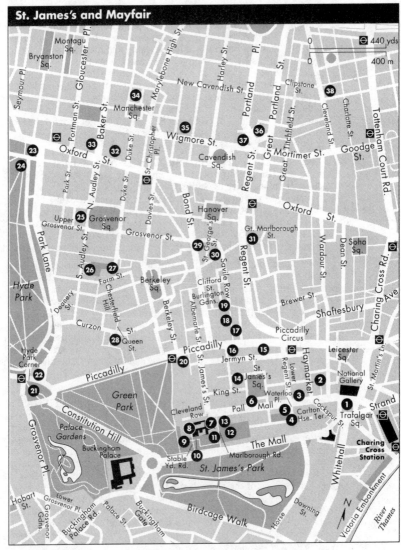

All Souls Church, **36**
Apsley House, **22**
Athenaeum, **5**
British Telecom Tower, **38**
Burlington Arcade, **18**
Burlington House, **17**
Church of the Immaculate Conception, **27**
Clarence House, **10**
Fortnum and Mason, **16**
Friary Court, **11**
Grosvenor Chapel, **26**
Grosvenor Square, **25**
Haymarket, **2**
Lancaster House, **9**
Langham Hotel, **37**
Liberty, **31**

London Library, **14**
Marble Arch, **23**
Marks and Spencer, **33**
Marlborough House, **12**
Museum of Mankind, **19**
Queen's Chapel, **13**
Reform Club, **6**
The Ritz, **20**
Royal Opera Arcade, **3**
St. George's Church, **30**
St. James's Church, **15**
St. James's Palace, **7**
Selfridges, **32**
Shepherd Market, **28**
Sotheby's, **29**
Speakers' Corner, **24**
Trafalgar Square, **1**

Wallace Collection, **34**
Waterloo Place, **4**
Wellington Arch, **21**
Wigmore Hall, **35**
York House, **8**

Next door are two James Barry–designed buildings, the **Travellers' Club** and the **Reform.** The latter is the most famous club, thanks partly to Jules Verne's Phineas Fogg, who accepted the around-the-world-in-80-days bet in its smoking room and was thus soon qualified to join the former. And—hallelujah—women can join the Reform. The **RAC Club** (for Royal Automobile Club, but it's never known as that), with its marble swimming pool, and the **Oxford and Cambridge Club** complete the Pall Mall quota; there are other, even older, establishments—Brooks's, the Carlton, Boodles, and White's (the oldest, founded in 1736)—in St. James's Street around the corner, alongside *the* gentlemen's bespoke (custom) shoemaker, Lobb's, and *the* hatter, James Lock.

Instead of turning right into St. James's Street, stay on Pall Mall until you are arrested by the surprisingly small Tudor brick **St. James's Palace,** with its solitary sentry posted at the gate. Matters to ponder as you look (you can't go in): It was named after a hospital for women lepers, which stood here during the 11th century; Henry VIII had it built; foreign ambassadors to Britain are still accredited to the Court of St. James's even though it has rarely been a primary royal residence; and the present queen made her first speech here.

Continue along Cleveland Row by the side of the palace to spy on a pair of current royal residences and a former one. First on the left is **York House,** home of the duke and duchess of Kent. A left turn into Stable Yard Road brings you to **Lancaster House,** built for the duke of York in the 1820s but more notable recently as the venue for the 1978 conference that led to the end of white rule in Rhodesia/Zimbabwe. On the other side of Stable Yard is **Clarence House,** home to England's best-loved royal (and practically the only scandal-free one), the Queen Mother. It was designed by Nash and built in 1825 for the duke of Clarence, who became William IV.

Now you come to the Mall. Look left to see the other facade of St. James's Palace, which was designed by Wren during the 17th century. Then turn left up Marlborough Road and you'll see the palace's open-sided **Friary Court.** Turn around, and there is **Marlborough House,** designed by Wren in 1709 for the duchess of Marlborough, who asked for something "strong plain and convenient" bearing no similarity to Blenheim Palace. Judge for yourself, but she must have been pleased with it because she remained there until she died in 1744. In front of the house is the **Queen's Chapel,** designed by Inigo Jones for the infanta of Castille when she was betrothed to Charles I in 1623. This was actually the first classical church in England, and attending a service is the only way you can get to delight in it. *Sun. services Easter–July: Holy Communion 8:30 AM, sung Eucharist or morning prayer 11:15.*

Turn left, then right into St. James's Street, and right again into King Street to penetrate to the heart of St. James's and do a spot of shopping. You'd best stick to browsing at 8 King Street, though, which is **Christie's,** the fine-art auctioneers who got £25 million for Van Gogh's *Sunflowers;* ditto No. 7, **Spink & Son,** best known for selling money (coins, banknotes, medals) but with an English and Asian art gallery worth perusing. Coming up on the left, Duke Street harbors further exclusive little art salons, but keep going straight for now, into **St. James's Square,** one of London's oldest and leafiest. It was the most snobbish address of all when it was laid out around 1670, with 14 resident dukes and earls installed by 1720. Since 1841, No. 14—one of the several 18th-century residences spared by World War II bombs—has housed the **London Library,** which, with its million or so volumes, is the best private humanities library in the land. You can go in and read the famous authors' complaints in the comments book—but not the famous authors' books, unless you join, for £100 a year.

Leave the square via Duke of York Street to reach **Jermyn Street,**
where the gentleman purchases his masculine paraphernalia. He
buys his shaving sundries and hip flask from Geo. F. Trumper, his
briar pipe from Astley's, his scent from Floris (for women, too—
both the Prince of Wales and his mother use Floris) or Czech &
Speake, his shirts from Turnbull & Asser, his deerstalker and pana-
ma from Bates the Hatter, and his cheeses from Paxton & Whitfield
(founded in 1740 and a legend among dairies). Shop your way east
along Jermyn Street, and you're practically in Piccadilly Circus,
ready for the next leg of our tour.

Piccadilly

In the early 17th century, Robert Baker, a humble tailor on the
Strand, sold an awful lot of picadils—collar ruffs that were all the
rage in courtly circles—and built a house with the proceeds. Snobs
dubbed his new-money mansion Piccadilly Hall, and the name stuck.
★ As for the "Circus" of **Piccadilly Circus,** that refers not to the menagerie of backpackers and camera clickers clustered around the steps
of **Eros,** but to the circular junction of five major roads.

Eros, London's favorite statue and symbol of the *Evening Standard*
newspaper, is not the Greek god of erotic love but the angel of Christian charity, commissioned in 1893 from the young sculptor Alfred
Gilbert as a memorial to the philanthropic earl of Shaftesbury. It
cost Gilbert £7,000 to cast the statue he called his "missile of kind-
ness" in the novel medium of aluminum, and since he was paid only
£3,000, he promptly went bankrupt and fled the country. (Don't
worry—he was knighted in the end.) Eros has lately done his best to
bankrupt Westminster Council, too, owing to some urgent leg sur-
gery and a new coat of protective microcrystalline synthetic wax.

Other than Eros, there's not much to see in this sometime hub of
London beyond a bank of neon advertisements, a large branch of
Tower Records, the tawdry Trocadero Centre (video arcades, food
courts, chain stores, and the Guinness World of Records), and a perpetual traffic jam. Look up to the east, though, for a glimpse of the
curve of Regent Street, to which we'll return in due course.

South of Regent Street, opposite the neon, is the wide, straight road
15 called **Piccadilly.** Walk west along it and you'll soon reach **St. James's
Church,** recessed from the street behind a courtyard filled, most
days, with a crafts market. Completed in 1684, it was the last of Sir
Christopher Wren's London churches, and his favorite. It also contains one of Grinling Gibbons's finest works, an ornate limewood
reredos (the screen behind the altar). A 1940 bomb scored a direct
hit here, but the church was completely restored, albeit with a fiber-
glass spire. It's a lively place, offering all manner of lecture series—
many on incongruously New Age themes—and concerts, mostly Baroque, as well as a brass-rubbing center.

Stay on the south side of Piccadilly and you'll pass a succession of
very expensive English emporia: **Simpson,** the gentlemen's outfit-
ters (behind a disturbingly reflectionless window); **Swaine, Adeney
& Brigg & Sons** for "umbrellas and whips"; **Hatchard's,** the booksell-
16 ers, with an 18th-century front; and **Fortnum and Mason,** the exclusive department store that supplies the queen's groceries. Legend
has it that Fortnum's stocks chocolate-coated red ants alongside the
glorious teas, marmalades, preserves, and tins of truffles and turtle
soup. Try to pass by at the stroke of the hour so you can see the can-
dy-colored automata of Mr. Fortnum and Mr. Mason bowing to a tin-
kly carillon above the main entrance.

17 Opposite Fortnum and Mason is **Burlington House,** built in the
Palladian style for the earl of Burlington around 1720, and one of the
few surviving mansions from that period. It is home to the **Royal**

Academy of Arts, which mounts major art exhibitions, usually years in the planning. The permanent collection (not all on show) includes at least one work by every academician past and present, including Gainsborough, Turner, and Constable, but its prize is, without doubt, a tondo (a sculpted disk) by Michelangelo of the Madonna and Child. The tondo is up the glass staircase in the Sackler Galleries (opened in 1991 and designed by another academician, Sir Norman Foster), where temporary exhibitions are held. Every June, the RA mounts the **Summer Exhibition,** a mishmash of sculpture and painting, both amateur and professional, from abstract expressionist to photo-realist (the bias is toward the latter), with about 1,000 things crammed into every cranny—it's an institution. Art weary now? Try the shop; it's one of the best museum stores in town. *Burlington House, Piccadilly, tel. 0171/439-7438 or 0171/439-4996 (recorded information). Admission varies according to exhibition. Open daily 10–6; closed Good Friday, Dec. 24–26, Jan. 1.*

*Available here, and at the other 11 places at which you can use it, is the **White Card**—a worthwhile investment for culture fiends, since it allows unlimited entrance for 3 (£14) or 7 (£23) days at all participating museums and galleries. The other places you can use the White Card are the Barbican Art Gallery, Courtauld Institute Galleries, Design Museum, Hayward Gallery, Imperial War Museum, London Transport Museum, Museum of London, Museum of the Moving Image, National Maritime Museum, Old Royal Observatory and Queen's House (Greenwich), Natural History Museum, Science Museum, and the V&A.*

The two sides of the Burlington House courtyard are occupied by several other learned societies: the Geological Society, Chemistry Society, Society of Antiquaries, and Royal Astronomical Society. Turning right as you exit, you'll find the entrance to one of Mayfair's enchanting covered shopping alleys, the **Burlington Arcade.** This one, built in 1819, is the second oldest in London. It's still patrolled by top-hatted beadles, who prevent you from singing, running, or carrying open umbrellas or large parcels (to say nothing of lifting English fancy goods from the mahogany-fronted shops).

At the other end of the arcade, in an extension at the back of Burlington House, is a place you will often—who knows why?—have practically to yourself, the **Museum of Mankind.** This overspill from the British Museum contains the best bits of the ethnographic collection, with amazing artifacts from Aztec, Mayan, African, and other non-Western civilizations beautifully displayed in miles of space. Long-running, imaginatively curated exhibitions are held on the first floor. When the long-awaited new British Library is up and running, the Department of Ethnography will be kicked back to the British Museum, so take advantage now. *6 Burlington Gdns., tel. 0171/437-2224. Admission free. Open Mon.–Sat. 10–5, Sun. 2:30–6; closed Good Friday, May Day, Dec. 23–26, Jan. 1.*

Retrace your steps to Piccadilly, turn right, and then turn right again into Albermarle Street to travel back to the early 19th century when electricity was young. In the basement of the Royal Institution is the **Faraday Museum,** a reconstruction of the laboratory where the physicist Michael Faraday discovered electromagnetic induction in 1831—with echoes of Frankenstein. *21 Albermarle St., tel. 0171/409-2992. Admission: £1 adults, 50p children. Open weekdays 1–4; closed public holidays.*

Cross the road on Piccadilly, turn right, and you'll soon be walking past the long, colonnaded front of the **Ritz** hotel, built in 1909, and meant to remind you of Paris. Beyond it is the 53-acre isosceles triangle of **Green Park,** the Mayfair hotel guests' jogging track. As with St. James's, Charles II made a public garden of the former royal hunting ground, and it, too, became fashionable—not the least among duelists; highwaymen; and, in the following century, hot-air balloonists. Nowadays you can see a tacky display of art on the railings and a nice one of daffodils in the spring.

The extreme west end of Piccadilly features the roaring traffic of **Hyde Park Corner**, the cyclist's nightmare. To cross here, you need to descend the pedestrian underpasses, following the signs to the **㉑ Wellington Arch**, marooned on its central island. This 1828 triumphal gateway by Decimus Burton almost wound up at the back door of Buckingham Palace, but here it stands instead, empty now of London's smallest police station, which occupied its cramped insides until 1992. A statue of Wellington was also moved, replaced by Adrian Jones's *Quadriga* in 1912.

㉒ Near the park, on the north side of Hyde Park Corner, is **Apsley House**—built by Robert Adam in the 1770s and later refaced and extended—where Wellington lived from the 1820s until his death in 1852. As the **Wellington Museum,** it has been kept as the Iron Duke liked it, his uniforms and weapons, his porcelain and plate, and his extensive art collection, partially looted during military campaigns, displayed heroically. Unmissable, in every sense, is the gigantic Canova statue of a nude (but fig-leafed) Napoléon Bonaparte, Wellington's archenemy. Apsley House got iron shutters in 1830 after rioters, protesting the duke's opposition to the Reform Bill (he was briefly prime minister), broke the windows. Yes, the British loved him for defeating Napoléon but mocked him with the name "Iron Duke"—it referred not to his military prowess, but to those shutters. *149 Piccadilly, tel. 0171/499–5676. Admission: £3 adults, £1.50 children and senior citizens. Open Tues.–Sun. 11–5.*

Mayfair

Mayfair, like St. James's and Soho, is precisely delineated—a trapezoid contained by Oxford Street and Piccadilly on the north and south, Regent Street and Park Lane on the east and west. Within its boundaries are streets broad and narrow, but mostly unusually straight and gridlike for London, making it fairly easy to negotiate. Real estate here is exorbitant, so this is embassy country and the site of luxury shops and swank hotels.

Starting where we just left off, at Hyde Park Corner, head north along the boundary of Hyde Park and risk your life crossing wide **Park Lane,** where drivers like to break the speed limit. You'll pass a succession of grand hotels: first, the modern blocks of the Inter-Continental and the Hilton; then the triangular Art Deco Dorchester; followed by the "old lady of Park Lane," the Grosvenor House Hotel, on the site of the earl of Grosvenor's 18th-century palace. After that, between Upper Grosvenor and Green streets, Nos. 93 to 99 plus No. 100, **Dudley House,** with their bow fronts and wrought-iron balconies, are the only survivors of Park Lane's early 19th-century glory days.

㉓ You have reached **Marble Arch,** the name of both the traffic whirlpool where Bayswater Road segues into Oxford Street and John Nash's 1827 arch, which was moved here from Buckingham Palace in 1851. Search the sidewalk by the arch to find the stone plaque that marks (roughly) the place where the Tyburn Tree stood for four centuries, until 1783. The Tyburn Tree was London's central gallows, a huge wooden structure with hanging space for 21. Hanging days were holidays, the spectacle supposedly functioning as a crime deterrent to the hoi polloi. It didn't work, though. Oranges, gingerbread, and gin were sold, alongside ballads and "personal favors," to vast, rowdy crowds, and the condemned, dressed in finery for their special moment, were treated more as heroes than as villains.

Cross over (or under—there are signs to help in the labyrinth) to the
(24) northeastern corner of Hyde Park, where **Speakers' Corner** harbors
a late-20th-century public spectacle. Here, on Sunday afternoons,
anyone is welcome to mount a soapbox and declaim on any topic. It's
an irresistible showcase of eccentricity, though sadly diminished
since the death in 1994 of the "Protein Man," who thought meat,
cheese, and peanuts led to uncontrollable acts of passion that would
destroy Western civilization. The pamphlets he sold for four decades
down Oxford Street are now collectors' items.

Ignoring Oxford Street for now, retrace your steps south along Park
(25) Lane and follow Upper Brook Street to **Grosvenor Square** (pronounced "Grove-na"), laid out in 1725–31 and as desirable an address today as it was then. Americans certainly thought so—from
John Adams, the second president, who as ambassador lived at No.
38, to Dwight D. Eisenhower, whose wartime headquarters was at
No. 20. Now the ugly '50s block of the **U.S. Embassy** occupies the entire west side, and a British memorial to Franklin D. Roosevelt
stands in the center. The little brick chapel used by Eisenhower's
(26) men during World War II, the 1730 **Grosvenor Chapel**, stands a couple of blocks south of the square on South Audley Street, with the
entrance to pretty **St. George's Gardens** to its left. Across the gardens is the headquarters of the English Jesuits, the mid-19th-centu-
(27) ry **Church of the Immaculate Conception**, known as Farm Street
because that is the name of the street on which it stands.

Continuing south toward Piccadilly, take Chesterfield Hill, then
Queen Street, and cross Curzon Street to enter, via the covered
(28) walkway at No. 47, **Shepherd Market.** This quaint and villagey tangle of streetlets was anything *but* quaint when Edward Shepherd
laid it out in 1735 on the site of the orgiastic, fortnight-long May Fair
(which gave the whole district its name). Now there are sandwich
bars, pubs and restaurants, boutiques and nightclubs, and a (fading)
red-light reputation in the narrow lanes.

Hit Curzon Street again and follow it east, taking Fitzmaurice Place
left into **Berkeley Square** (pronounced to rhyme with "starkly"). Not
many of its original mid-18th-century houses are left, but look at
Nos. 42–46 (especially No. 44, which the architectural historian Sir
Nikolaus Pevsner thought was London's finest terraced house), and
Nos. 49–52 to get some idea of why it was once London's top address—not that it's in the least humble now. The 200-year-old plane
trees, which dignify ugly showrooms and offices, presumably inspired that sentimental ballad about a nightingale singing here.

Leave via Bruton Street on the east side and continue to **Bond
Street,** divided into northern "New" (1710) and southern "Old"
(1690) halves. The stretch of New Bond Street you have entered
(29) boasts **Sotheby's,** the world-famous auction house, at No. 35, but
there are other opportunities to flirt with financial ruin on Old Bond
Street: the mirror-lined Chanel store, the vainglorious marble acres
of Gianni Versace, and the boutique of his more sophisticated compa-
triot Gucci, plus Tiffany's British outpost and art dealers Colnaghi,
Léger, Thos. Agnew, and Marlborough Fine Arts. **Cork Street,**
which parallels the top half of Old Bond Street, is where London's
top dealers in contemporary art have their galleries—you're welcome to browse, but be dressed well. Royal personages buy baubles
from Asprey & Co. at the beginning of New Bond Street, with many
designers' shops (plus the more affordable fashion store, Fenwicks)
continuing all the way up.

Before you reach Oxford Street, turn right into Brook Street (the
composer Handel lived at No. 25), which leads to Hanover Square.
Turning right down St. George Street brings you to the porticos of
(30) **St. George's Church,** where Percy Shelley and George Eliot, among
others, had their weddings. A right turn after the church down Mill

Street brings you into the tailors' mecca of **Savile Row,** the fashionable spot for the bespoke suit since the mid-19th century.

Regent and Oxford Streets

John Nash and his patron, the Prince Regent—the future George IV—had grand plans for **Regent Street,** which was conceived as a kind of ultra-catwalk from the prince's palace, Carlton House, to Regent's Park (then called Marylebone Park). The section between Piccadilly and Oxford Street was to be called the Quadrant and lined with colonnaded purveyors of "articles of fashion and taste," in a big P.R. exercise to improve London's image as the provincial cousin of smarter European capitals. The scheme was never fully implemented, and what there was fell into such disrepair that, early this century, Aston Webb (of the Mall route) collaborated on the redesign you see today.

It is still a major shopping street, but one with a peculiar dearth of goods one wants to buy. Exceptions exist: **Hamleys,** the gigantic toy ❸❶ emporium, is fun, and since 1875 there has been **Liberty,** which originally imported silks from the East, then diversified to other Asian goods, and is now best known for its "Liberty print" cottons, its jewelry department, and—still—its high-class Asian imports. The stained-glass-lit mock-Tudor interior, with beams made from battleships, is worth a look.

Shopping continues to dominate as you reach **Oxford Circus** toward the north end of Regent Street. Turn left into **Oxford Street.** The reasons for this thoroughfare's reputation as London's main shopping drag may well elude you as you inch through the crowds (they're marshaled by police at Christmastime) passing jeans store after jeans store after tacky "designer bargain" emporium. But two rea- ❸❷ sons to shop Oxford Street remain, and they are **Selfridges** and ❸❸ **Marks and Spencer.**

Harry Gordon Selfridge came to London from Chicago in 1906 and opened his store, with its row of massive Ionic columns, in 1909. Now British-run, Selfridges rivals Harrods in size and stock, but its image of lesser glamour has been tenacious. It stands toward the Marble Arch end of the street, close by the flagship branch of everyone's favorite chain store, Marks and Spencer (usually known by its pet names M&S or Marks & Sparks)—supplier of England's underwear, purveyor of woollies (sweaters, that is), and producer of dishes passed off as homemade at dinner parties. This place has by far the highest turnover of any shop in the land, so expect crowds at all times. Nearer Oxford Circus, **John Lewis,** another flagship of another major chain of department stores, is known for its dressmaking fabrics and notions and its slogan "Never Knowingly Undersold." Off Oxford Street near Bond Street tube station, to the south and north, respectively, are **South Molton Street** and **St. Christopher's Place,** two little pedestrians-only streets that yield further goodies (*see* Chapter 5, Shopping for Bargains).

Take care not to exhaust yourself with consumer activities because something far more edifying awaits you around the corner, off Duke Street (to the right of Selfridges), in Manchester Square. The ❸❹ **Wallace Collection,** assembled by four generations of marquesses of Hertford and given to the nation by the widow of Sir Richard Wallace, bastard son of the fourth, is important, exciting, undervisited—and free. As at the Frick Collection in New York, the setting here, Hertford House, is part of the show. The fine late-18th-century mansion, built for the duke of Manchester, was completely renovated in the late 1970s, so that treading its deep carpets and ascending its glorious white marble sweep of stairs transports you far, far from the shoe stores and branches of the Gap that you recently left behind.

The first marquess was a patron of Sir Joshua Reynolds, the second bought Hertford House, the third—a flamboyant socialite—favored Sèvres porcelain and 17th-century Dutch painting; but it was the eccentric fourth marquess who, from his self-imposed exile in Paris, really built the collection, snapping up Bouchers, Fragonards, Watteaus, and Lancrets for a song (the French Revolution having rendered them dangerously unfashionable), augmenting these works with furniture and sculpture, and sending his son Richard out to do the deals. With 30 years of practice behind him, Richard Wallace continued acquiring treasures on his father's death, scouring Italy for majolica and Renaissance gold and then moving most of it to London. Look for Rembrandt's portrait of his son, the Rubens landscape, the Van Dycks, and the Canalettos; the French rooms; and, of course, the porcelain, and don't forget to say hello to Frans Hals's *Laughing Cavalier* in the Big Gallery. *Hertford House, Manchester Sq., tel. 0171/935-0687. Admission free. Open Mon.-Sat. 10-5, Sun. 2-5; closed Good Friday, May Day, Dec. 24-26, Jan. 1.*

35 Take a left up Wigmore Street from Duke Street, passing **Wigmore Hall,** the freshly renovated concert hall that the piano-maker Friedrich Bechstein built in 1901 (pick up a schedule for its excellent and varied concert series). Continue all the way back to Regent Street at the point where it becomes Portland Place.

Portland Place, the elegant throughway to Regent's Park, was London's widest street in the 1780s when the brothers Robert and James Adam designed it. The first sight to greet you there, drawing the eye around the awkward corner, is the succulently curvaceous **36** portico and pointy Gothic spire of **All Souls Church,** one part of Nash's Regent Street scheme that remains. It is now the venue for innumerable concerts and Anglican services, broadcast to the nation by the British Broadcasting Corporation. The 1931 block of **Broadcasting House,** next door, is home to the BBC's five radio stations. It curves, too, if less beautifully, and features an Eric Gill sculpture of Shakespeare's Ariel (aerial—get it?) over the entrance, from which the playful sculptor was obliged to excise a portion of phallus lest it offend public decency—which the modified model did in any case.

37 The **Langham Hotel** across the street was built in 1864 to resemble a Florentine palace and duly played host to exiled royalty (Napoléon III of France and Haile Selassie of Ethiopia, for example) and the beau monde of the next 85 years until it fell afoul of fashion (new luxury hotels were built farther west) and then, in 1940, a German land mine. Now it has been restored and reopened by the Hilton group.

Turn right about halfway up Portland Place into New Cavendish Street and left onto Great Portland Street, proceed as far as Clipstone Street, and look to your right. That giant glass pencil is **38** **British Telecom Tower,** imposed on London by the Post Office in 1965 (everyone still calls it the Post Office Tower) to field satellite phone calls and beam radio and TV signals around. It has a habit of popping up on the skyline from the most surprising locations, but here it reveals its full 620 feet. A terrorist bomb went off upstairs in 1975, and the great view from the top has been off-limits ever since.

Soho and Covent Garden

Numbers in the margin correspond to points of interest on the Soho and Covent Garden map.

Yet another quadrilateral—this one described by Regent Street, Coventry/Cranbourn streets, Charing Cross Road, and the eastern half of Oxford Street—encloses Soho, the most fun part of the West End. This appellation, unlike the New York neighborhood's similar one, is not an elision of anything, but a blast from the past—derived (as far as we know) from the shouts of "So-ho!" that royal huntsmen in Whitehall Palace's parklands were once heard to cry. One of Charles II's illegitimate sons, the duke of Monmouth, was an early resident, his dubious pedigree setting the tone for the future: For many years Soho was London's strip show/peep show/clip joint/sex shop/brothel center. The mid-'80s brought legislation that granted expensive licenses to a few such establishments and closed down the rest; most prostitution had already been ousted by the 1959 Street Offences Act. Only a cosmetic smear of red-light activity remains now, plus a shop called "Condomania" and one or two purveyors of couture fetishwear for outfitting trendy club goers.

These clubs, which cluster around the Soho grid, are the diametric opposite of the St. James's gentlemen's museums—they cater to youth, change soundtracks every month, and have tyrannical fashion police at the door. Another breed of Soho club is the strictly members-only media haunts (the Groucho, the Academy, the Soho House, Fred's), salons for carefully segregated strata of high-income hipsters. The same crowd populates the astonishing selection of restaurants, but then so does the rest of London and all its visitors—because Soho is gourmet country.

It was after World War I, when London households relinquished their resident cooks en masse, that Soho's gastronomic reputation was established. It had been a cosmopolitan area since the first wave of immigrants, the French Huguenots, who arrived during the 1680s. More French came fleeing the revolution during the late 18th century and then the Paris Commune of 1870, followed by Germans, Russians, Poles, Greeks, and (especially) Italians and, much later, Chinese. Pedestrianized Gerrard Street, south of Shaftsbury Avenue, is the hub of London's compact **Chinatown,** which boasts restaurants, dim- sum houses, Chinese supermarkets, and February New Year's celebrations, plus a brace of scarlet pagoda-style archways and a pair of phone booths with pictogram dialing instructions.

Soho, being small, is easy to explore, though it's also easy to mistake one narrow, crowded street for another, and even Londoners get lost here. We enter from the northwest corner, **Oxford Circus.** From here, head south about 200 yards down Regent Street, turn left into Great Marlborough Street, and head to the top of Carnaby Street.

The '60s synonym for swinging London, **Carnaby Street** fell into a postparty depression, reemerging sometime in the '80s as the main drag of a public-relations invention called West Soho. Blank stares would greet anyone asking directions to such a place, but it is geographically logical, and the tangle of streets—Foubert's Place, Broadwick Street, Marshall Street—do cohere, at least, in a type of merchandise (youth accessories, mostly, with a smattering of designer boutiques). Broadwick Street is also notable as the birthplace, in 1758, of the great visionary poet and painter William Blake at No. 74. At age 26 Blake came back for a year to sell prints next door, at No. 72 (now an ugly tower block), and then remained a Soho resident in Poland Street.

Turn right off Broadwick Street into Berwick (pronounced "Berrick") Street, famed as central London's best fruit and vegetable market. Then step through tiny Walker's Court (ignoring the notorious hookers' bulletin board); cross Brewer Street, named for two extinct 18th-century breweries; and you'll have arrived at Soho's hip hangout, Old Compton Street. From here, Wardour, Dean, Frith, and Greek streets lead north, all of them bursting with the aforementioned restaurants and clubs. Take either of the latter two to

❶ **Soho Square,** laid out about 1680 and fashionable during the 18th century. Only two of the original houses still stand, plus the 19th-

Soho and Covent Garden

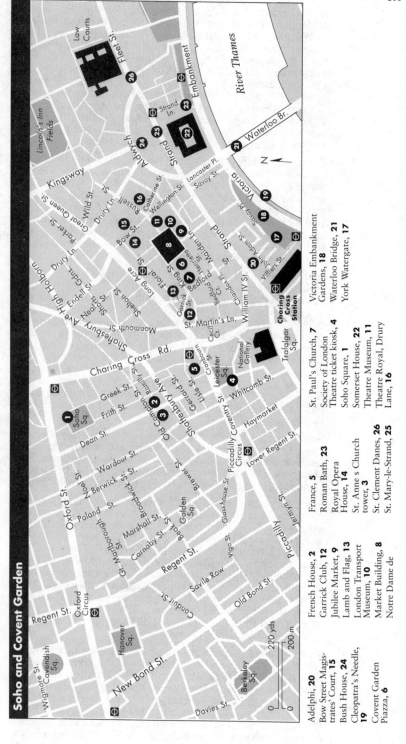

Adelphi, **20**
Bow Street Magistrates' Court, **15**
Bush House, **24**
Cleopatra's Needle, **19**
Covent Garden Piazza, **6**

French House, **2**
Garrick Club, **12**
Jubilee Market, **9**
Lamb and Flag, **13**
London Transport Museum, **10**
Market Building, **8**
Notre Dame de

France, **5**
Roman Bath, **23**
Royal Opera House, **14**
St. Anne's Church tower, **3**
St. Clement Danes, **26**
St. Mary-le-Strand, **25**

St. Paul's Church, **7**
Society of London Theatre ticket kiosk, **4**
Soho Square, **1**
Somerset House, **22**
Theatre Museum, **11**
Theatre Royal, Drury Lane, **16**

Victoria Embankment Gardens, **18**
Waterloo Bridge, **21**
York Watergate, **17**

century central garden. It's now a place of peace and offices (among them Paul McCartney's music publishers, Bloomsbury Publishing).

In the other direction from Old Compton Street is a longstanding Gallic outpost, recognizable by the tricolor fluttering outside on ❷ Dean Street, the **French House.** This pub has been crammed with people ever since de Gaulle's Free French Forces rendezvoused here during World War II. Nowadays the crowd isn't French—it's Soho trendies and peculiar bohemians, some heading for the trendy restaurant upstairs. No pints of beer here, but you can get a decent *vin ordinaire* or a glass of pastis beneath the signed photos of French boxers. Opposite the French House is all that remains of once-fa- ❸ mous **St. Anne's Church,** probably the work of Wren. A German bomb in 1940 spared only the tower and the graveyard behind it on Wardour Street.

The street you now face is Shaftesbury Avenue, the heart of theaterland, and across which you'll find Chinatown.

South of Shaftesbury Avenue and Gerrard Street is **Leicester Square** (no, not "lay-sess-ter" but "lester"), of which it is no compliment to say that it is showing no sign of its great age. Looking at the neon of the major movie houses, the fast-food outlets (plus a useful Häagen-Dazs café), and the disco entrances, you'd never guess it was laid out around 1630. By the 19th century it was already bustling and disreputable, and now it's usually the only place that's crowded after midnight—with suburban teenagers, Belgian backpackers, and London's swelling ranks of the homeless. That said, it is not a threatening place, and the liveliness can be quite cheering. In the middle are statues of Shakespeare, Hogarth, Reynolds, and Charlie Chaplin, and underneath is an invisible new £22-million electrical substation. One landmark certainly worth visiting ❹ is the **Society of London Theatre ticket kiosk,** on the southwest corner, which sells half-price tickets for many of that evening's performances (*see* Theater in Chapter 6, The Arts and Nightlife). On the ❺ northeast corner, in Leicester Place, stands **Notre Dame de France,** with a wonderful mural by Jean Cocteau in one of its side chapels.

Charing Cross Road runs west of Leicester Square. A bibliophile's dream, it's lined with bookstores—new and secondhand, general and specialist. Although it does not qualify as a Soho street, check out little **Cecil Court,** running east off Charing Cross Road before it hits Trafalgar Square, for some of the best of the bookshops.

Covent Garden

The best place to begin your rounds of this ever-evolving neighborhood is in its center, the former **Covent Garden Market,** now often ❻ referred to as the **Piazza** that it became in 1980. It's close to Covent Garden tube (just stroll south down James Street). The easiest way to find the market building from Charing Cross Road is to walk down Cranbourn Street, next to Leicester Square tube, then down Long Acre, and turn right at James Street.

This has always been the sort of neighborhood alluded to as "colorful." It was originally the "convent garden" belonging to the Abbey of St. Peter at Westminster (later Westminster Abbey). The land was given to the first earl of Bedford by the Crown after the Dissolution of the Monasteries in 1536. The earls—later promoted to dukes—of Bedford held on to the place right up until 1918, when the 11th duke managed to offload what had by then become a liability. In between, the area enclosed by Long Acre, St. Martin's Lane, Drury Lane, and assorted streets north of the Strand had gone from the height of fashion (until the nobs moved west to brand-new St. James's) to a period of arty-literary bohemia during the 18th century, followed by an era of vice and mayhem, to become the vegetable supplier of London once more when the market building went up in the 1830s, followed by the Flower Market in 1870 (Eliza Dolittle's alma mater in Shaw's *Pygmalion* and Lerner and Loewe's musical version, *My Fair Lady*).

Still, it was no Mayfair, what with 1,000-odd market porters spending their 40 shillings a week in the alehouses, brothels, and gambling dens that had never quite disappeared. By the time the Covent Garden Estate Company took over the running of the market from the 11th duke, it seemed as if seediness had set in for good, and when the fruit-and-vegetable trade moved out to the bigger, better Nine Elms Market in Vauxhall in 1974, it left a decrepit wasteland. But this is one of London's success stories: The (sadly defunct) Greater London Council stepped in with a dream of a rehabilitation scheme—not unlike the one that was tried, less successfully, in the Parisian equivalent, Les Halles. By 1980, the transformation was complete. Now read on . . .

Go all the way through the market—we'll return in a minute—exiting stage right to cross the Piazza (maybe pausing to watch the street entertainers, who have passed auditions for this coveted spot) **7** to **St. Paul's Church.** This 1633 work of the great Inigo Jones has always been known as "the actors' church," thanks to the several theaters in its parish, and well-known actors often read the lessons at services. The matching tall, terraced houses Jones designed to form a quadrangle with the church are long since history.

With your back to St. Paul's portico (the setting for *Pygmalion*'s **8** opening scene), you get a good view of the restored 1840 **market building** around which Covent Garden pivots. Inside, the shops are mostly higher-class clothing chains, plus a couple of cafés and some knickknack stores that are good for gifts. There's a superior crafts market on most days, too. If you turn right, you'll reach the indoor **9** **Jubilee Market,** with stalls selling clothing, army-surplus gear, more crafts, and more knickknacks. At yet another market off to the left (on the way back to the tube), the leather goods, antiques, and secondhand clothing stalls are a little more exciting. In the summer it may seem that everyone you see around the Piazza (and the crowds are legion) is a fellow tourist, but there is still plenty of office life in the area, and Londoners continue to flock here.

Two entertaining museums stand at the southeastern corner of the **10** square. First, in the old Flower Market, is the **London Transport Museum,** which tells the story of mass transportation in the capital and is much better than it sounds. It is particularly child-friendly, with lots of touch-screen interactive material, live actors in costume (including a Victorian horse-dung collector); old rolling stock; period smells and sounds; and, best of all, a tube-driving simulator. There's also a café and a shop selling the wonderful old London Transport posters, plus mugs, socks, bow ties, and so on, printed with the elegant London tube map, designed by Harry Beck in 1933 and still in use today. *Piazza, tel. 0171/379–6344. Admission: £3.95 adults, £2.50 children 5–16 and senior citizens, children under 5 free. White Card valid. Open daily 10–6; closed Dec. 24–26. Tube: Covent Garden.*

11 Next door is the **Theatre Museum,** which aims to re-create the excitement of theater itself. There are usually programs in progress that allow children to make a mess with makeup or have a giant dressing-up session. Permanent exhibits depict the history of the English stage from the 16th century to Mick Jagger's jumpsuit, with tens of thousands of theater playbills and sections on such topics as Hamlet through the ages and pantomime—the peculiar British theatrical tradition whereby men dress as ugly women (as distinct from RuPaul), and girls wear tights and play princes. There's a little theater in the bowels of the museum and a ticket desk for "real" theaters

around town, plus a café and a good bookstore. *7 Russell St., tel.
0171/836–7891. Admission: £3 adults, £1.50 children 5–14 and senior citizens. Open Tues.–Sun. 11–7; closed Good Friday, Dec. 24–
26, Jan. 1. Tube: Covent Garden.*

The best way to explore the little streets around the Piazza is to follow your nose, but here are a few suggested directions to point it in,
with landmarks.

You could start off, wearing your shopping hat, on **Neal Street,** which
begins north of Long Acre catercorner to the tube station and is
closed to traffic halfway down. In Neal Street you can buy everything you never knew you needed—apricot tea, sitars, vintage flying jackets, silk kimonos, Alvar Aalto vases, halogen desk lamps,
shoes with heels lower than the toes, collapsible top hats, and so on.
To the left off Neal Street, on Earlham Street, is Thomas Neal's—a
new, upmarket, designerish clothing and housewares mall, which,
despite trying hard, is ever underpopulated. It's named after the
founder (in 1693) of the star-shape cobbled junction of tiny streets
just past there, called **Seven Dials**—a surprisingly residential enclave, with lots going on behind the tenement-style warehouse facades. Turning left into the next street off Neal Street, Shorts
Gardens, you come to Neal's Yard (note the comical, water-operated
wooden clock), originally just a health-foods wholesaler, now an entire holistic village with therapy rooms, an organic bakery and
dairy, a great vegetarian café, and a medical herbalist's shop remi-
niscent of a medieval apothecary.

From Seven Dials, veer 45 degrees south into Mercer Street, turning right on Long Acre, then left into Garrick Street. Here stands a
⓬ stray from clubland (the gents' version), the **Garrick Club.** Named
for the 18th-century actor and theater manager David Garrick, it is,
because of its literary-theatrical bent, more louche than its St.
James's brothers, and famous actors, from Sir Laurence Olivier
down, have always been proud to join—along with Dickens, Thack-
⓭ eray, and Trollope, in their time. Find the **Lamb and Flag** down
teeny Rose Street to the left. Dickens drank in this pub, better
known during its 17th-century youth as the Bucket of Blood owing
to the bare-knuckles boxing matches upstairs. (You'll find that many
London pubs claim Dickens as a habitué, and it's unclear whether
they lie or the author was the city's premier sot. *See* Chapter 3,
Where to Eat on a Budget.)

From Rose Street, turn right into Floral Street, another shopping
spot, especially good for high-fashion menswear and for the Sanctuary, a women-only day spa, with parrots, palms, and pool. At the
⓮ other end you'll emerge onto Bow Street, right next to the **Royal Opera House.** In fact, for the entire length of the block between James
and Bow streets you've been walking past the theater's 1982 extension, which added much-needed rehearsal and dressing-room space
to the building designed in 1858 by E. M. Barry, son of Sir Charles,
the House of Commons architect. This one is the third theater on the
site. The first opened in 1732 and burned down in 1808; the second
opened a year later under the aegis of one John Anderson, only to
succumb to fire in 1856. Anderson, who had lost two theaters already, had an appalling record when it came to keeping the lime-
lights apart from the curtains.

Despite government subsidies, tickets for the Royal Opera are
pricey, though the expense is unlikely to lead to riots as it did in
1763, 1792, and for *61 days* of protest in the Old Price Riots of 1809,
when the cost of rebuilding inflated the cost of seats. (The public
won.) Many British and world premiers have been staged here (including the world's first public piano recital in 1767), and the Royal
Opera attracts all the glittering divas on the international circuit.

Nowadays you can see some of them for free, when selected summer performances are relayed live to a giant screen in the Piazza.

⑮ Opposite the Royal Opera's Bow Street facade is the **Bow Street Magistrates' Court,** from which the prototype of the modern police force once operated. Known as the Bow Street Runners (because they chased thieves on foot), they were the brainchild of the second Bow Street magistrate—none other than Henry Fielding, the author of *Tom Jones* and *Joseph Andrews*. The late-19th-century edifice on the site went up during one of the market-improvement drives. It now houses three courts, including that of the metropolitan chief magistrate, who hears all extradition applications.

Continuing on, and turning left into Russell Street, you reach Drury Lane, home to London's best-known auditorium and one of its larg-
⑯ est, the **Theatre Royal, Drury Lane;** its entrance is on Catherine Street. Since World War II, its forte has been musicals (*Miss Saigon* is the current resident; past ones have included *The King and I*, *My Fair Lady*, *South Pacific*, *Hello Dolly*, and *A Chorus Line*)—though David Garrick, who managed it from 1747 to 1776, made its name by reviving the works of the obscure William Shakespeare. It enjoys all the romantic accessories of a London theater—a history of fires (it burned down three times, once in a Wren-built incarnation), riots (in 1737, when a posse of footmen demanded free admission), attempted regicides (George II in 1716 and his grandson George III in 1800), and even sightings of a phantom (in the Circle, matinees).

The Strand and Embankment

South of Covent Garden, the ¾-mile-long traffic-clogged **Strand** is one of London's oldest streets. It was already lined with mansions seven centuries ago, when it was a mere Thames-side bridle path. In 1706 Thomas Twining, the tea tycoon, moved his shop into No. 216 (it's still there); this shop was closely followed by a slew of coffee houses, frequented by Boswell and Johnson, which persisted for most of that century. Remember Judy Garland doing Burlington Bertie in Chaplin drag, walking down the Strand with gloves in hand, in *A Star Is Born?* William Hargreaves's song was a popular number in the Strand music halls that put the street on the map again in the early 1900s. Now its presence on maps is about all that the characterless Strand has to recommend it, beyond one or two high spots that we'll return to after strolling by the river.

Starting at Charing Cross Station at the southern end of the Strand, take Villiers Street down to the Thames. On Watergate Walk, at the
⑰ western end of Victoria Embankment, stands the **York Watergate.** This was once the grand river entrance to York House, the duke of Buckingham's mansion, built in 1625 and about the oldest building extant around here; it marks the place where the river used to flow before the road was built. A riverside road had seemed a good plan ever since Wren had come up with the idea after the Great Fire of 1666, but nobody got around to it until Sir Joseph Bazalgette set to work on the **Victoria Embankment** two centuries later. Bazalgette, incidentally, is better known for providing London with the sewer system still largely in use; his likeness can be admired on the bronze bust right there by Hungerford Bridge.

Between the York Watergate and the Strand section of the embank-
⑱ ment is the triangular handkerchief-like **Victoria Embankment Gardens,** where office sandwich-eaters and people who call it home coexist at lunchtime. If you walk through to the river, you come upon London's *oldest thing*, predating its arbitrary namesake and
⑲ London itself by centuries: **Cleopatra's Needle.** The 60-foot pink granite obelisk was erected at Heliopolis, in Lower Egypt, in about 1475 BC, then moved to Alexandria, where Mohammed Ali, the Turkish viceroy of Egypt, rescued it from its fallen state in 1819 and

presented it to the British. The British, though grateful, had not the faintest idea how to get the 186-ton gift home, so they left it there for years until an expatriate English engineer contrived an iron pontoon to float it to London via Spain. Future archaeologists will find an 1878 "time capsule" underneath, containing the morning papers, several Bibles, a railway timetable, some pins, a razor, and a dozen photos of Victorian pinup girls.

㉒ Cross the gardens northwest from there toward the Strand, and you enter the **Adelphi.** This regal riverfront row was the work of all four brothers Adam (John, Robert, James, and William—hence the name, from the Greek *adelphoi,* meaning brothers), London's Scottish architects. All the late-18th-century design stars were roped in to beautify the interiors, but the grandeur gradually eroded, and today few of the 24 houses remain; 7 Adam Street is the best.

㉑ Circumnavigate the Strand by sticking to the embankment walk, and you'll soon reach **Waterloo Bridge,** where (weather permitting) you can catch some of London's most glamorous views, toward both the City and Westminster around the Thames bend. Look past the bridge and you'll see the grand 18th-century classical river facade of **㉒** **Somerset House,** which you enter from the Strand. Within lurks both horror and heaven, the former in a vast compilation of civil servants (cf. the red-tape-bestrewn Circumlocution Offices in Dickens's *Little Dorrit*), the latter the **Courtauld Institute Galleries,** which moved there in 1990.

Founded in 1931 by the textile maven Samuel Courtauld, this is London's finest Impressionist and post-Impressionist collection, with bonus post-Renaissance works thrown in. Botticelli, Breughel, Tiepolo, and Rubens are represented, but the younger French painters (plus Van Gogh) are the stars—here, for example, are Manet's *Bar at the Folies-Bergère* and *Déjeuner sur l'Herbe* (a companion to the bigger version at the Musée d'Orsay in Paris). *The Strand, tel. 0171/873–2526. Admission: £3 adults, £1.50 children, students, and senior citizens. White Card valid. Open Mon.–Sat. 10–6, Sun. 2–6; closed public holidays. Tube: Temple, Embankment.*

㉓ Slinking north up narrow Strand Lane between Somerset House and **King's College** (a branch of London University), you'll come upon a curious little redbrick plunge-pool known as the **Roman Bath.** It's probably about a thousand years younger than Roman, but nobody is quite sure. To see it, you have to peer in the window at No. 5. Dickens may inadvertently have named it, in *David Copperfield,* though nobody seems quite sure of that, either.

㉔ Now you're back on the Strand, with the main entrance of Somerset House at your back, looking at the **Aldwych,** a great big croissant of a potential traffic accident, with a central island on which stand three hulking monoliths: India House, Melbourne House, and the handsome 1935 neoclassical **Bush House,** headquarters of the BBC World Service. Bush House shows its best face to Kingsway, to the north, with a pair of massive columns, and statues celebrating "friendship between English-speaking peoples."

㉕ Dwarfed by Bush House but prettier by far, and stranded (oops) in the traffic on islands in the Strand to the west, are two churches. The 1717 **St. Mary-le-Strand,** James Gibbs's (of St.-Martin-in-the-Fields fame) first public building, was inspired by the Baroque churches of Rome that had impressed Gibbs during his studies **㉖** there. Wren's **St. Clement Danes** (with a tower appended by Gibbs) is dedicated to the Royal Air Force. Its 10 bells peal the tune of the nursery rhyme "Oranges and lemons,/Say the bells of St. Clements . . ." even though the bells in the rhyme belong to St. Clements, Eastcheap. Inside is a book listing 1,900 American airmen who were killed during World War II.

Bloomsbury and Legal London

Numbers in the margin correspond to points of interest on the Bloomsbury and Legal London map.

To the north and northeast of the area we just investigated lie these two loosely delineated neighborhoods. The first is best known for its famous flowering of literary-arty bohemia during this century's first three decades, the Bloomsbury Group, and for the British Museum and the University of London, which dominate it now. The second sounds as exciting as, say, a center for accountancy or dentists, but don't be put off, it's more interesting than you may suppose.

Bloomsbury

Let's get the Bloomsbury Group out of the way, since you can't visit them and nothing exists to mark their territory beyond a sprinkling of blue plaques. (London has about 400 of these government-sponsored tablets commemorating persons who enhanced "human welfare or happiness" and have been dead for at least 20 years.) There's also a plaque in Bloomsbury Square, saying nothing about this elite clique of writers and artists except that they lived around here.

The chief Bloomsburies were Virginia Woolf, T.S. Eliot, E.M. Forster, Vanessa and Clive Bell, Duncan Grant, Dora Carrington, Roger Fry, John Maynard Keynes, and Lytton Strachey, with satellites including Rupert Brooke and Christopher Isherwood. They agreed with G.E. Moore's philosophical notion that "the pleasures of human intercourse and the enjoyment of beautiful objects . . . form the rational ultimate end of social progress." True to their beliefs, when they weren't producing beautiful objects, the friends enjoyed much human intercourse, as has been exhaustively documented, not the least in Virginia Woolf's own diaries. All you need do to find out more about them is to read the Review supplements of the Sunday broadsheets, which are forever running Bloomsbury exposés as if they were fresh gossip.

Bloomsbury Square was laid out in 1660 and is therefore the earliest Bloomsbury square, although none of the original houses remains; what is most remarkable about it now is that you can always find a parking spot in the huge underground garage underneath. You'll find the square by exiting the tube at Tottenham Court Road—a straight, ugly street where London buys its electrical appliances, hi-fi equipment, and computer accessories—and taking Great Russell Street east. You may never reach the square, however, because

★ ❶ you will have had to resist entering the **British Museum.**

Allow plenty of time here. There are 2½ miles of floor space inside, split into nearly 100 galleries of astonishing artifacts and treasures, some as old as humankind itself, that were bought and donated, but mostly "discovered" and looted, from everywhere in the world. It started in 1753, when Sir Hans Sloane, physician to Queen Anne and George II, bequeathed his personal collection of curiosities and antiquities to the nation and then quickly grew, thanks to enthusiastic kleptomaniacs after the Napoleonic Wars—most notoriously the seventh earl of Elgin, who lifted marbles from the Parthenon and Erechtheum while on a Greek vacation between 1801 and 1804. Although Lord Elgin did a great thing in saving the marbles for posterity, their continuing presence in the British Museum is a source of embarrassment to many British subjects, who believe the Greeks should now have their "Elgin Marbles" back, as, indeed, do the Greeks.

British Museum, **1**

Dickens House
Museum, **6**

Gray s Inn, **8**

Hospital for Sick
Children, **7**

Inner Temple, **14**

Lincoln's Inn, **10**

Middle Temple, **15**

Old Curiosity Shop, **11**

Percival David Founda-
tion of Chinese Art, **4**

Prince Henry's Room, **17**

Royal Courts of
Justice, **13**

Sir John Soane's
Museum, **12**

Staple Inn, **9**

Temple Bar
Memorial, **16**

Temple Church, **18**

Thomas Coram
Foundation, **5**

University College, **3**

University of London, **2**

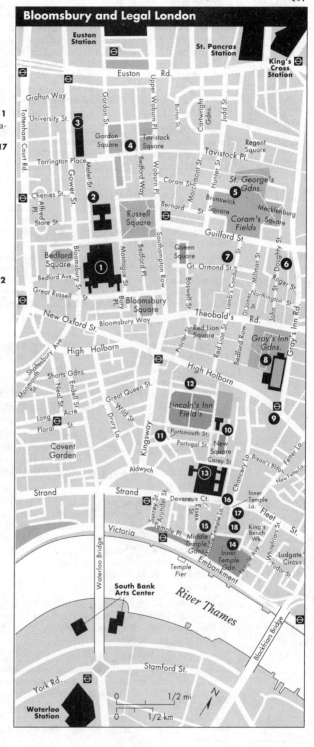

Bloomsbury and Legal London

The enormous building, with its Classical Greek–style facade featuring figures representing the Progress of Civilization, was finished in 1847, the work of Sir Robert Smirke. Ascending the steps, you go straight into the main entrance hall, where you can pick up a floor plan. Wherever you go there are marvels, but certain objects and collections are more important, rarer, older, or downright unique, and since you may wish to include them in your wanderings, here follows a highly edited résumé (in order of encounter) of the BM's greatest hits:

Close to the entrance hall, in the south end of Room 25, is the **Rosetta Stone,** found in 1799, and carved in 196 BC with a decree of Ptolemy V in Egyptian hieroglyphics, demotic, and Greek. It was this multilingual inscription that provided the French Egyptologist Jean-François Champollion with the key to deciphering hieroglyphics.

Maybe the **Elgin Marbles** oughtn't to be here, but since they are—and they are, after all, among the most graceful and heartbreakingly beautiful sculptures on earth—you can find them in Room 8, west of the entrance. The best part is what remains of the Parthenon frieze that girdled the interior of Athena's temple on the Acropolis, carved around 440 BC. (The handless, footless Dionysus who used to recline along the east pediment is especially well known.) While you're in the west wing, you can see one of the Seven Wonders of the Ancient World—in fragment form, unfortunately—in Room 12: the **Mausoleum of Halicarnassus.** This 4th-century tomb of Mausolus, king of Caria, was the original "mausoleum."

Also close to the entrance, but east, in Rooms 30 and 31 in the part of the British Library (*see below*) open to the public, are two of the four existing copies of that prototype census and manual of early British law, King John's 1215 charter, the **Magna Carta,** as well as the spectacularly illuminated 7th-century **Lindisfarne Gospels,** the work of a monk called Eadfrith. Also on display are handwritten manuscripts by, among others, Jane Austen, William Wordsworth, and John Lennon.

Upstairs are some of the most perennially popular galleries, especially beloved by children: Rooms 60 and 61, where the **Egyptian Mummies** are exhibited. You'll find here the preserved corpses not only of humans but of a menagerie of animal companions discovered alongside them.

Proceeding clockwise, you'll come to Room 40, above the main entrance, where the **Mildenhall Treasure** glitters. This haul of 4th-century Roman silver tableware was found beneath the sod of a Suffolk field in 1942. Next door, in Room 41, is the equally splendid **Sutton Hoo Treasure,** which was buried at sea with (they think) Redwald, king of the Angles, in the 7th century and excavated from a Suffolk field in 1938–39; it includes swords and helmets, bowls and buckles, all encrusted with jewels.

In Room 37 lies Pete Marsh, so named by the archaeologists who unearthed the **Lindow Man** from a Cheshire peat marsh. He was ritually slain, probably as a human sacrifice, in the 1st century and lay perfectly pickled in his bog until 1984.

Since 1759, the **British Library** has also been on this site, but in an imminent revolution in the world of English letters, the whole thing is to be decanted into its new home in St. Pancras after years of delay. The year 1991 was the intended moving date for the almost literally countless (somewhere around 18 million, actually) volumes, but the building wasn't finished; the funding ran out; there were problems with the new stacks; and, well, the operation will probably not have started by the time you read this. The British Library is entitled to a free copy of every single book, periodical, newspaper, and map published in the United Kingdom—a gift of George II, along with his Royal Library—which translates into 2 new miles of shelf space per year. Needless to say, room at the old library ran out long ago, and most of its books are not housed here. A Reader's Ticket for access to the library and entrance to the much-loved circular, copper-dome **Reading Room** is available only by written application, with proof of the serious intent of your research required. *Great Russell St., tel. 0171/636–1555 or 0171/580–1788 (recorded information). Admission free. 1½-hour guided tours, £6 per person; twice a day in winter, four times daily in summer. Phone for times. Open Mon.–Sat. 10–5, Sun. 2:30–6; closed Good Friday, May Day, Dec. 23–26, Jan. 1. Tube: Tottenham Court Road, Holburn, Russell Square.*

Time Out The museum's self-service restaurant and café gets very crowded but serves a reasonable selection of not overly mass-produced meals beneath a plaster cast of a part of the Parthenon frieze that Lord Elgin didn't remove. *Open Mon.–Sat. noon–4:15, Sun. 2:45–5:15. Coffee shop open Mon.–Sat. 10–3.*

Around the University of London

Leaving the museum via the back exit leads you to Montague Place, which you should cross to Malet Street, straight ahead, to reach the **University of London.** This relatively youthful institution grew out of the need for a nondenominational center for higher education (Oxford and Cambridge both demanded religious conformity to the Church of England); it was founded by Dissenters in 1826, with its first examinations held 12 years later. Jews and Roman Catholics were not the only people admitted for the first time to an English university—women were, too, though they had to wait 50 years (until 1878) to sit for a degree. The building you see here dates only from 1911. Previously, this branch of academe had borrowed Somerset House (which now houses the Courtauld Collection), Burlington House (now the Royal Academy), then Burlington House's extension (now the Museum of Mankind).

On the left after you pass the university buildings is the back of the **Royal Academy of Dramatic Art,** or RADA (its entrance is on Gower Street), where at least half the most stellar British thespians got their training. **University College** follows at the top of Malet Place—a satisfyingly classical edifice by the architect of the National Gallery, William Wilkins, with its main entrance also on Gower Street. Within its portals is the **Slade School of Fine Art,** which did for many of Britain's artists what RADA did for its actors. There is a fine collection of sculpture by one of the alumni, John Flaxman, on view inside. You can also see more Egyptology, if you didn't get enough at the BM, in the **Petrie Museum** (reached from Malet Place), which contains one of London's weirder treasures: the clothed skeleton of one of the university's founders, Jeremy Bentham, who bequeathed himself to the college.

Circumventing the university and heading south down Gordon Street, you reach **Gordon Square,** which Virginia Woolf, the Bells, John Maynard Keynes (all, severally, at No. 46), and Lytton Strachey (at No. 51) called home for a while. Here also is another of the university's collections, the **Percival David Foundation of Chinese Art,** dominated by ceramics, from the Sung to Qing dynasties—10th to 19th century, in other words. *53 Gordon Sq., tel. 0171/387–3909. Admission free. Open weekdays 10:30–5 (sometimes closed 1–2 for lunch); closed weekends and bank holidays. Tube: Russell Square.*

Continuing south down busy Woburn Place, bypass Russell Square, Bloomsbury's biggest, on the right, and veer left down Guilford Street to reach the **Thomas Coram Foundation** in the 7-acre **Coram's**

Fields. Captain Thomas Coram devoted half his life to setting up the sanctuary and hospital for London's street orphans he named the Foundling Hospital; it moved to Hertfordshire in 1926. Coram was a remarkable man, a master mariner and shipbuilder, who, having played a major role in the colonization of Massachusetts, returned to London in 1732 to sights he could not endure—abandoned babies and children "left to die on dung hills." Petitioning the lunching ladies of his day and their lords, he raised the necessaries to set up what became the most celebrated good cause around, thanks partly to the sparkling benefactors he attracted. Handel gave an organ to the chapel, which he played himself in fund-raising performances of his *Messiah*, and the chapel, in turn, became *the* place to be seen worshiping on a Sunday. Coram's great friend William Hogarth was one of several famous hospital governors, and his portrait of the founder hangs alongside other works of art (including paintings by Reynolds and Gainsborough) and mementos in the museum that now stands on the site of the hospital. Sadly, at press time, all this was off-limits to the public, until the governors manage to find a fresh crop of volunteers to man the front of the house—an indefinite period, in other words. *40 Brunswick Sq., tel. 0171/278–2424. Closed to visitors, but call for the latest information. Tube: Russell Square.*

Charles Dickens was often among the chapel congregation, since he lived a couple of blocks away, at 42 Doughty Street (turn left south of Coram's Fields on Guilford Place, then right), which is now the **Dickens House Museum.** Blue plaques bearing his name would litter the city if every place Dickens lived had survived, but Doughty Street is the only one still standing and would have had a real claim to his fame in any case, since he wrote *Oliver Twist* and *Nicholas Nickleby* and finished *Pickwick Papers* here between 1837 and 1839. The house looks exactly as it would have looked in Dickens's day, complete with first editions, letters, and desk, plus a treat for Lionel Bart fans—his score of *Oliver. 48 Doughty St., tel. 0171/405–2127. Admission: £3 adults, £2 senior citizens and students, £1 children under 15. Open Mon.–Sat. 10–5; closed national holidays, Dec. 24–Jan. 1. Tube: Russell Square.*

Two streets west, parallel to Doughty Street, is pretty **Lamb's Conduit Street** (whose pub, the Lamb, Dickens inevitably frequented); off it runs Great Ormond Street, where you will find another savior of children, the **Hospital for Sick Children.** Like Coram a century before, Dr. Charles West, its founder, was horrified at the inadequate provision made in London for the welfare of children; some 21,000 were dying every year. In 1929, Peter Pan gave the hospital a new lease on life—or rather his creator, Sir James Barrie, did, by donating the royalties from the play until 50 years after his death. (A special Act of Parliament enabled the gift to continue to this day.) Lately, the hospital—like many in London—has been in financial difficulties again, but a new generation of benefactors has saved the day for now, and Princess Di came out of her self-imposed seclusion early in 1994 to open the long-awaited new wing.

Legal London—The Inns of Court

At the bottom of Lamb's Conduit Street you reach Theobald's Road, where you enter the time-warp territory of interlocking alleys, gardens and cobbled courts, town houses and halls, where London's legal profession grew up. The Great Fire of 1666 razed most of the city but spared the buildings you are about to explore, and the whole neighborhood oozes history. What is best about the area is that it lacks the commercial veneer of other historic sites, mostly because it is still the center of London's legal profession. Barristers, berobed and bewigged, may add an anachronistic frisson to your sightseeing, but they're only on their way to work.

They are headed for one of the four Inns of Court: **Gray's Inn, Lincoln's Inn, Middle Temple,** and **Inner Temple.** Those arcane names are simply explained. The inns were just that: lodging houses for the lawyers who, back during the 14th century, clustered together here so everyone knew where to find them and soon took over the running of the inns themselves. The temples were built on land owned by the Knights Templar, a chivalric order founded during the First Crusade in the 11th century; their 12th-century Temple Church still stands here. Few barristers (British for trial lawyers) still live in the inns, but nearly all keep chambers (British for barristers' offices) here, and all are still obliged to eat a requisite number of meals in the hall of "their" inn during training—no dinner, no career. They take exams, too.

⑧ The first inn you reach is the least architecturally interesting and the one most damaged by German bombs in the '40s, but **Gray's Inn** still has its romantic associations. In 1594, Shakespeare's *Comedy of Errors* was performed for the first time in its hall—which was lovingly restored after the World War II bombing and has a fine Elizabethan screen of carved oak. You must make advance arrangements to view the hall of Gray's Inn, but you can stroll around the secluded and spacious gardens, first planted by Francis Bacon in 1606. *Holborn, tel. 0171/405–8164. Visits only by advance written application to the librarian. Chapel open weekdays 10–4; closed national holidays. Tube: Holburn, Temple.*

You emerge from Gray's Inn onto **High Holburn** (pronounced "Hoebun"), heavy with traffic, since it (with the Strand) is the main route from the City to the West End and Westminster. Once it *was* the west end, or at least one of London's main shopping drags, and **Hatton Garden,** running north from·Holburn Circus and still the center of London's diamond and jewelry trade, is a reminder of that.

⑨ Another ghost of former trading is **Staple Inn**—not an inn of court, but the former wool staple, where wool was weighed and traded and its merchants were lodged. It is central London's oldest surviving Elizabethan half-timbered building, and thanks to extensive restoration, with its overhanging upper stories, oriel windows, and black gables striping the white walls, looks the same as it must have in 1586 when it was brand-new.

Keep walking west and turn left down tiny Great Turnstile Row to reach one of the oldest, best-preserved, and most comely of the inns,

⑩ **Lincoln's Inn.** There's plenty to see—from the Chancery Lane Tudor brick gatehouse to the wide-open, tree-lined, atmospheric **Lincoln's Inn Fields** and the 15th-century **Chapel** remodeled by Inigo Jones in 1620. The wisteria-clad **New Square,** London's only complete 17th-century square, is not the newest part of the complex; the oldest-looking buildings are—the 1845 **Hall** and **Library,** which you must obtain the porter's permission to enter. Pass the Hall and continue around the west side of New Square, and you'll see an archway leading to **Carey Street.** You have just headed "straight for Queer Street." Since the bankruptcy courts used to stand here, you can divine what the old expression means. *Chancery La., tel. 0171/405–1393. Gardens and chapel open weekdays 12:30–2:30 (the public may also attend Sun. service at 11:30 in the chapel during legal terms); closed national holidays. Guided tours available. Tube: Chancery Lane.*

"Queer Street" leads you round into Portugal Street, where, at No. 13–14, stands a place of overwhelming cuteness, which a sign announces is **The Old Curiosity Shop.** The teeny, red-roof 16th-century

⑪ shop is probably one of the rare places in London that Dickens did *not* frequent, but it sure looks like his old curiosity shop, despite the orange-brick office block that dwarfs it.

Recross to the north side of Lincoln's Inn Fields to find a museum
that nobody who visits it ever forgets. **Sir John Soane's Museum,**
guaranteed to raise a smile from the most blasé and footsore tourist,
hardly deserves the burden of its dry name. Sir John, architect of
the Bank of England, bequeathed his house to the nation on condition that nothing be changed. We owe him our thanks, since he obviously had enormous fun with his home, having had the means to
finance great experiments in perspective and scale and to fill the
space with some wonderful pieces. In the Picture Room, for instance, two of Hogarth's *Rake's Progress* series are among the
paintings on panels that swing away to reveal secret gallery pockets
with more paintings. Everywhere mirrors and colors play tricks
with light and space, and split-level floors worthy of a fairground fun
house disorient you. In a basement chamber sits the vast 1300 BC
Sarcophagus of Seti I, lit by a domed skylight two stories up. When
Sir John acquired this priceless object for £2,000, he celebrated with
a three-day party. *13 Lincoln's Inn Fields, tel. 0171/405–2107. Admission free. Open Tues.–Sat. 10–5; closed national holidays.
Tube: Holburn, Temple.*

Walking the other way on Carey Street brings you to the vast Victorian Gothic pile containing the nation's principal Law Courts, the
Royal Courts of Justice, whose 1,000-odd rooms run off 3½ miles of
corridor all the way through to the Strand. Here are heard the most
important civil law cases—that's everything from divorce to fraud,
with libel in between—and you can sit in the viewing gallery to
watch any trial you like, for a live version of Court TV. The more
dramatic criminal cases are heard at the Old Bailey (*see* Temple Bar
to Ludgate Hill in The City, *below*). Other sights to witness include
the 238-foot-long main hall and the compact exhibition of judges'
robes. *The Strand, tel. 0171/936–6000. Admission free. Open weekdays 9–4:30; closed Aug.–Sept., national holidays. Tube: Temple.*

Leaving the Law Courts by the main door, cross the Strand and you
will be teetering on the edge of the City, at Temple Bar, ready to
enter **Inner Temple** and **Middle Temple,** collectively known as—you
guessed it—**Temple.** The exact point of entry into the City is marked
by a young (1880) bronze griffin, the **Temple Bar Memorial.** He is the
symbol of the City, having replaced (sadly) a Wren gateway (*see*
Temple Bar to Ludgate Hill in The City, *below*). In the buildings opposite you'll see an elaborate stone arch through which you pass into
Middle Temple Lane, past a row of 17th-century timber-frame
houses, and on into Fountain Court on the right. This lane runs all
the way to the Thames, more or less separating the two Temples,
past the sloping lawns of Middle Temple Gardens, on the east border
of which you'll find the Elizabethan **Middle Temple Hall.** If it's open,
don't miss that hammer-beam roof, among the finest in the land. *Tel.
0171/353–4355. Open weekdays 10–noon and (when not in use) 3–4.
Tube: Temple.*

You'll find an alternative entrance to the lawyers' sanctum farther
east where the Strand becomes Fleet Street (which we visit on the
next tour). Your landmark is the Jacobean half-timbered house
known as **Prince Henry's Room,** built in 1610 to celebrate the investi-
ture of Henry, James I's eldest son, as Prince of Wales, and marked
with his coat of arms and a "PH" on the ceiling. You can go in to visit
the small Samuel Pepys exhibition. *17 Fleet St., tel. 0171/936–2710.
Open Mon.–Sat. 11–2. Closed public holidays. Tube: Temple.*

The gateway next door leads down Inner Temple Lane as far as
Temple Church, built by the Knights Templar during the 12th century and featuring "the Round"—a rare circular nave. The Red
Knights (so called after the red crosses they wore—you can see them
in effigy around the nave) held their secret initiation rites in the
crypt here. Having started poor, holy, and dedicated to the protec-
tion of pilgrims, they grew rich from showers of kingly gifts, until in

the 14th century they were accused of heresy, blasphemy, and sodomy; thrown into the Tower; and stripped of their wealth. You may suppose the church to be thickly atmospheric, but Victorian and postwar restorers have tamed the antique mystery. Still, it's a fine Gothic-Romanesque church, whose 1240 chancel ("the Oblong") has been called perfect. *The Temple, tel. 0171/353–8462. Open daily 10–4; closed national holidays. Tube: Temple.*

The gorgeous gardens of the Inner and Middle Temples are irritatingly off-limits to the public, but it's possible to see them, plus other secret sights, by investing in one of the **Wig and Pen Club's Legal Tours.** The club is another of those St. James's-style affairs, this time for "men of justice, journalists, and businessmen of the City" (plus former presidents Nixon and Reagan), which has its home in the only Strand building to have survived the Great Fire of 1666. The tours include meals, refreshments, and honorary membership for the day (even for women) and are guided by experts. *229 Strand, tel. 0171/583–7255. Cost: £50 (half-day) or £70.50 (full day).*

The City

Numbers in the margin correspond to points of interest on the City map.

If you went on the previous tour, you will already have entered the City of London. You may have assumed you had done so when your plane touched down at Heathrow, but note that capital letter: the City of London is not the same as the city of London. The capital-C City is an autonomous district, separately governed since William the Conqueror started building the Tower of London, and despite its compact size (you may hear it referred to as the "Square Mile," which is almost accurate), it remains the financial engine of Britain and one of the world's leading centers of trade.

The City is also London's most ancient part, although there is little remaining to remind you of that fact beyond a scattering of Roman stones. It was Aulus Plautius, Roman ruler of Britain under Claudius, who established the Romans' first stronghold on the Thames halfway through the first century AD. The name "Londinium," though, probably derives from the Celtic *Lyn-dun,* meaning "fortified town on the lake," which suggests a far earlier settlement. Not much is known about the period between AD 410, when the Roman legions left, and the 6th century, when the Saxons arrived, but it was really after Edward the Confessor moved his court to Westminster in 1060 that the City gathered momentum. As Westminster took over the administrative role, the City was free to develop the commercial heart that still beats strong.

The Romans had already found Londinium's position handy for trade—the river being navigable yet far enough inland to allow for its defense—but it was the establishment of crafts guilds in the Middle Ages, followed in Tudor and Stuart times by the proliferation of great trading companies (the Honourable East India Company, founded in 1600, was the star), that really started the cash flowing. King John had confirmed the City's autonomy by charter in 1215, and its commerce and government fed off each other, the leaders of the former electing the leaders of the latter. This is still largely the case: The Corporation of London has control over the Square Mile and elects a Lord Mayor, just as it did in the Middle Ages, when the famous folk hero Richard Whittington was four times (not thrice, as in *Dick Whittington,* the pantomime) voted in.

Three times the City has faced devastation—and that's not counting the "Black Monday" of 1992, when sterling crashed. The Great Fire of 1666 spared practically none of the labyrinthine medieval streets—a blessing in disguise, actually, since the Great Plague of

The City

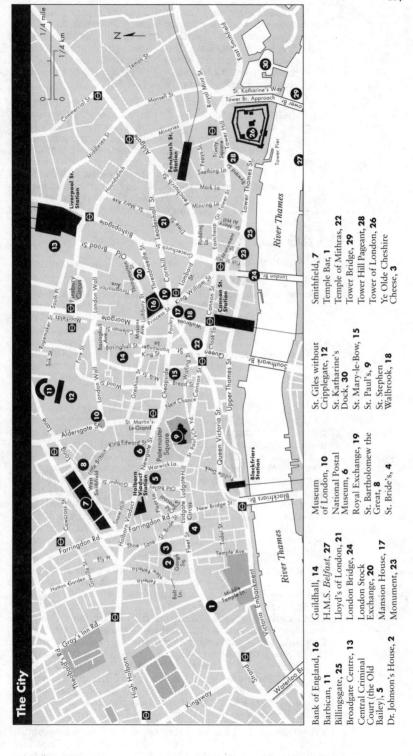

Bank of England, **16**
Barbican, **11**
Billingsgate, **25**
Broadgate Centre, **13**
Central Criminal
Court (the Old
Bailey), **5**
Dr. Johnson's House, **2**

Guildhall, **14**
H.M.S. *Belfast*, **27**
Lloyd's of London, **21**
London Bridge, **24**
London Stock
Exchange, **20**
Mansion House, **17**
Monument, **23**

Museum
of London, **10**
National Postal
Museum, **6**
Royal Exchange, **19**
St. Bartholomew the
Great, **8**
St. Bride's, **4**

St. Giles without
Cripplegate, **12**
St. Katharine's
Dock, **30**
St. Mary-le-Bow, **15**
St. Paul's, **9**
St. Stephen
Walbrook, **18**

Smithfield, **7**
Temple Bar, **1**
Temple of Mithras, **22**
Tower Bridge, **29**
Tower Hill Pageant, **28**
Tower of London, **26**
Ye Olde Cheshire
Cheese, **3**

the year before had wiped (or driven) out most of the population and left a terrible mess in the cramped, downright sordid houses. With the wind in the west, they said, you could smell London from Tilbury. The fire necessitated a total reconstruction, in which Sir Christopher Wren had a big hand, contributing not only his masterpiece, St. Paul's Cathedral, but 49 further parish churches (*see* "Wren and the Great Fire of London" in Chapter 9, Portraits of London).

The third wave of destruction, after the plague and the fire, was, of course, dealt by the German bombers of World War II, who showered the City with 57 days and nights of special attention, wreaking as much havoc as the Great Fire had managed. The ruins were rebuilt, but slowly, and with no overall plan, leaving the City a patchwork of the old and the new, the interesting and the flagrantly awful. Since a mere 8,000 or so people call it home, the financial center of Britain is deserted outside the working week, with restaurants shuttered and streets forlorn and windswept. Do this tour on a weekday—there's little to see unless you see it in action.

Temple Bar to Ludgate Hill

Begin at the gateway to the City—and we mean that literally. Until the 18th century there were eight such gates, all but one of which survive in name only (Cripplegate, Ludgate, Bishopsgate, Moorgate, and so on). The surviving one, just to be confusing, is a gate ❶ neither in name nor in form, being called **Temple Bar** and having evolved from the chain between wooden posts that it was during the 13th century into the bronze griffin you see today on the Strand opposite the **Royal Courts of Justice.** Panels around the base recall earlier entrances, as does the ritual still performed when the sovereign wants to enter the City: She has to ask the Lord Mayor's permission, which he grants by letting her hold his Sword of State.

Temple Bar, then, marks the western edge of the Square Mile, which does cover 677 acres (a square mile is 640), though not in a remotely straight-sided fashion. The curvy shape described by its boundaries—Smithfield in the north, Aldgate and Tower Hill in the east, and the Thames on the south—resembles nothing so much as an armadillo, with Temple Bar at snout level.

Walking, as it were, toward the tail, you will soon find yourself on **Fleet Street,** which follows the course of, and is named after, one of London's ghost rivers. The Fleet, so called by the Anglo-Saxons, spent most of its centuries above ground as an open sewer, offending local noses until banished below in 1766. It still flows underfoot, now a sanctioned section of London's sewer system. The street's sometime nickname, "Street of Shame," has nothing to do with the stench. It refers to the trade that made it famous: the press. Since the end of the 15th century, when Wynkyn de Worde set up England's first printing press here, and especially after 1702, when the first newspaper, the *Daily Courant*, moved in, followed by (literally) all the rest, Fleet Street has been synonymous with newspaper journalism. The papers themselves all moved out in the 1980s, but the British press is still collectively known as "Fleet Street." (Don't miss the black-glass-and-chrome Art Deco *Daily Mirror* building.)

Turn left on Bolt Court to reach Gough Square, where Samuel Johnson lived between 1746 and 1759, in the worst of health, compiling his famous dictionary in the attic. Like Dickens, he lived all over ❷ town, but, like Dickens's House, **Dr. Johnson's House** is the only one of his abodes that remains today. It is a shrine to the man who was possibly more attached to London than anyone else, ever, and includes a first edition of his dictionary among the Johnson-and-Boswell mementos. *17 Gough Sq., tel. 0171/353–3745. Admission: £3* *adults, £1 children under 18, and £2 senior citizens. Open May–Sept., Mon.–Sat. 11–5:30; Oct.–Apr., Mon.–Sat. 11–5; closed national holidays. Tube: Chancery Lane, Temple.*

One of the places Dr. Johnson drank (like Dickens, he is claimed by many a pub) was his "local" around the corner in Wine Office Court, **❸ Ye Olde Cheshire Cheese,** which retains a venerable open-fires-in-tiny-rooms charm when not too packed with tourists. Among 19th-century writers who followed Johnson's footsteps to the bar here were Mark Twain and, yes, Charles Dickens.

Back on Fleet Street, you come to the first of Wren's city churches—one of the bomb-damaged ones, reconsecrated only in 1960 after a **❹** 17-year restoration: **St. Bride's.** As St. Paul's, Covent Garden is the actor's church, so St. Bride's belongs to journalists, many of whom have been buried or memorialized here, as reading the wall plaques will tell you. Even before the press moved in, it was a popular place to take one's final rest. By 1664 the crypts were so crowded that Samuel Pepys had to bribe the grave digger to "justle together" some bodies to make room for his deceased brother. Now the crypts house a museum of the church's rich history and a bit of Roman sidewalk. *Fleet St., tel. 0171/353–1301. Admission free. Open Mon.–Sat. 9–5, Sun. between the services at 11 and 6:30. Tube: Chancery Lane.*

The end of Fleet Street is marked by the messy traffic intersection called **Ludgate Circus,** which you should cross to Ludgate Hill to reach **Old Bailey,** second on the left. At the top, on the site of the courts we are about to visit, **Newgate Prison** stood from the 12th century right until the beginning of this one. Few survived for long in the version pulled down in 1770. Those who didn't starve were hanged, pressed to death in the Press Yard, or succumbed to the virulent gaol (the archaic British spelling of "jail") fever—any of which must have been preferable to a life in the stinking, subterranean, lightless Stone Hold or to suffering the robberies, beatings, and general victimization endemic in what Henry Fielding called the "prototype of hell." The next model lasted only a couple of years before it was torn down by insane mobs during the anti-Catholic Gordon Riots of 1780, to be replaced by the Newgate that Dickens visited several times (in between pubs) and used in several novels—Fagin ended up in the Condemned Hold here in *Oliver Twist*, from which he would have been taken to the public scaffold that replaced the Tyburn Tree and stood outside the prison until 1868.

Instead of a hanging, the modern visitor can watch a trial by jury in **❺** the **Central Criminal Court,** better known as the Old Bailey, which replaced Newgate in 1907. The most famous and most interesting feature of the solid Edwardian building is the gilded statue of blind Justice perched on top, scales in her left hand, sword in her right. Ask the doorman which current trial is likely to prove juicy, if you're that kind of ghoul—you may catch the conviction of the next Crippen or Christie (England's most notorious wife murderers, both tried here). *Public Gallery open weekdays 10–1 and 2–4; queue forms at the Newgate St. entrance. Check the day's hearings on the sign outside. Tube: Blackfriars.*

From mass murderers to stamp collectors . . . A right turn on Newgate Street at the top of Old Bailey, then a left onto King Edward **❻** Street brings you to the **National Postal Museum.** This landmark for philatelists was founded in 1965, but the collection is as old as the postal service itself and is one of the world's best. *King Edward Bldg., King Edward St., tel. 0171/239–5420. Admission free. Open Mon.–Thurs. 9:30–4:30, Fri. 9:30–4; closed national holidays. Tube: St. Paul's.*

The road turns into Little Britain farther along, then emerges at **❼ Smithfield,** London's main meat market. Nowadays the meat is

Perfect vacations.
Some assembly required.

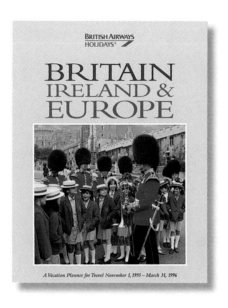

Who better to design your dream vacation
than you? Especially with our Britain
Ireland & Europe vacation planner.

It covers everything.

Like places to stay in the city and the country,
theatre tickets, sightseeing and auto rentals,
to name a few.

So call your travel agent or give
us a ring at 1-800-AIRWAYS.
You'll make the choices, we'll make it happen.

BRITISH AIRWAYS
HOLIDAYS®

Reality check. Call home.

—— *AT&T USADirect® and World Connect®. The fast, easy way to call most anywhere.* ——

Take out AT&T Calling Card or your local calling card.** Lift phone. Dial AT&T Access Number
for country you're calling from. Connect to English-speaking operator or voice prompt.
Reach the States or over 200 countries. Talk. Say goodbye. Hang up. Resume vacation.

Austria⁺†††....................	022-903-011	**Luxembourg**............................	0-800-0111	**Turkey**⁺............................	00-800-12277
Belgium⁺.........................	0-800-100-10	**Netherlands**⁺....................	06-022-9111	**United Kingdom**................	0500-89-0011
Czech Republic⁺..............	00-420-00101	**Norway**	800-190-11		
Denmark	8001-0010	**Poland**†♦⁺.....................	0◊010-480-0111		
Finland	9800-100-10	**Portugal**†	05017-1-288		
France...............................	19-0011	**Romania**⁺	01-800-4288		
Germany..........................	0130-0010	**Russia**⁺†(Moscow)................	155-5042		
Greece⁺...........................	00-800-1311	**Slovak Rep.**⁺..................	00-420-00101		
Hungary⁺........................	00◊-800-01111	**Spain**●...............................	900-99-00-11		
Ireland	1-800-550-000	**Sweden**	020-795-611		
Italy⁺...............................	172-1011	**Switzerland**⁺	155-00-11		

AT&T
Your True Choice

**You can also call collect or use most U.S. local calling cards. Countries in bold face permit country-to-country calling in addition to calls to the U.S. World Connect® prices consist of USADirect® rates plus an additional charge based on the country you are calling. Collect calling available to the U.S. only. *Public phones require deposit of coin or phone card. †May not be available from every phone. †††Public phones require local coin payment during call. ♦Not available from public phones. ◊Await second dial tone. ⁺Dial 010-480-0111 from major Warsaw hotels. ●Calling available to most European countries. ©1995 AT&T.

For a free wallet sized card of all AT&T Access Numbers, call: 1-800-241-5555.

dead, but up to the middle of the 19th century, livestock was sold here, by human meatheads, who liked to get blind drunk and stampede their herds around the houses—"like a bull in a china shop," which is where that phrase comes from. This "smooth field" was already a market in the 12th century, but the building you see today, modeled on the Victorian Crystal Palace, was not opened until 1868. Although threatened by various European Community directives, not to mention the disappearance of the artisan butcher, Smithfield still bustles like nowhere else, frenetic porters (actor Michael Caine's father was one) slinging sides of beef about, dripping blood down their aprons, and then repairing to pubs that have special early alcohol licenses for breakfast. Visitors, although welcome, had better get up very early because the show's over by 9:30, keep out of the way or get sworn at, and not be vegetarian.

Backtracking a few steps down Little Britain, you'll see on the left a perfect half-timbered gatehouse atop a 13th-century stone archway. Enter here to reach one of London's oldest churches, the Norman **St. Bartholomew the Great.** Along with its namesake on the other side of the road, St. Bartholomew's Hospital, the church was founded by Rahere, Henry I's court jester. At the Dissolution of the Monasteries, Henry VIII had most of it torn down, so that the Romanesque choir is all that survives from the 12th century. The hospital across the street, although one of London's most famous—and despite protests, is in the process of "an orderly run-down and disposal" as part of a government reorganization of the British Health Service.

St. Paul's Cathedral

You can slip around by the back route to reach the City's star sight by recrossing Newgate Street and continuing straight through Cathedral Place, or you can go all the way around via Ludgate Hill, but whichever way you approach **St. Paul's,** your first view of it will take your breath away. In fact, the dome—the world's third largest—will already be familiar, since you see it peeping through on the skyline from many an angle.

The cathedral is, of course, Sir Christopher Wren's masterpiece, completed in 1710 after 35 years of building and much argument with the royal commission and then, much later, miraculously (mostly) spared by the World War II bombs. Wren had originally been commissioned to restore Old St. Paul's, the Norman cathedral that had replaced, in its turn, three earlier versions, but the Great Fire left so little of it behind that a new cathedral was deemed necessary.

Wren's first plan, known as the New Model, did not make it past the drawing board, while the second, known as the Great Model, got as far as the 20-foot oak rendering you can see here today before being rejected, too, whereupon Wren is said to have burst into tears. The third, however, known as the **Warrant Design** (because it received the royal warrant), was accepted, with the fortunate coda that the architect would be allowed to make changes as he saw fit. Without that, there would be no dome, since the approved design had featured a steeple. Parliament felt that building was proceeding too slowly (in fact, 35 years is lightning speed, as cathedrals go) and withheld half of Wren's pay for the last 13 years of work. Wren was pushing 80 when Queen Anne finally coughed up the arrears.

When you enter and see the **dome** from the inside, you may find that it seems smaller than you expected. You aren't imagining things; it *is* smaller, and 60 feet lower, than the lead-covered outer dome. Between the inner and outer domes is a brick cone, which supports the familiar 850-ton lantern, surmounted by its golden ball and cross. Nobody can resist making a beeline for the dome, so we'll start beneath it, standing dead center, on top of Wren's memorial, which his

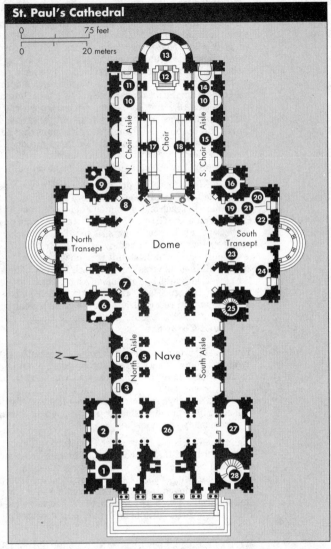

son composed and had set into the pavement and which reads suc-
cinctly: *Lector, si monumentum requiris, circumspice*—"Reader, if
you seek his monument, look around you."

Now climb the 259 spiral steps to the **Whispering Gallery.** This is the
part of the cathedral with which you bribe children, who are fascinated by the acoustic phenomenon: Whisper something to the wall
on one side, and a second later it transmits clearly to the other side,
107 feet away. The only problem is identifying "your" whisper from
the cacophony of everyone else's, since this is a popular game. Look
down onto the Nave from here and up to the frescoes of St. Paul by
Sir James Thornhill (who nearly fell off his ladder while painting
them), before ascending farther to the **Stone Gallery,** which encir-
cles the outside of the dome and affords a spectacular panorama of
London. Go up again (careful—you will have tackled 627 steps altogether) and you reach the **Golden Gallery,** from which you can view
the lantern through a circular opening called the oculus.

Back downstairs there are the inevitable monuments and memorials to see, though fewer than one may expect, since Wren didn't want his masterpiece cluttered up. The poet John Donne, who had been dean of St. Paul's for his final 10 years (he died in 1631), lies in the south choir aisle, his monument the only one remaining from Old St. Paul's. The vivacious choir-stall carvings nearby are the work of Grinling Gibbons, as is the organ, which Wren designed and Handel played. The painters Sir Joshua Reynolds and J. M. W. Turner are commemorated, as is George Washington. The American connection continues behind the high altar in the **American Memorial Chapel**, dedicated in 1958 to the 28,000 GIs stationed in England who lost their lives in World War II.

A visit to the **crypt** brings you to Wren's tomb, the black marble sarcophagus containing Admiral Nelson (who was pickled in alcohol for his final voyage here from Trafalgar) and an equestrian statue of the duke of Wellington atop his grandiose tomb. *Tel. 0171/248–2705. Admission to cathedral, ambulatory (American Chapel), crypt, and treasury: £2.50 adults, £2 senior citizens, £1.50 children; to galleries: £3 adults, £2.50 senior citizens, £2 children; combined ticket: £5 adults, £4 senior citizens, £3 children. Cathedral open for sightseeing Mon.–Sat. 8:30–4:30 (closed occasionally for special services); ambulatory, crypt, and galleries open Mon.–Sat. 9:30–4:15. Tube: St. Paul's.*

Surrounding St. Paul's is . . . nothing. Various plans to redevelop the area, which was flattened by bombing and obviously rebuilt in a hurry, have been dogged by bickering and delay for decades. This situation is gradually going to change, however, when the ugly '60s building on Ludgate Hill, Juxon House, makes way for a more sensitive development that is nearly through the planning stage. The new St. Paul's approach will include the reinstallation of Sir Christopher Wren's 1672 Temple Bar gateway close to its original site as the City's western gateway. (At the moment, it's moldering in a suburban park.)

The Museum of London and the Barbican

Find Little Britain yet again, taking its right fork to cross Aldersgate Street to **London Wall,** named for the Roman rampart that stood along it. It's a dismal street, now dominated by postmodern architect Terry Farrell's late-'80s follies, but about halfway along you can see a section of 2nd-to-4th-century wall at St. Alphege Garden. There's another bit in an appropriate spot back at the start of London Wall, outside the **Museum of London,** which you can view better from a window inside the museum itself, near the Roman monumental arch the museum's archaeologists reconstructed a mere two decades ago. Anyone with the least interest in how this city evolved will adore the museum, especially the reconstructions and the dioramas—like the ones of the Great Fire (flickering flames! sound effects!), a 1940s air-raid shelter, a Georgian prison cell, and a Victorian street complete with fully stocked shops. There are plenty of treasures (the Cheapside Hoard of Jacobean jewelry shouldn't be missed), costumes, furniture, and domestic paraphernalia to flesh it all out, and galleries proceed chronologically for easy comprehension. *London Wall, tel. 0171/ 600–3699. Admission: £3.50 adults, £1.75 children under 18 and senior citizens, £8.50 family ticket (up to 2 adults and 3 children); admission free 4:30–6. All tickets allow unlimited return visits for three months. White Card valid. Open Tues.–Sat. 10–6, Sun. noon–6; closed Good Friday, Dec. 24–25.*

North of the museum is the enormous concrete maze Londoners love to hate—the **Barbican,** home of the Royal Shakespeare Company and its two theaters, the London Symphony Orchestra and its auditorium, the Guildhall School of Music and Drama, a major gallery for touring exhibitions, two cinemas, a convention center, and apartments for a hapless two-thirds of the City's residents (mostly part time). The name comes from a defensive fortification of the City, and defensive is what the Barbican's apologists (including architects Chamberlain, Powell, and Bon) became when the complex was finally opened in 1982, after 20 years of building. An epidemic of jokes ensued about getting lost forever in the Barbican's bowels. A hasty rethink of the contradictory signposts and nonsensical "levels" was performed, and navigatory yellow lines materialized, Oz-like, on the floors, but it didn't help much—the Barbican remains difficult to navigate. Time has mellowed the elephant-gray concrete into a darker blotchy brownish-gray, and Londoners have come to accept the place, if not exactly love it, because of its contents. Actors rate the theaters' acoustics especially high, and the steep bank of the seating makes for a good stage view. The visiting exhibitions are often worth a trek, as are the free ones in the foyer.

Negotiating the windy walkways of the deserted residential section, then descending in elusive elevators to the lower depths of the Centre (where the studio auditorium, the aptly named Pit, is located), spotting stray sculptures and water gardens, receiving electric shocks from the brass rails—all this has its perverse charm, but there is one unadulterated success in the Barbican, though unfortunately it's not often open to the public. Secreted on an upper floor is an enormous, lush conservatory in a towering glass palace, big enough for full-grown trees to flourish. *Silk St., tel. 0171/638-4141. Admission free. Open Mon.-Sat. 9 AM-11 PM, Sun. noon-11. Gallery: admission £4.50 adults, £2.50 children and senior citizens. White Card valid. Open Mon.-Sat. 10-7:30, Sun. and national holidays noon-7:30. Conservatory: admission 80p adults, 60p children and senior citizens; open weekends noon-5:30 when not in use for private functions (always call first). Tours (minimum 10 people; book in advance), tel. 0171/628-0183; cost: £3.50 adults, £2.50 children and senior citizens. RSC backstage tours, tel. 0171/628-3351. Tube: Moorgate, Barbican.*

South of the Barbican complex stands one of the few City churches to have withstood the Great Fire, only to succumb to the Blitz bombs three centuries later, **St. Giles without Cripplegate.** The tower and a few walls survived; the rest was rebuilt to the 16th-century plan in the 1950s, and now the little church struggles hopelessly for attention amid the Barbican's towers, whose parishioners it tends. Past parishioners included Oliver Cromwell, married here in 1620, and John Milton, buried here in 1674.

Before heading south to the City's financial heart, detour east to see one of the more successful recent development schemes, the **Broadgate Centre,** at the north end of Old Broad Street, hanging on the tails of the redeveloped **Liverpool Street Station.** In contrast to the Barbican, this collection of offices, shops, and restaurants got good notices as soon as it opened in 1987, especially for its circular courtyard surrounded by hanging gardens. The courtyard is iced over in winter to become London's only outdoor skating rink; it hosts bands and performers in summer.

The Guildhall and the Financial Center

Back on London Wall, turn south into Coleman Street and then right onto Masons Avenue to reach Basinghall Street and the **Guildhall,** symbolic nerve center of the City. The Corporation of London ceremonially elects and installs its Lord Mayor here, as it has done for 800 years. The Guildhall was built in 1411, and though it failed to avoid either the 1666 or 1940 flames, its core survived, with a new roof sensitively appended in the 1950s and further cosmetic embellishments added in the '70s.

The fabulous hall is a psychedelic patchwork of coats of arms and banners of the City Livery Companies, which inherited the mantle of the medieval trade guilds, which invented the City in the first place. Actually, this honor really belongs to two giants, Gog and Magog, the pair of mythical beings who founded ancient Albion and who glower upon the prime minister's annual November banquet from their west gallery grandstand in 9-foot painted limewood form.

The 94 modern Livery Companies are more than symbolic banner bearers, since they fund education and research in the trades they represent, and many offer apprenticeships. Most are modern and useful, like the Vintners', Plaisterers', Grocers', and Insurers' companies. Other, older ones have had to change with the times and diversify—the Tallow Chandlers' Company has gone into the oil trade, and the Paviors' Company, no longer required to dispose of scavenging pigs, now concentrates on street construction. *Gresham St., tel. 0171/606–3030. Admission free. Open Mon.–Sat. 10–5; closed national holidays. Tube: St. Paul's, Moorgate, Bank, Mansion House.*

The 1970s west wing houses the **Guildhall Library**—mainly City-related books and documents, plus a collection belonging to one of the Livery Companies, **the Worshipful Company of Clockmakers,** with over 600 timepieces on show, including a skull-faced watch that belonged to Mary, Queen of Scots. *Tel. 0171/606–3030. Admission free. Open weekdays 10–5; closed national holidays. Tube: St. Paul's, Moorgate, Bank, Mansion House.*

As you might guess, many streets around here were named for their own medieval craft guilds, including the dairymen's lane, Milk Street, which you now follow south to **Cheapside.** Chepe being Old English for "market," you might also divine that this street was where the bakers of Bread Street, the cobblers of Cordwainers Street, the goldsmiths of Goldsmith Street, and all their brothers gathered to sell their wares.

⓯ You now come to another symbolic center of London, **St. Mary-le-Bow,** Wren's 1673 church; the spire survives intact. The bells are the symbolic part, since a Londoner must be born within the sound of them to qualify as a true cockney. The origin of that idea was probably the curfew rung on the Bow Bells during the 14th century, even though "cockney" only came to mean Londoner three centuries later, and then it was an insult.

Walk to the east end of Cheapside. Here seven roads meet and financial institutions converge in a tornado of fiscal activity that is bereft of life on weekends. Turn to your left, and you will be facing the cita-
⓰ del-like **Bank of England,** known familiarly for the past couple of centuries as "The Old Lady of Threadneedle Street," after someone's parliamentary quip. The bank, which has been central to the British economy since 1694, manages the national debt and the foreign exchange reserves, issues banknotes, sets interest rates, looks after England's gold, and regulates its banking system. Sir John Soane (*see* Legal London—The Inns of Court, *above*) designed the neoclassical hulk in 1788, wrapping it in windowless walls (which are all that survives of his building) to suggest a stability that the ailing economy of the post-Thatcher years tends to belie. The larger history of this economy and the role that the Bank of England played in it are traced in the **Bank of England Museum.** *Bartholomew La., tel. 0171/601–5545. Admission free. Open Easter–Sept., weekdays 10–5, Sun. and public holidays 11–5; Oct.–Easter, weekdays 10–6; closed public holidays Oct.–Easter. Tube: Bank, Monument.*

With your back to the bank you will see the mid-18th-century Palladian facade of the lord mayor's abode, **Mansion House.** What you won't see is the colonnaded Egyptian Hall or the cell where the suffragette Emmeline Pankhurst was held early in this century or any of the state rooms where the mayor entertains his fellow dignitaries, since the building is closed to public scrutiny.

At the mayor's back door stands the parish church that many think is Wren's best, **St. Stephen Walbrook,** on the street of the same name. You may be beginning to think that *every* Wren church shares that distinction, but this one really does shine, by virtue of its practice dome, which predates the big one at St. Paul's by some 30 years. Two inside sights warrant investigation: Henry Moore's 1987 central stone altar, which sits beneath the dome ("like a lump of Camembert," say critics), and, well, a telephone—an eloquent tribute to that genuine savior of souls, Rector Chad Varah, who founded the Samaritans, givers of phone help to the suicidal, here in 1953.

The third **Royal Exchange** to inhabit the isosceles triangle between Threadneedle Street and Cornhill was blessed by Queen Victoria at its 1844 opening. Sir William Tite designed the massive templelike building, its pediment featuring 17 limestone figures (Commerce, plus merchants) supported by eight sizable Corinthian columns, to house the then-thriving futures market. This market moved on (*see below*), leaving the Royal Exchange, which you may no longer enter, a monument to money.

In back of the Bank of England, at the start of Old Broad Street, is yet another venerable trading institution that has completely changed, the **London Stock Exchange.** A mere 14 years after this building opened (again, the third on its site), it was rendered practically useless, when the "Big Bang," the stock market crash of late 1986, put a stop to trading in equities on the floor. The London Traded Options Market persisted in one corner, which visitors could observe from the Viewing Gallery, until security-consciousness following an IRA bomb in July 1990 closed *it* down. The building was due to close anyway because in February 1992 the last bastion of the jobbers and brokers of the stock exchange floor merged with the London International Financial Futures Exchange (LIFFE, pronounced "life"), and they all packed up their phones and decamped to deal at **Cannon Bridge Station** in nearby Cousin's Lane (tel. 0171/623–0444; tours available by arrangement), leaving the dealing floor at the Stock Exchange echoing with red-suspendered, stripe-shirted '80s phantoms. All you can visit there now is the reception desk, where a long-suffering security guard says that you can't go in and somewhat tetchily hands over an information booklet.

Continue along Cornhill to Leadenhall Street. The final tale of fiscal fortunes on this route is contained in what most agree is the most exciting recent structure London can boast, the **Lloyd's of London** tower, Richard Rogers's (of Paris Pompidou Centre fame) 1986 masterpiece. The building is a fantastic steel-and-glass medium rise of six towers around a vast atrium, with Rogers's trademark inside-out ventilation shafts, stairwells, gantries, and so on partying all over the facades. It is definitely best seen at night, when cobalt and lime spotlights make it leap out of the deeply boring gray skyline like Carmen Miranda at a funeral.

The institution that commissioned this fabulous £163-million fun house has been trading in insurance for two centuries and is famous the world over for several reasons: It (1) started in a coffee house; (2) insured Marilyn Monroe's legs; (3) has accepted no corporate responsibility for losses, which are carried by its investors; (4) has its "Names"—the rich people who underwrite Lloyd's losses; and (5) seemed unassailable for a long time until recently—losses in 1990 were £2.9 billion. The 1990 losses caused the financial ruination of many Names, and worse; according to reports (possibly hyperbolic), more than 30 of the unfortunates were so devastated by the loss of an apparently safe investment that they committed suicide.

Lloyd's has been allowed to continue trading, however, and claims that good times are coming in the not-too-distant future. Meanwhile, the viewing galleries over the trading floor and the museum of Lloyd's history, containing the Lutine Bell, which heralds important announcements (one ring for bad news), have all been closed to the public—not on account of recent misfortunes, but as insurance against future ones, in the form of bombs. *1 Lime St., tel. 0171/623–7100.*

Mithras, the Monument, and London Bridge

Now we leave the money markets and return briefly to Roman London, which you may have learned more about in the Museum of London. The museum funds an archaeological department, which has been patiently piecing together a picture of the 2nd-to-4th-century City for the past few decades, with one recent and exciting find currently in the process of assimilation: the remains of an amphitheater, discovered a decade ago on a building site by the Guildhall. It must have been one of Londinium's major attractions.

❷ Another, minor place of pilgrimage in the Roman City was unearthed on another building site in 1954 and taken, at first, for an early Christian church. In fact, worshipers at the **Temple of Mithras** were not at all keen on Christ; they favored his chief rival during the 3rd and 4th centuries, Mithras, the Persian god of light. Mithraists aimed for all the big virtues, but still were not appreciated by early Christians, from whom their sculptures and treasures had to be concealed. These devotional objects are now on display at the Museum of London, while here, on Queen Victoria Street, not far from the Bank of England, you can see the foundations of the temple itself.

❸ Moving along a few centuries, the next shrine you pass, after a sharp left turn into Cannon Street, commemorates the "dreadful visitation" of the Great Fire of 1666. Known simply as **Monument**, this is the world's tallest isolated stone column—the work of Wren, who was asked to erect it "on or as neere unto the place where the said Fire soe unhappily began as conveniently may be." And so here it is—at 202 feet, exactly as tall as the distance it stands from Farriner's baking house in Pudding Lane, where the fire started. Above the viewing gallery (311 steps up—better than any StairMaster) is a flaming bronze urn, and around it a cage for the prevention of suicide, which was a trend for a while during the 19th century. *Monument St., tel. 0171/626–2717. Admission: £1 adults, 25p children. Open Apr.–Sept., weekdays 9–5:30, weekends 2–5:30; Oct.–Mar., Mon.–Sat. 9–3:30. Tube: Monument.*

❹ Just south of Monument is the latest **London Bridge.** This one dates from only 1972; it replaced the 1831 Sir John Rennie number that now graces Lake Havasu City, Arizona, the impulse purchase of someone at the McCulloch Oil Corporation, who (rumor has it) was under the impression that he'd bought the far more picturesque Tower Bridge. The version before that one, the first in stone and the most renowned of all, stood for 600 years after it was built in 1176, the focus of many a gathering thanks to the shops and houses crammed along its length, not to mention the boiled and tar-dipped heads of traitors that decorated its gatehouse after they were removed at the Tower of London. Before that time, the Saxons had put up a wooden bridge; it collapsed in 1014, which was probably the origin of "London bridge is falling down." Nobody is sure of the exact location of the earliest London Bridge—the Roman version around which London grew—but it was certainly close to the 100-foot-wide, three-span, prestressed concrete cantilever one that you see today.

25 Turn left onto Lower Thames Street and you'll come to **Billingsgate,** London's principal fish market for 900 years—until 1982, when the market moved to the Isle of Dogs farther east and the developers moved in here, leaving a sanitized, if pretty, shell, which at press time had yet to find a tenant. Next door is the Custom House, built early in the last century.

The Tower of London

You'll have spotted the most famous of the City's sights already, since it's an easy five-minute walk from the Custom House: the ★ **26** **Tower of London.** The Tower, as it's generally known, has top billing on every tourist itinerary for good reason. Nowhere else does London's history come to life as vividly as in this minicity of melo-dramatic towers, which is stuffed to bursting with heraldry and treasure, the intimate details of lords and dukes and princes and sovereigns etched in the walls (literally in some places, as you'll see) and quite a few pints of royal blue blood spilled on the stones. Be warned that visitor traffic at the sight of sights is copious, meaning not only lines for the best bits, but a certain dilution of atmosphere, which can be disappointing if you've been fantasizing scenes from *Elizabeth and Essex.* At least you need no longer spend all day in line for the prize exhibit, the Crown Jewels, since they have been transplanted to a new home where moving walkways hasten your progress at the busiest times.

The reason the Tower holds the royal gems is that it is still one of the royal palaces, although no monarch since Henry VIII has called it home. The Tower has also housed the Royal Mint, the Public Re-cords, the Royal Menagerie, and the Royal Observatory, although its most renowned and titillating function has been, of course, as a jail and place of torture and execution.

A person was mighty privileged to be beheaded in the peace and se-clusion of **Tower Green** instead of before the mob at Tower Hill. In fact, only seven people were ever important enough—among them Anne Boleyn and Catherine Howard, the second and fifth of Henry VIII's six wives; Elizabeth I's friend Robert Devereux, earl of Essex; and the nine-days queen, Lady Jane Grey, aged 17. Tower Green's other function was as a corpse-dumping ground when the chapel just got too full. You can see the executioner's block, with its charming forehead-size dent, and his axe—along with the equally famous rack, where victims were stretched, and the more obscure scavenger's daughter, which pressed a body nearly to death, plus assorted thumbscrews, iron maidens, etc.—in the **Martin Tower,** which stands in the northeast corner.

Before we go any farther, you should know about the excellent free and fact-packed tours that depart every half hour or so from the Mid-dle Tower. They are conducted by the 42 yeoman warders, better known as "Beefeaters"—ex-servicemen dressed in resplendent navy-and-red (scarlet-and-gold on special occasions) Tudor outfits. Beefeaters have been guarding the Tower since Henry VII ap-pointed them in 1485. One of them, the yeoman ravenmaster, is re-sponsible for making life comfortable for the eight ravens who live in the Tower—an important duty, since if they were to desert the Tow-er (goes the legend), the kingdom would fall.

In the prime position stands the oldest part of the Tower and the most conspicuous of its buildings, the **White Tower.** This central keep was begun in 1078 by William the Conqueror; by the time it was com-pleted, in 1097, it was the tallest building in London, underlining the might of the victorious Normans. Henry III (1207–72) had it white-

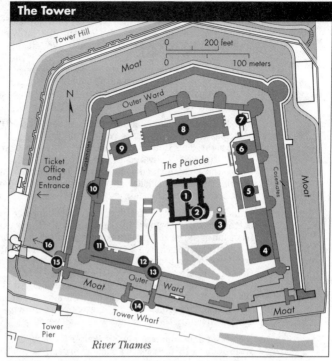

The Tower

washed, which is where the name comes from, and then used it to house his menagerie, including the polar bear that the king of Norway had given him.

The spiral staircase—winding clockwise to help the right-handed swordsman defend it—is the only way up, and here you'll find the **Royal Armouries,** Britain's national museum of arms and armor, with about 40,000 pieces on display. One of the Tower's original functions was as arsenal, supplying armor and weapons to the kings and their armies. Henry VIII started the collection in earnest, founding a workshop at Greenwich as a kind of bespoke tailor of armor to the gentry, but the public didn't get to see it until the second half of the 17th century, during Charles II's reign—which makes the Tower Armouries Britain's oldest public museum.

Here you can see weapons and armor from Britain and the Continent, dating from Saxon and Viking times right up to our own. Among the highlights are four of the armors that Henry VIII commissioned to fit his ever-increasing bulk, plus one for his horse. The medieval warhorse was nothing without his *shaffron,* or head protector, and here you'll find a 500-year-old example, one of the oldest pieces of horse armor in the world. Don't miss the tiny armors on the third floor—one belonging to Henry's son (who survived to become Edward VI), and another only just over 3 feet tall. In the **New Armouries,** added in the 17th century, are examples of almost every weapon made for the British soldier from the 17th to the 19th century.

Most of the interior of the White Tower has been much altered over the centuries, but the **Chapel of St. John,** downstairs from the armouries, is unadulterated 11th-century Norman—very rare, very simple, and very beautiful. Underneath it is "Little Ease," the cell where Guy Fawkes (*see* The Houses of Parliament in Westminster and Royal London, *above*) was held, chained to a ring in the floor.

The other fortifications and buildings surrounding the White Tower date from the 11th to the 19th century. Starting from the main entrance, you can't miss the **moat.** Until the duke of Wellington had it drained in 1843, this was a stinking, stagnant mush, obstinately resisting all attempts to flush it with water from the Thames. Now there's a little raven graveyard in the grassed-over channel, with touching memorials to some of the old birds (who are not known for their kind natures, by the way, and you risk a savage pecking if you try to befriend them).

Across the moat, the **Middle Tower** and the **Byward Tower** form the principal landward entrance, with **Traitors' Gate** a little farther on to the right. This London equivalent of Venice's Bridge of Sighs was where the boats delivered prisoners to their cells, and so it was where those condemned to death got their last look at the outside world. During the period when the Thames was London's chief thoroughfare, this was the main entrance to the Tower.

Immediately opposite Traitors' Gate is the former Garden Tower, better known since about 1570 as the **Bloody Tower.** Its name comes from one of the most famous unsolved murders in history, the saga of the "little princes in the Tower." In 1483 the boy king, Edward V, and his brother Richard were left here by their uncle, Richard of Gloucester, after the death of their father, Edward I. They were never seen again, Gloucester was crowned Richard III, and in 1674 two little skeletons were found under the stairs to St. John's Chapel. The obvious conclusions have always been drawn—and were, in fact, even before the skeletons were discovered.

Another famous inmate was Sir Walter Raleigh, who was kept here from 1603 to 1616. It wasn't such an ordeal, as you'll see when you visit his spacious rooms, where he kept two servants, had his wife and two sons live with him (the younger boy was christened in the Tower chapel), and amused himself by writing his *History of the World*. Unfortunately, he was less lucky on his second visit in 1618, which terminated in his execution at Whitehall.

Next to the Bloody Tower is the circular **Wakefield Tower,** which dates from the 13th century and once contained the king's private apartments. It was the scene of another royal murder in 1471, when Henry VI was killed midprayer. Henry founded Eton College and King's College, Cambridge, and they haven't forgotten: Every May 21, envoys from both institutions mark the anniversary of his murder by laying white lilies on the site.

The shiniest, the most expensive, and the most famous exhibits here are, of course, the **Crown Jewels,** now housed in the **Duke of Wellington's Barracks.** In their new setting you get so close that you could lick the gems (if it weren't for the wafers of bulletproof glass), and they are enhanced by new laser lighting, which almost hurts the eyes with sparkle. Before you meet them in person, you are given a high-definition-film preview, along with a few scenes from Elizabeth's 1953 coronation.

It's commonplace to call these baubles priceless, but it's impossible not to drop your jaw at the notion of their worth. They were, in fact, lifted once—by Colonel Thomas Blood, in 1671—though only as far as a nearby wharf. The colonel was given a royal pension instead of a beating, fueling speculation that Charles II, short of ready cash as usual, had his hand in the escapade somewhere. These days security is as fiendish as you'd expect, since the jewels—even though they would be literally impossible for thieves to sell—are *so* priceless that they're not insured.

A brief résumé of the top jewels: The finest is the **Royal Sceptre,** containing the earth's largest cut diamond, the 530-carat Star of Africa. This diamond is also known as Cullinan I, having been cut from the

South African Cullinan, which weighed 20 ounces when dug up from a De Beers mine at the beginning of the century. Another chip off the block, Cullinan II, is on the **Imperial Crown of State** that Prince Charles is due to wear at his coronation—the same one that Elizabeth II wore in her coronation procession; it was made for Victoria's coronation in 1838. Aside from its 2,800 diamonds, it features the Black Prince's ruby, which Henry V was supposed to have worn at Agincourt, and is actually an imposter—it's no ruby, it's a semiprecious spinel. The other famous gem is the Koh-i-noor, or "Mountain of Light," which adorns the **Queen Mother's crown.** When Victoria was presented with this gift horse in 1850, she looked it in the mouth, found it lacking in glitteriness, and had it chopped down to almost half its weight.

The little chapel of **St. Peter ad Vincula** can be visited only as part of a yeoman-warder tour. The third church on the site, it conceals the remains of some 2,000 people who were executed at the Tower, Anne Boleyn and Catherine Howard among them. Being traitors, they were not so much buried as dumped under the flagstones, but the genteel Victorians had the courtesy to rebury their bones during renovations.

One of the more evocative towers is **Beauchamp Tower,** built west of Tower Green by Edward I (1272–1307). It was soon designated a jail for the higher class of miscreant, including Lady Jane Grey, who is thought to have added her Latin graffiti to the many inscriptions carved by prisoners that you can see here.

Just south of the Beauchamp Tower is an L-shape row of half-timbered Tudor houses, with the **Queen's House** at the center. Built for the governor of the Tower in 1530, this place saw the interrogation or incarceration of several of the more celebrated prisoners, including Anne Boleyn and the Gunpowder Plot conspirators. The Queen's House also played host to the Tower's last prisoner, Rudolph Hess, the Nazi who parachuted into London in 1941 to seek asylum.

Don't forget to stroll along the battlements before you leave; from them, you get a wonderful overview of the whole Tower of London. As you'll agree at this point, the expensive admission is worth the outlay. *H. M. Tower of London, tel. 0171/709–0765. Admission: £7.95 adults, £5.95 senior citizens, £5.25 children under 15, £21.95 family (2 adults, 3 children, or 1 adult, 4 children). Small additional admission charge to the Fusiliers Museum. Open Mar.–Oct., Mon.–Sat. 9:30–6:30, Sun. 2–6; Nov.–Feb., Mon.–Sat. 9:30–5; closed Good Friday, Dec. 24–26, Jan. 1. For tickets to Ceremony of the Keys (the locking of the main gates, nightly at 10), write well in advance to the Resident Governor and Keeper of the Jewel House, Queen's House, H. M. Tower of London, EC3. Give your name, the dates you wish to attend (including alternate dates), and the number of people (up to 7) and enclose a self-addressed stamped envelope. Yeoman-warder guides leave daily from the Middle Tower, subject to weather and availability, at no charge (but a tip is always appreciated), about every 30 min until 3:30 in summer, 2:30 in winter. Tube: Tower Hill.*

From the riverside, walk to the front of the Tower: There is a good
㉗ view across the river to **HMS** *Belfast* and the new building developments along the south bank of the Thames (*see* Butler's Wharf to Old St. Thomas's in The South Bank, *below*).

To the west of the Tower is London's first "dark-ride" museum, the
㉘ **Tower Hill Pageant,** where automated cars take you past mock-ups of scenes from most periods of London's past, complete with "people," sound effects, and even smells. There's also an archaeological museum with finds from the Thames, set up by the Museum of London. *Tower Hill Terrace, tel. 0171/709–0081. Admission: £5.45 adults, £3.45 children under 16 and senior citizens. Open Apr.–Oct., daily*

9:30–5:30; Nov.–Mar., daily 9:30–4:30; closed Dec. 25. Tube: Tower Hill.

Tower Bridge and St. Katharine's Dock

★ ㉙ The eastern edge of the City is rich indeed in symbols of London, as you will gather when you stagger out from the Tower only to be confronted with the aptly named **Tower Bridge.** Despite its venerable, nay medieval, appearance, Tower Bridge is a Victorian youngster that celebrated its centenary in June 1994. Constructed of steel, then clothed in Portland stone, it was deliberately styled in the Gothic persuasion to complement the Tower next door and is famous for its enormous bascules—the "arms" that open to allow large ships through. Nowadays large ships rarely do so, but when river traffic was dense, the bascules were raised about five times a day.

The bridge's 100th-birthday gift was a new exhibition, one of London's most imaginative and fun. You are conducted in the company of "Harry Stoner," an animatronic bridge-construction worker worthy of Disneyland, back in time to witness the birth of the Thames's last downstream bridge. History and engineering lessons are painlessly absorbed as you meet the ghost of the bridge's architect, Sir Horace Jones, see the bascules work, and wander the walkways with their grand upstream–downstream views annotated by interactive video displays. Be sure to hang on to your ticket and follow the signs to the Engine Rooms for part two, where the original steam-driven hydraulic engines gleam and a cute rococo theater is the setting for an Edwardian music-hall production of the bridge's story. *Tel. 0171/403–3761. Admission: £5 adults, £3.50 children under 15 and senior citizens. Open Apr.–Oct., daily 10–6:30; Nov.–Mar., daily 10–5:15 (last entry 1¼ hrs before closing); closed Good Friday, Dec. 24–25, Jan. 1. Tube: Tower Hill.*

㉚ You've left the City now, but still worth a look is **St. Katharine's Dock,** which you reach from the wharf underneath Tower Bridge. Finished in 1828, St. Katharine's thrived until container ships and their cargoes grew too big for the little river docks to handle, and it was shut down in 1968. Developers moved in and created this enclave of shops and luxury apartments, whose inhabitants moor their luxury yachts in the marina alongside a few old Thames sailing barges (which you can charter) and the converted-warehouse Dickens Inn, with its waterside terrace. (Dickens did not drink here.)

The East End

Numbers in the margin correspond to points of interest on the East End map.

Whitechapel and Spitalfields, Shoreditch, Mile End, and Bethnal Green began as separate villages, melding during the population boom of the 19th century—a boom that was shaped by French Huguenot and Jewish refugees; by poverty; and, in the past several decades, by a growing Bengali community. If you visit on a Sunday morning, the East End has a festive air: About half the neighborhood sprouts hundreds of market stalls (especially in and around Middlesex Street, Brick Lane, and Columbia Road). After shopping, you could have brunch among cows and sheep on a farm and then play at being Georgians in a restored, candlelit 18th-century town house. You would miss out on a few weekday-only sights, but—as a Victorian peep-show barker might have said—you pays yer money and you takes yer choice. Our tour begins in Whitechapel, enters Spitalfields, heads north to Bethnal Green, and then goes south through Mile End back to Whitechapel.

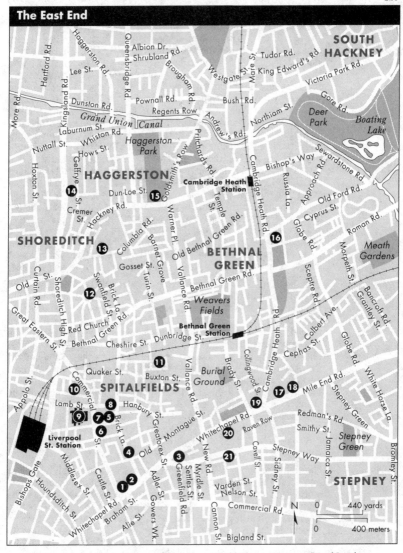

The East End

Whitechapel

The easiest way to reach Whitechapel High Street is via the District Line to Aldgate East tube (one stop past Tower Hill, where the previous tour ended). Whitechapel is where the Salvation Army was founded and the original Liberty Bell was forged, but what everyone remembers about it is that its Victorian slum streets were stalked by **Jack the Ripper.** Accordingly, we begin at the site of **George Yard Buildings,** where the notorious slasher's first victim, Martha Turner, was discovered in August 1888, punctured 29 times by his knife. Turning left out of the tube station, you come immediately to the place behind which George Yard Buildings used to stand: ❶ **Bloom's,** the United Kingdom's most famous kosher restaurant, run by the same family for over 70 years. You can clog your arteries here with *heimische* latkes, gefilte fish, and Bloom's famous salt beef, all at bargain rates (90 Whitechapel High St., tel. 0171/247–6001; meals served Sun.–Thurs. 11–9:30, Fri. 11–2). Sephardic Jews settled around here during the late 17th century, but the biggest wave of Jewish refugees were those fleeing the pogroms of Eastern Europe between the 1880s and the outbreak of World War I. Though most of London's Jews have now moved out of the East End, they have a sort of potted history written into the walls around here, as you will see.

Practically next door is the striking 1901 Art Nouveau arched doorway of the **Whitechapel Gallery.** The gallery has an international reputation for its shows, often on the cutting edge of contemporary art. The American "action painter" Jackson Pollock showed here in the '50s, the pop artist Robert Rauschenberg exhibited here in the '60s, and David Hockney had his first solo show here in the '70s. More recently the Tate Gallery visited the Whitechapel and bought the American Bill Viola's powerful video installation, the *Nantes Triptych,* which shows Viola submerged underwater, his wife giving birth on one side, his mother dying in a hospital on the other. Other exhibitions highlight the local community and culture, and there are programs of lectures, too. *Whitechapel High St., tel. 0171/ 377–0107. Admission free (fee for some exhibitions). Open Tues.– Sun. 11–5, Wed. 11–8. Closed Dec. 25–26, Jan. 1, and for installations of exhibits. Tube: Aldgate East.*

Continue east until you reach Fieldgate Street on the right, where ❸ you'll find the **Whitechapel Bell Foundry,** responsible for some of the world's better-known chimes. Before moving to this site in 1738, the foundry cast Westminster Abbey's bells (in the 1580s), but its biggest work, in every sense, was the 13-ton Big Ben, cast in 1858 by George Mears, which required 16 horses to transport from here to Westminster. Its other important work was casting the original Liberty Bell (now in Philadelphia) in 1752, and both the Liberty Bell and Big Ben can be seen in pictures, along with exhibits about bell making, in a little museum in the shop. You can even buy a small table bell (for about £36) if they are in stock, though the actual foundry is off-limits. *34 Whitechapel Rd., tel. 0171/247–2599. Admission free. Open weekdays 8:30–5:30; closed public holidays. Tube: Aldgate East.*

Retracing your steps, turn right from Whitechapel Road into ❹ Osborn Street, which soon becomes **Brick Lane.** In its time, this long, narrow street has seen the manufacture of bricks (during the 16th century, when it was named), beer, and bagels, but nowadays it is the center of the East End's Bengali community. (You can still get the bagels, though, at No. 159, the 24-hour **Beigel Bake.**) All along here you'll see shops selling psychedelic saris and stacks of sticky Indian sweets; video stores renting Indian movies; and Bengali, Bangladeshi, and Pakistani restaurants, well known among Londoners for the most authentic and least expensive curries in town. On Sunday morning the entire street is packed with stalls in a market parallel to the more famous **Petticoat Lane** (*see* Street Markets in Chapter 5, Shopping for Bargains), three blocks to the west on Middlesex Street—it was renamed by the prudish Victorians circa 1830.

Brick Lane and the narrow streets running off it offer a paradigm of the East End's development. Its population has always been in flux, with some moving in to find refuge here as others were escaping its poverty. Just before the start of Brick Lane, you can take a short detour (turn left, then right) to see the birthplace of one who did just that. **Flower and Dean Street,** past the ugly 1970s housing project on Thrawl Street and once the most disreputable street in London, was where Abe Sapperstein, founder of the *Harlem Globetrotters*, was born in 1908.

Spitalfields

Fournier Street, two blocks into Brick Lane, displays over two centuries' worth of such changes. The French Huguenots fled to Spitalfields after the Edict of Nantes (which had allowed them religious freedom in Catholic France) was revoked in 1685. The neighborhood gave them not only religious sanctuary but also work in the nascent silk industry, and those who became master weavers grew rich. Most of the early 18th-century Huguenot silk weavers' houses along the north side of Fournier Street have been restored by conservationists. Others still contain textile sweatshops—only now the ❺ workers are Bengali. On the corner of Brick Lane is the **Jamme Masjid,** where local Muslims worship. *Umbra summus* ("We are shadows"), announces the inscription above the entrance, an apt epitaph for the successive communities who have had temporary claim on the building. Built in 1742 as a Huguenot chapel, it was converted to a Methodist church in 1809, only to become the Spitalfields Great Synagogue when the Orthodox Machzikei Hadath sect bought it in 1897.

❻ At the other (west) end of Fournier Street, on the left, towers **Christ Church, Spitalfields,** Wren's associate Nicholas Hawksmoor's 1729 masterpiece. Hawksmoor built only six London churches; this one was commissioned as part of Parliament's 1711 "Fifty New Churches Act." The idea was to score points for the Church of England against such Nonconformists as the Protestant Huguenots. (It must have worked; in the churchyard, you can still see some of their gravestones, with epitaphs in French.) The silk industry declined as 19th-century machinery made hand weaving obsolete, and the church fell into disrepair, its gardens acquiring a reputation as a tramps' ground (and the sobriquet "Itchy Park"). By 1958 the structure was crumbling to bits and had to be closed. It was saved from demolition—but only just—and reopened in 1987, though restoration work won't be complete until 1998 or so. Until then, opening hours are restricted, but there are occasional evening concerts (and a music festival in June) and always a fine view of the colonnaded portico and tall spire from Brushfield Street to the west. *Commercial St., tel. 0171/377–0287. Admission free (charge for concerts). Open weekdays noon–2:30; Sun. services. Tube: Aldgate East.*

Follow Wilkes Street north of the church, where you'll find more 1720s Huguenot houses, and turn immediately right into **Princelet Street,** once important to the Jewish settlers. No. 19 is now the ❼ **Spitalfields Heritage Centre,** dedicated to research on local immigrant communities and the preservation of the neighborhood's historic buildings. Huguenots rented the 1720 house—it still has their silk-weaving attic—but in 1870 the little **United Friends Synagogue** was grafted onto the back. You can still see its wooden ark, pulpit, seats, and boards listing benefactors, complete with Hebrew errors. London's third-oldest (purpose-built) synagogue sometimes houses exhibitions and presents videos about the Jewish East End; otherwise, the Heritage Centre remains rather erratic as a museum, since it is in the process of (underfunded) restoration. *19 Princelet St., tel. 0171/377-6901. Admission free. Normally open weekdays 10–5, but phone first.*

Farther along Princelet Street, where No. 6 now stands, the first of several thriving **Yiddish Theaters** opened in 1886, playing to packed houses until the following year, when disaster struck. A false fire alarm during a January performance ended with 17 people being crushed to death and so demoralized the theater's actor-founder, Jacob Adler, that two months later he moved his troupe to New York, where he played a major role in founding that city's great Yiddish theater tradition—which, in turn, had a significant effect on Hollywood.

Now you reach Brick Lane again. Turn left; at Hanbury Street is the ❽ **Black Eagle Brewery,** the only one of the several East End breweries still standing. And a handsome example of Georgian and 19th-century industrial architecture it is, too, along with its mirrored 1977 extension. It belonged to Truman, Hanbury, Buxton & Co., which in 1873 was the largest brewery in the world (the English always did like their bitter). The building now houses the East End Tourism Trust offices and the modern Truman brewery's administration. You can't go in except to look at the old stables and vat house on the east side. Opposite, however, the old brewery canteen has been turned into the little **Brick Lane Music Hall,** a cute and shabby theater serving an *echt* East End dinner (latkes feature on most menus) and an old-fashioned laugh-a-minute cabaret show. *Brewery: 91 Brick La. Music Hall: 152 Brick La., tel. 0171/377-8787; dinner and show £15–£20, Wed.–Sat. 7:30 PM. Tube: Aldgate East, Shoreditch.*

As you stroll safely west down Hanbury Street, reflect that it was here, in 1888, behind a seedy lodging house at No. 29, that **Jack the Ripper** left his third mutilated murderee, "Dark" Annie Chapman. A double murder followed, and then, after a month's lull, came the death on this street of Marie Kelly, the Ripper's last victim and his most revolting murder of all. He had been able to work indoors this time, and Kelly, a young widow, was found strewn all over the room, charred remains of her clothing in the fire grate. Of course, Jack the Ripper's identity has never been discovered, although to this day theories are still bandied about.

Hanbury Street becomes Lamb Street, where you'll find the two ❾ northern entrances to **Spitalfields Market.** Fruit and vegetables were sold here from the mid-17th century until 1991, but it has now been transmogrified into something far more exciting. Until the 3-acre glass-roof market buildings are redeveloped in 1999, they have been leased to the folks who invented Camden Lock (*see* Shopping Districts and Street Markets in Chapter 5, Shopping for Bargains), and the whole place now overflows with crafts and design shops and stalls, a sports hall, restaurants and bars, and different markets every day of the week. The nearer the weekend, the busier it all gets, culminating in the Sunday arts-and-crafts and greenmarket. The latest additions are an opera house and a swimming pool, and events are staged all the time, including the sculptor Andrew Logan's annual Alternative Miss World extravaganza, where drag queens replace beauty queens, in May, and the hip fetish and clubwear Alternative Fashion Show in March. *65 Brushfield St., tel. 0171/ 247-6590. Admission free. Open daily 10–7; market stalls weekdays 11–2, weekends 9–4. Tube: Liverpool Street.*

Retracing your steps east on Lamb Street and then turning left on Commercial Street will bring you to Folgate Street, where, in a restored early 18th-century terrace, one of London's most extraordi-❿ nary experiences awaits you at **Dennis Sever's House.** Sever, a performer-designer-scholar from Escondido, California, has dedicated his life not only to the restoration of his Georgian house but also to raising the ghosts of a fictitious Jervis family who might have inhabited it over two centuries. Sever himself lives a replica of Georgian life, without electricity but with a butler in full 18th-century livery to light the candles and lay the fires—for the Jervises. Three evenings a week he stages a performance, or a "time-travel experience," of philosophical bent, trailing the Jervises through 10 rooms and five generations (from 1724 to 1919, to be precise), always missing them by moments. Sever's stunning house, sans Jervises, is also open one Sunday afternoon a month. *18 Folgate St., tel. 0171/247–4013. Admission: £5 Sun., £30 evenings. Reservations essential. No children. Open first Sun. of the month 2–5; 3 performances per wk (days vary) 7:30 PM–10:20 PM. Tube: Liverpool Street.*

Head back to Brick Lane, turn left, make the third right into Pedley Street, and you won't believe your ears. The source of the moos, bleats, and quacks is **Spitalfields City Farm,** which is just what it sounds like—a sliver of rural England squashed between housing projects. It's one of about a dozen such places in London, which exist to educate city kids in country matters. Available are pony rides, local history tours by horse and cart, a Sunday brunch, summer barbecues, and an altogether surreal experience. *Pedley St., tel. 0171/247–8762. Admission free. Open Tues.–Sun. 9:30–5:30. Sun. brunch 11–3; barbecue June–Sept. (approx.), Wed. 7 PM (call to confirm). Horse-and-cart tours, Sun. 11 and 2:30 (weather permitting), start at £3 adults, £1.50 children. Tube: Shoreditch, Liverpool Street.*

Bethnal Green

It's about a half-mile walk to the next few sights. If you go back west through Folgate Street, you reach Shoreditch High Street, where you can catch Bus 22a, 22b, or 149 north to Kingsland Road. If you walk—an especially good plan on Sunday—cross Bethnal Green Road at the north end of Brick Lane and turn left and then right onto Club Row (which was one enormous pet market until it was closed down in the 1980s by animal-rights campaigners), which leads to **Arnold Circus.** Suddenly you're standing in a perfect circle of arts-and-crafts–style houses around a raised bandstand in the middle. This is the center of the Boundary Estate—"model" housing built by Victorian philanthropists and do-gooders for the slum-dwelling locals and completed as the century began.

Two streets north (running west to east) is **Columbia Road,** the reason you should consider skipping the bus ride Sunday. Once a week this street gets buried under forests of potted palms, azaleas, ivy, ficus, freesias, tiger lilies, carnations, roses, and hosts of daffodils in London's main plant-and-flower market. Prices are ultralow, and lots of the Victorian shop windows around the stalls are filled with wares—terra-cotta pots, vases, gardening tools, hats, and antiques. *Open Sun. 7 AM–2 PM. Tube: Old Street.*

Cross Hackney Road and slip up Waterson Street to wide, busy Kingsland Road, where soon, on the right, you'll come to a row of early 18th-century almshouses: the **Geffrye Museum.** This small, perfectly formed museum re-creates domestic English interiors of every period from Elizabethan through postwar '50s utility, all in sequence, so you walk through time. The best thing about the Geffrye (named after the 17th-century lord mayor of London whose land this was) is that its rooms are not the grand parlors of the gentry one normally sees in historic houses but copies of real family homes, as if talented movie-set designers had been let loose instead of academic museum curators. There's also a walled, scented herb garden and a full program of accessible lectures, including regular "bring a room to life" talks, and a new set of 20th-century rooms is in the offing. *Kingsland Rd., tel. 0171/739–9893. Admission free.*

Open Tues.–Sat. 10–5, Sun. and bank holiday Mon. 2–5. Period
room talks: Sat. 2 and 3:30. Closed Good Friday, Dec. 24–26, Jan.
1. Tube: Liverpool Street, then bus 2A, 22B, 67, 149, or 243.

Head east about 500 yards on Hackney Road (Cremer Street, south
⑮ of the museum, gets you there), and you come to the **Hackney City**
Farm. This one is smaller than Spitalfields' (*see above*), and so are its
animals. Bees and butterflies are the stars here, along with the
kinds of wildflowers they like, as well as an ecologically sound pond.
If you're walking this route, drop in and buy a pot of London honey.
1A Goldsmiths Row, tel. 0171/729–6381. Admission free. Open
Tues.–Sun. 10–4:30. Tube: Bethnal Green.

Going south down Warner Place (across Hackney Road opposite the
farm entrance) takes you to Old Bethnal Green Road, at the end of
which a right turn brings you to a primary-colored sign announcing
⑯ the **Bethnal Green Museum of Childhood.** The East End outpost of
the Victoria and Albert museum, this entire iron, glass, and brown-
brick building was transported here from South Kensington in 1875;
since then, believe it or not, its contents have grown into the biggest
toy collection *in the world*. The central hall is a bit like the Geffrye
Museum zapped into miniature, since here are dollhouses (some royal) of every period. Each genre of plaything has its own enclosure, so
if teddy bears are your weakness, you need not waste time on the
train sets. The museum's title is justified upstairs, in the recently
opened, fascinating—and possibly unique—social-history-of-child-
hood galleries. *Cambridge Heath Rd., tel. 0181/980–4315. Admis-*
sion free. Open Mon.–Thurs. and Sat. 10–5:50, Sun. 2:30–5:50.
Free art workshops for children over 3: Sat. 11 and 2. Closed May
Day holiday, Dec. 24–26, Jan. 1. Tube: Bethnal Green.

Mile End

Now you can either catch Bus 106 or 253 or walk south about half a
mile down Cambridge Heath Road as far as the Mile End Road.
Turning left, you'll find four historical landmarks that provide more
food for thought than thrills for the senses. On the north side of the
street, a redbrick student hostel cunningly conceals its interesting
⑰ origin as the **Trinity Almshouses,** built (possibly with Wren's help) in
1695 for "28 decayed Masters and Commanders of Ships or ye wid-
ows of such," bombed during World War II, and restored by the London County Council. Behind, even better concealed, is the oldest
Jewish cemetery in Britain, founded by the Sephardic community in
1657 after Cromwell allowed them back into the country. (If you
would like to view the cemetery, call the United Synagogues Cemetery Maintenance Department, tel. 0171/790–1445.)

On the south side of the street stands the third visually uninterest-
ing landmark—a stone inscribed "Here William Booth commenced
the work of the Salvation Army, July 1865." It marks the position of
the first Sally Army platform, while back on the north side a few
⑱ steps past the almshouses, a **statue of William Booth** stands on the
very spot where the first meetings were held.

Turn around now, and on the northwest corner of Cambridge Heath
Road you'll see a Victorian pub with the completely un-p.c. name of
⑲ **The Blind Beggar.** You've just beheld the sites of the first Sally
Army platform and the first Sally Army meetings; this den of iniquity was where William Booth preached his first sermon. Booth didn't
supply the pub's main claim to fame, though. The Blind Beggar's
real notoriety dates only from March 1966, when Ronnie Kray—one
of the Kray twins, the former gangster kings of London's East End
underworld—shot rival "godfather" George Cornell dead in the sa-
loon bar.

The hulk of a building opposite Whitechapel tube, a few yards west
of the pub, is the **Royal London Hospital.** The hospital was founded
in 1740, and its early days were as nasty as its then-neighborhood
near the Tower of London. Waste was carried out in buckets and
dumped in the street; bedbugs and alcoholic nurses were problems,
but according to hospital records, nobody died—they were "re-
lieved." Anyone who lived but refused to give thanks to both the hospital committee and God went on a blacklist, banned from further
treatment. In 1759, the hospital moved to a new building, the core of
the one you see today. By then it had become the best hospital in
London, and it was enhanced further by the addition of a small medical school in 1785 and 70 years later, an entire state-of-the-art medical college. Thomas John Barnado, who went on to found the famous
Dr. Barnado's Homes for Orphans, came to train here in 1866. Ten
years later, with the opening of a new wing, the hospital became the
largest in the United Kingdom, and now, though mostly rebuilt
since World War II, it remains one of London's most capacious.

Behind the buildings, the **Royal London Hospital Archives** have displays of medical paraphernalia, objects, and documentation to illus-
trate the 250-year history of this East London institution. *Crypt of
St. Augustine with St. Philip's Church, Newark St., tel. 0171/377–
7000, ext. 3364. Admission free. Open weekdays 10–4:30; closed
Dec. 24–26, Jan. 1. Tube: Whitechapel.*

The South Bank

*Numbers in the margin correspond to points of interest on the South
Bank map.*

If you head back to Tower Bridge, cross it, and follow the river upstream, you soon enter London's oldest "suburb," **Southwark.** Just
across the river from London Bridge yet conveniently outside the
City walls and laws, it was the ideal location for the taverns and
cockfighting arenas that served as after-hours entertainment in the
Middle Ages. By Shakespeare's time it had become a veritable den
of iniquity, famous above all for the "Southwark stews," or brothels,
and for being very rough. The Globe Theatre, in which Shakespeare
acted and held shares, was one of several established here after theaters were banished from the City in 1574 for encouraging truancy
in young apprentices and being generally rowdy and insubordinate.
The Globe was as likely to stage a few bouts of bearbaiting as the
latest play by Shakespeare.

Southwark was heavily bombed during World War II and then ne-
glected for a few decades while more central parts of London were
repaired. The active ports had moved downstream by then anyway,
so Southwark's 19th-century warehouses and winding alleys had little to recommend them to developers. This circumstance began to
change when theater returned to the Bankside environs (Bankside
is the street along the South Bank from Southwark to Blackfriars
Bridges) in the form of the national arts complex that opened downstream in 1976, but it took another decade or so for developers and
local authorities to catch on to the potential farther east. Now the
pockets of the new and the renovated—Gabriel's Wharf, London
Bridge City, Hay's Galleria, Butler's Wharf—have practically con-
nected to form a South Bank that even Londoners, who have an atti-
tude problem about crossing the river, have been known to admire
and even frequent.

Butler's Wharf to Old St. Thomas's

Start your walk scenically at the end of **Tower Bridge** opposite the
one where our City tour finished, finding the steps on the east (left)
side that descend to the start of a pedestrians-only street, Shad

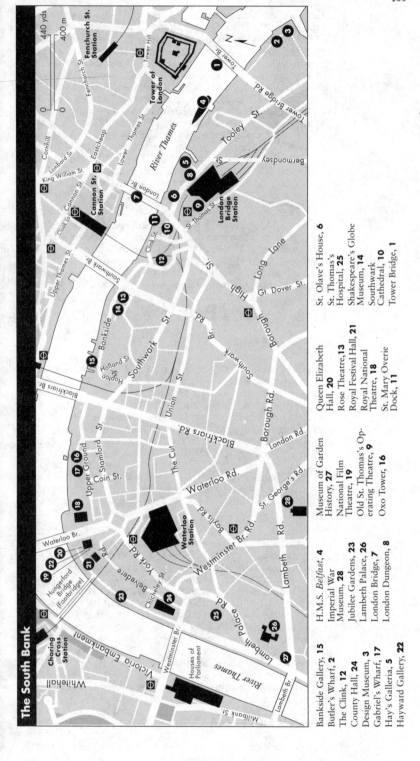

The South Bank

440 yds
400 m

Tower Br.

Fenchurch St. Station

Fenchurch St.

Tower Hill

Tower of London

N

Tower Bridge Rd.

Lower Thames St.

River Thames

Tooley St.

Bermondsey St.

Cornhill

Lombard St.

King William St.

Cannon St.

Eastcheap

Lower Thames St.

Cannon St. Station

London Br.

London Bridge Station

St. Thomas St.

Clink St.

Southwark Br.

Upper Thames St.

Long Lane

Gt. Dover St.

Bankside

Southwark St.

Borough High St.

Hopton St.

Holland St.

Union St.

Southwark St.

Blackfriars Br.

The Cut

Coin St.

Stamford St.

Upper Ground

Waterloo Rd.

Blackfriars Rd.

Borough Rd.

London Rd.

Waterloo Br.

Waterloo Station

Waterloo Rd.

Westminster Br. Rd.

Bayliss Rd.

St. George's Rd.

Lambeth Rd.

York Rd.

Belvedere Rd.

Chicheley St.

Hungerford Bridge (Footbridge)

Charing Cross Station

Victoria Embankment

Whitehall

Westminster Br.

Lambeth Palace Rd.

Houses of Parliament

River Thames

Millbank St.

Lambeth Br.

Bankside Gallery, **15**
Butler's Wharf, **2**
The Clink, **12**
County Hall, **24**
Design Museum, **3**
Gabriel's Wharf, **17**
Hay's Galleria, **5**
Hayward Gallery, **22**

H.M.S. *Belfast*, **4**
Imperial War
Museum, **28**
Jubilee Gardens, **23**
Lambeth Palace, **26**
London Bridge, **7**
London Dungeon, **8**

Museum of Garden
History, **27**
National Film
Theatre, **19**
Old St. Thomas's Op-
erating Theatre, **9**
Oxo Tower, **16**

Queen Elizabeth
Hall, **20**
Rose Theatre, **13**
Royal Festival Hall, **21**
Royal National
Theatre, **18**
St. Mary Overie
Dock, **11**

St. Olave's House, **6**
St. Thomas's
Hospital, **25**
Shakespeare's Globe
Museum, **14**
Southwark
Cathedral, **10**
Tower Bridge, **1**

Thames. Now turn your back on the bridge and follow this quaint path between cliffs of good-as-new warehouses. These warehouses were once the seedy, dingy, dangerous shadowlands where Dickens killed off evil Bill Sikes in *Oliver Twist* but are now part of **Butler's Wharf,** an '80s development that is maturing gracefully. Many apartments in its deluxe loft-style warehouse conversions and swanky new blocks still lack inhabitants, but there *is* life here, thanks partly to London's saint of the stomach, Sir Terence Conran (also responsible for Bibendum and Quaglino's—*see* St. James's in Chapter 3, Where to Eat on a Budget). Conran gave it his "Gastrodrome" of four restaurants, a vintner's, a deli, a bakery, and who knows what else by now. You'll find it to your left.

Conran was also responsible for the other success on this riverside site, the **Design Museum,** which you come to next. Opened in 1989, it's the first museum in the world to elevate the everyday design we take for granted to the status of exhibit, slotting it into its social and cultural context. On the top floor, the **Collection** traces the evolution of mass-produced goods, with cases full of telephones and washing machines, plates and hi-fi equipment, computers and Coke bottles, and plenty of backup material from ads to films. Alongside the Collection, the regularly revamped **Review** looks deeply into a particular aspect of the consumer durable. Special exhibitions are held downstairs on the first floor, and there's also a program of lectures and events, as well as the very good **Blueprint Café** with its own river terrace. *Butler's Wharf, tel. 0171/403–6933. Admission: £4.50 adults, £3.50 children and senior citizens. White Card valid. Open daily 10:30–5:30; closed Dec. 24–26, Jan. 1. Tube: Tower Hill, then walk across the river.*

Turn around and veer away from the river, just before you get back to Tower Bridge, along Horsleydown Lane, and then follow Tooley Street. Turn right at Morgan Lane, and you'll be hit by the unlikely spectacle of a vast gray battleship—**HMS *Belfast*,** at 656 feet one of the largest and most powerful cruisers the Royal Navy ever had. The *Belfast* played a role in the D-day landings off Normandy, left for the Far East after the war, and has been becalmed here since 1971. On board there's an outpost of the Imperial War Museum, which tells the Royal Navy's story from 1914 to the present and shows you what life on board a World War II battleship was like, from mess decks and bakery, punishment cells, and operations room to engine room and armaments. *Morgan's La., Tooley St., tel. 0171/ 407–6434. Admission: £4 adults, £3 senior citizens, £2 children under 16. Open mid-Mar.–Oct., daily 10–5:30; Nov.–mid-Mar., daily 10–4; closed Dec. 24–26, Jan. 1. Tube: London Bridge.*

From the *Belfast*, take a short riverside stroll to reach **Hay's Galleria.** Hay's Wharf was built by Thomas Cubitt in 1857 on the spot where the port of London's oldest wharf had stood since 1651. It was known as "London's larder" on account of the edibles landed here until it wound down gradually and closed in 1970. In 1987 it was reborn as this Covent Gardenesque parade of bars and restaurants, offices, and shops, all weatherproofed by an arched glass atrium roof supported by tall iron columns. The centerpiece is a fanciful kinetic sculpture by David Kemp, *The Navigators*, which looks like the skeleton of a pirate schooner crossed with a dragon and spouts water from various orifices. Inevitably, jugglers, string quartets, and crafts stalls abound. This courtyard hub of the developing **London Bridge City** needed all the help it could get in its early days, but it has settled in nicely now with its captive crowd of office workers from the adjacent new developments.

Step out onto Tooley Street again, and you come upon the former Hay's Wharf offices, an exciting black-and-white-and-gold-striped Art Deco block built in 1931 by H. S. Goodhart-Rendel and called **St. Olave's House** after the church it replaced. The shiny square edifice has far more style than the newer buildings around it and quite puts them to shame. At the end of Tooley Street (difficult to see how, but the name is a corruption of St. Olave's) stands the 1972 version of **⑦ London Bridge.**

Coming up to the left on the same street is the gory, grisly, grue- **⑧** some **London Dungeon.** Here realistic waxwork people are sub- jected in graphic detail to all the historical horrors that the Tower of London merely suggests. Tableaux depict famous bloody mo- ments—like Anne Boleyn's decapitation or the martyrdom of St. George—alongside the torture, murder, and ritual slaughter of more anonymous victims, all to a soundtrack of screaming, wailing, and agonized moaning. London's times of deepest terror—the Great Fire and the Great Plague—are brought to life, too, and so are its public hangings. And did you ever wonder what a disembowelment actually looks like? See it here. Children absolutely adore this place, which is among London's top tourist attractions and usually fea- tures long lines. Spend your money elsewhere if you're not accompa- nied by children—this is no bargain. *28–34 Tooley St., tel. 0171/403- 0606. Admission: £6.95 adults, £4 children under 14, and £5.50 sen- ior citizens. Open Apr.–Sept. daily 10–5:30, Oct.–Mar. daily 10– 4:30; closed Dec. 24–26. Tube: London Bridge.*

To continue the theme of pain and blood after the dungeons, turn left into Joiner Street underneath the arches of London's first (1836) railway and then right onto St. Thomas Street, where you'll find the **⑨ Old St. Thomas's Operating Theatre.** This is all that remains of one of England's oldest hospitals, which stood here from the 12th century until the railway forced it to move in 1862, and was where women went under the knife. The theater was bricked up and forgotten for a century but has now been restored and turned into an exhibition of early 19th-century medical practices: the operating table onto which the gagged and blindfolded patients were roped; the box of sawdust underneath for catching their blood; the knives, pliers, and hand- saws the surgeons wielded; and—this was a theater in the round— the spectators' seats. Next door is a sweeter show: the **Herb Garret,** with displays of medicinal herbs used in the same period. *9A St. Thomas St., tel. 0171/955–4791. Admission: £2 adults, £1.50 senior citizens, £1 children. Open Tues.–Sun. 10–4.; closed Dec. 15–Jan. 5. Tube: London Bridge.*

Southwark Cathedral to Coin Street

⑩ Just across Borough High Street you reach **Southwark Cathedral** (pronounced *suth-uck*). Despite its still-standing 12th-century parts (which make it the second-oldest Gothic church in London, next to Westminster Abbey) and its remarkable memorials, not to mention a program of lunchtime concerts, it is little visited. It was promoted to cathedral status only in 1905; before then, it had been the priory church of St. Mary Overie (as in "over the water," on the South Bank). Look for the gaudily renovated 1408 tomb of the poet John Gower, a friend of Chaucer, and for the Harvard Chapel, named after John Harvard, founder of the college, who was baptized here in 1608. Another notable buried here is Edmund Shakespeare, brother of William.

Walk down Cathedral Street to the water, and you'll be in another of **⑪** the South Bank's recent office developments, **St. Mary Overie Dock.** The three-masted topsail schooner *Kathleen & May,* kept in an en- closed dock, maintains the maritime theme. Early this century hun- dreds like it hauled cargoes of coal, cement, timber, and even gunpowder around the British coast, but now the *Kathleen & May* is the only one left. You can normally board it to view an exhibition about this brand of seafaring life, plus a rare film of the ship itself under sail, although it was closed at press time. *St. Mary Overie*

Dock, tel. 0171/403–3965. Admission: £1 adults, 50p children under 16 and senior citizens. Open daily 10–5; closed Dec. 25, Jan. 1. Call to check if it reopened. Tube: London Bridge.

Incorporated in the St. Mary Overie development is the west wall, with rose window outline, of Winchester House, palace of the bishops of Winchester until 1626. Attached to this palace was a prison whose name still serves as a general term for jail: **the Clink.** One of five Southwark prisons, it was the first to detain women, most of whom were "Winchester Geese"—another euphemism the bishops donated to the language, meaning prostitutes. The oldest profession was endemic in Southwark, especially around the bishops' area of jurisdiction, known as "the Liberty of the Clink." Their graces' sensible solution was to license prostitution, rather than ban it, but a Winchester goose who flouted the rules ended up, of course, in the Clink. Now there is a museum tracing the history of prostitution in the Liberty—complete with an R-rated section—and showing what the Clink was like during its 16th-century prime. *1 Clink St., tel. 0171/403–6515. Admission: £2 adults, £1 children and senior citizens. Open daily 10–6. Closed Dec. 25–26. Tube: London Bridge.*

Shakespeare's Globe Theatre was also within the Liberty, and if you continue to the end of Clink Street onto Bankside, the paved riverside walk, and under Southwark Bridge, you will come to a reconstruction of it. First, though, turn left up Rose Alley, where in 1989 the remains of another famous Jacobean theater, the **Rose Theatre,** were unearthed. Depending, however, on what stage (no pun intended) the office development that will surround the preserved foundations has reached, there may not be much to see.

The next little alley is New Globe Walk, and it is here that you'll find **Shakespeare's Globe.** For more than two decades, until he died in 1993, the American actor and film director Sam Wanamaker worked ceaselessly to raise funds for this ambitious project. In addition to an exact replica of Shakespeare's open-roofed Globe Playhouse (built in 1599, incinerated in 1613), using authentic Elizabethan materials and craft techniques—green oak timbers joined only with wooden pegs and mortice and tendon joints; plaster made of lime, sand, and goat's hair; and the first thatched roof in London since the Great Fire—he planned a second, indoor theater, which is being built to a design of the 17th-century architect Inigo Jones. The whole thing stands a hundred yards from the original Globe on the appropriate site of the 17th-century Davies Amphitheatre, admittedly more a bullbaiting, prizefighting sort of venue than a temple to the legitimate stage, but at least Samuel Pepys immortalized it in his diaries. Until the theater is completed this summer, there's a fascinating tour to be had, showing the construction in progress. Once finished, the Globe will be a celebration of the great bard's life and work, an actual rebirth of his "Great Wooden O" (see *Henry V*), where his plays will be presented in natural light (and sometimes rain) to 1,000 people on wooden benches in the "bays" and to 500 "groundlings," standing on a carpet of filbert shells and clinker, just as they did nearly four centuries ago. For any theater buff, this stunning project is unmissable. *New Globe Walk, Bankside, tel. 0171/ 928–6406. Admission: £4 adults, £2.50 children under 18, and £3 senior citizens. Open daily. 10–5. Performances commence June 1996. Call for schedule. Closed Dec. 24–25. Tube: Mansion House, then walk across Southwark Bridge.*

About 100 yards farther along Bankside you reach the reconstruction of the Globe Playhouse itself, followed by the 17th-century **Cardinal's Wharf,** where, as a plaque explains, Wren lived while St. Paul's Cathedral was being built. Next you pass by **Bankside Power Station,** which is to become the new Tate Gallery by the year 2000, and arrive at **Bankside Gallery,** a modern building in which two artistic societies—the Royal Society of Painter-Printmakers and the

Royal Watercolour Society—have their headquarters. Together they mount exhibitions of current members' works, usually for sale, alongside artists' materials and books. *48 Hopton St., tel. 0171/928–7521. Admission: £3.50 adults, children under 15 free, and £2 senior citizens. Open Tues.–Sat. 10–5, Sun. 1–5; closed Dec. 24–Jan. 2, Easter. Tube: Blackfriars, then walk across the bridge.*

You have now reached your fourth bridge on this tour, **Blackfriars Bridge,** which you pass beneath to join the street called Upper Ground. You may notice the **Oxo Tower** to your left, with what looks like a giants' game of ticktacktoe written in windows on its summit. In fact, it's a 1928 ploy to circumvent billboard-advertising regulations: Oxo was—and is—a brand of beef bouillon (and now it also has a free ad in Fodor's). Just before it, by the bridge, is a modern pub remarkable only for its name, **Doggett's Coat and Badge.** Each July the boat race of the same name, founded by an actor named Thomas Doggett in 1716, still runs from Cadogan Pier in Chelsea to London Bridge, making it the oldest annual event in British sports.

Between the pub and the tower, you pass yet another (fairly) new development, but one of an entirely different character from the foregoing business behemoths. **Coin Street Community Builders,** as their name suggests, is a nonprofit action group formed by local residents during the mid-'70s to create family housing and public spaces out of land that would otherwise have gone to commercial developers. You can see the human-scale homes and gardens they've already built since 1984 and the adjacent Stamford Wharf, which they plan to make into a haven of housing, performance spaces, crafts workshops, and restaurants. In the meantime they've set up **Gabriel's Wharf,** a dinky marketplace of shops and cafés, where about 15 designers sell jewelry, ceramics, toys, etc. and music is staged in summer.

The South Bank Arts Complex

The next section involves a single bridge, but several hours. At least, for anyone with any feeling for the arts it does, since the concrete congregation on either side of Waterloo Bridge is London's chief arts center. Continue along Upper Ground to reach the first of its buildings, the **Royal National Theatre,** a low-slung, multilayered block the color of heavy storm clouds. You may be forgiven for believing you made a mistake and wandered back to the Barbican— and, indeed, Londoners generally felt the same way about Sir Denys Lasdun's brutalist function-dictates-form building when it opened in 1976, as they would a decade later about the far nastier Barbican. But whatever its merits or demerits as a landscape feature (and architects have given it an overall thumbs up), the Royal National Theatre—still abbreviated colloquially to the preroyal warrant NT— has wonderful insides.

There are three auditoriums in the complex. The biggest one, the **Olivier,** is named after Sir Laurence, chairman of the first building commission and first artistic director of the National Theatre Company, formed in 1962. (From the first proposal for a national theater for Britain and the 1949 formation of that building commission, an entire century passed.) The **Lyttleton** theater, unlike the Olivier, has a traditional proscenium arch, while the little **Cottesloe** mounts studio productions and new work in the round. Interspersed with the theaters are various levels of foyer, where exhibitions are shown, bars and restaurants are frequented, and free entertainment is provided, and the whole place is lively six days a week. The Royal National Theatre Company does not rest on its laurels. It attracts many of the nation's top actors (Anthony Hopkins, for one, does time here) in addition to launching future stars. Since it's a repertory company, you'll have several plays to choose from even if your

London sojourn is short, but, tickets or not, wander round and catch the buzz. *South Bank, tel. 0171/928–2252 (box office). Hour-long tours of the theater backstage (tel. 0171/633–0880) Mon.–Sat. at 10:15, 12:30, and 5:30; £3.50 adults, £2.50 children and senior citizens. Foyers open Mon.–Sat. 10 AM–11 PM; closed Dec. 24–25. Tube: Waterloo.*

Keep walking along the wide path. You'll find distractions all over here, especially in summer—secondhand bookstalls, entertainers, arrogant pigeons, and a series of plaques annotating the buildings ⑲ opposite. Underneath Waterloo Bridge is the **National Film Theatre** (or NFT). Its two movie theaters boast easily the best repertory programming in London, favoring rare, obscure, foreign, silent, forgotten, classic, noir, or short films over blockbusters. Technically it's a film club, but you can easily join for the modest fee of 40p. There's a third cinema inside MOMI, or the **Museum of the Moving Image,** but if you reckon you'll just have a quick look around before you catch a movie here, think again. MOMI may be the most fun of all London's museums, and you will get stuck for at least a couple of hours. The main feature is a history of cinema from 4,000-year-old Javanese shadow puppets to Spielbergian special effects, and as good as the displays are, the supporting program is even better, and it stars *you.* Actors dressed as John Wayne or Mae West or usherettes or chorus girls pluck you out of obscurity to read the TV news or audition for the chorus line or fly like Superman over the Thames. They also perform, mime, improvise, and generally bring celluloid to life, while all around, various screens show clips from epoch-making giants like Hitchcock and Eisenstein, plus newsreels and ads. Techies can learn focus-pulling and satellite beaming, artists can try animation, and eggheads can explore ethical issues like censorship and documentary objectivity. Needless to say, this is always a big hit with children. *South Bank Centre, tel. 0171/401–2636. Admission: £5.50 adults, £4 children and senior citizens, £4.70 students, £16 family (2 adults, 4 children). White Card valid. Open daily 10–6, last admission 5 PM; closed Dec. 24–26. Tube: Waterloo.*

The next building you come to contains one medium and one small ⑳ concert hall, the **Queen Elizabeth Hall** and the **Purcell Room,** respectively. Both offer predominantly classical recitals of international caliber, with due respect paid to 20th-century composers and the more established jazz and vocal artists. Next on riverside is the ㉑ largest auditorium, the **Royal Festival Hall,** with superb acoustics and a 3,000-plus capacity. It is the oldest of the blocks, raised as the centerpiece of the 1951 Festival of Britain, a postwar morale-boosting exercise. The London Philharmonic resides here; symphony orchestras from the world over often visit; and choral works, ballet, serious jazz and pop, and even film with live accompaniment are also staged. As at the NT, there is a multiplicity of foyers, with free rotating exhibitions, several eating stations, and an excellent bookstore.

㉒ Finally, tucked behind the concert halls, is the **Hayward Gallery,** one of the city's major art-exhibition spaces, its bias fixed firmly in this century. This stained and windowless bunker has come in for the most flak of all the buildings, enduring constant threats to flatten it and start again, but it's still here, topped by its multicolored neon tube sculpture, the most familiar feature on the South Bank skyline. *South Bank Complex, tel. 0171/928–3144. Admission varies according to exhibition. White Card valid. Open daily 10–6, Tues. and Wed. until 8; closed Good Friday, May Day, Dec. 25–26, Jan. 1. Tube: Waterloo.*

Westminster Bridge to the Imperial War Museum

Now make your way to the final two bridges on this tour, eyes glued to the opposite bank for the quintessential postcard vista of the Houses of Parliament, best in the late afternoon when the last westerly rays silhouette the towers and catch on the waves of the Thames—if it's not raining.

㉓ This view is good from **Jubilee Gardens,** the rectangle of grass planted in 1977 to mark the queen's 50th year on the throne; it is the site of arts festivals and often, during summer, a visiting circus. It
㉔ gets better as you pass **County Hall,** a curved, colonnaded neoclassical hulk that took 46 years (1912–58; two world wars interfered) to build and was home to London's local government, the Greater London Council (or GLC, which mutated out of the London County Council in 1965) until it disbanded in 1986. Since then the issue of whether a new citywide governing body would enhance London has been contentious. (It's politicians who wrangle; most Londoners would like to have one.)

㉕ Past Westminster Bridge the river is fronted by **St. Thomas's Hospital,** which few bother to look at since you are now finally at the spot precisely opposite Westminster Hall. You may remember the remains of Old St. Thomas's from the Southwark leg of this tour; here is where the hospital reopened, in 1868, to the specifications of the founder of the first school of nursing, the Lady with the Lamp, Florence Nightingale. Most of it was bombed to rubble in the Blitz and then rebuilt to become one of London's teaching hospitals. Since 1989 it has also housed the **Florence Nightingale Museum,** where you can learn all about the most famous nursing reformer. Here is a reconstruction of the barracks ward at Scutari (Turkey), where she tended soldiers during the Crimean War (1854–56) and earned her nickname; here is a Victorian East End slum cottage showing what she did to improve living conditions among the poor; and here is the Lamp. *2 Lambeth Palace Rd., tel. 0171/620–0374. Admission: £2.50 adults, £1.50 children and senior citizens. Open Tues.–Sun. and public holidays 10–4; closed Good Friday, Easter, Dec. 25–26, Jan. 1. Tube: Waterloo, or Westminster and walk over the bridge.*

Having seen the remains of the palace of the Bishops of Winchester
㉖ at St. Mary Overie Dock, you now arrive at **Lambeth Palace,** a bishop's palace that is still standing, complete with (occasionally) a resident archbishop. For 800 years this has been the London base of the archbishop of Canterbury, top man in the Church of England. Much of the palace is hidden behind great walls, and even the Tudor gatehouse, visible from the street, is closed to the public, but you can stand here and absorb the historical vibrations echoing from such momentous events as the 1381 storming of the palace during the Peasants' Revolt against the poll tax (a modern version of which Thatcher recently reinstated, whereupon modern riots ensued, and the tax was sheepishly repealed) and the 1534 clash of wills when Thomas More refused to sign the Oath of Supremacy claiming that Henry VIII (not the pope) was the head of the English Church, was sent to the Tower, and executed for treason the following year.

Adjacent to the palace is **St. Mary's,** which you certainly can visit. It belongs to the Tradescant Trust, which is named after John Tradescant (c. 1575–1638), botanist extraordinaire, who brought to these shores the lilac, larch, jasmine, and spiderwort (named Trad-
㉗ escantia in his honor), and which founded the **Museum of Garden History** here when the old church was deconsecrated in 1977. In the nave are changing exhibitions with horticultural themes, supplemented by a reconstructed—or regrown—17th-century knot garden. Tradescant's tomb in the graveyard is carved with scenes from his worldwide plant-discovery tours and surrounded with the plants he discovered. Near it, William Bligh, captain of the *Bounty*, is bur-

ied, which suits the theme—the *Bounty* was on a breadfruit-gathering mission in 1787 when the crew mutinied. *Lambeth Palace Rd., tel. 0171/261–1891. Admission free; donations welcome. Open weekdays 11–3, Sun. 10:30–5; closed mid–Dec.–early Mar. Tube: Waterloo.*

En route to the next museum, if you take a detour to the right off Lambeth Road, you could be "doing the Lambeth Walk" down the street of the same name. A cockney tradition ever since the 17th century, when there was a spa here, the Sunday stroll was immortalized in a song from the 1937 musical *Me and My Gal*, which recently was a hit all over again in the West End and on Broadway. A little farther east along Lambeth Road you reach an elegant domed and colonnaded building, erected in the early 19th century to house the Bethlehem Hospital for the Insane, better known as the infamous Bedlam. In fact, though, by 1816, when the patients were moved to this location, they were no longer kept in cages to be taunted by tourists (see the final scene of Hogarth's *Rake's Progress* at Sir John Soane's Museum for an idea of how horrific it was), since reformers—and George III's madness—had effected more humane confinement.

The pair of giant guns outside have nothing to do with the restraint of patients, however, since Bedlam moved to Surrey in 1930. The building now houses the **Imperial War Museum.** Pacifists, don't stop reading. Despite its title, this museum of 20th-century warfare does not glorify bloodshed but attempts to evoke what it was like to live through the two world wars. Of course, there is hardware for martial boys—a Battle of Britain Spitfire, a German V2 rocket, tanks, guns, submarines—but there is an equal amount of war art (by David Bomberg, Henry Moore, John Singer Sargent, and Graham Sutherland, to name a few), poetry, photography, and documentary film footage. One very affecting exhibit is *The Blitz Experience*, which is what it sounds like—a 10-minute taste of an air raid in a street of acrid smoke with sirens blaring and searchlights glaring. More recent wars attended by British forces are thoughtfully commemorated, too, right up to the Gulf War of 1991. *Lambeth Rd., tel. 0171/416–5000. Admission: £3.90 adults, £2.90 senior citizens, £1.95 children under 16. White Card valid. Open daily 10–6; closed Dec. 24–26, Jan. 1. Tube: Lambeth North.*

Chelsea and Belgravia

Numbers in the margin correspond to points of interest on the Chelsea and Belgravia map.

It would be unfair to London to pretend that there's nothing of interest south of the river between Lambeth and Battersea, but space forbids its exploration here, so we gloss over such sights as Kennington's cricket valhalla, **the Oval;** the new wholesale fruit-and-vegetable market at **Nine Elms,** Vauxhall, into which Covent Garden was decanted; the no-longer-used four-chimney landmark **Battersea Power Station,** beloved by Londoners out of all proportion to its usefulness (which is negligible—nobody will buy it); and big, beautiful **Battersea Park** and aim directly for the third bridge upstream from Lambeth Bridge to return to the north bank.

Chelsea

❶ Albert Bridge, a hybrid cantilever-suspension model, went up in 1873 and is probably London's favorite (except to those trapped on it daily by rush-hour traffic) on account of its prettiness, especially when fairy-lit by night. On its north side is Chelsea, a neighborhood as handsome as its real estate is costly. Strolling its streets you will often notice gigantic windows adorning otherwise ordinary houses.

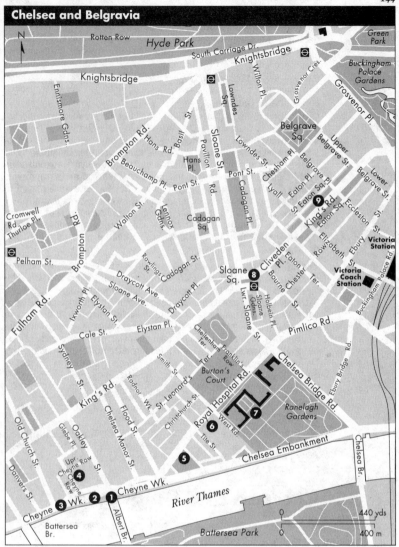

Chelsea and Belgravia

Albert Bridge, **1**

Carlyle's House, **4**

Chelsea Physic
Garden, **5**

Cheyne Walk, **2**

Eaton Square, **9**

National Army
Museum, **6**

Royal Court Theatre, **8**

Royal Hospital, **7**

Thomas More statue, **3**

They are now mostly used to hike property values a few notches higher, but these remnants of Chelsea's 19th-century bohemian days once lit artists' studios; many famous artists and writers have lived here. Latterly Chelsea—especially the King's Road—gave birth to Swinging '60s London and then to '70s punk youth culture. The '90s version is not really the center of anything, but it's hard not to like walking it.

Stretching in both directions from Albert Bridge is very expensive ❷ **Cheyne Walk** (it rhymes with "rainy"), featuring some beautiful Queen Anne houses (particularly Norman Shaw's ornamental 1876 Cheyne House, to the right) and a storm of blue plaques marking famous ex-residents' abodes. George Eliot died at No. 4 in 1880; Dante Gabriel Rossetti annoyed the neighbors of No. 16 with his peacock collection (there's still a clause in the lease banning the birds); and at Carlyle Mansions (after the King's Head and Eight Bells pub), Henry James died and T.S. Eliot and Ian Fleming lived. The western reaches was painters' territory, most notably James McNeill Whistler, who lived at No. 96 and then at No. 101, and J. M. W. Turner, who used No. 119 as a retreat, shielding his identity behind the name Admiral "Puggy" Booth.

Also toward the western end, outside the church of All Saints, is a ❸ golden-faced **Thomas More** (who wouldn't sign the Oath of Supremacy at Lambeth Palace in 1534 and was executed as a traitor; *see* Westminster Bridge to the Imperial War Museum in The South Bank, *above*), looking pensive and beatific on a throne facing the river, in a 1969 addition to the walk. Double back and turn left into Cheyne ❹ Row to reach one literary residence you can visit. **Carlyle's House** was a thriving salon of 19th-century authors, who were attracted by the fame of Thomas Carlyle (who wrote a then-blockbuster, since all-but-forgotten history of the French Revolution and founded the London Library) and by the wit of his wife, the poet Jane Carlyle. Dickens, Thackeray, Tennyson, and Browning were regular visitors, and you can see the second-floor drawing room where they met just as they saw it, complete with leather armchair, decoupage screen, fireplace, and oil lamps, all in ruddy Victorian hues. *24 Cheyne Row, tel. 0171/352–7087. Admission: £2.90 adults, £1.45 children under 17. Open Apr.–Oct., Wed.–Sun. and public holidays 11–5 (last admission 4:30); closed Good Friday, Dec. 24–26, Jan. 1. Tube: Sloane Square, then walk down King's Rd., or take bus 11, 19, 22, 49, 219, or 249.*

At the point where the east end of Cheyne Walk runs into Royal Hospital Road, gardeners and herbalists should make a beeline for the ❺ **Chelsea Physic Garden,** first planted by the Society of Apothecaries in 1673 for the study of medicinal plants and still in use for the same purpose today. These herbs, shrubs, and flowers, planted to a strict plan but tumbling rurally over the paths nevertheless, are interspersed with woodland areas; England's first rock garden; and ancient trees, some of which were tragically uprooted in a 1987 hurricane. In the middle stands a statue of Sir Hans Sloane, Queen Anne and George II's physician, whose collection formed the basis of the British Museum and who saved the garden from closure in 1722, making sure nobody would ever be allowed to build over it. *Swan Walk, 66 Royal Hospital Rd., tel. 0171/352–5646. Admission: £3.50 adults, £1.30 children under 16 and students. Open Apr.–Oct., Sun. and Wed. 2–5; daily noon–5 during the Chelsea Flower Show in the 3rd wk of May. Tube: Sloane Square and then walk down King's Rd., or take bus 11, 19, 22, 49, 219, or 249.*

Turn right after the garden on Royal Hospital Road. The Imperial War Museum (*see* Westminster Bridge to the Imperial War Museum in The South Bank, *above*) tells of British warfare during this centu- ❻ ry; the **National Army Museum** covers the history of British land forces from the Yeoman of the Guard (the first professional army, founded in 1485 and ancestors of the Tower's Beefeaters) to the present. Again, a great deal of effort is made to convey the experience of those who lived through the wars, and a visit should enhance anyone's grasp of London's history and its personages. *Royal Hospital Rd., tel. 0171/730–0717. Admission free. Open Mon.–Sat. 10–5:30, Sun. 2–5:30; closed Good Friday, May Day, Dec. 24–26, Jan. 1. Tube: Sloane Square.*

❼ Royal Hospital Road takes its name from the institution next door to the museum, the magnificent **Royal Hospital.** Charles II founded this hospice for elderly and infirm soldiers in 1682—some say after a badgering from his softhearted, high-profile mistress, Nell Gwynn, but more probably as an act of expedience, since his troops had hitherto enjoyed not so much as a meager pension and were growing restive after the civil wars of 1642–46 and 1648. Charles wisely appointed the great architect of burned-out City churches, Sir Christopher Wren, to design this small village of red brick and Portland stone, set in manicured gardens (which you can visit) surrounding the "Figure Court"—named after the 1692 bronze figure of Charles II dressed up as a Roman soldier—and the Great Hall (dining room) and chapel. The chapel is enhanced by the choir stalls of Grinling Gibbons (who did the bronze of Charles, too), and the Great Hall, by a vast oil of Charles on horseback by Antonio Verrio, and both are open to inspection.

No doubt you will run into some of the 400-odd residents. Despite their advancing years, these "Chelsea Pensioners" are no shrinking violets. In summer and for special occasions they wear dandy scarlet frock coats with gold buttons and breastfuls of medals and natty tricorne hats, and, being of proved good character (a condition of entry, along with old age and loyal service), may offer to show you around—in which case you may wish to supplement their daily beer and tobacco allowance with a tip.

May is the big month at the Royal Hospital. The 29th is **Oak Apple Day,** when the pensioners celebrate Charles II's birthday by draping oak leaves on his statue and parading around it in memory of a hollow oak tree that expedited the king's miraculous escape from the 1651 Battle of Worcester. In the same month the **Chelsea Flower Show,** the year's highlight for thousands of garden-obsessed Brits, is also held here (*see* Festivals and Seasonal Events in Chapter 1, Essential Information). *Royal Hospital Rd., tel. 0171/730–0161. Admission free. Open Mon.–Sat. 10–noon and 2–4, Sun. 2–4; closed national holidays and Sun. Oct.–Mar. Tube: Sloane Square.*

A left turn up Franklin's Row and Cheltenham Terrace brings you to famous **King's Road,** where the miniskirt was born in the '60s and Vivienne Westwood and Malcolm McLaren clothed the Sex Pistols in bondage trousers from their shop, Sex, in 1975, thus spawning punk rock. Westwood, Britain's most innovative fashion star, still has her shop at No. 430, where the road kinks. Both boutique and neighborhood are called **World's End,** possibly because Chelseaites believe that's what it does here—the less-fancy Fulham begins around this stretch. The other end of King's Road, leading into Sloane Square, has various fashion stores (no longer style-setters, on the whole) and some rather good antiques shops and markets along the way; check out **Antiquarius** at No. 135–141.

The **Pheasantry,** at No. 152, is recognizable by some over-the-top Grecian statuary in a fancy portico. Named during its mid-19th-century pheasant-breeding days, it had a phase from 1916 to 1934 as a ballet school where Margot Fonteyn and Alicia Markova learned the first position. Now it's a club-restaurant haunted by the braying breed of Chelsea yuppie, dubbed "Sloane Rangers" by '80s style-watchers. **Peter Jones** department store marks the exit from the north of Chelsea and the beginning of Belgravia: Sloane Square.

You may remember Sir Hans Sloane from the Chelsea Physic Garden, which he saved for posterity, and the British Museum, which his collection started. This is his territory, since he bought the manor of Chelsea in 1712, and Sloane Square, laid out late that century,
8 is named in his honor. Of chief interest here now is the **Royal Court Theatre,** dedicated to new work that has seen many a first night of future star playwrights. It was here that John Osborne's *Look Back in Anger* premiered in 1956. Fifty years earlier, many of George Bernard Shaw's plays had their first public airings here, too.

Belgravia

The neighborhood between Sloane Square and Hyde Park Corner is aristocratic **Belgravia,** with King's Road and Knightsbridge its southern and northern borders; Sloane Street and Grosvenor Place its western and eastern ones; and vast Belgrave Square, home to many embassies, in the middle. Belgravia is relatively young: It was built between the 1820s and the 1850s by the builder-developer-entrepreneur Thomas Cubitt (who had as great an influence on the look of London in his day as Wren and Nash had in theirs), under the patronage of Lord Grosvenor, and was intended to rival Mayfair for spacious snob value and expense.

Well, it did, and it does. The grand, white-stucco houses have not
9 changed at all since the mid-19th century, and **Eaton Square** remains such a desirable address that the rare event of one of its houses coming on the market makes all the property pages. Its most famous residents were fictional: The enduringly popular period soap, *Upstairs Downstairs*, was set here.

Knightsbridge, Kensington, and Holland Park

Numbers in the margin correspond to points of interest on the Knightsbridge, Kensington, and Holland Park map.

East of Belgravia and north of Chelsea lies salubrious Knightsbridge, with approximately equal doses of elite residential streets and ultra-shopping opportunities. To *its* east is one of the highest concentrations of important artifacts anywhere, the "museum mile" of South Kensington, with the rest of Kensington offering peaceful strolls, a noisy main street, and another palace. The Holland Park neighborhood is worth visiting for its big, fancy, tree-shaded houses and its exquisite and surprising park. This is an all-weather tour—museums and shops for rainy days, grass and strolls for sunshine.

Knightsbridge

When you surface from the Knightsbridge tube station—one of London's deepest—you are immediately engulfed among the angry drivers, professional shoppers, and ladies-who-lunch who make up the local population. If you're in a shopping mood—and we're talking window-shopping, unless you intend to blow your entire dining budget—**Harvey Nichols**—right at the tube—has six floors of total fashion, and **Sloane Street,** leading south, is strung with the boutiques of big-name French and English designers.

1 There's no point pretending you don't want to see **Harrods,** so we'll head there next, going west down Brompton Road and soon colliding with the store's domed terra-cotta Edwardian bulk, outlined in thousands of white lights by night. The 15-acre Egyptian-owned store's sales weeks are world-class, and the store is as frenetic as a stock market floor, since its motto, *Omnia, omnibus, ubique*

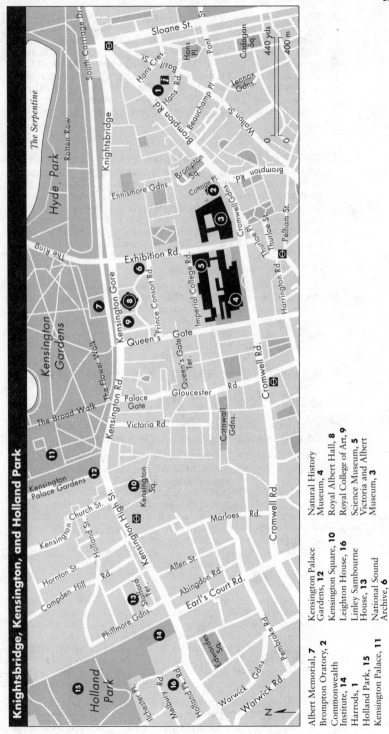

Knightsbridge, Kensington, and Holland Park

Sloane St.

Hans Cres.
Basil St.
Pont St.
Cadogan Sq.

440 yds
400 m

Hans Pl.
Lennox Gdns.
Walton St.

South Carriage Dr.

Hans Rd.
Beauchamp Pl.

Brompton Rd.

Knightsbridge

Rotten Row

The Serpentine

Hyde Park

Brompton Sq.

Ennismore Gdns.

Cottage Pl.
Cromwell Gdns.
Brompton Rd.
Pelham St.

Thurloe Pl.
Thurloe St.

The Ring

Exhibition Rd.

Imperial College Rd.

Harrington Rd.

Kensington Gardens

Kensington Gore
Prince Consort Rd.

Queen's Gate

Queen's Gate Ter.

Gloucester Rd.

Cromwell Rd.

The Flower Walk

Kensington Rd.

Palace Gate

Victoria Rd.

Cornwall Gdns.

The Broad Walk

Kensington Palace Gardens

Kensington Church St.

Holland St.

Kensington High St.

Kensington Sq.

Marloes Rd.

Cromwell Rd.

Hornton St.

Campden Hill Rd.

Allen St.

Stafford Ter.

Abingdon Rd.

Earl's Court Rd.

Phillimore Gdns.

Holland Park

Ilchester Pl.

Melbury Rd.

Holland Pk. Rd.

Edwardes Sq.

Warwick Gdns.

Pembroke Rd.

Warwick Rd.

N

Albert Memorial, **7**
Brompton Oratory, **2**
Commonwealth Institute, **14**
Harrods, **1**
Holland Park, **15**
Kensington Palace, **11**

Kensington Palace Gardens, **12**
Kensington Square, **10**
Leighton House, **16**
Linley Sambourne House, **13**
National Sound Archive, **6**

Natural History Museum, **4**
Royal Albert Hall, **8**
Royal College of Art, **9**
Science Museum, **5**
Victoria and Albert Museum, **3**

What to do when your *money* is done traveling before you are.

Don't worry. With **MoneyGram**,^{SM} your parents can send you money in usually 10 minutes or less to more than 19,000 locations in 80 countries. So if the money you need to see history becomes history, call us and we'll direct you to a **MoneyGram**^{SM} agent closest to you.

USA: **1-800-MONEYGRAM**   Canada: **1-800-933-3278**   France: **05-905311**
Germany: **0130-8-16629**   England: **0800-89-7198**   Spain: **900-96-1218**

or call collect **303-980-3340**

("everything, for everyone, everywhere") is not too far from the truth. Visit the pet department, a highlight for children, and don't miss the extravagant **Food Hall,** with its stunning Art Nouveau tiling in the neighborhood of meat and poultry, which continues in the fishmonger's territory, where its glory is rivaled by displays of the sea produce itself. This is the place to acquire your green-and-gold souvenir Harrods bag, since food prices are surprisingly competitive. Go as early as you can to avoid the worst of the crowds. From Harrods, continue west down the Brompton Road, pausing at Beauchamp ("Bee-chum") Place and Walton Street if shopping is your intention.

❷ Presently, at the junction of Brompton and Cromwell roads, you come to the pale, Italianate **Brompton Oratory,** a product of the English Roman Catholic revival of the late 19th century, led by John Henry Cardinal Newman (1801–90), who established this oratory in 1884 and whose statue you see outside. A then-unknown 29-year-old architect, Herbert Gribble, won the competition to design the place, an honor that you may assume went to his head when you see the vast, incredibly ornate interior. The interior is punctuated by treasures far older than the church itself, like the giant Twelve Apostles in the nave, carved from Carrara marble by Giuseppe Mazzuoli in the 1680s and brought here from Siena's cathedral. New and dastardly treasure was also found here, in the side altar, when the second pillar to the left of the pietà was unmasked as a "dead-letter box"—a hot line from secret agents to the KGB.

South Kensington

You are now in museum territory. (The neighborhood's three large museums, incidentally, can be reached via a long underground passage from the South Kensington tube.)

★ ❸ The next building along, at the start of Cromwell Road, is the first of the colossal museums of South Kensington, the **Victoria and Albert,** recognizable by the copy of Victoria's Imperial Crown it wears on the lantern above the central cupola, and always referred to as the V&A. It showcases the applied arts of all disciplines, all periods, all nationalities, and all tastes and is a wonderful, generous place to get lost in, full of innovation and completely devoid of pretension. The collections are so catholic that confusion is a hazard—one minute you're gazing on the Jacobean oak 12-foot-square four-poster **Great Bed of Ware** (one of the V&A's most prized possessions, given that Shakespeare immortalized it in *Twelfth Night*); the next, you're in the 20th-century end of the equally celebrated **Dress Collection,** coveting a Jean Muir frock you could actually buy at Harrods.

Prince Albert, Victoria's adored consort, was responsible for the genesis of this permanent version of the 1851 Great Exhibition, and his queen laid its foundation stone in her final public London appearance in 1899. From the start, the V&A had an important role as a research institution, and that role continues today, with many resources available to scholars, designers, artists, and conservators. Two of the latest are the **Textiles and Dress 20th Century Reference Centre,** with ingenious space-saving storage systems for thousands of bolts of cloth, and the **Textile Study Galleries,** which perform the same function for 2,000 years' worth of the past.

Follow your own whims around the 7 miles of gallery space, but try to reach the new and spectacular **Glass Gallery,** where a collection spanning four millennia is reflected between room-size mirrors, under young designer Danny Lane's breathtaking glass balustrade. *Cromwell Rd., tel. 0171/938–8500. Suggested contribution: £4.50 adults, £1 children and senior citizens. White Card valid. Open Mon. noon–5:50, Tues.–Sun. 10–5:50; closed Good Friday, May Day, Dec. 24–26, Jan. 1. Tube: South Kensington.*

The museum that follows provides clues to its contents in relief panels scattered across its outrageously ornate French Romanesque-style terra-cotta facade. Alfred Waterhouse, the architect of the **Natural History Museum,** carved living creatures to the left of the entrance and extinct ones to the right, a categorization that is sort of continued in reverse inside, with **Dinosaurs** on the left and the **Ecology Gallery** on the right. Both these newly renovated exhibits (the former with life-size *moving* dinosaurs, the latter complete with a moonlit "rain forest") make essential viewing in a museum that realized it was getting crusty and has consequently invested millions overhauling itself in recent years.

The **Creepy Crawlies Gallery** features a nightmarish superenlarged scorpion, yet ends up making tarantulas cute (8 out of 10 animal species, one learns here, are arthropods). Other wonderful bits include the **Human Biology Hall,** which you arrive in through a birth-simulation chamber; the full-size blue whale; and, in the east wing, once the separate Geological Museum, an earthquake machine (not for L.A. residents) in the **Earth Galleries.** Understandably, this place usually resembles grade-school recess. *Cromwell Rd., tel. 0171/ 938–9123. Admission: £5 adults, £2.50 children under 17 and senior citizens, £13.50 family (2 adults, 4 children). Admission free weekdays 4:30–5:50, weekends 5–5:50. White Card valid. Open Mon.– Sat. 10–5:50, Sun. 11–5:50; closed Dec. 24–26, Jan. 1. Tube: South Kensington.*

⑤ The last of the three big museums, the **Science Museum,** stands behind the Natural History Museum in a far plainer building. This one features even more hands-on exhibits, with entire schools of children apparently decanted inside to play with them; but it is, after all, painlessly educational. Highlights include the **Launch Pad** gallery, which demonstrates basic scientific principles (try the beautiful plasma ball, where your hands attract "lightning"—if you can get them on it); the **Computing Then and Now** show, which gets the most crowded; *Puffing Billy,* the oldest train in the world; and the actual **Apollo 10** capsule, which took U.S. astronauts around the moon in 1969 and now sits beside a mock-up moon base in the space-exploration segment. Food technology, medical history, flight, navigation, transport, meteorology—all these topics are explored, and the entire height of the museum is used for a **Foucault's Pendulum** that has been there, in perpetual motion thanks to the movement of the earth, from the start. *Exhibition Rd., tel. 0171/938–8000. Admission: £4.50 adults, £2.40 children under 15 and senior citizens. White Card valid. Open Mon.–Sat. 10–6, Sun. 11–6; closed Dec. 24– 26, Jan. 1. Tube: South Kensington.*

Turn left to continue north up Exhibition Road, a kind of unfinished cultural main drag that was Prince Albert's conception, toward the road after which British moviemakers named their fake blood, Kensington Gore. Near the end on the left is the aural outpost of the **⑥** British Library, the **National Sound Archive,** in which you may listen to the queen who made this entire tour possible: The million recordings held here include one of Victoria speaking sometime in the 1880s, but you have to book in advance to hear her or anyone else. There's a small exhibit of early recording equipment and ephemera, too. *29 Exhibition Rd., tel. 0171/589–6603. Admission free. Open weekdays 10–5 (Thurs. 10–9); closed public holidays, Dec. 24–26, Jan. 1. Tube: South Kensington.*

Having heard Victoria, you can now see Albert, across Kensington Gore in the grandiose temple that his grieving widow had erected on the spot where his Great Exhibition had stood a mere decade before his early death from typhoid in 1861. To tell the truth, all you can **⑦** actually see of the **Albert Memorial** is the world's tallest freestanding piece of scaffolding, since the intricate structure housing the 14-foot bronze statue of Albert is undergoing a £14 million renovation—including a pure gold-leaf coat donated by an anonymous benefactor—not due to be finished until the year 2000.

Just opposite, on the south side of the street, stands a companion—
⑧ and, this time, shriekingly visible—memorial, the **Royal Albert Hall.** The Victorian public donated funds to build this domed, circular 8,000-seat auditorium (as well as the Albert Memorial), but more money was raised by selling 1,300 future seats at £100 apiece—not for the first night, but for every night for 999 years. (Some descendants of purchasers still use the seats.) The Albert Hall is best known and best loved for its annual July–September Henry Wood Promenade Concerts (the "Proms"), with bargain standing (or promenading or sitting-on-the-floor) tickets sold on the night of the world-class classical concerts. London also enjoys the "Erics," when rock guitarist Eric Clapton performs for adoring fans for 10 days there every February. *Kensington Gore, tel. 0171/589–3203. Admission varies according to event. Tube: South Kensington.*

The building adjacent to the Albert Hall could hardly contrast more sharply with all this sentimental Victoriana: the glass-dominated
⑨ **Royal College of Art,** designed by Sir Hugh Casson in 1973. Famous in the '50s and '60s for processing David Hockney, Peter Blake, and Eduardo Paolozzi, the RCA is still one of the country's foremost art schools, and there's usually an exhibition, lecture, or event here open to the public. *Kensington Gore, tel. 0171/584–5020. Admission free. Open weekdays 10–6; phone first to check exhibition details. Tube: South Kensington.*

Kensington

You've already entered Kensington, but now you're drawing closer to the heart of it. It first became the *Royal* Borough of Kensington (and Chelsea) by virtue of a king's asthma. William III, who suffered terribly from the Thames mists over Whitehall, decided in 1689 to buy Nottingham House in the rural village of Kensington so that he could breathe more easily; besides, his wife and comonarch, Mary II, felt confined by water and wall at Whitehall. Courtiers, functionaries, and society folk soon followed where the crowns led, and by the time Queen Anne was on the throne (1702–14), Kensington was overflowing. In a way, it still is, since most of its grand houses, and the later, Victorian ones of Holland Park, have been divided into apartments, or else are serving as foreign embassies.

⑩ Begin with a stroll around the covetable houses of **Kensington Square,** laid out around the time William moved to the palace up the road and therefore one of London's oldest squares. A few early 18th-century houses remain, with Nos. 11 and 12 the oldest. Return to Kensington High Street up Derry Street, with the offices of London's local paper, the *Evening Standard*, on the right and what was once Derry and Tom's department store—it closed down in the '70s—on the left. The best feature of the store was its magical roof garden, complete with palm trees, ponds, and flamingos; the roof garden is still there, now part of a nightclub owned by Richard Branson, the high-profile London figure who also owns Virgin Atlantic Airways.

Follow the road east until you reach Kensington Gardens, where
⑪ **Kensington Palace** stands close to the western edge. It did not enjoy a smooth passage as a royal residence. Twelve years of renovation were needed before William and Mary could move in; it continued to undergo all manner of refurbishment during the next three monarchs' times. By coincidence, these monarchs happened to suffer ignominious deaths. First, William III fell off his horse when it stumbled on a molehill and succumbed to pleurisy in 1702. Then, in 1714, Queen Anne (who, you may recall, was fond of brandy) suffered an apoplectic fit brought on by overeating. Next, George I, the

first of the Hanoverian Georges, had a stroke as a result of "a surfeit of melons"—admittedly not at Kensington, but in a coach to Hanover, in 1727. Worst of all, in 1760, poor George II burst a blood vessel while on the toilet (the official line was, presumably, that he was on the throne).

The best-known royal Kensington story, though, concerns the 18-year-old Princess Victoria of Kent, who was called from her bed in June 1837 by the archbishop of Canterbury and the lord chamberlain. Her uncle, William IV, was dead, they told her, and she was to be the queen. The **state rooms** where Victoria had her ultrastrict upbringing are currently being renovated and will reopen in spring 1997, depicting the life of the royal family through the past century. *Kensington Gdns., tel. 0171/937–9561. Closed for renovation.*

Behind the palace runs one of London's rare private roads, guarded and gated both here and at the other end by Notting Hill Gate, **⑫ Kensington Palace Gardens.** If you walk it, you will see why it earned the nickname "Millionaires' Row"—it is lined with palatial white-stucco houses designed by a selection of the best architects of the mid-19th century. The novelist William Makepeace Thackeray, author of *Vanity Fair*, died in 1863 at No. 2—a building that now houses an embassy (Israeli), as do most of the others. **Kensington Church Street** also leads up to Notting Hill Gate, with the little 1870 St. Mary Abbots Church on its southwest corner and a cornucopia of expensive antiques in its shops all along the way.

Rather than walk the traffic-laden Kensington High Street, take the longer, scenic route, first turning left off Kensington Church Street into Holland Street and admiring the sweet 18th-century houses (Nos. 10, 12–13, and 18–26 remain). As you cross Hornton Street, you'll see to your left an orange-brick 1970s building, the Kensington Civic Centre (donor of parking permits, home of the local council), and Holland Street becomes the leafy Duchess of Bedford's Walk, with **Queen Elizabeth College,** part of London University, on the right.

Turn left before Holland Park into Phillimore Gardens (perhaps detouring east into Phillimore Place to see No. 44, where Kenneth Grahame, author of *The Wind in the Willows*, lived from 1901 to **⑬** 1908), then left again into Stafford Terrace to reach **Linley Sambourne House.** The Victorian Society has perfectly preserved this 1870s home of the political cartoonist Edward Linley Sambourne, complete with William Morris wallpaper and illustrations from the (recently defunct) satirical magazine *Punch*, including many of Sambourne's own, adorning the walls. *18 Stafford Terr., tel. 0181/ 994–1019. Admission: £3 adults, £1.50 children under 16. Open Mar.–Oct., Wed. 10–4, Sun. 2–5. Tube: High Street Kensington.*

Step back to High Street, turn right, pass the gates of Holland Park (we'll enter them soon), and you'll see one of London's more eccentric structures—the swimming-pool-blue walls and asymmetric **⑭** copper tent roof of the **Commonwealth Institute.** A wander round the open-plan walkways of this lovable museum is like a trip around the world, or at least around the 50 Commonwealth nations, with lifestyles and histories of other continents captured in dioramas and displays that are more like art than education, although education is an important part of the work done at this vibrant institute (it hosts a lot of music, art, and film events, too). Work should be well under way by now on the new first-floor "Wonders of the World" exhibit, which owes more to Disneyworld than to the world of museum curators—passenger cars travel through simulations of a coral reef, a Caribbean storm, an African safari, underground volcanic eruptions, and the like. This exhibit is due to open in spring 1996 (at which point, expect a sharp increase in price). *230 Kensington High St., tel. 0171/603–4535. Admission: £1 adults, 50p children. Open*

Mon.–Sat. 10–5, Sun. 2–5; closed Good Friday, Dec. 24–26, Jan. 1. Tube: High Street Kensington.

Holland Park

Stepping through the gates you just passed, you will find yourself in a haven of wildlife, flora, and even culture, **Holland Park.** These former grounds of the Jacobean **Holland House** opened to the public only in 1952; since then, many treats have been laid on within its 22 hectares. Holland House itself was nearly flattened by World War II bombs, but the east wing remains, now incorporated into a youth hostel and providing a fantastic stage for the April–September **Open Air Theatre** (box office, tel. 0171/602–7856). The glass-walled **Orangery** also survived to host art exhibitions and wedding receptions, while next door, the Garden Ballroom has become the **Belvedere** restaurant (*see* Kensington and Notting Hill Gate in Chapter 3, Where to Eat on a Budget).

From the Belvedere's terrace you see the formal **Dutch Garden,** planted by Lady Holland in the 1790s with the first English dahlias. North of that are woodland walks, lawns populated by peacocks and guinea fowl and the odd emu, a fragrant rose garden, great banks of rhododendrons and azaleas (which bloom profusely in May), a well-supervised children's **Adventure Playground,** and even a **Japanese water garden,** legacy of the 1991 London Festival of Japan. If that's not enough, you can watch cricket on the **Cricket Lawn** on the south side or tennis on several courts.

Exit the park at the gate by the tennis courts (near the Orangery) onto Ilchester Place, follow Melbury Road a few yards, and turn right onto Holland Park Road to reach **Leighton House.** The main reason to tour the home of Frederic Leighton—painter, sculptor, and president of the Royal Academy, who was endowed with a peerage by Victoria (unfortunately, he died a month later)—is the incredible **Arab Hall.** George Aitchison designed this Moorish fantasy in 1879 to show off Leighton's valuable 13th- to 17th-century Islamic tile collection, and, adorned with marble columns, dome, and fountain, it is exotic beyond belief. The rest of the rooms are more conventionally, stuffily Victorian, but they feature many paintings by Leighton, plus Edward Burne-Jones, John Millais, and other leading Pre-Raphaelites. *12 Holland Park Rd., tel. 0171/602–3316. Admission free. Open Mon.–Sat. 11–5; closed national holidays. Tube: Holland Park.*

During the late 19th century, **Melbury Road** was a veritable colony of artists, though the Victorian muse they followed failed to appeal to later sensibilities, so they're now an obscure bunch—except Dickens's illustrator, Marcus Stone, who had No. 8 built in 1876. From here you could turn right onto Addison Road (just off our map) to see the Technicolor tiles rioting over Sir Ernest Debenham's "Peacock House" at No. 8 (he founded the eponymous Oxford Street department store). If you continue north, you reach the plane tree–lined Holland Park Avenue, main thoroughfare of an expensive residential neighborhood and good for a pleasant stroll.

Hyde Park, Kensington Gardens, and Notting Hill

Numbers in the margin correspond to points of interest on the Hyde Park, Kensington Gardens, and Notting Hill map.

Many Londoners, not to mention visitors, love the city above all for its huge chunks of green, which cut right through the middle of town. The two we visit here together form by far the biggest of central London's royal parks (Richmond Park, in the far west, is larger; *see* Richmond in The Thames Upstream, *below*). It's probably been centuries since any major royal had a casual stroll here, but the parks remain the property of the Crown, and it was the Crown that saved them from being devoured by the city's late-18th-century growth spurt.

★ **Hyde Park,** along with the smaller St. James's and Green Parks to the east, started as Henry VIII's hunting grounds. Henry had no altruistic intent but—you could say—stole the land for his pleasure, from the monks at Westminster at the 1536 Dissolution of the Monasteries. James I was more generous and allowed the public in at the beginning of the 17th century, as long as they were "respectably dressed." Nowadays, as summer visitors can see, you may wear whatever you like—a bathing suit will do.

North of the parks—which are separate, although the boundary is virtually invisible—lie Bayswater, Queensway, and Notting Hill, the last of which is a multicultural neighborhood that has really come into its own in the past few years.

Hyde Park

Where else would you enter Hyde Park but at Hyde Park Corner? The most impressive of the many entrances is here, beside Apsley House (*see* Piccadilly in St. James's and Mayfair, *above*). Officially
❶ it's the Hyde Park Screen, but it's usually called **Decimus Burton's Gateway** because it was Burton who designed this triple-arched monument in 1828. The next gate to the north was a 90th-birthday gift to Elizabeth, the Queen Mother (who is as old as the century), and we don't know what she thought of it. Public reception of the
❷ gaudy unicorns-and-lions-rampant **Queen Mother's Gate,** wrought in scarlet-, cobalt-, white-, and gold-painted metal, was derisive, but see what you think.

Your first landmark in all the greenery is a sand track that runs
❸ along the south perimeter, called **Rotten Row.** It was Henry VIII's royal path to the hunt—hence the name, a corruption of *route du roi.* Contemporary horses still use it, ridden by the rich who own them, the fairly well-heeled who hire them, or the Household Caval-
❹ ry who ride for the queen. You can see the latter's **Knightsbridge Barracks**—a high rise and a long, low, ugly red block—to the left. This is the brigade that mounts the guard at the palace, and you can see them leave to perform this duty, in full regalia, plumed helmet and all, at around 10:30 AM or await the return of the exhausted ex-guard about noon.

You can follow either Rotten Row or Serpentine Road west, or you can stray over the grass, but the next landmark to find is the long, narrow,
❺ man-made (in 1730) lake, the **Serpentine.** It is a beloved lake, much frequented in summer, when the south shore **Lido** resembles a beach and the water is dotted with hired rowboats. If you rise very early, you might catch the Serpentine Swimming Club—a band of eccentrics who are guaranteed to appear on TV at the first hard frost each winter, since they dive in here at 6 AM every day of the year, breaking the ice first if necessary. Walk the bank, and you will soon reach the
❻ picturesque stone **Serpentine Bridge,** built in 1826 by George Rennie.

Kensington Gardens

❼ In passing the bridge, you leave Hyde Park and enter **Kensington Gardens.** On the south side of the bridge is the **Serpentine Gallery,** which hangs several exhibitions of modern work a year, often very avant-garde, indeed, and always worth a look. *Kensington Gardens, tel. 0171/402–6075. Admission free. Open daily 10–6; closed Christmas wk. Tube: Lancaster Gate.*

Hyde Park, Kensington Gardens, and Notting Hill

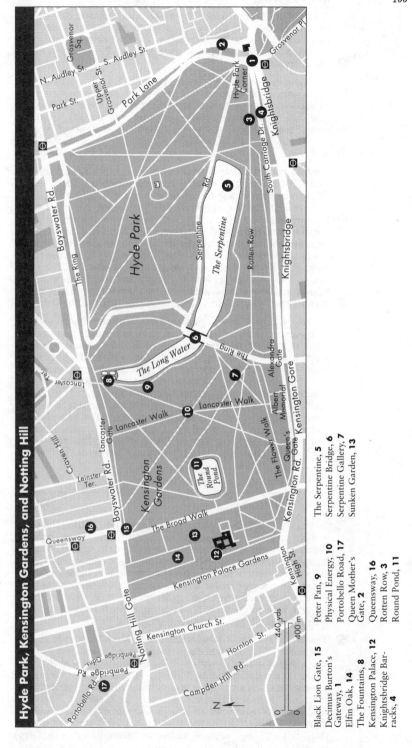

Black Lion Gate, **15**
Decimus Burton's Gateway, **1**
Elfin Oak, **14**
The Fountains, **8**
Kensington Palace, **12**
Knightsbridge Barracks, **4**

Peter Pan, **9**
Physical Energy, **10**
Portobello Road, **17**
Queen Mother's Gate, **2**
Queensway, **16**
Rotten Row, **3**
Round Pond, **11**

The Serpentine, **5**
Serpentine Bridge, **6**
Serpentine Gallery, **7**
Sunken Garden, **13**

Kensington Gardens is more formal than its neighbor, since it was first laid out as palace grounds. Continue along the south bank of the lake, called the Long Water on this side of the bridge, to the top, to reach the formal, paved Italian garden called, for obvious reasons, **❽ The Fountains.**

On your way, you will have passed a statue that children have loved since George Frampton cast it in 1912—a bronze of the boy who lived **❾** on an island in the Serpentine and never grew up, **Peter Pan.** His creator, J. M. Barrie, lived at 100 Bayswater Road, not 500 yards from here. There's another statue worth seeking southwest of Peter at the intersection of several paths: George Frederick Watts's 1904 **❿** bronze of a muscle-bound horse and rider, entitled **Physical Energy.**

Next on your westward stroll comes another water feature, the **⓫ Round Pond,** a magnet for model-boat enthusiasts and duck feeders. You may happen on an exciting remote-controlled shipwreck or ice thick enough for skating, which is allowed here. Next you reach **⓬ Kensington Palace** (*see* Kensington, *above*), with an early 19th-cen- **⓭** tury **Sunken Garden** north of it, complete with a living tunnel of lime trees and golden laburnum. **The Broad Walk** between the pond and the palace runs south-to-north, from the bottom to the top of the park. Following it all the way north to the Bayswater Road, you'll see, on the left, a **playground** full of the kind of children who have nannies and whose nannies take them to the remains of a tree carved **⓮** with scores of tiny woodland creatures, Ivor Innes's **Elfin Oak.**

⓯ Leaving the park by **Black Lion Gate,** you are almost opposite **⓰** Bayswater's main drag, **Queensway,** a rather peculiar, cosmopolitan street of ethnic confusion, late-night cafés and restaurants, a skating rink, and the Whiteleys shopping-and-movie mall. The road expresses Bayswater's nature quite aptly: This is a neighborhood that looks fancy, with its grand white-stucco terraced houses and leafy squares, but is somewhat disreputable, as demonstrated by the 1963 Profumo sex scandal—involving a government minister, a teenage showgirl, and a Soviet naval attaché—which unfurled behind closed Bayswater doors and toppled a government (see the movie *Scandal* for the whole story). You'll notice dozens of identical medium-priced hotels along the streets east of Queensway, but probably won't notice the prostitution, of which there's a certain amount still going on around here.

Notting Hill

As you walk west, the Bayswater Road turns into **Notting Hill Gate,** a wide, windy crossroads of functional shops. Turn right at Pembridge Road, however, and you've reached the start of a happening neighborhood, a trendsetting square mile of multiethnicity, music, and markets, with lots of see-and-be-seen-in restaurants and the younger, more egalitarian and adventurous versions of the Cork Street commercial modern-art galleries. The style-watching media dub the musician/novelist/filmbiz/drug-dealer/fashion-victim local residents and hangers-out Notting Hillbillies.

⓱ The famous **Portobello Road** starts soon on the left and runs about a mile north. What it's famous for is its Saturday antiques market, which begins around Chepstow Villas and continues for about three blocks before giving way to fruit-and-vegetable stalls. Lining the sloping street are also dozens of antiques shops and indoor markets, open most days (*see* Chapter 5, Shopping for Bargains). Where the road levels off, youth culture kicks in and continues to the **Westway** overpass ("flyover" in British), where London's best flea market (high-class, vintage, antique, and secondhand clothing and jewelry) is held Friday and Saturday, then on up to Goldbourne Road. There's a strong West Indian flavor to Notting Hill, with a Trinidadstyle **Carnival** centered along Portobello Road on the August bank-holiday weekend. *Tube: Notting Hill Gate, Ladbroke Grove.*

Regent's Park and Hampstead

Numbers in the margin correspond to points of interest on the Regent's Park and Hampstead map.

This walk is a long one. We start at the Georgian houses superimposed on medieval Maryburne, where London's most overpopulated tourist attraction now lies, and continue around John Nash's Regency facades, and his park, home now to everything from elephants to softball. Next, we visit North London's canalside youth center, then climb up to the city's prettiest, most expensive "village," which wraps around its most bucolic park, before finishing, fittingly, at its most famous cemetery. You may well want to divide this tour into segments, using the notoriously inefficient Northern Line of the tube to jump between neighborhoods.

Begin at the tube station whose name will thrill the Sherlock Holmes fan: **Baker Street.** It sits on **Marylebone Road** (pronounced "Marra-le-bun"), remarkable for its permanent traffic jam. The aforementioned Conan Doyle reader may wish to pay homage to the fictional detective, who lived at 221B Baker Street. Walking past the Abbey National Building Society's head office at Abbey House, 215–229 Baker Street (sparing a thought for the poor mail-room attendant who still wades through letters asking Holmes and Watson for ❶ help), you reach No. 237–9, the **Sherlock Holmes Museum,** distinguishable by the actor dressed as a Victorian policeman outside and by the sign that claims this as 221B, though we know it's lying. Inside, "Holmes's housekeeper" conducts you into a series of Victorian rooms, full of Sherlockabilia. *"221B" Baker St., tel. 0171/935–8866. Admission: £5 adults, £3 children under 16 and senior citizens. Open daily 10–6; closed Dec. 25, Jan. 1. Tube: take a guess.*

Around the corner again on Marylebone Road, follow the line of tour buses to one of London's busiest and most overpriced sights, ❷ **Madame Tussaud's.** It is nothing more, nothing less, than the world's premier exhibition of lifelike waxwork models of celebrities. Madame T. learned her craft while making death masks of French Revolutionary victims and in 1835 set up her first show of the famous ones near this spot. Nowadays, superstars of entertainment, in their own hall of the same name, outrank any aristocrat in popularity, along with the newest segment, The Spirit of London, a "time taxi ride" that visits every notable Londoner from Shakespeare to Benny Hill. But top billing still goes to the murderers in the Chamber of Horrors, who stare glassy eyed at you—this one from the electric chair, that one next to the tin bath where he dissolved several wives in quicklime. What, aside from ghoulish prurience, makes people stand in line to invest in London's most expensive museum ticket? It must be the thrill of rubbing shoulders with Shakespeare, Martin Luther King Jr., the queen, and the Beatles—most of them dressed in their own clothes—in a single day. *Marylebone Rd., tel. 0171/935–6861. Admission: £8.25 adults, £6.25 senior citizens, £5.25 children under 15; or joint ticket with planetarium (see below). Open Sept.–June, weekdays 10–5:30, weekends 9:30–5:30; July–Aug., daily 9:30–5:30; closed Dec. 25. Tube: Baker Street.*

❸ Next door is the green dome of the **London Planetarium,** which could hardly provide greater contrast with the waxworks (though you can save a bit of cash by combining them in a single visit). The stars here, of course, are the ones in the sky, simulations of which are projected on the dome's insides by the Digistar Mark 2 projector

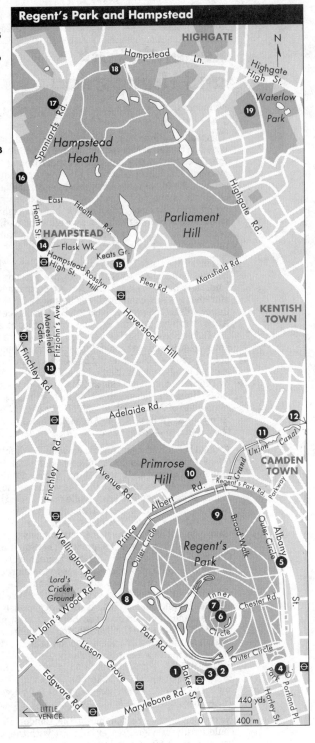

Regent's Park and Hampstead

and accompanied by gosh-wow-fancy-that narration. The shows, which change daily, are good enough to make children addicted to astronomy. The Space Trail of interactive planet and spacecraft models is also worth seeing, and there are occasional laser shows and rock-music extravaganzas. *Marylebone Rd., tel. 0171/486–1121. Admission: £4 adults, £3.10 senior citizens, £2.50 children under 15. Joint ticket with Madame Tussaud's: £9.40 adults, £7.95 senior citizens, £5.65 children. Shows every 40 min, weekdays 12:40–4:40, weekends 10:40–5:20; extra shows during school vacations. Tube: Baker Street.*

Now, hope for good weather because the next leg of the tour keeps you outdoors. Continuing east up Marylebone Road, you pass by **Harley Street**—an English synonym for private (as opposed to state-funded) medicine, since it's lined with the consulting rooms of the country's top specialist doctors. Next you reach the first part of John Nash's impressive Regent's Park scheme, the elegantly curva-
❹ ceous **Park Crescent.** Nash planned it as a full circus at the northern end of his ceremonial route from St. James's, but only this southern semicircle was built (1812–18). It was later wrecked during World War II, reconstructed, and rebuilt behind the repaired facade in the 1960s—as, indeed, were all the Nash houses you will see around the park. Crossing the street, you enter **Regent's Park** at the Outer Circle.

Regent's Park and the Zoo

This, the youngest of London's great parks, was laid out in 1812 by John Nash, working, as ever, for his patron, the Prince Regent (hence the name), who was crowned George IV in 1820. The idea was to re-create the feel of a grand country residence close to the center of town, with all those magnificent white-stucco terraces facing the park. As you walk the Outer Circle, you'll see how successfully Nash's plans were carried out, although the center of it all, a palace for the prince, was never built—George was too busy fiddling with the one he already had, Buckingham Palace.

The most famous and impressive of Nash's terraces, appearing soon on your right, was extra ornamental, since it would have been in the
❺ prince's line of vision from the planned palace. **Cumberland Terrace** has a central block of Ionic columns surmounted by a triangular Wedgwood-blue pediment that is like a giant cameo. Snow-white statuary personifying Britannia and her empire (the work of the on-site architect, James Thomson) further single it out from the pack.

Turn left into the park from this road. As in all London parks, plant-ing is planned with the aim of having something in bloom in all sea-sons, but if you hit the park in May, June, or July, head first to the
❻ **Inner Circle.** Your nostrils should lead you to **Queen Mary's Gardens,** a fragrant 17-acre circle that riots with roses in summer and heath-ers, azaleas, and evergreens in other seasons. Close by is the
❼ **Open-Air Theatre,** which has been mounting mostly Shakespearean productions since 1932. *A Midsummer Night's Dream* is the one to catch—never is that enchanted Greek wood more lifelike than it is here, augmented by genuine bird squawks. The park can get chilly, so bring a blanket—and rain stops the play only when heavy, so an umbrella may be wise, too. *Open Air-Theatre, Regent's Park, tel. 0171/486–2431. Open June–Aug. Tube: Baker Street, Regent's Park.*

Rejoin the **Broad Walk** from Chester Road, look west past the mock-Tudor prefab tearoom, and before you stretches what is practically London's only uninterrupted open vista. From here you can watch a Technicolor sunset over the minaret and glittery gilt dome of the
❽ **London Central Mosque** on the far west side of the park, or—if it's a summer evening or a Sunday afternoon—witness a remarkable re-

cent phenomenon. Wherever you look, the sport being enthusiastically played (subject to the ritual annual banning by the park authorities) is not cricket but softball, now Britain's fastest-growing participant sport (bring your mitt). Actually, you're likely to see cricket, too.

Continue along the Broad Walk, and you will reach an institution that opened in 1828, peaked in the 1950s (when more than 3 million visitors passed through its turnstiles every year), but recently faced the prospect of closing its gates forever: the **London Zoo.** The problems started when animal-crazy Brits, apparently anxious about the morality of caging wild beasts, simply stopped visiting. But the zoo fought back, pulling heartstrings with a *Save Our Zoo* campaign and tragic predictions of mass euthanasia for homeless polar bears and, at the 11th hour, found commercial sponsorship that was generous enough not only to keep the wolves from the door (or the wolves indoors) but to fund a great big modernization program.

Zoo highlights that will remain include the **Elephant and Rhino Pavilion,** which closely resembles the South Bank Arts Complex; the graceful **Snowdon Aviary,** spacious enough to allow its tenants free flight; and the 1936 **Penguin Pool,** where feeding time sends small children into raptures. Plans include the construction of a desert swarming with locusts; a rainforest alive with butterflies, bats, and hummingbirds; and a cave lit by fireflies. This being the headquarters of the Zoological Society of London, much work is done here in wildlife conservation, education, and the breeding of endangered species, and the new funding will enable even more emphasis to be placed on these spheres and more displays to help explain them to visitors. The first step along this road is the new **Children's Zoo,** which shows how people and animals live together and features domestic animals from around the world. *Regent's Park, tel. 0171/722–3333. Admission: £6.95 adults, £5.95 senior citizens, £4.95 children under 14, under 4 free. Penguin feed, 2:30; aquarium feed, 2:30; reptile feed, 2:30 Fri. only; elephant bath, 3:45. Open summer, daily 9–6; winter, daily 10–4; closed Dec. 25. Tube: Camden Town, and bus 74.*

From here, you can take the water bus and spy on the back gardens along the **Grand Union Canal** (which everyone calls the Regent's Canal) to Little Venice. Don't get *too* excited—the canal you're on (constructed 1812–20) is the only one there is, but this peaceful little bit of London does have an atmosphere unique to it, with enormous white wedding-cake houses set back from the banks, and it's a good strolling location. (For more on canal trips, *see* Important Contacts A to Z in the Gold Guide, *above.*)

North of the zoo, cross Prince Albert Road to **Primrose Hill,** a high point (literally, at 206 feet), and the best place to be on the night of November 5, when London's biggest bonfire burns a Guy Fawkes effigy (*see* The Houses of Parliament in Westminster and Royal London, *above*), and there's a spectacular fireworks display. Heading east from here (Regent's Park Road, then left down Parkway is the easiest route) brings you to the center of Camden Town, the neighborhood that, according to recent censuses, houses London's highest concentration of single people in their 20s.

This demographic will quickly become obvious as you flail in seas of creative haircuts and store after store of identical T-shirts, clompy boots, vintage frocks, and cheap leathers. Camden definitely has its charms, though. Gentrification has been layered over a once overwhelmingly Irish neighborhood, vestiges of which coexist with the youth culture: the Inverness Street fruit-and-vegetable market alongside the Arlington House homeless shelter, architects' offices, and antiques stores. Dominating everything are the markets that brought in the crowds. Turning left at the foot of Parkway, and bat-

tling north along Camden High Street (actually, the crowds are un-
❶ bearably dense only on the weekend), you reach **Camden Lock,**
which is indeed a pair of locks on the Grand Union Canal, now developed into a vast market that sells just about everything, but mostly
crafts, clothing (vintage, ethnic, and young designer), and antiques.

Escaping the mayhem is easy if you take the canal towpath in either
direction. Going west—a green and pleasant stroll in summer—you
reach Regent's Park in no time, with some fancy houses to admire
along the way. The easterly walk is less scenic by far, but interesting: You pass by housing projects and light-industrial buildings on
the way to **King's Cross,** site of one of London's main train stations,
of the new British Library building, of vast acres belonging to British Rail (where a massive redevelopment scheme has currently
stalled), and of the city's highest concentration of streetwalkers.

About a mile along the towpath, in a former ice-storage house, is the
❷ quirky little **London Canal Museum.** Here you can learn about the
rise and fall of London's once extensive canal network: the trade, the
vessels, and the way of life. Outside, on the Battlebridge Basin,
float the gaily painted narrow boats of modern canal dwellers—a
few steps and a world away from what remains one of London's least
salubrious neighborhoods, despite recent police action to clean up
street activities like drug dealing and prostitution. *12–13 New
Wharf Rd., tel. 0171/713–0836. Admission: £2.50 adults, £1.25 children and senior citizens. Open Apr.–Sept., Tues.–Sun. 10–4; call
for winter hours; closed national holidays. Tube: King's Cross.*

Hampstead

You can take a detour to the unlovely Swiss Cottage environs to stop
❸ off at the **Freud Museum.** The father of psychoanalysis lived here for
only a few months, between his escape from Nazi persecution in his
native Vienna in 1938 and his death in 1939. Many of his possessions
emigrated with him and were set up by his daughter Anna (herself a
pioneer of child psychoanalysis) as a shrine to her father's life and
work. Four years after Anna's death in 1982, the house was opened
as a museum. It replicates the atmosphere of Freud's famous consulting rooms, particularly through the presence of the Couch.
You'll find Freud-related books, lectures, and study groups here,
too. *20 Maresfield Gdns., tel. 0171/435–2002. Admission: £2.50
adults, £1.50 senior citizens, children under 12 free. Open Wed.–
Sun. noon–5; closed Easter, Dec. 24–26, Jan. 1. Tube: Swiss Cottage, Finchley Road.*

If you skip Freud's house, three stops on the Northern Line from
Camden Town tube (make sure you take the Edgware branch) will
plant you squarely 181 feet below central Hampstead, in London's
deepest tube station. The cliché about **Hampstead** is that it is just
like a pretty little village—albeit one with designer shops, expensive French delicatessens, restaurants, cafés, cinemas, and so on. In
fact, like so many London neighborhoods, Hampstead did start as a
separate village, when plague-bedeviled medieval Londoners fled
the city to this clean hilltop 4 miles away. By the 18th century, its
reputation for cleanliness had spread so far that its water was being
bottled and sold to the hoi polloi down the hill as the Perrier of its
day. That was the beginning of Hampstead's heyday as an artistic
and literary retreat that attracted many famous writers, painters,
and musicians to its leafy lanes—as it still does today. Just strolling
around here is rewarding: Not only are the streets incredibly picturesque, they also harbor some of London's best Georgian buildings.

❹ The best, and most concentrated, collection is strung along **Church
Row,** said to be London's most complete Georgian street. At the
west end is the 1745 "village" church of **St. John's,** where the painter
John Constable is buried. **Flask Walk** is another pretty street, nar-

row and shop lined at the High Street end, then widening after you pass The Flask—the pub it is named for, which, in turn, is named for the flasks that contained the therapeutically clean Hampstead spa water. The pub has a pretty courtyard, by the way. Nearby **Well Walk** was where the spring surfaced, its place now marked by a dried-up fountain. John Constable lived here, as well as John Keats and, later, D. H. Lawrence.

⑮ Keats moved on in 1818, though, to what is now known as **Keats House** in, well, Keats Grove. Here you can see the plum tree under which the young Romantic poet composed the *Ode to a Nightingale*, many of his original manuscripts, his library, and other possessions he managed to acquire in his short life. He died in Rome of consumption, aged 25, two years after moving in here. *Keats House, Wentworth Pl., Keats Grove, tel. 0171/435-2062. Admission free. Open Apr.–Oct., weekdays 10–6, Sat. 10–5, Sun. and national holidays 2–5; Nov.–Mar., weekdays 1–5, Sat. 10–5, Sun. 2–5; closed 1 hour at lunch and Easter, May Day, Dec. 24–26, Jan. 1. Tube: Hampstead.*

However pretty the houses may be, the nicest thing about Hampstead is **Hampstead Heath,** which spreads for miles to the north and is utterly wild in parts. On the southwest corner stands the rebuilt **⑯** version of a famous inn, **Jack Straw's Castle.** The inn is named after the Peasant Revolt leader who hid out and was captured here in 1381 after destroying Sir Robert Hales's residence and Priory, the Prior of St. John. Hales was hated for enforcing the poll tax, which led to the uprising.

Another historic pub stands off the northwest edge of the Heath, on **⑰** Hampstead Lane. The **Spaniards Inn** is, in contrast to Jack Straw's Castle, little changed since the early 18th century, when (they say) the notorious highwayman Dick Turpin hung out here. Keats also drank here, as did Shelley and Byron—but not Dickens. When his eternal pub crawl brought him up to Hampstead, Dickens preferred Jack Straw's Castle.

The main sight on the Heath, aside from the woods, ponds, and over-**⑱** all rural bliss, is **Kenwood House.** This magnificent mansion was first built in 1616 and remodeled by Robert Adam in 1764. Adam refaced most of the exterior and added the glorious library, which, with its curved, painted ceiling and gilded detailing, is the highlight of the house. The other unmissable part is the **Iveagh Bequest**—a collection of paintings that the earl of Iveagh gave the nation in 1927, starring a Rembrandt self-portrait and works by Reynolds, Van Dyck, Hals, Gainsborough, Vermeer, and Turner. In front of the house, a graceful lawn slopes down to a little lake crossed by a dinky bridge—all in perfect 18th-century upper-class taste. Nowadays the lake is dominated by its **concert bowl,** which stages a popular summer series of orchestral concerts, including at least one performance of Handel's *Music for the Royal Fireworks*, complete with fireworks. *Hampstead La., tel. 0181/348-1286. Admission free. Open Easter–Sept., 10–6, Oct.–Easter, 10–4; closed Christmas. Tube: Golder's Green, then bus 210.*

To the east of Hampstead, and also topping a hill, is the former village of **Highgate,** which has some fine houses, especially along its Georgian High Street, and retains a peaceful period atmosphere. **⑲** What it is most famous for is **Highgate Cemetery,** a sprawling early Victorian graveyard featuring many an overwrought stone memorial, especially on its older, west side—which can be visited only by a tour given by the Friends of Highgate Cemetery, a group of volunteers who virtually saved the place from ruin. The shady streets of the dead, Egyptian Avenue and the Circle of Lebanon on the west side, are particularly Poe-like, but the famous graves are mostly on the newer, less atmospheric east side, which is still in use and may be wandered freely. Karl Marx's enormous black bust is probably the most visited place, but George Eliot is also buried here. This is not London's oldest cemetery—that distinction belongs to Kensal Green, with its spine-chilling catacombs and Gothic mausolea (*see* Off the Beaten Track, *below*). *Swains La., Highgate, tel. 0181/340–1834. Admission: east side, £1; west side tour, £2. East side open Apr.–Oct., daily 10–4:45; Oct.–Mar., daily 10–3:45. West side tours: Apr.–Oct., weekdays 2 PM and 4 PM, weekends periodically 11–4; Nov.–Mar., weekdays noon, 2, and 3; weekends periodically 11–3. Closed Dec. 25 and for funerals. Tube: Archway.*

Greenwich

Numbers in the margin correspond to points of interest on the Greenwich map.

About 8 miles downstream—which means seaward, to the east—from central London lies a neighborhood you'd think had been designed to provide the perfect day out. **Greenwich** is another of London's self-contained "villages," the only one with unique and splendid sights surrounding the residential portion. Sir Christopher Wren's Royal Naval College and Inigo Jones's Queen's House reach architectural heights; the Old Royal Observatory measures time for our entire planet; and the Greenwich Meridian divides the world in two—you can stand astride it with one foot in either hemisphere. The National Maritime Museum and the proud clipper ship *Cutty Sark* are thrilling to seafaring types, and landlubbers can stroll the green acres of parkland that surround the buildings, the quaint 19th-century houses, and the weekend crafts and antiques markets.

The journey to Greenwich is fun itself, especially if you approach by river, arriving to the best possible vista of the Royal Naval College, with the Queen's House behind. On the way, the boat glides past famous sights on the London skyline (there's a guaranteed spine chill on passing the Tower) and ever-changing docklands, and there's always a cockney navigator enhancing the views with wiseguy commentary. The trip takes about an hour from Westminster Pier (next to Big Ben) and 25 minutes from the Tower of London. (*See* Guided Tours in Chapter 1, Essential Information).

The least interesting, but fastest, route to Greenwich is on the Network SouthEast train from Charing Cross, which takes about 10 minutes. This is London's oldest railway line, but you can also take the newest: the Docklands Light Railway (DLR). The DLR, a high-speed elevated track, which opened in 1987, connects with the tube network at Bank; alternatively, you can pick it up at Tower Gateway, a two-minute walk from the Tower Hill tube stop. The DLR brings you to Island Gardens, exactly opposite the Royal Naval College, with the finest possible view, of course. You can't miss the squat little circular brick building with its glass-domed roof. This is also the entrance to the Greenwich Foot Tunnel, where an ancient elevator takes you down to a walkway under the Thames that brings you up close to the *Cutty Sark*.

Since the pleasure boats also land hereabouts, we'll start at this romantic tea clipper, which happens to provide a great way into the
❶ Greenwich riches. The *Cutty Sark* was built in 1869, one of fleets and fleets of similar wooden tall-masted clippers, which plied the seven seas during the 19th century, trading in exotic commodities—tea, in this case. The *Cutty Sark*, the last to survive, was also the fastest, sailing the China–London route in 1871 in only 107 days. Now the photogenic vessel lies in dry dock, a museum of one kind of seafaring life—and not a comfortable kind for the 28-strong crew, as you'll see. The collection of figureheads is amusing, too. *King Wil-*

Greenwich

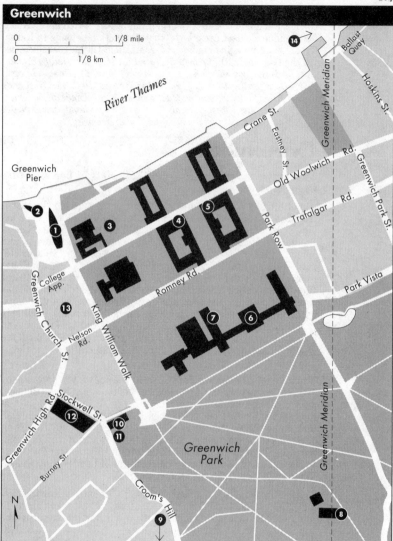

0   1/8 mile
0   1/8 km

River Thames

Greenwich Pier

Crane St.

Eastney St.

Old Woolwich Rd.

Greenwich Meridian

Ballast Quay

Hoskins St.

Greenwich Park St.

Trafalgar Rd.

Park Row

College App.

Greenwich Church St.

Nelson Rd.

King William Walk

Romney Rd.

Park Vista

Greenwich High Rd.

Stockwell St.

Burney St.

Croom's Hill

Greenwich Park

Greenwich Meridian

N

College Chapel, **5**
Covered Crafts
Market, **13**
Cutty Sark, **1**
Fan Museum, **11**
Gipsy Moth IV, **2**
Greenwich Antique
Market, **12**
Greenwich Theatre, **10**
National Maritime
Museum, **7**
Old Royal
Observatory, **8**
Painted Hall, **4**
Queen's House, **6**
Ranger's House, **9**
Royal Naval College, **3**
Thames Barrier, **14**

liam Walk, tel. 0181/858–3445. Admission: £3.25 adults, £2.25 children under 16 and senior citizens. Open Apr.–Sept., Mon.–Sat. 10–6, Sun. and public holidays noon–6; Oct.–Mar., Mon.–Sat. 10–5, Sun. and public holidays noon–5. Last admission 30 min. before closing. Closed Dec. 24–26.

2 While you're there, don't miss the adjacent dry-docked *Gipsy Moth IV,* the boat in which Sir Francis Chichester achieved the first single-handed circumnavigation of the globe in 1966. Inside you'll see the tiny space the sailor endured for 226 days and the ingenious way everything he needed was installed. The queen knighted him on board here, using the same sword with which the previous Elizabeth had knighted that other seagoing Francis, Sir Francis Drake, three centuries before. *King William Walk, tel. 0181/858–3445. Admission: 50p adults, 30p children and senior citizens. Open Apr.–Oct., Mon.–Sat. 10–6, Sun. noon–6; closed Nov.–Mar.*

Now that you have some salt in your veins, you can begin to penetrate the heart of Greenwich. By continuing along King William
3 Walk, you come to the wrought-iron gates of the **Royal Naval College,** which Wren began in 1694 as a home, or hospital (cf. the Royal Hospital in Chelsea), for ancient mariners, but which became this school for young ones in 1873. You'll notice how the blocks part to reveal the Queen's House across the central lawns. Wren, with the help of his assistant, Hawksmoor, was at pains to preserve the river vista from the house, and there are few more majestic views in London than the awe-inspiring symmetry he achieved. Behind the col-
4 lege are two buildings you can visit. The **Painted Hall,** the college's dining hall, derives its name from the baroque murals of William and Mary (reigned 1609–1782) and assorted allegorical figures, the whole supported by trompe l'oeil pillars that Sir James Thornhill (who decorated the inside of St. Paul's dome, too) painted between
5 1707 and 1717. In the opposite block stands the **College Chapel,** which was rebuilt after a fire in 1779 and is altogether lighter, in a more restrained, neo-Grecian style. At Christmas 1805, Admiral Nelson's body was brought from the battle of Trafalgar to lie in state here. *Royal Naval College, King William Walk, tel. 0181/858–2154. Admission free. Open Fri.–Wed. 2:30–4:45.*

From the south end of the Royal Naval College, you approach the
6 building that Wren's majestic quadrangles frame, the **Queen's House.** The queen whom Inigo Jones began designing it for in 1616 was James I's Anne of Denmark, but she died three years later, and it was Charles I's French wife, Henrietta Maria, who inherited the building when it was completed in 1635. It is no less than Britain's first classical building—the first, that is, to use the lessons of Italian Renaissance architecture—and is therefore of enormous importance in the history of English architecture. Inside, the Tulip Stair, named for the fleur-de-lys–style pattern on the balustrade, is especially fine, spiraling up, without a central support, to the Great Hall. The Great Hall itself is a perfect cube, exactly 40 feet in all three directions, and decorated with paintings of the Muses, the Virtues, and the Liberal Arts. *Admission: £4.95 adults, £2.95 children, £3.95 senior citizens, including National Maritime Museum and Old Royal Observatory. Open Mon.–Sat. 10–6, Sun. noon–6; closed Good Friday, May Day, Dec. 24–27, Jan. 1. White Card valid.*

The Queen's House forms part of Greenwich's star attraction, the
7 **National Maritime Museum,** which you come to now. The place contains everything to do with the British at sea, in the form of paintings, models, maps, globes, sextants, uniforms (especially the one Nelson died in at Trafalgar, complete with bloodstained bullet hole), and—best of all—actual boats, including a collection of ornate, gilded royal barges. *Romney Rd., tel. 0181/858–4422. Admission and opening hours same as Queen's House above.*

Now head up the hill in Greenwich Park overlooking the Naval College and Maritime Museum to the **Old Royal Observatory,** founded in 1675 by Charles II. That same year, Wren built it for John Flamsteed, the first Astronomer Royal, but the red ball you see on its roof has been there only since 1833. The ball drops every day at 1 PM, and you can set your watch by it, as the sailors on the Thames always have. In fact, nearly everyone sets his or her watch by it, since this "Greenwich Timeball" and the Gate Clock inside the observatory are the most visible manifestations of Greenwich Mean Time, since 1884 the ultimate standard for time around the world. Also here is the **Prime Meridian,** a brass line laid on the cobblestones at zero degrees longitude, one side being the eastern hemisphere, and the other, the western hemisphere. In 1948, the Old Royal Observatory lost its official status: London's glow had grown too intense, and the astronomers moved to Sussex, while the Astronomer Royal decamped to Cambridge. They left various telescopes, chronometers, and clocks for you to view in their absence. *Greenwich Park, tel. 0181/858–4422. Joint admission with National Maritime Museum (see above). Opening hours as for the National Maritime Museum.*

Greenwich Park itself is one of London's oldest royal parks. It had been in existence for well over 200 years before Charles II commissioned the French landscape artist Le Nôtre (who was responsible for Versailles and for St. James's Park) to redesign it in what was, in the 1660s, the latest French fashion. The Flower Garden on the southeast side and the deer enclosure nearby are particularly pleasant. Look also for **Queen Elizabeth's Oak** on the east side, around which Henry VIII and his second queen, Anne Boleyn, Elizabeth I's mother, are said to have danced.

Just outside the park boundaries, on the southwest side, stands the **Ranger's House,** a handsome early 18th-century mansion, which was the Greenwich park ranger's official residence during the 19th century and now houses collections of Jacobean portraits and early musical instruments. Concerts are regularly given here. *Chesterfield Walk, Blackheath, tel. 0181/853–0035. Admission free. Open daily Apr.–Sept. 10–6, Oct.–Mar. 10–4 except for 1 hour at lunch; closed Good Friday, Dec. 24–26, Jan. 1.*

Walking back through the park toward the river, you'll enter the pretty streets of Greenwich Village to the west. There are plenty of bookstores and antiques shops for browsing, and, at the foot of Crooms Hill, the modern **Greenwich Theatre.** Officially a West End theater, despite its location, it mounts well-regarded, often star-spangled productions. *Tel. 0181/858–7755.*

Immediately opposite the theater, in two newly restored houses dating from the 1820s, is the highly unusual **Fan Museum.** The 2,000 fans here, which date from the 17th century onward, constitute the world's only such collection, and the history and purpose of these often exquisitely crafted objects are explained satisfyingly. It was the personal vision—and fan collection—of Helene Alexander that brought it into being in 1991, and the workshop and conservation and study center that she has also set up ensure that this anachronistic art will have a future. *10–12 Croom's Hill, tel. 0181/858–7879. Admission: £2.50 adults, £1.50 children under 15 and senior citizens. Open Tues.–Sat. 11–4:30, Sun. noon–4:30; closed Dec. 24–26, Jan. 1.*

If you're visiting on a weekend, there are two excellent markets. The **Greenwich Antique Market** (open 8–4), on Burney Street near the museum and theater, has a lot of bric-a-brac and books and is well known among the cognoscenti as a good source of vintage clothes. The Victorian **Covered Crafts Market** (open 9–5) you'll find by the *Cutty Sark,* on College Approach. As you'd expect, this one features crafts, but there are more of the sort of ceramics, jewelry, knitwear, and leather goods that you may actually want to own than is common in such places, and you get to buy them off the people who made them. The goods at these markets are mostly reasonably priced, indeed.

A few miles farther downstream—another 25-minute boat ride away (though you can also get here by Network SouthEast trains from Greenwich or Charing Cross to Charlton)—is the amazing **Thames Barrier,** a mammoth piece of civil engineering that will come in handy if the water table ever again rises as high as it did in 1928 and 1953 and London is threatened with another flood. This curiously haunting ¼-mile-long barrier, with its 10 upstanding steel gates, contains enough concrete to build 10 miles of six-lane freeway and looks like a cross between the Sydney Opera House and a line of submerged alien beings. You can't visit the control room, but there's an exhibition, with videos explaining why it's necessary and how it works, and you can walk along the riverbank close to it, though the best view is from out on the river. Also here is **Hallett's Panorama,** an incongruous re-creation, with oils and sculpture, of the city of Bath, and the Soviet navy's largest submarine, the 1967-vintage **U-475 Foxtrot,** moored at nearby Long's Wharf. *Unity Way, off Woolwich Rd., tel. 0181/854–1373. Admission (including Hallett's Panorama): £2.50 adults, £1.55 children and senior citizens. Open weekdays 10:30–5, weekends 10:30–5:30; closed Dec. 25–26, Jan. 1. Russian submarine, admission: £3.95 adults, £2 children. Open daily 10–6; closed Dec. 25–26, Jan. 1.*

The Thames Upstream

The Thames is Britain's longest river. It winds its way through the Cotswolds, beyond the "dreaming spires" of Oxford and past majestic Windsor Castle—far more the lazy, leafy country river than the dark gray urban waterway you see in London. Once you leave the city center, going west, or upstream, you reach a series of former villages—Chiswick, Kew, Richmond, and Putney—that, apart from the roar of aircraft coming in to land at Heathrow a few miles farther west, still retain a peaceful, almost rural atmosphere, especially in places where parkland rolls down to the riverbank. In fact, it was really only at the beginning of this century that these villages expanded into London proper. The royal palaces and grand houses that dot the area were built not as town houses but as country residences with easy access to London by river.

Each of the places we list here could easily absorb a whole day of your time (Hampton Court is especially huge), and it may be wise to resist attempting to see everything. Access is fairly easy: The District Line of the Underground runs out to Kew and Richmond, as does Network SouthEast from Waterloo, which also serves Twickenham and Hampton Court. Chiswick House can be reached by tube to Turnham Green and then by the E3 bus or by tube to Hammersmith and Bus 290.

Of course, the best, if slowest, way to go is by river. Boats depart Westminster Pier (just by Big Ben) for Kew (1½ hours), Richmond (2–3 hours), and Hampton Court (4 hours) several times a day in summer and less frequently from October through March. As you can tell from those sailing times, the boat trip is worth taking only if you make it an integral part of your day out, and even then, be aware that it can get very breezy on the water and that the scenery going upstream is by no means constantly fascinating. *Westminster Pier, tel. 0171/930–4097.*

Chiswick and Kew

Chiswick is the nearest of these Thames-side destinations to London, with Kew just a mile or so beyond it. Much of Chiswick today is a nondescript suburb developed at the beginning of this century. But, incongruously stranded among the terraced houses, a number of fine 18th-century houses and a charming little village survive. The peacock of the flock is **Chiswick House,** built circa 1725 by the earl of Burlington as a country residence in which to entertain friends and as a kind of temple to the arts. It is the very model of a Palladian villa, inspired by the Villa Capra near Vicenza in northeastern Italy. The house fans out from a central octagonal room in perfect symmetry, guarded by statues of Burlington's heroes, Palladio himself and his disciple Inigo Jones. Burlington's friends— Pope, Swift, Gay, and Handel, among others—were well qualified to adorn a temple to the arts.

This is the Lord Burlington of Burlington House, Piccadilly, home of the Royal Academy and, of course, Burlington Arcade. It goes without saying that he was a great connoisseur and an important patron of the arts, but he was also an accomplished architect in his own right, fascinated—obsessed even—by the architecture and art of the Italian Renaissance and ancient Rome, with which he'd fallen in love during his Italian grand tour (every well-bred boy's rite of passage). Along with William Kent (1685–1748), who designed the interiors and the rambling gardens here, Burlington did an awful lot to disseminate the Palladian ideals around Britain: Chiswick House sparked enormous interest, and you'll see these forms reflected in hundreds of subsequent English stately homes, both small and large. *Burlington La., tel. 0181/995–0508. Admission: £2.30 adults, £1.70 senior citizens, £1.15 children under 16. Open Apr.–Sept., daily 10–6; Oct.–Mar., daily 10–4; closed 1 hour at lunch and Dec. 25–26, Jan. 1. Tube: Turnham Green.*

Close to Chiswick House, but unprotected from the six-lane Great West Road, which remains a main route to the West Country, is **Hogarth's House,** where the painter lived from 1749 until his death in 1764. Although the poor house is besieged by the surrounding traffic, it contains a little museum consisting mostly of the amusingly moralistic engravings for which Hogarth is best known, including the most famous one, *The Rake's Progress* series of 1735. *Hogarth La., tel. 0181/994–6757. Admission free. Open Apr.–Sept., Mon.– Sat. 11–6, Sun. 2–6; Oct.–Mar., Mon.–Sat. 11–4, Sun. 2–4; closed Good Friday, first 3 wks of Sept., last 3 wks of Dec., Jan. 1. Tube: Turnham Green.*

Church Street (reached by an underpass) is the nearest thing to a sleepy country village street in all of London, despite its proximity to the Great West Road. Follow it down to the Thames and turn left at its foot to reach the sturdy 18th-century riverfront houses of **Chiswick Mall.** The half-mile walk along here takes you far away from London and into a world of elegance and calm.

There's a similarly peaceful walk to be had about a mile to the west, along the 18th-century river frontage of **Strand-on-the-Green,** whose houses look over the narrow towpath to the river, their tidy brick facades covered with wisteria and roses in summer. Strand-on-the-Green ends at Kew Bridge, opposite which is **Kew Green,** where local teams play cricket on summer Sundays. All around it are fine 18th-century houses and, in the center, a church in which the painters Gainsborough and John Zoffany (1733–1810) are buried.

The village atmosphere of Kew is still distinct, making this one of the most desirable areas of outer London. What makes Kew famous, though, are the Royal Botanic Gardens, known simply as **Kew Gardens:** a spectacular 300 acres of public gardens, containing more than 60,000 species of plants. In addition, this is the country's leading botanical institute, with strong royal associations. Until 1840, when Kew Gardens was handed over to the nation, it had been the grounds of two royal residences: the White House (formerly Kew House) and Richmond Lodge, or the Dutch House. George II and Queen Caroline lived at Richmond Lodge in the 1720s, while their eldest son, Frederick, Prince of Wales, and his wife, Princess Augusta, came to the White House during the 1730s.

The royal wives were keen gardeners. Queen Caroline got to work on her grounds, while Frederick's pleasure garden next door was developed as a botanic garden by his widow after his death. Caroline introduced all kinds of "exotics," foreign plants brought back to England by botanists. She was aided by a skilled head gardener and by the architect Sir William Chambers, who built a series of temples and follies, of which the crazy 10-story **Pagoda** (1762), visible for miles around, is the star turn. The celebrated botanist Sir Joseph Banks (1743–1820) then took charge of Kew, which developed rapidly in both its roles—as a beautiful landscaped garden and as a center of study and research.

In 1802, George III, who had been brought up largely at Kew, united the two estates, knocking down the White House, which he intended to rebuild on a more lavish scale, and living in the Dutch House meanwhile. But George was, famously, losing his reason, and the new palace never got built. The Dutch House became known as **Kew Palace** and remains to this day quietly domestic. The little formal gardens to its rear were redeveloped in 1969 as a 17th-century garden. These, too, are a pleasure to see, with their trim hedges, statuary, and carefully laid-out plants and flowers. *Tel. 0181/940–3321. Admission: £1.20 adults, 90p senior citizens, 80p children under 16. Open Apr.–Sept., daily 11–5:30.*

It is not the palace that makes anyone remember a visit to Kew, though, but the two great 19th-century greenhouses filled with tropical plants, many of which have been there as long as their housing. Both the **Palm House** and the **Temperate House** were designed by Sir Decimus Burton, the first opening in 1848, the second in 1899 (though it had been begun 40 years earlier). The older Palm House, with its ornate cast-iron supports and curvaceous glass walls, is generally more celebrated than the later building, although on its completion the latter was the biggest greenhouse in the world and today contains the biggest greenhouse plant in the world, a Chilean wine palm rooted in 1846. You can climb the spiral staircase almost to the roof and look down on this and the dense tropical profusion from the walkway.

The **Princess of Wales Conservatory,** the latest and the largest plant house at Kew, was opened in 1987 by Princess Diana. Under its bold glass roofs, designed to maximize energy conservation, there are no fewer than 10 climatic zones, their temperatures all precisely controlled by computer. Within a few minutes you can move from the humid pool-and-swamp habitats, where the Amazon water lily flourishes, to the cloud-forest zone, which reproduces the conditions on the upper reaches of tropical mountains, through to the savanna of eastern Africa.

The **Centre for Economic Botany** is housed in the newly constructed Joseph Banks Building, the majority of which is devoted to Kew's research collection on economic botany and to its library. But the public can enjoy exhibitions here on the theme of plants in everyday life. *Admission free. Open Mon.–Sat. 9:10–4:30, Sun. 9:30–5:30.*

The plant houses make Kew worth visiting even in the depths of winter, but in spring and summer the gardens come into their own. In late spring, the woodland nature reserve of **Queen Charlotte's Cottage Gardens** is carpeted in bluebells; a little later, the **Rhododen-**

dron Dell and the **Azalea Garden** become swathed in brilliant color. High summer features glorious displays of roses and water lilies, while fall is the time to see the heather garden, near the pagoda. Whatever time of year you visit, something is in bloom, and your journey is never wasted. *Royal Botanic Gardens, tel. 0181/940–1171. Admission: £4 adults, £2 senior citizens and students, £1.50 children under 16. Gardens open at 9:30 daily, greenhouses at 10; closing time varies according to sunset, usually 4 PM in winter, later in summer. Tube: Kew Gardens.*

Osterley Park

You reach **Osterley Park** by getting off the Piccadilly Line five stops before Heathrow Airport, then making a 15-minute walk from the station. A unique hybrid of Tudor and 18th-century architecture, Osterley was built in the 1560s, then tinkered with extensively by Robert Adam two centuries later. The result is a Tudor brick mansion with a pepper-pot tower at each corner and a sweeping central staircase leading to an incongruous Doric-columned doorway with a carved pediment. The inside is maximum Adam, down to much of the furniture. The architect himself described it as being all "delicacy, gaiety, grace, and beauty," with "fanciful figures and winding foliage." Sir Horace Walpole, on the other hand, found much of it "too theatric"—an attribute rather in its favor if you don't have to live in it but are just visiting. The outrageously elaborate neo-Gothic blue, green, and gold ceiling (with matching frilly window blinds and handloomed carpet) in the Drawing Room and the all-over fresco work of the Etruscan Room ("like Wedgwood's vase," said Walpole) are nothing if not arresting. When it all gets to be too much, you can retire to the gardens, designed by William Chambers (who was responsible for much of Kew Gardens, too), with an Adam greenhouse. *Isleworth, tel. 0181/560–3918. Admission: £3.50 adults, £1.75 children under 16. Open Apr.–Oct., Wed.–Sat. 1–5, Sun. 11–5; closed Nov.–Mar.*

Richmond

Named after the palace Henry VII built here in 1500, **Richmond** is still a welcoming and extremely pretty riverside "village" with many handsome (and mountainously expensive) houses; many antiques shops; a Victorian theater; and, best of all, the biggest of London's royal parks, **Richmond Park.** Charles I enclosed this one in 1637, as was done with practically all the parks, for hunting purposes. Unlike the others, however, Richmond Park still has wild red and fallow deer roaming its 2,470 acres of grassland and heath, among the oldest oaks you're likely to see—vestiges of the medieval forests that once encroached on London from all sides. **White Lodge,** inside the park, was built for George II in 1729. Edward VIII was born here; now it houses the Royal Ballet School. You can walk from the park past the fine 18th-century houses in and around **Richmond Hill** to the river, admiring first the view from the top. At the Thames, you may notice Quinlan Terry's recent **Richmond Riverside** development, which met with the approval of England's architectural adviser, Prince Charles, for its classical facades and was vilified by many others for playing it safe.

Ham House and Marble Hill House

To the west of Richmond Park, overlooking the Thames and nearly opposite the oddly named Eel Pie Island, stands **Ham House.** The house was built in 1610 by Sir Thomas Vavasour, knight marshal to James I, then refurbished later the same century by the duke and duchess of Lauderdale, who, although not particularly nice (a contemporary called the duchess "the coldest friend and the most violent enemy that ever was known"), managed to produce one of the finest houses in Britain at the time. Now that £2 million has been sunk into restoring Ham House—a project overseen by the National Trust—its splendor can be appreciated afresh. The formerly empty library has been filled with 17th- and 18th-century volumes; the original decorations in the Great Hall, Round Gallery, and Great Staircase have been replicated; and all the furniture and fittings, on permanent loan from the V&A, have been cleaned and restored. The 17th-century gardens, too, merit a visit in their own right. You can reach Ham from Richmond on Bus 65 or 371 or by one of Greater London's most pleasant rural walks, along the eastern riverbank south from Richmond Bridge for half an hour or so. *Ham St., Richmond, tel. 0181/940–1950. Admission: £4 adults, £2 children under 16 and senior citizens; admission to gardens free. Open Mar.–Oct., Sat.–Wed. 1–5; Nov.–Dec., weekends 1–5. Closed Jan.–Feb.*

On the northern bank of the Thames, almost opposite Ham House, stands another mansion, this one a near-perfect example of a Palladian villa. **Marble Hill House** was built in the 1720s by George II for his mistress, the "exceedingly respectable and respected" Henrietta Howard. Later the house was occupied by Mrs. Fitzherbert, who was secretly married to the Prince Regent (later George IV) in 1785. Marble Hill House was restored in 1901 and opened to the public two years later, looking very much like it did in Georgian times. A ferry service operates during the summer from Ham House across the river; access by foot is via a half-hour walk south along the west bank from Richmond Bridge. *Richmond Rd., Twickenham, tel. 0181/892–5115. Admission free. Open Easter–Sept., daily 10–6; Oct.–Easter, daily 10–4; closed Dec. 24–25, Jan. 1.*

Hampton Court Palace

Some 20 miles from central London, on a loop of the Thames upstream from Richmond, lies **Hampton Court,** one of London's oldest royal palaces, more like a small town in size, and requiring a day of your time to do it justice. The magnificent Tudor brick house was begun in 1514 by Cardinal Wolsey, the ambitious and worldly lord chancellor (roughly, prime minister) of England and archbishop of York. He wanted it to be the absolute best palace in the land, and in this he succeeded so effectively that Henry VIII grew deeply envious, whereupon Wolsey felt obliged to give Hampton Court to the king. Henry moved in in 1525, adding a great hall and chapel, and proceeded to live much of his rambunctious life here. James I made further improvements at the beginning of the 17th century, but by the end of the century the palace was getting rather run-down. Plans were drawn up by the joint monarchs William III and Mary II to demolish the building and replace it with a still larger and more splendid structure in conscious emulation of the great palace of Versailles outside Paris. However, the royal purse wouldn't stretch quite that far. It was decided to keep the original buildings but add a new complex adjoining them at the rear, for which Wren was commissioned, and his graceful South Wing is one of the highlights of the whole palace. (A severe fire badly damaged some of Wren's chambers in 1986, but they were restored and opened again in 1992, with some of the Tudor features he had covered up uncovered again.) William and, especially, Mary loved Hampton Court and left their mark on the place—see their fine collections of Delftware and other porcelain.

The site beside the slow-moving Thames is perfect. The palace itself, steeped in history, hung with priceless paintings, full of echoing cobbled courtyards and cavernous Tudor kitchens, complete with deer pies and cooking pots—not to mention the ghost of Catherine Howard, who is still abroad, screaming her innocence (of adul-

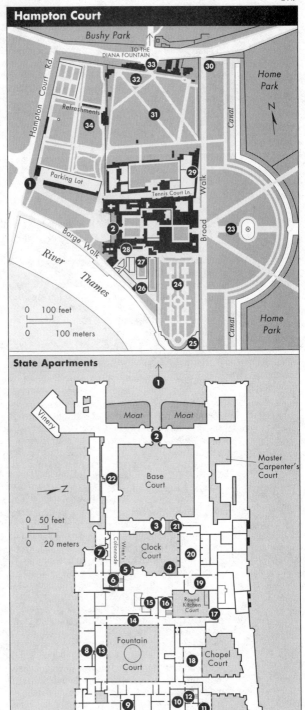

Hampton Court

State Apartments

tery) to an unheeding Henry VIII—is set in a fantastic array of ornamental gardens, lakes, and ponds. Among the horticultural highlights are an Elizabethan Knot Garden; Henry VIII's Pond Garden; the enormous conical yews around the Fountain Garden; and the Great Vine near the Banqueting House, planted in 1768 and still producing Black Hamburg grapes, which you can buy in season. Best of all is the celebrated maze, which you enter to the north of the palace. It was planted in 1714 and is truly fiendish.

Royalty ceased living here with George III; poor George preferred the seclusion of Kew, where he was finally confined in his madness. The private apartments that range down one side of the palace are now occupied by pensioners of the Crown. Known as "grace and favor" apartments, they are among the most covetably positioned homes in the country, with a surfeit of peace and history on their doorsteps. *East Molesey, tel. 0181/977–8441. Admission: apartments and maze £7 adults, £5.30 senior citizens, £4.70 children under 16; maze only £1.75 adults and senior citizens, £1.10 children; grounds free. State apartments open Apr.–Oct., Tues.–Sun. 9:30–6, Mon. 10:15–6; Nov.–Mar., Tues.–Sun. 9:30–4:30, Mon. 10:15–4:30; grounds open daily 8–dusk. Closed Good Friday, Dec. 24–25, Jan. 1.*

Off the Beaten Track

Regent's Canal From **Camden Lock,** follow the tow path of the **Regent's Canal** (*see* Regent's Park and Hampstead, *above*) east for a fascinating view of London and Londoners at home. The canal runs past the elegant houses of Islington and then through increasingly less prosperous areas, eventually reaching the Thames at Limehouse. There's a great deal of interest for the curious observer—private homes and semisecret back gardens running down to the water, wide views south to the tower blocks of the City, and old industrial areas. The canal runs alongside Victoria Park in Hackney, one of the capital's first public parks. Follow it the other way, and you're led the back way around the perimeter of Regent's Park and on through Paddington (part posh villas, part housing projects) to Little Venice, literally one of London's more hidden backwaters. Refresh yourself at the picturesque Bridge House pub (Delamere Terr.). There are numerous exits from the canal towpath to the surrounding streets.

Docklands London's most rapidly changing neighborhood has emerged from what only a decade ago was an even less frequented area—partly low-cost residential, partly working docks, partly wasteland. Now it houses national newspaper offices, a brand-new riverside business community containing Britain's tallest building, sports facilities, and even a farm. Its boundaries are roughly defined by **Tower Bridge** and the **Design Museum** to the west (*see* Butler's Wharf to Old St. Thomas's in The South Bank, *above*), and **London City Airport** and the **Royal Docks** to the east, though the area inside a loop of the Thames called the **Isle of Dogs** is of the most interest. Take the hightech **Docklands Light Railway** (DLR) to Crossharbour (change at Bank) and pick up a free map at the **London Docklands Visitors Centre,** where an exhibition, information desk, and film introduce the area. *3 Limeharbour, Isle of Dogs, tel. 0171/512–1111. Open weekdays 9–6, weekends and holidays 10–4:30. Bus tours of the area depart Tues. at 2, Thurs. at 10:30, Sun. at 11:30.*

Off-season, the upbeat tone is belied by the absence of crowds, and indeed, Docklands is by no means an unmitigated success story. More than 16,000 new homes have been constructed, but many remain unsold, and much of the 28 million square feet of commercial and industrial development lies empty. **Canary Wharf,** with its 50-story **Tower** (1 Canada Sq.) by the architect of New York City's World Trade Center, Cesar Pelli, is the most notorious development project Britain has seen in years. Olympia & York, the Canadian developers, went bust; bomb scares closed the observation deck; the arts funding ran out; shops stayed unrented; jokes were made. But here are waterfront promenades and pubs, a new London piazza called **Cabot Square,** a large concert hall, and a (rather unexciting) shopping mall. *Canary Wharf Visitor Center, Cabot Pl. E, tel. 0171/ 418–2000.*

A different approach is to get off the DLR at **Island Gardens** for a spectacular view across the river to the Naval College of Greenwich—which you can walk to via the **Greenwich Foot Tunnel** under the Thames. There's a small information center next to the DLR station (open weekdays 10–4:30). Or on a summer evening, you can bring a picnic to the Isle of Dogs and watch cricket in **Millwall Park** across Manchester Road. North of the park, **Mudchute Farm** is a real working farm, complete with animals and a riding school. *E. Ferry Rd., tel. 0171/515–5901. Admission free. DLR: Mudchute.*

Dulwich   **Dulwich Village** in southeast London has handsome 18th-century houses strung out along its main street. Most of the land around here belongs to the Dulwich College Estate—founded in the early 17th century by the actor Edward Alleyn—which keeps strict control of modern development. The village is a pleasant place to wander on a sunny summer day. **Dulwich Park** is a well-kept municipal park with a particularly fine display of rhododendrons in late May. Opposite the park gates is the **Dulwich Picture Gallery,** a lovely small gallery with works by Rembrandt, Van Dyck, Rubens, Poussin, and Gainsborough, among others; the gallery was designed by Sir John Soane (*see* Bloomsbury and Legal London, *above*). To get to Dulwich, take the Network South East surface train from Victoria to West Dulwich or from London Bridge to North Dulwich. *College Rd., tel. 0181/693–5254. Admission: £2 adults, children under 16 free, £1 senior citizens. Open Tues.–Fri. 10–1 and 2–5, Sat. 11–5, Sun. 2–5; closed national holidays.*

If you have enough energy left after exploring Dulwich and the Picture Gallery, walk through the park and then south for about half a mile to another delightful small museum, the **Horniman Museum.**

The Royal Air   **The Royal Air Force Museum** in north London is a must for flying and
Force Museum   military enthusiasts. The story of the R.A.F. is told in great detail, and there are uniforms, guns, and radar equipment on display, as well as detailed sections on World War I and World War II exploits, including the work of the Bomber Command. The **Battle of Britain Museum** in the same complex (no extra charge) explains how the R.A.F. fought off the German Luftwaffe in 1940. The nearest tube stop is Colindale, a 15-minute walk from the museum. *Grahame Park Way, Hendon, tel. 0181/205–2266. Admission: £5.20 adults, £2.60 children under 16 and senior citizens. Open daily 10–6; closed Dec. 25–26, Jan. 1.*

North   After you visit the Thames Barrier (*see* Greenwich, *above*), make
Woolwich   your way east into Woolwich, take the open-deck car ferry across
Old Station   the river, and visit the **North Woolwich Old Station Museum.** This
Museum   museum has displays on the history of railways in east London, as well as locomotives, rolling stock, and a reconstructed 1910 booking office. Return to central London by overground train from North Woolwich. *Pier Rd., N. Woolwich, tel. 0171/474–7244. Admission free. Open Mon.–Sat. 10–5, Sun. and national holidays 2–5; telephone to check Christmas and Easter week opening times.*

Kensal Green   Heralding itself as "London's first Necropolis," this west London
Cemetery   cemetery was established in 1832 and beats the more famous Highgate for atmosphere, if only because it's less populated with live people. Within its 77 acres are more freestanding mausolea than in any other cemetery in Britain, some of them almost the size of small churches, and most of them constructed while their future oc-

cupants were still alive. Those who balked at burial but couldn't afford a mausoleum of their own could opt for a position in the catacombs, and these, with their stacks of moldering caskets, are a definite highlight for seekers of the macabre, though they can be seen only as part of a tour. In the cemetery you will find the final resting places of the novelists Trollope, Thackeray, and Wilkie Collins; of the great engineer Isambard Kingdom Brunel; and of Decimus Burton, Victorian architect of the Athenaeum Club, the Wellington Arch, the Kew Gardens greenhouses, and many other bits of London you'll have just seen. To get here, take the Bakerloo line tube to Kensal Green, then Bus 18, which stops outside the gates. *Harrow Rd. W10, tel. 0181/969–0152. Suggested donation: £2. Open Mon.–Sat. 9–5:30, Sun. 10–5:30 (times may vary Nov.–Feb., so call first). 2-hr guided tours (including catacombs) Mar.–Oct., weekends 2:30; Oct.–Feb., Sun. 2. Catacomb tours first Sun. of the month; phone for times.*

5 Shopping for Bargains

Shopping is almost as big a priority in London as sightseeing, but you have to know where and when to go to pick up a bargain. Generally, the sale seasons are January and June, although they seem to be starting earlier each year, especially since the recession hit.

There are other new phenomena in the world of fashion: the emergence of permanent sale shops, of upscale secondhand clothing emporia, and of "warehouse sales." These last happen when one designer, or a group of them, offload the previous season's collections to make space for new stock. Previously the jealously guarded secret of those who work in the fashion world, they are now advertised discreetly in *Time Out* and the *Evening Standard*, so keep your eyes peeled. The same function is served by the handful of sale shops you'll find listed here. There's no stigma to buying secondhand clothes these days (and it's better for the environment), especially when they are *couture* castoffs whose owners merely fancied a change—and several shops exist for the purpose of this transaction, too.

Fashion aside, London's shopping possibilities are limitless, especially to resourceful customers who are prepared to take their chances in uncharted, out-of-the-way neighborhoods and at street markets. Books are particularly good buys here (ask Helene Hanff). Every main street seems to have its share of publishers' surplus outlets, but it's secondhand and vintage volumes to which we refer. These are not necessarily cheaper than in the United States, but there's always the chance that your diligent search will root out a dusty first edition or the long-out-of-print paperback you've been looking for. Something similar could be said for "antiquing," too. See below for likely hunting grounds.

The following listings lie somewhere between overview and tour. We've tried to find establishments that offer good value, which—as any smart shopper knows—does not always mean that their prices are the lowest. A bargain is only a bargain when you really want it.

Shopping Districts

Camden Town Around Camden Lock and the other weekend markets, an impressive array of complementary shops has emerged over recent years. The style will suit those of bohemian tendencies, with crafts both made by British designers and imported from sunnier continents. The area is good for cheap clothing of the T-shirts-boots-and-vintage type.

Chelsea Chelsea means first and foremost the King's Road, less glamorous now than a few years ago, and no longer a mecca for those in search of up-to-the-minute fashion. Chelsea is pricey, with antiques, fashions, and home furnishings aimed at the moneyed residents. Clothing can be a good buy.

Covent Garden Crafts shops, clothing stores, and design-conscious retailers have made a natural home for themselves here, especially in and around the elegantly restored 19th-century market. But this is one of those delightful areas where simply strolling around, window shopping, and people watching are as much fun as the shopping itself.

Hampstead For picturesque peace and quiet with your shopping, stroll around here midweek. Upscale clothing stores and representatives of the better chains share the half dozen streets with cozy boutique-size shops for the home and stomach.

Kensington Antiques are the real draw here, especially up Kensington Church Street, but you'd better be serious—the prices certainly will be. Kensington High Street itself is a smaller, less crowded version of Oxford Street, with some good-quality mid-price clothing shops and larger stores at the east end.

Knightsbridge Home of Harrods, one of the world's best-known department stores, Knightsbridge prices are way up there. Neighboring areas—Sloane Street, Walton Street, Beauchamp Place, and, especially, Brompton Cross—are packed with gorgeous shops and provide what may be the best of the capital's window shopping.

Mayfair Mayfair means Bond Street (Old and New), South Molton Street, Savile Row, and the Burlington Arcade, in an area lying between Piccadilly and Oxford Street. The emphasis is very much on traditional British goods, international brand names, and the poshest designers' wares. Prices and quality are tiptop.

Oxford Street Despite its claim to be Britain's premier shopping street, Oxford Street is to be endured rather than enjoyed. Selfridges, Marks and Spencer, and John Lewis are all good department stores here, while little St. Christopher's Place and Gees Court, almost opposite the Bond Street tube, add a chic touch. But otherwise the crowds, the noise, the traffic, and the unmistakable tattiness of stretches of Oxford Street itself combine to produce a very much less-than-lovely atmosphere.

Piccadilly Though the actual number of shops here is really quite low for a street of its length—after all, Green Park takes up almost half of one side—Piccadilly still boasts a number of classy outfits: Simpsons, Hatchards, and Fortnum and Mason chief among them. Classiness does not come cheap, but the elegant Burlington and Royal Arcades are unmissable, just for looking.

Regent Street The wide, elegant sweep of Regent Street provides a far more pleasant way to get into a crowd than neighboring Oxford Street, though most of the shops are expensively average. Exceptions are Hamleys, the vast toy emporium, and Liberty, probably the city's most appealing department store.

Shopping A (Mayfair, Soho, and Covent Garden)

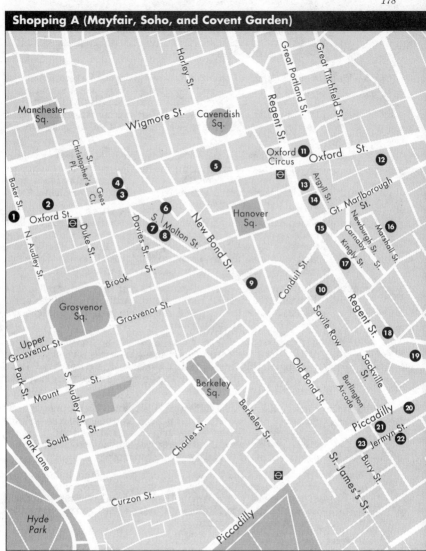

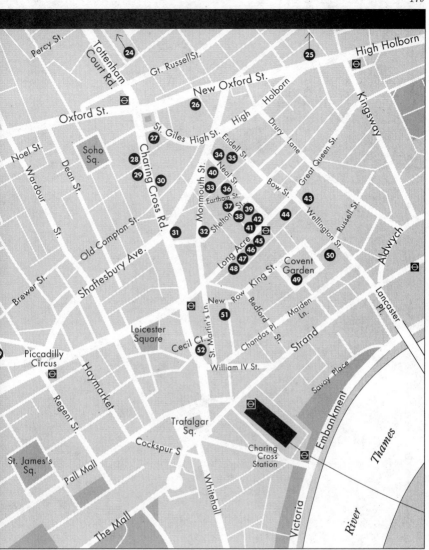

180

Shopping B (Kensington, Knightsbridge, and Chelsea)

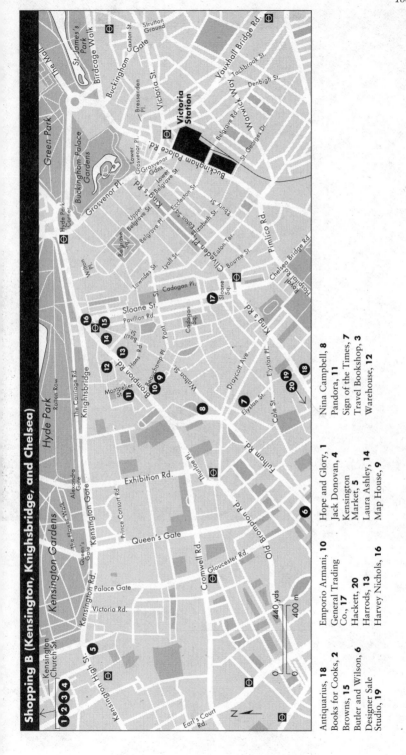

Antiquarius, **18**
Books for Cooks, **2**
Browns, **15**
Butler and Wilson, **6**
Designer Sale
Studio, **19**

Emporio Armani, **10**
General Trading
Co., **17**
Hackett, **20**
Harrods, **13**
Harvey Nichols, **16**

Hope and Glory, **1**
Jack Donovan, **4**
Kensington
Market, **5**
Laura Ashley, **14**
Map House, **9**

Nina Campbell, **8**
Pandora, **11**
Sign of the Times, **7**
Travel Bookshop, **3**
Warehouse, **12**

NOW THE FASTEST WAY OVER THE CHANNEL MAY BE UNDER IT.

At speeds of up to 200 mph, the Eurostar train takes you from downtown London to downtown Paris in just 3 hours – the same amount of time it takes by plane. But without the hassles of cabs, traffic jams or weather delays.

What's more, Eurostar's first class service costs less than most airline business class trips.

And we're ready to go when you are – with at least 10 departures daily.

For information and reservations contact your travel agent or call **1-800-EUROSTAR**.

THE EUROSTAR TRAIN. THE BETTER WAY TO FLY ACROSS THE CHANNEL.

Eurostar is a service provided together by the railways of Belgium, Britain and France.

This guidebook teaches you how to budget your money.

This page is for slow learners.

We all make mistakes. So if you happen to find yourself making a costly one, call Western Union. With them, you can receive money from the States within minutes at any of our European locations. Plus, it's already been converted into the appropriate currency.

Just call our numbers in Austria 0222 892 0380, Belgium 02 753 2150, Denmark 800 107 11, Finland 9 800 20440, France 161 43 54 46 12, Germany 069 2648201, 0681 933 3328, Greece 01 687 3850, Ireland 1 800 395 395,* Italy 039 6 167016840, Netherlands 06 0566,* Poland 22 37 1826, Spain 93 301 1212, Sweden 020 741 742, United Kingdom 0 800 833 833,* or if you're in the United States 1 800 325 6000.*

And since nobody's perfect, you might want to keep these numbers in your wallet, for those times when nothing else is in there.

WESTERN UNION | MONEY TRANSFER®

The fastest way to send money worldwide.™

St. James's Though his suits may be made in Savile Row, this is where the English gent comes for the rest of his clothes. Superb shoes, classic shirts, silk ties, magnificent hats, and all manner of accessories have kept St. James's a front runner for timeless English clothes. Naturally the prices mirror the quality.

Specialty Stores

Antiques London can provide a fruitful vacation for any antiques buff, whether you're buying or browsing. For a chance at finding something you can afford, street markets are best, especially Bermondsey, Camden Passage, and Portobello (*see* Street Markets, *below*). We've listed a couple of distinctly *un*affordable places, too, because they're like tiny museums.

Antiquarius (131–141 King's Rd., SW3, tel. 0171/351–5353) at the Sloane Square end of the King's Road is an indoor antiques market with over 200 stalls that offer a wide variety of collectibles, including metalware, meerschaum pipes, ceramics, and art nouveau bric-à-brac. Prices are fair, which is to say sometimes accessible. *Tube: Sloane Square.*

A real find for any enthusiast is the **Gallery of Antique Costume and Textiles** (2 Church St., NW8, tel. 0171/723–9981). Here you can forage at leisure amid tapestries, shawls, table linens, and, above all, costumes. Nothing after the 1930s. *Tube: Edgeware Road.*

For any collector of china and glass who also has a taste for history, **Hope and Glory** (131A Kensington Church St., W8, tel. 0171/727–8424) is fascinating. The stock here is of commemorative china and glass from 1887 to the present, with some affordable lesser pieces. *Tube: Notting Hill Gate.*

Jack Donovan (93 Portobello Rd., W11, tel. 0171/727–1485) is unique for its mechanical antiques: music boxes, polyphons, caged songbirds, and all manner of vintage automata. *Tube: Notting Hill Gate.*

Books Charing Cross Road is London's booksville, with a couple of dozen stores there or thereabout. The many antiquarian booksellers tend to look daunting, but there are many new bookshops, too. Especially large, though it has to be the most chaotic and confusing shop in London, with a staff that doesn't know anything, is **Foyle** (#119, tel. 0171/437–5660). **Waterstone** (#121–125, tel. 0171/434–4291) is part of a reliable chain with long hours and a program of author readings and signings. **Hatchards** (187–188 Piccadilly, WC2, tel. 0171/434–2543) and **Dillons** (82 Gower St., WC1, tel. 0171/636–1577) both have not only a huge stock, but also a well-informed staff to help you choose. *Tube: Charing Cross.*

Books for Cooks (4 Blenheim Cres., W11, tel. 0171/221–1992) and its near neighbor, **The Travel Bookshop** (#13, tel. 0171/229–5260), are exactly what they say, and worth the trip for enthusiasts. Travel books and maps are the specialty of **Stanford** (12 Long Acre, WC2, tel. 0171/836–1321); art books of **Zwemmer** (24 Litchfield St., WC2, tel. 0171/240–1559) just off Charing Cross Rd.; and sci-fi, fantasy, horror, and comic books of **Forbidden Planet** (71 New Oxford St., WC1, tel. 0171/836–4179.) *Tube: Tottenham Court Road.*

Back on the Charing Cross Road, **Silver Moon** at #64 (tel. 0171/836–7906) is an accessible and friendly women's bookshop. Just off the south end is Cecil Court, a pedestrians-only lane where every shop is a specialty bookstore. If you go book-hunting just once, make it here. **Marchpane** (#16, tel. 0171/836–8661) stocks covetable rare and antique illustrated children's books; **Dance Books** (#9, tel. 0171/836–2314) has—yes—dance books; and **Pleasures of Times Past** (#11, tel. 0171/836–1142) indulges the collective nostalgia for Victoriana. At the north end, **Sportspages** (Caxton Walk, tel. 0171/240–9604) is

London's only sports bookshop—it's so comprehensive there's even a good baseball section. *Tube: Charing Cross.*

Try **Bloomsbury Book Auctions** (3–4 Harwick St., EC1, tel. 0171/833–2636) every other Thursday at 1 PM for everything from illuminated manuscripts to cases of old paperbacks. *Tube: Angel.*

Clothing The resourceful shopper can really clean up on the bargains in this field. Any merchandise that takes your fancy comes within reach in January and June, and a couple of the shops we list below are known for their especially juicy sales. London is one of the world's fashion capitals, and every designer you've ever heard of is sold here somewhere. It's also a center for innovation, street fashion, and exciting young design. Many an exciting young designer first sold a collection at a London street market, so don't go just by the label and you could discover a future star.

Dress Agencies At these elegant boutiques, women offload their expensive, unworn (or nearly) designer mistakes to be resold, usually at less than half the original cost.

Pandora (16–22 Cheval Pl., SW7, tel. 0171/589–5289), one of the first of the breed, stocks the crème de la crème: from Europe, YSL, Valentino, Chanel; New York's Donna Karan; and even the odd Bruce Oldfield from London. As you'd expect from those names, prices are high. *Tube: Knightsbridge.*

Up in Hampstead, **Designs** (60 Rosslyn Hill, NW3, tel. 0171/435–0100) stocks some new clothes among the pristine MaxMara, Krizia, Moschino, and Marella numbers. *Tube: Hampstead.*

Sign of the Times (17 Elystan St., SW3, tel. 0171/589–4774) couldn't be more aptly named. Affluent women flog their Alaias, Conrans, Ozbeks, and Chanels so they can go to Browns' sale (*see below*) and buy some more. *Tube: South Kensington.*

Designer Sale Shops Browns (*see below*) consistently collects London's most covetable clothing, and its **Labels for Less** (50 S. Molton St., W1, tel. 0171/409–3011) offers the rejects at up to 75% off. *Tube: Bond Street.*

The Chelsea **Designer Sale Studio** (241 King's Rd., SW3, tel. 0171/351–4171) has been a fixture for almost a decade, selling mainly Italian womenswear. Armani, Byblos, Genny, Basile, and Versace are usually around. *Tube: Sloane Square.* (Consult the phone book for other branches.)

In **Harvey Nichols** (109 Knightsbridge, SW1, tel. 0171/235–5000), the premier (but expensive) department store for fashion, there is a permanent sale department somewhere—they keep moving it. Visit the store's Personal Shopping adviser, for a free consultation, and she'll help you meet your budget. (*See* Department Stores, *below.*) *Tube: Knightsbridge.*

Susanna Vida's longstanding basement, **Venus** (below **On Show**, 19 Shorts Gdns., WC2, tel. 0171/379–1426), has an amazing selection of the more eccentric and avant-garde British designers' samples and surplus: Westwood, Galliano, Hamnett, Conran—all the greats. *Tube: Covent Garden.*

For men, a shop to check out when Paul Smith's sale (*see below*) doesn't work for you, **Arrivals** (28A Floral St., WC2, tel. 0171/379–0646) stocks young British and Italian designers—Ross Perez, Vestium Officina, Custo—at 25%–50% off. *Tube: Covent Garden.*

Womenswear Sales Lines form during the first days of the famous sales at **Browns** (23–27 S. Molton St., W1, tel. 0171/493–1230; 6C Sloane St., SW1, tel. 0171/491–7833) and the staff relax their sneers a teeny bit. Here are Jean Muir, Jil Sander, Alaia and Conran and Karan and Ozbek, Gigli, Gaultier, etc., etc. Sales here start a little after the rest of the pack's. *Tube: Bond Street.*

Nicole Farhi (25 St. Christopher's Pl., W1, tel. 0171/486–3416, and branches) has the knack of designing exactly what women covet. Her wearable—no, *edible*—classic but funky suits and separates in natural fibres and subtle colors are worth the investment at their sale price. *Tube: Bond Street.*

Though its house-label stuff in particular is not prohibitively priced, it's still worth waiting for the sales to visit **Whistles** (The Market, Covent Garden, WC2, tel. 0171/379–7401, and branches) because its up-to-the-second designs date quickly and prices drop heavily. There's also a permanent sale branch in St. Christopher's Place. *Tube: Covent Garden.*

Menswear Sales
Browns (*see above*) also has a men's shop. Katharine Hamnett, Joseph, and Gigli are among the designers stocked. *Tube: Bond Street.*

British retailer **Paul Smith** (Floral St., WC2, tel. 0171/379–7133) has definitive versions of snappy casual jackets, suits, shirts, and knitwear, plus accessories, shoes, and knickknacks. *Tube: Covent Garden.*

The best suits are Italian, and the best Italian is Armani, they say. Decide for yourself at **Emporio Armani** (187–91 Brompton Rd., SW3, tel. 0171/823–8818). *Tube: Knightsbridge.*

Farther along, at 87 Brompton Road, you collide with **Harrods** (*see* Department Stores, *below*), whose famous sale is partly famous for its menswear.

Good-value Shops
Anokhi (22 Wellington St., WC2, tel. 0171/836–0663) stocks colorful printed cottons and raw silks, commissioned in Rajasthan and made into wearable separates that look more expensive than they are. *Tube: Covent Garden.*

The Hat Shop (58 Neal St., WC2, tel. 0171/836–6718, and other branches). A store with rows of cubbyholes brimming with ladies' and men's hats for every occasion, from feasts to funerals. Friendly assistants to help you with that difficult choice. The shop is so tiny that only 10 people are allowed in at a time. *Tube: Covent Garden.*

Jigsaw (21 Long Acre, Covent Garden, WC2, tel. 0171/240–3855, and other branches) is popular for its separates that don't sacrifice quality to fashion, are reasonably priced, and suit women in their twenties to forties. *Tube: Covent Garden.*

Kensington Market (49–53 Kensington High St., W8) is the diametric opposite of sober British stiff-upper-lip antifashion. For over two decades it has been a principal purveyor of the constantly changing, frivolous, hip London street style. Hundreds of stalls—some shop-size, others tiny—are crammed into this building, where you can get lost for hours trying to find the good bits. *Tube: Kensington High Street.*

Laura Ashley (256–258 Regent St., W1, tel. 0171/437–9760; 47 Brompton Rd., SW3, tel. 0171/823–9700, and other branches). Design from the firm founded by the late high priestess of English traditional. Country dresses, blouses, and skirts, plus wallpapers and fabrics in dateless patterns that rely heavily on flowers, fruit, leaves, or just plain stripes, that have captured the nostalgic imagination of the world. *Tube: Oxford Circus (Regent St.), Knightsbridge (Brompton Rd.)*

Marks & Spencer (458 Oxford St., W1, tel. 0171/935–7954, and 173 Oxford St., W1, tel. 0171/437–7722). This major chain of stores is an integral part of the British way of life—sturdy practical clothes, good materials and workmanship, and basic accessories, all at moderate, though not bargain basement, prices. "Marks and Sparks," as they are popularly known, have never been renowned for their high style, though that is changing as they continue to bring in (anonymously) big-name designers to spice up their ranges. Of the two major branches on Oxford Street, #458 near Marble Arch has by far the highest turnover of any shop in the United Kingdom.

Paddy Campbell (8 Gees Ct., W1, tel. 0171/493–5646). Campbell designs elegant matching separates in natural fabrics and subtle colors. Prices are reasonable for this level of workmanship, and the staff will alter garments for a perfect fit. *Tube: Bond Street.*

Warehouse (19 Argyll St., W1, tel. 0171/437–7101). Warehouse stocks practical, stylish, reasonably priced separates, in easy fabrics and lots of fun colors. The finishing isn't so hot, but style, not substance, counts here, and the shop's youthful fans don't seem to mind. The stock changes very quickly, so it always presents a new face to the world. Also at 76 Brompton Road, SW3, as well as other locations. *Tube: Oxford Circus.*

Menwear **Blazer** (36 Long Acre, WC2, tel. 0171/379–6258, and 117 Long Acre, WC2, tel. 0171/379–0456) stocks stylish, medium-priced formal wear at the first branch and a casual range at the second. Clothes tend toward the classic, but with style-conscious details and rich colors. *Tube: Covent Garden.*

Hackett (65B New King's Rd., SW6, tel. 0171/371–7964, and other branches) started as a posh thrift store, recycling cricket flannels, hunting pinks, Oxford brogues, and similar Britishwear. Now they make their own, and they have become a genuine—and very good—gentlemen's outfitter. *Tube: Sloane Square.*

Moss Bros. (88 Regent St., WI, tel. 0171/494–0666). "Moss Bross," as you will always hear this store called, made their name renting out tuxedos, complete morning suits for fancy weddings, and all kinds of formal wear for the busy man—and woman—on the move. *Tube: Oxford Circus (Regent St.)*

Sam Walker (41 Neal St., WC2, tel. 0171/240–7800) provides a refined way to buy secondhand clothes. He specializes in men's vintage clothing at prices that *almost* reflect their near-museum quality. Naturally, most of the stock is well pre–World War II and carries period nostalgia in every fold. There's also a women's version, called **Rebecca,** at #66. *Tube: Covent Garden.*

Tom Gilbey (2 New Burlington Pl., W1, tel. 0171/734–4877) is a custom tailor, but the exciting part of his shop is the Waistcoat Gallery, where exquisite vests, some in silk or brocades or embroidered by hand, others marginally plainer, are essential accessories for the dandy. Though not inexpensive, they are worth it. *Tube: Oxford Circus.*

Turnbull & Asser (71 & 72 Jermyn St., W1, tel. 0171/930–0502) is *the* custom shirtmaker. Unfortunately for those of average means, the first order must be for a minimum of six shirts, from around £100 each. But there's a range of less expensive, still exquisitely made ready-to-wear shirts, too. *Tube: Piccadilly Circus.*

Crafts In the wake of the current interest in alternative ways of living, health foods, and preserving the environment, there has been an enormous increase in public awareness of the value of traditional crafts. London now boasts many stores devoted to selling the best craftwork available.

Some of the best British potters joined to found the **Craftsmen Potters Shop** (7 Marshall St., W1, tel. 0171/437–7605) as a cooperative venture to market their wares. The result is a store that carries a wide spectrum of the potter's art, from thoroughly practical pitchers, plates, and bowls to ceramic sculptures. Prices range from the reasonable to way up. *Tube: Oxford Circus.*

Craftworks (31 Southend Rd., NW3, tel. 0171/431-4337) is a haven packed with handmade table- and glassware, ceramics, candlesticks, wall hangings, and mirrors from all over the world—and also from just down the road. Prices are reasonable. *Tube: Hampstead.*

At **Contemporary Applied Arts** (43 Earlham St., WC2, tel. 0171/836-6993), a mixed bag of designers and craftspeople display their wares over two floors. Anything from glassware and jewelry to furniture and lighting can be found here. *Tube: Covent Garden.*

True to its name, **Naturally British** (13 New Row, WC2, tel. 0171/240-0551) is a good spot to find British crafts, from small, low-priced pottery or wood items to larger pieces, such as gloriously carved rocking horses with high price tags on their aristocratic manes. *Tube: Covent Garden.*

Anyone with an eye for the decorative attractions of Italian marbled paper will find **Nina Campbell** (9 Walton St., SW3, tel. 0171/225-1011) a must. Address books, all kinds of desk equipment and stationery, Edwardian-inspired lamps, and fluffy cushions make very tempting gifts. *Tube: Knightsbridge.*

Gifts Of course, virtually anything from any shop in this chapter has gift potential, but these selections lean toward stores with a lot of choice, both in merchandise and price. Chances are you'll want the recipients of your generous bounty to know how far you traveled to procure it for them, so our suggestions tend toward identifiable Britishness. You should also investigate the possibilities in the shops attached to the major museums, most of which offer far more than racks of souvenir postcards. Some of the best are at the **British Museum**, the **V&A**, the **Royal Academy**, and the **London Transport Museum** (*see* Exploring London, Chapter 4, *above*).

The Armoury of St. James's (17 Piccadilly Arcade, SW1, tel. 0171/493-5082). The Armoury is a fascinating wee store bursting with impeccably painted toy soldiers, old medals, and military prints. A must for the nostalgia enthusiast. *Tube: Piccadilly Circus.*

Fortnum & Mason (181 Piccadilly, W1, tel. 0171/734-8040), the queen's grocer, is, paradoxically, the most egalitarian of gift stores, with plenty of irresistibly packaged luxury foods, stamped with the gold "by appointment" crest, for under £5. Try the teas, preserves, blocks of chocolate, tins of pâté, or boxes of Duchy Originals oatcakes—like Paul Newman, the Prince of Wales has gone into the retail food business with these. *Tube: Green Park.*

General Trading Co. (144 Sloane St., SW1, tel. 0171/730-0411). With a dozen departments to explore, even the most finicky shopper will find something to delight or amuse in this Aladdin's cave. General Trading Company buyers travel the world—especially the Far East—to discover new suppliers, and their merchandise includes French glass, Indian crafts, Italian lighting fixtures, Chinese toys, and English bone china. Although you can spend as little as £5, or as much as your credit card will stretch to, every debutante has her wedding list here, and that's who this shop really caters to. *Tube: Sloane Square.*

Hamleys (188–196 Regent St., W1, tel. 0171/734-3161). Six floors of toys and games for both children and adults. The huge stock ranges from traditional teddy bears to computer games and all the latest technological gimmickry. Try to avoid it at Christmas, when police have to rope off a section of Regent Street for Hamleys customers. *Tube: Oxford Circus.*

Maison (47–49 Neal St., WC2, tel. 0171/240-2822) is a cool, spacious two floors of homage to design. Among the gorgeous goods displayed like museum pieces are lots of witty ideas for presents, from the sublime (Alvar Aalto vases) to the ridiculous (chocolate sardines). *Tube: Covent Garden.*

Neal Street East (5 Neal St., WC2, tel. 0171/240–0135) isn't big on British, but this importer of Oriental everything does carry stock with universal appeal. There are several floors of what you'd expect in the way of woks, chopsticks, bowls, books, kimonos, and toys, but also glorious lacquered boxes, woven baskets, silk flowers, Japanese kites, amber and silver jewelry, and loads of fun gifts for under a fiver. *Tube: Covent Garden.*

Penhaligon's (41 Wellington St., WC2, tel. 0171/629–1416) is a block south of the Royal Opera House in Covent Garden. William Penhaligon—court barber at the end of Queen Victoria's lengthy reign—blended perfumes and toilet waters in the back of his shop, using essential oils and natural, indeed often exotic, ingredients. Today Penhaligon's still makes its traditional preparations—including soaps, talc, and bath oils—following William Penhaligon's original notes, and the elegantly packaged (and very pricey) products and equally sumptuous shops both retain a look of high Victoriana. Also at 55 Burlington Arcade, W1; 69 Moorgate, EC2; and 20A Brook Street, W1. *Tube: Piccaddilly Circus.*

Ray Man (29 Monmouth St., WC2, tel. 0171/240–1776), for "Eastern Musical Instruments" is probably the only place in Europe you can buy an *erh hu*, which is, of course, a two-stringed coconut fiddle. It's an amazing place, perfect for gifts for the weird. You can pick up a set of ankle bells or pan pipes for a song. *Tube: Covent Garden.*

The Tea House (15A Neal St., WC2, no phone). Any shop that's devoted to the British national drink has to be worth a visit, and this one certainly is. There's tea of all kinds on sale, plus "teaphernalia," as they call it—strainers, infusers, cozies (to keep the pot warm), trivets (to protect the table), and an enormous teapot and tea book collection. Prices are very reasonable. *Tube: Covent Garden.*

Jewelry Jewelry—precious, semiprecious, and totally fake—can be had by just rubbing an Aladdin's lamp in London's West End. Of the department stores, Liberty and Harvey Nichols are particularly known for their fashion jewelry, but here are a few more suggestions for baubles, bangles, and beads.

All that glitters at **Butler and Wilson** (20 South Molton St., W1, tel. 0171/409–2955) isn't gold. This store is cleverly designed to set off its irresistible costume jewelry to the very best advantage—against a dramatic black background. It has some of the best displays in town, and keeps very busy marketing silver, diamanté, French gilt, and pearls by the truckload. The sales are especially fine, with 50% off at least half the entire stock. *Tube: Bond Street.* Also at 189 Fulham Road, SW3, tel. 0171/352–3045; *tube: South Kensington.*

Cartier (175 New Bond St., W1, tel. 0171/528–7419). The very essence of Bond Street is captured by this exclusive jeweler, which also sells glassware, leather goods, and stationery. It combines royal connections—Cartier's was granted its first royal warrant in 1902—with the last word in luxurious good taste. Many of the Duchess of Windsor's trinkets first saw the light of day here. One for voyeurs only. *Tube: Bond Street.*

Garrard (112 Regent St., W1, tel. 0171/734–7020) has connections with the royal family going back to 1722 and is still in charge of the upkeep of the Crown Jewels. But it is also a family jeweler and offers an enormous range of items, from antique to modern, exorbitant to affordable. *Tube: Oxford Circus.*

The Outlaws Club (49 Endell St., WC2, tel. 0171/379–6940) stocks the work of around 100 designers, with prices ranging from a few pounds up to £200. All the pieces are stylish and the store has been a favorite with fashion writers for a decade. *Tube: Covent Garden.*

Linen Among the traditional crafts that can still be bought in London, fine linen ranks high. Again, many of the department stores, Liberty and Harrods among them, carry a fair range of linen goods, but at a price.

The Linen Cupboard (21 Great Castle St., W1, tel. 0171/629–4062) is stacked with piles of sheets and towels of all sorts and has by far the lowest-priced fine Irish linens and Egyptian cottons in town. *Tube: Oxford Circus.*

Prints For a gift to take home, a memento of London, or just the delight of owning a beautiful old object, prints are hard to beat. We list here two out of the many print shops in central London. If you want to do some concentrated print browsing, visit Cecil Court, just north of Trafalgar Square, where there are several shops close together.

Grosvenor Prints (28–32 Shelton St., WC2, tel. 0171/836–1979). Shelton Street lies in the tangle of streets northwest of Covent Garden, where many attractive stores have established themselves. Grosvenor Prints sells antiquarian prints, but with an emphasis on views and architecture of London—and dogs! It's an eccentric collection, and the prices range widely, but the stock is so odd that you are bound to find something interesting and unusual to meet both your budget and your taste. *Tube: Covent Garden.*

The Map House (54 Beauchamp Pl., SW3, tel. 0171/589–4325) is an old established store, and is one of the best places in London to root out a special old map or print. Antique maps can run from a few pounds to several thousand, but the Map House also has excellent reproductions of maps and prints, especially of botanical subjects and cityscapes. *Tube: Knightsbridge.*

Department Stores

London's department stores range from Harrods—which every tourist is obliged to visit—through many serviceable middle-range stores, devoted to the middle-of-the-road tastes of the middle class, to a few cheapjack ones that sell merchandise you would find at a better rate back home. Most of the best and biggest department stores are grouped in the West End around Regent Street and Oxford Street, with two notable exceptions out in Knightsbridge.

We begin with our favorite, **Liberty** (200 Regent St., W1, tel. 0171/734–1234), easily the most splendid store on Regent Street, and one of London's most attractive. Liberty is a labyrinthine building, full of nooks and crannies, all stuffed with goodies like a dream of an eastern bazaar. Famous principally for its fabrics, it also has an Oriental department, rich with color; menswear that tends to the traditional; and womenswear that stresses the chic and recherché. It is a store hard to resist, where you may well find an original gift—especially one made from those classic Liberty prints. Prices are high, but so is the quality. *Tube: Oxford Circus.*

A short distance from Liberty, two blocks west on Oxford Street, is **John Lewis** (278 Oxford St., W1, tel. 0171/629–7711), a store whose motto is "Never knowingly undersold," and for sensible goods at sensible prices this store is hard to beat. For the visitor to London who's handy with the needle, John Lewis has a wonderful selection of dress and furnishing fabrics. Many's the American home with John Lewis drapes. *Tube: Oxford Circus.*

Ten blocks west on Oxford Street—crowded blocks in the middle of the day or at sale time—lies **Selfridges** (400 Oxford St., W1, tel. 0171/629–1234). This giant, bustling store is London's upscale version of Macy's and was started early this century by an American. If this all-rounder has an outstanding department, it has to be its Food Hall, or else its frenetic cosmetics department that seems to perfume the air the whole length of Oxford Street. In recent years, Selfridges has made a specialty of high-profile popular designer fashion. Even more important for the visitor to town, there's a branch of the London Tourist Board on the premises, a theater ticket counter, and a branch of Thomas Cook, the travel agent, in the basement. *Tube: Marble Arch.*

Harrods (87 Brompton Rd., SW1, tel. 0171/730–1234), the only English department store classed among monuments and museums on every visitor's list, hardly needs an introduction. In fact, its Englishness is tentative, since it is owned by the Egyptian Al Fayed brothers—but who cares? It is as swanky and plush and deep carpeted as ever, its spectacular food halls are alone worth the trip, and it stands out from the pack for fashion these days, too. You can forgive the store its immodest motto, *Omnia, omnibus, ubique* ("everything, for everyone, everywhere"), since there are more than 230 departments, including a pet shop rumored to supply anything from aardvarks to zebras (on request) and the toy department—sorry, *kingdom*—which does the same for plush versions. During the pre-Christmas period and the sales, the entire store is a menagerie. The traditional tourist thing to do is to buy a box of matches or a hairnet or anything for about 20p, just so you get one of the distinctive dark-green-and-gold shopping bags. *Tube: Knightsbridge.*

Harvey Nichols (109 Knightsbridge, SW1, tel. 0171/235–5000) is just a few blocks from Harrods, but is not competing on the same turf, since its passion is fashion, all the way. There are five floors of it, including departments for dressing homes and men, but the woman who invests in her wardrobe is the main target. Accessories are strong suits, especially jewelry, hats, scarves, and makeup—England's first MAC counter here was 10-deep for months. (*See* Designer Sale Shops, *above*). *Tube: Knightsbridge.*

Street Markets

The street markets of London are not only great places for bargains—or at least you can kid yourself that they are!—but are full of bedouin Londoners, from the Cockney stallholders selling vegetables or antiques, their Jaguars parked in a nearby street, to the locals out buying their Sunday dinners. The markets are also a rich source of free entertainment, tasty snacks, and insights into the way London works. Naturally there is a lot of junk on sale, imported plastic from Hong Kong or cheesecloth shirts from Bombay, but there is also a seemingly endless supply of plates, cut glass, Victorian jewel boxes, brass candlesticks, and the like. Depending on the kind of market, you may well catch some of that antique Cockney badinage you've heard in the movies, though today's stallholders are more likely to be about as friendly as New York cab drivers.

Street markets are mainly a weekend pastime, and, as many of them are open on Sunday morning, they provide something to do on a day that can be extremely dull and dreary in London. A wander through one of the markets, followed by a good Sunday lunch, then an afternoon in a park or by the river, makes a classic London way of cheering up the sabbath.

Bermondsey (Tower Bridge Rd., SE1). Also known as the New Caledonian Market, this is one of London's largest market sites. There are hundreds of stalls selling a wealth of junk and treasures from Britain's attics. Note that this market is held on Friday only starting at the unearthly hour of 4 AM, and it's then that the really great buys will be snapped up. You should still be able to find a bargain or two if you turn up a bit later. *To get there, take the #15 or #25 bus to*

Aldgate, then a #42 over Tower Bridge to Bermondsey Sq., or take the tube to London Bridge and walk. Open Fri. 4 AM–1 PM.

Camden Lock Market (NW1). Even though its character has changed along with its development into something half touristy, half teenage meat market, this remains just the place to pick up an unusual and inexpensive gift, and it's still a picturesque area to wander around, with its cobbled courtyards and the attractive lock itself. There's an antiques market here on Saturday and Sunday, though the individual crafts shops are open during the week as well. It does get horribly crowded on weekends, and some find the entire neighborhood simply too funky. *Take the tube or #24 or #29 bus to Camden Town. Shops open Tues.–Sun. 9:30–5:30, stalls on weekends 8–6.*

Camden Passage (Islington, N1). The endless rows of little antiques shops here are the places to head for, particularly if you're interested in silverware and jewelry, though the market is by no means confined to these alone. Saturday and Wednesday are the big days for stalls; during the rest of the week only the shops are open. *A #19 or #38 bus or tube to the Angel will get you there. Open Wed. and Sat. 8:30–3.*

Greenwich Antiques Market (Greenwich High Rd., SE10). If you're planning to visit Greenwich, then combine your trip with a wander around this open-air market near St. Alfege Church. You'll find one of the best selections of secondhand and antique clothes in London—quality tweeds and overcoats can be had at amazing prices. But, as in any self-respecting London market, you'll also find a wide range of other items, from the worthless to the wonderful. The market for antiques is open on Saturday and Sunday only. *Take a British Rail train to New Gate Cross and then a #117 bus, or a bus direct to Greenwich. Antiques, crafts, and clothes weekends 9–5; fruit and vegetables weekdays 9–5.*

Leadenhall Market (EC3). The draw here is not so much what you can buy—plants and food, mainly—as the building itself. It's a handsome late-Victorian structure, ornate and elaborate, with lashings of atmosphere. *To get there take the tube to Bank or Monument. Open weekdays 9–5.*

Petticoat Lane (Middlesex St., E1). Petticoat Lane doesn't actually appear on the map, but it's the commonly used name of this famous Sunday market on Middlesex Street. Look for quality, cut-rate fashion clothes and leatherwear in the warehouse between Goulston and Middlesex streets. There are also luxury goods, such as cameras, videos, and stereos, at exceptional prices. *Liverpool St., Aldgate, or Aldgate East tubes are the closest. Open Sun. 9–2.*

Portobello Market (Portobello Rd., W11). Saturday is the best day to search the stalls for treasure in the way of silverware, curios, porcelain, and jewelry. There are 1,500 dealers, meaning that bargains are still possible, especially very early. Saturdays are always crowded, and there are street entertainers and an authentic hustle-and-bustle atmosphere. You'll find that the first section of the market that you come to has the highest-quality merchandise (and the highest prices), while the farther you walk—and it spreads a long way—the more bric-a-brac you see. At the Westway (elevated road), the flea market takes over. The whole area is London's hippest. *Take a #52 bus or the tube to Ladbroke Grove or Notting Hill Gate. Fruit and vegetables Mon.–Wed. and Fri. 8–5, Thurs. 8–1; antiques Fri. 8–3; both on Sat. 6–5.*

Spitalfields (Brushfield St., E1). Until it eventually becomes shops and offices, the developers of Camden Lock have got hold of the old three-acre indoor fruit market near Petticoat Lane and installed food, crafts and clothes stalls, cafés, performance and sports facilities, and a city farm. *Directions as for Petticoat Lane, above. Open weekdays 11–3, Sun. 9–3.*

VAT Refunds

To the eternal fury of Britain's storekeepers, who struggle under cataracts of paperwork, Britain is afflicted with a 17½% Value Added Tax. Foreign visitors, however, need not pay VAT if they take advantage of the Personal Export Scheme. Of the various ways to get a VAT refund, the most common are **Over the Counter** and **Direct Export.** Note that though practically all larger stores operate these schemes, information about them is not always readily forthcoming, so it is important to ask. Once you have gotten on the right track, you'll find that almost all the larger stores have export departments that will be able to give you all the help you need.

The easiest and most usual way of getting your refund is the **Over the Counter** method. There is normally a minimum of £75, below which VAT cannot be refunded. You must also be able to supply proof of your identity—your passport is best. The sales clerk will then fill out the necessary paperwork, VAT Form 407. Keep the form and give it to Customs when you leave the country. Lines at major airports are usually long, so leave plenty of time. The form will then be returned to the store and the refund forwarded to you, minus a small service charge, usually around $3. You can specify how you want the refund. Generally, the easiest way is to have it credited to your charge card. Alternatively, you can have it in the form of a sterling check, but your bank will charge a fee to convert it. Note also that it can take up to eight weeks to receive the refund.

The **Direct Export** method—whereby you have the store send the goods to your home—is more cumbersome. You must have the VAT Form 407 certified by Customs, police, or a notary public when you get home and then send it back to the store. It, in turn, will refund your money.

If you are traveling to any other EC country from Britain, the same rules apply, except in France, where you can claim your refund as you leave the country.

However, in 1988 the **Tourist Tax-Free Shopping** service came into operation. This service, which uses special VAT refund vouchers, rather than Form 407, expedites your refund, provided that you make your purchases at a store (identified by the red, white, and blue Tax-Free for Tourists sign) offering the service. If you are going on from Britain to the Continent, you can even get cash refunds. Full details and a list of stores offering the Tax-Free service are available from the British Tourist Authority, 551 Fifth Avenue, New York, NY 10036, and the British Travel Centre, 12 Regent Street, London SW1Y 4PQ.

Clothing Sizes

Men Suit and shirt sizes in the United Kingdom and the Republic of Ireland are the same as U.S. sizes.

Women *Dresses and* *Coats*							
U.S.	4	6	8	10	12	14	16
U.K./Ireland	6	8	10	12	14	16	18

Blouses and *Sweaters*							
U.S.	30	32	34	36	38	40	42
U.K./Ireland	32	34	36	38	40	42	44

Shoes							
U.S.	4	5	6	7	8	9	10
U.K./Ireland	2	3	4	5	6	7	8

6 The Arts and Nightlife

The Arts

To find out what's on, check the extensive listings in the weekly magazine *Time Out*, which also prints reviews, or pick up the free fortnightly *London Theatre Guide* from cinemas and theaters, bookshops, cafés, and so forth. The *Evening Standard* also carries listings, especially the Friday edition, as do the "quality" Sunday papers and the Friday and Saturday *Independent*, *Guardian*, and *Times*. You'll find a rack overflowing with leaflets and flyers in most cinema and theater foyers, too.

Theater Although the price of a seat rarely falls below a tenner, London's West End theaters still pull in enough custom to cause a mini traffic jam each night before the house lights dim and the curtain rises. From Shakespeare to the umpteenth year of *Les Misérables* (or *The Glums*, as it's affectionately known), the West End has what visitors think of as London's theater. But there's more to see in London than the offerings of the Charing Cross Road Theaterland and the national companies.

Of the 100 or so legitimate theaters in the capital, only about 30 are "West End," while the remainder go under the blanket title of "Fringe." Much like New York's Off- and Off-Off-Broadway, Fringe Theater encompasses everything from off-the-wall "physical theater" pieces to first runs of new plays and revivals of old ones. Recently, for instance, you could catch an evening of one-act Chekhov comedies; a Sunday morning musical "Brechtfest" (breakfast and newspaper included); productions of Pinter, Zola, and Kundera; a Rodgers and Hammerstein musical adaptation of a Steinbeck story; a dramatization of *The Motown Story;* an Irish storyteller and balladeer; any amount of improvisations; and several Shakespeare productions. And that's merely scratching the surface. Fringe is undoubtedly the best way to "do" London theater on a budget, without missing out on the happening shows.

Theaters and Concert Halls

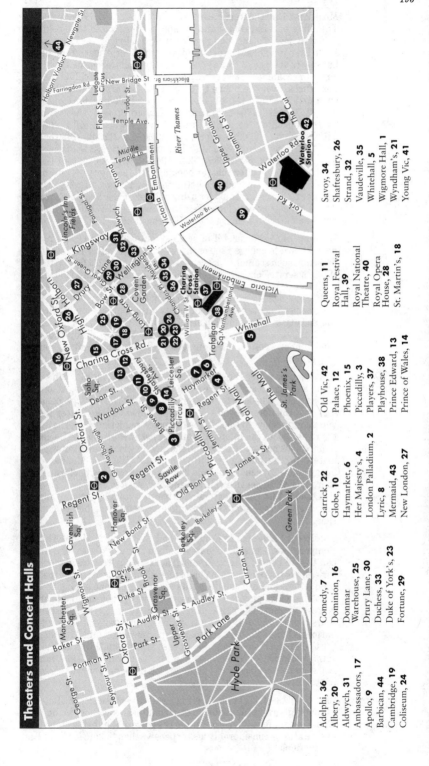

Adelphi, **36**
Albery, **20**
Aldwych, **31**
Ambassadors, **17**
Apollo, **9**
Barbican, **44**
Cambridge, **19**
Coliseum, **24**

Comedy, **7**
Dominion, **16**
Donmar Warehouse, **25**
Drury Lane, **30**
Duchess, **33**
Duke of York's, **23**
Fortune, **29**

Garrick, **22**
Globe, **10**
Haymarket, **6**
Her Majesty's, **4**
London Palladium, **2**
Lyric, **8**
Mermaid, **43**
New London, **27**

Old Vic, **42**
Palace, **12**
Phoenix, **15**
Piccadilly, **3**
Players, **37**
Playhouse, **38**
Prince Edward, **13**
Prince of Wales, **14**

Queens, **11**
Royal Festival Hall, **39**
Royal National Theatre, **40**
Royal Opera House, **28**
St. Martin's, **18**

Savoy, **34**
Shaftesbury, **26**
Strand, **32**
Vaudeville, **35**
Whitehall, **5**
Wigmore Hall, **1**
Wyndham's, **21**
Young Vic, **41**

Most West End theaters have matinees twice a week (Wednesday or Thursday and Saturday) and evening performances that begin at 7:30 or 8; performances on Sunday are rare. Prices vary, but in the West End you should expect to pay from £6 for a seat in the upper balcony to at least £20 for a good one in the stalls (orchestra) or dress circle (mezzanine). Tickets may be booked at the individual theater box offices, over the phone by credit card, or through ticket agents such as **First Call** (tel. 0171/240–7941) or **Ticketmaster** (tel. 0171/413–3321 or 800/775–2525 from the United States); these usually charge a booking fee. **Keith Prowse** has a New York office (234 W. 44th St., Suite 1000, New York, NY 10036, tel. 212/398–1430 or 800/669–8687), as does **Edwards & Edwards** (1 Times Sq. Plaza, 12th Floor, New York, NY 10036, tel. 212/944–0290 or 800/223–6108). All the larger hotels offer theater bookings, but as they tack on a hefty service charge, you would do better visiting the box offices yourself. You might, however, consider using one particular booking line that doubles the price of tickets: **West End Cares** (tel. 0171/976–8100) donates half of what it charges to AIDS charities.

Warning: Be *very* careful of scalpers outside theaters; they have been known to charge £200 or more for a sought-after ticket. If you buy from such scalpers, you could easily end up with a forged ticket. While a service charge is legitimate, scalping certainly isn't, especially since the vast majority of theaters have some tickets (returns and "house seats") available on the night of performance. If you have a bad experience with a scalper, contact the Development Officer at the Society of West End Theatres (Bedford Chambers, The Piazza, Covent Garden, WC2E 8HQ, tel. 0171/836–3193). They probably can't get you a refund, but your letter will help stamp out scalpers in the future.

Discount Sometimes matinees are cheaper, and if you are what's known in En-
Tickets gland as a "concession," there are usually reduced rates, as long as you have ID. These rates are for students, OAPs (old age pensioners), and the unemployed—sometimes called "UB40s" after the ID you need to show to qualify for the price reduction. Alternatively, the ticket booth (no telephone) on the southwest corner of Leicester Square sells **half-price tickets** on the day of performance for approximately 45 theaters (subject to availability). It's open Monday–Saturday noon–2 for matinees and 2:30–6:30 for evening performances; there is a £1.50 service charge, and only cash is accepted. In addition, most West End theaters offer bargain standby seats to anyone prepared to line up at the box office an hour or so before curtain time.

West End The **Royal Shakespeare Company** and the **Royal National Theatre Company** perform at London's two main arts complexes, the **Barbican Centre** (Tube: Barbican) and **The National Theatre** (Tube: Waterloo), respectively. Both companies mount consistently excellent productions and are usually a safe option for anyone having trouble choosing which play to see. There is standing room available at the largest National Theatre auditorium, the Olivier, as well as standby seats for nonsellouts. The Lyttleton's Wednesday matinees are the bargain shows, while at the more experimental studio theater, the Cottesloe, restricted-view seats cost about two-thirds of the full rate. Both RSC theaters at the Barbican offer £7 last-minute standbys, which carry the obvious risk of being unavailable when it's too late to go see something else.

Fringe Shows can be straight plays, circus, comedy, musicals, readings, or productions every bit as polished and impressive as those in the West End—except for their location and the price of the seat. Fringe tickets are always considerably less expensive than tickets for West End productions.

Concerts The ticket prices to symphony-size orchestral concerts are fortu-
nately still relatively moderate, usually ranging from £5 to £15. If
you can't book in advance, then arrive at the hall an hour before the
performance for a chance at returns.

The London Symphony Orchestra is in residence at the **Barbican
Arts Centre** although other top orchestras—including the Philhar-
monia and the Royal Philharmonic—also perform here. The **South
Bank Arts Complex,** which includes the **Royal Festival Hall,** the
Queen Elizabeth Hall, and the small **Purcell Room**, forms another
major venue; the Royal Festival Hall is one of the finest concert halls
in Europe. Between the Barbican and South Bank, there are concert
performances almost every night of the year. The Barbican also features chamber music concerts, with such celebrated orchestras as
the City of London Sinfonia.

For a different concert-going experience, as well as the chance to
take part in a great British tradition, try the **Royal Albert Hall** during the Promenade Concert season: eight weeks lasting from July to
September. Special "promenade" (standing) tickets usually cost half
the price of normal tickets and are available at the hall on the night
of the concert. Another summer pleasure is the outdoor concert series by the lake at **Kenwood** (Hampstead Heath; tel. 0181/348–6684).
Concerts are also part of the program at the open-air theater in **Holland Park** (no phone). Check the listings for details.

You should also look for the lunchtime concerts that take place all
over the city in smaller concert halls, the big arts center foyers, and
churches; they usually cost under £5 or are free and will feature
string quartets, singers, jazz ensembles, or gospel choirs. **St.
John's, Smith Square** and **St. Martin-in-the-Fields** are two of the
more popular locations. Performances usually begin about 1 PM and
last an hour.

Concert Hall **Barbican Arts Centre,** Barbican, EC2Y 8DS, tel. 0171/638–8891
Box Office (reservations); 0171/628–2295 (information)
Information **Royal Albert Hall,** Kensington Gore, SW7 2AP, tel. 0171/589–8212
St. John's, Smith Sq., SW1P 3HA, tel. 0171/222–1061
St. Martin-in-the-Fields, Trafalgar Sq., WC2N 4JJ, tel. 0171/839–
8362
South Bank Arts Complex, South Bank, SE1 8XX, tel. 0171/928–
2252
Wigmore Hall, 36 Wigmore St., W1H 9DF, tel. 0171/935–2141

Opera The main venue for opera in London is the **Royal Opera House** (Covent Garden), which ranks in importance with the Metropolitan Opera House in New York. Prices range from about £5 in the upper
slips ("the gods") to way over £100 for the best seat. The least expensive way to see (we use the verb loosely) a production here is to get in
line at 10 AM for the 65 rear amphitheatre seats that the house keeps
back. New productions, big-name singers, and crowd pleasers attract
enormous lines for these cheap seats. You can phone the box office first
to get some idea of your chances.

English-language productions are staged at the **Coliseum** in St. Martin's Lane, home of the English National Opera Company. Prices
here are generally lower than at the Royal Opera House, ranging
from around £8 to £48, and productions are often innovative and exciting. There are several ways to save on a seat. Concessions (*see*
Theater, *above*) qualify for standby seats at around £15 three hours
before curtain, but must buy in person and are limited to one ticket.
Saturdays there are a few excellent seats (stalls and dress circle) at
£28, and for weekday performances (except first nights) there are
special seats available from 10 AM the same day at £25.

Ballet The Royal Opera House is also the home of the world-famous **Royal
Ballet.** Prices are slightly more reasonable for the ballet than they

are for the opera, but bookings should be made well in advance, as tickets sell out fast. Standing room tickets on sellout nights cost around £2, starting at 6:30 PM, and there are also 65 rear amphitheatre seats at £11.50—one per person, obtainable only in person—on sale from 10:30 AM. The **English National Ballet** and visiting international companies perform at the Coliseum and the Royal Festival Hall from time to time. The **London City Ballet** is based at **Sadler's Wells Theatre,** which also hosts various other ballet companies and regional and international modern dance troupes. Prices here are much cheaper than at Covent Garden, at around £5–£20.

Opera and **Coliseum,** St. Martin's La., WC2N 4ES, tel. 0171/632–8300
Ballet **Royal Opera House,** Covent Garden, WC2E 9DD, tel. 0171/304–
Box Office 4000
Information **Sadler's Wells,** Rosebery Ave., EC1R 4TN, tel. 0171/713–6000

Dance Contemporary dance thrives in London, with innovative young choreographers and companies constantly emerging (and then, it often seems, moving to New York). Michael Clark was one of the first of the new wave; Yolanda Snaith and choreographer Lea Anderson's troupe, the Cholmondeleys (pronounced "Chumleys"), are a few more examples of home-grown talent. In addition to the many Fringe theaters that mount the odd dance performance, the following theaters showcase contemporary dance:

The Place, 17 Duke's Rd., WC1, tel. 0171/387–0031
Riverside Studios, Crisp Rd., W6, tel. 0181/741–2255
Sadler's Wells (*see* Opera and Ballet, *above*)

Movies Despite the video invasion, West End movies continue to do good business. Most of the major houses (Odeon, MGM, etc.) are congregated in the Leicester Square/Piccadilly Circus area, where tickets cost £6–£9. Mondays and matinees are sometimes better buys at around £4, and there are also fewer crowds. Prices drop to around £5 as you get out of the West End, and are even lower in the suburbs, but unless you're staying there, any savings could be eaten up by transportation costs.

Movie clubs and repertory cinemas screen a wider range of movies, including classics, Continental, and underground, as well as rare or underestimated masterpieces. Some charge a membership fee of under £1. One of the best is the **National Film Theatre** (in the South Bank Arts Complex; tel. 0171/928–3232), where the London Film Festival is based in the fall; there are also lectures and presentations. Daily memberships cost 40p. Other notable rep cinemas include the **Everyman** (Hollybush Vale, Hampstead, tel. 0171/435–1525; membership 60p/year) and the **Riverside** (*see* Fringe Theater, *above*).

The **Institute of Contemporary Arts** (the Mall, tel. 0171/930–3647) contains two cinemas (one is tiny). The **French Institute** (17 Queensbury Pl., SW7, tel. 0171/589–6211) and **Goethe Institute** (Princes Gate, SW7, tel. 0171/581–3344) show French and German films, respectively, usually free of charge. Films are also shown irregularly at many of the national museums; normally there is no charge for these showings, either.

Nightlife

You can have fun on a budget in London after dark, but it isn't easy. You can thank the ancient licensing laws: They prohibit the sale of alcohol after 11 PM, except where a special license has been awarded. In practice this means that most places with an after-hours license make you pay for the privilege of drinking, even if you don't want to drink, and there's a cover charge almost everywhere. Another problem is getting around, since tubes stop running around midnight. Night buses are the young Londoner's method of transportation, and Trafalgar Square, through which they nearly all pass, often resembles a nightclub extension at 2 AM on a weekend. (Make sure to pick up bus maps if you want to avoid paying cab fare.) *Time Out* is the best source of up-to-date information about the fast-changing club scene. At press time, for instance, free early-evening Latin dance lessons had become a trend—you could pick up the moves to use later on the dance floor. Midweek clubs are always a few pounds cheaper than on the weekends.

Bars   **The Atlantic.** This vast, glamorous, wood-floored basement caused a revolution when, in early 1994, it became the first central London bar to be granted a late, late alcohol license. It's had its day as *the* place to be seen, but the table service and the intimate Dick's Bar—an art deco cocktail lounge—are still great. *20 Glasshouse St., W1, tel. 0171/734–4888. Open Mon.–Sat. noon–3 AM, Sun. noon–11 PM. Tube: Piccadilly Circus.*

Beach Blanket Babylon. In Notting Hill, close to Portobello market, this always packed singles bar is distinguishable by its fanciful decor—like a fairy-tale grotto or a medieval dungeon visited by the gargoyles of Notre Dame. *45 Ledbury Rd., W11, tel. 0171/229–2907. Open noon–11 PM daily. Tube: Notting Hill Gate.*

Cabaret   **Comedy Café.** Talent nights, jazz, and video karaoke, but mostly stand-up comedy, take place at this popular dive in the City. Admission charges are occasionally waived. There's food available in the evenings and usually a late license (for alcohol). *66 Rivington St., EC2, tel. 0171/256–1242. Admission free–£7. Open Wed., Thurs. 7:30 PM–1 AM, Fri.–Sat. 7:30 PM–2 AM. MC, V. Tube: Old Street.*

Comedy Store. This is the improv factory where the United Kingdom's funniest stand-ups cut their teeth, now relocated to a bigger and better place. The name performers and new talent you'll see may be strangers to you, but you're guaranteed to laugh. *Haymarket House, Oxendon St., SW1, tel. 0171/344–4444 or 01426/914433 for information. Admission: £8–£9. Shows Tues.–Thurs., Sun. at 8, Fri.–Sat. at 8 and midnight. Tube: Piccadilly Circus.*

Jazz   **100 Club.** The best for blues, trad, and Dixie, plus the occasional straight rock-and-roll, this Oxford Street subterranean has the correct paint-peeling, smoke-choked, dance-inducing atmosphere. There's a food counter most nights. *100 Oxford St., W1, tel. 0171/636–0933. Admission: £4–£10, depending on the night. Open Mon., Wed. 7:30–midnight, Thurs.–Sat. 8:30 PM–1 AM, Sun. 7:30–11:30. No credit cards. Tube: Oxford Circus.*

Jazz Cafe. This palace of high-tech cool in a converted bank in bohemian Camden has its problems—you often have to stand in line, and there never seems to be enough seating—but still it remains an essential hangout for fans of the mainstream end of the repertoire. Varied line-ups of international musicians, free Saturday lunchtime jazz, and good food make the (easy) journey north worthwhile. *5–7 Pkwy., NW1, tel. 0171/916–6000. Admission: £7–£12, depending on the band. Open Mon.–Sat. 7 PM–late (time varies). Reservations advised for balcony restaurant. AE, DC, MC, V. Tube: Camden Town.*

Pizza Express. It may seem strange, since Pizza Express is the capital's best-loved (small) chain of pizza houses, but this is one of London's principal jazz venues, with music every night except Monday in the basement restaurant. The underground interior is darkly lit, the line-ups (often featuring visiting U.S. performers) are interesting, and the Italian-style thin-crust pizzas are great! *10 Dean St., W1, tel. 0171/437–9595. Admission: £6–£9, depending on band. Open from noon for food; music from 9:30 PM to 1 AM Tues.–Sun. Reservations advised; essential some nights. AE, DC, MC, V. Tube: Leicester Square.*

Ronnie Scott's. The legendary Soho jazz club, since its opening in the early '60s, has been attracting all the big names. It's usually packed and hot, the food isn't great, service is slow—because the staff can't move through the crowds, either—but the atmosphere can't be beat, and it's probably still London's best, although, at these prices, you'll want to be sure you like the performer. Musicians Union members qualify for a reduced rate. *47 Frith St., W1, tel. 0171/439–0747. Admission £10–£12 non-members. Open Mon.–Sat. 8:30 PM–3 AM, Sun. 8 PM–11:30 PM. Reservations advised; essential some nights. AE, DC, MC, V. Tube: Leicester Square.*

South Bank. A certain kind of really big name (Carla Bley, Jan Garbarek, Richard Thompson) end up here, the Royal Festival Hall, or the Queen Elizabeth Hall. What you lose in atmosphere, you gain in accoustical clarity. *Waterloo, tel. 0171/928–8800. Admission: £7.50–£15. Jazz concerts usually start 7:30 PM; call for this week's events. Reservations essential. AE, MC, V. Tube: Waterloo.*

The Vortex. In the wilds of Stoke Newington, a very happening, liberal-arts neighborhood, with tons of Asian vegetarian-type restaurants, is this showcase venue for the healthy British jazz scene, with an emphasis on advanced, free, and improvised work. *Stoke Newington Church St., N16, tel. 0171/254–6516. Admission £4–£6. Open most nights 8 PM–11 PM. (No tube).*

Nightclubs **Café de Paris.** This former gilt and red velveteen ballroom still looks like a disreputable tea-dance hall but hosts fun nights for 20- to 30-somethings who dress the part. At press time, Wednesdays were for a slightly older crowd; Fridays were called **Sex.** But ring for current details. *3 Coventry St., W1, tel. 0171/287–3602. Admission: £5–£12. Open. Wed. 10 PM–4 AM, Thurs.–Sat. 11 PM–6 AM. No credit cards. Tube: Piccadilly Circus.*

Camden Palace. This is the student tourist's first stop, though some nights are hipper than others. Still, it would be difficult to find a facial wrinkle, even if you could see through the laser lights and find your way around the three floors of bars. There's often a live band. *1A Camden High St., NW1, tel. 0171/387–0428. Admission: £3–£9. Open Tues.–Sat. 9 PM–3 AM. Tube: Mornington Crescent.*

Heaven. London's premier (mainly) gay club is the best place for dancing wildly for hours. A state-of-the-art laser show and a large, throbbing dance floor complement a labyrinth of quieter bars and lounges and a snack bar. *Under the Arches, Craven St., WC2, tel. 0171/839–3852. Admission: £4–£8 depending on the night. Call for opening times (approx. 10 PM–3 AM). MC, V. Tube: Charing Cross.*

The Limelight. Home away from home for most Americans. It is owned by New York Limelighter Peter Gatien and situated, like its New York counterpart, in an old church. One of London's most popular nightspots, it offers lots of one-nighter shows and special events. *136 Shaftesbury Ave., WC2, tel. 0171/434–0572. Admission: weekdays £7, Sat. £10. Open Mon.–Sat. 9:30 PM–3 AM. Tube: Leicester Square.*

Palookaville. Conveniently close to Covent Garden tube, this basement restaurant/bar charges a cover only on Friday and Saturday. It's popular with office people for after-hours drinks. You won't write home about the food or the undemanding music—usually there's a jazz trio or similar live band—but you might about the friendly, mellow ambience. *13A James St., WC2, tel. 0171/240–5857. Admission: £2 Mon.–Wed., £3 Thurs., £4 Fri. and Sat. Open Mon.–Wed. 5:30 PM–12:30 AM, Thurs.–Sat. 5:30 PM–1:30 AM. MC, V. Tube: Covent Garden.*

The Wag. This tenacious representative of Soho's club circuit takes on a different character according to which night it is and which DJ is spinning. One extremely loud, sweaty floor houses bars and dance spaces, and a quieter, cooler one, a restaurant serving dinner and breakfast. *33–35 Wardour St., W1, tel. 0171/437–5534. Admission: £4–£9, depending on the night. Open Mon.–Thurs. 10:30 PM–3 AM, Fri. and Sat. 10:30 PM–6 AM. No credit cards. Tube: Leicester Square.*

Rock **The Astoria.** Very central and quite hip, this place hosts bands that there's a buzz about and has late club nights. *157 Charing Cross Rd., W1, tel. 0171/434–0403. Admission around £8–£12. Check listings for opening times. Tube: Tottenham Court Road.*

The Forum. This ex-ballroom with balcony and dance floor packs them in and attracts the best medium-to-big-name performers, too. *9–17 Highgate Rd., NW5, tel. 0171/284–0303. Admission: around £8–£12. Open most nights 7–11. Tube: Kentish Town.*

The Roadhouse. True to its name, this cavernous place beneath the Jubilee Market pays homage to the American dream of the open road, with a Harley behind the bar and much memorabilia. The music fits the feel-good, tuneful, middle-of-the-road end of the R&B/blues/rock/soul spectrum. Great fajitas. *Jubilee Hall, Covent Garden, WC2, tel. 0171/240–6001. Admission: £3–£6. Open Mon.– Thurs. 5:30 PM–1 AM; Fri., Sat. 5:30 PM–2 AM. AE, MC, V. Tube: Covent Garden.*

Shepherd's Bush Empire. London's newest major venue was converted from the BBC TV theater, where Terry Wogan, England's Johnny Carson, recorded his show for years and years. Now it hosts the same kind of medium–big names as the north London Forum. *Shepherd's Bush Green, W12, tel. 0181/740–7474. Admission: £8– £12. Open 7:30–11. AE, MC, V. Tube: Goldhawk Road.*

Subterania. Home of Notting Hillbillies everywhere—that is, the hip and cool bohemians of the neighborhood—this large, medium-tech balconied club never welcomes mainstream bands but books the top musicians in any alternative genre from all over the world. *12 Acklam Rd., W10, tel. 0181/960–4590. Admission: £6–£8. Call for hours; bands play Tues.–Thurs. MC, V. Tube: Ladbroke Grove.*

Weekly events are listed in *Time Out* or in one of the rock magazines, such as *New Musical Express, Melody Maker,* or *Sounds,* available every Thursday.

7 Excursions from London

Sometimes you've just got to get out of the Old Smoke, and just because you're only here for two weeks doesn't mean you, too, won't feel the urge to see trees and sky and stately homes. Follow any of these itineraries, and you'll feel like you've added another week of vacation, such is the change of pace you'll experience. England is so much more than its capital—a fact that Londoners tend to forget.

All five of these places are comfortably—and inexpensively—within range of London and are best reached by train, though a bus is a viable alternative if you choose to go to Cambridge and Windsor. Be sure to call ahead for times.

Bath

Getting There By **train** from Paddington station to Bath Spa: journey time 1 hour 20 minutes; trains about once an hour. By **National Express coach** (tel. 0171/730–0202) from Victoria Coach Station: journey time 3 hours; coaches about every 2 hours.

Tourist Information **Bath Tourist Information Centre** is on Bath Street in the Colonnades (tel. 01225/462–831).

Exploring It is impossible to convey the heartbreaking beauty of Bath, an unsullied Georgian city, which looks for all the world as if its chief architect, John Wood; its principal dandy, "Beau" Nash; and the beloved author who enshrined it in her novels, Jane Austen, might still be walking there. Just as in Venice, stepping out of the train station brings you right to the center, and Bath is compact enough to explore easily on foot. A single day is sufficient for you to look your fill on the glorious yellow stone buildings, tour the Roman baths, and stop for tea, though it will give you only a brief taste of the thriving cultural life that still goes on in this vibrant place.

Follow signs from the train station to the **Pump Room and Roman Baths.** The Romans settled here in AD 43, which was when they built this temple to Minerva, goddess of wisdom. However, legend has it that the first taker of the sacred waters in their baths was King Lear's leprous father, Prince Bladud, in the 9th century BC (he was cured). The waters continue to gush and can still be taken. Below the gorgeous and recently restored 18th-century Pump Room (take a look at *Mansfield Park, Emma, Northhanger Abbey* et al.) is a museum of objects found during excavations. *Abbey Churchyard, tel. 01225/461–111. Admission: £5 adults, £3 children. Open Mon.–Sat. 9:30–5, Sun. 10:30–5.*

Next door is **Bath Abbey,** commissioned by God. Really. The current design came like a vision to a bishop in a dream and was built by the Vertue brothers in the 16th century, although there's been an abbey on this site since the 8th century. In the **Heritage Vaults** is a museum of archeological finds, including the remains of an 800-year-old woman, and a model of 13th-century Bath. Look up at the fan-vaulted ceilings in the nave and the carved angels on the newly restored West Front. *Tel. 01225/446–300, Heritage Vaults, tel. 01225/422–462. Admission free. Open Mon.–Sat. 10–4.*

Head north up Union Passage to Milsom and Gay streets. The entire route is thrillingly aesthetic, but the best part is at the top (and Bath is built on a hill, so take that literally). Gay Street leads up into a perfectly circular ring of Bath stone houses, known as **The Circus,** designed by John Wood, and completed after his death by his son. It serves as an appetizer for the breathtaking experience that awaits west of here, off Brock Street. **Royal Crescent** is the most famous sight in Bath, and you can't help but see why. Designed by John Wood the younger, it is perfectly proportioned and beautifully sited, with a sweeping view over parkland. **Number 1 Royal Crescent** is reconstructed inside exactly as Beau Nash would have had it circa 1765. *Tel. 01225/428–126. Admission: £3 adults, £2.50 senior citizens and children. Open Mar. 2–Oct., daily 10:30–5; Nov.–Dec. 11, daily 10:30–4. Closed Dec. 12–Mar. 1, Good Friday.*

On the east side of The Circus are more thrills for Austen readers, the much-mentioned **Assembly Rooms,** which now contain the self-explanatory **Museum of Costume.** *Bennett St., tel. 01225/461–111. Open Apr.–Sept., Mon.–Sat. 9:30–6, Sun. 10–6; Oct.–Mar., Mon.–Sat. 10–5, Sun. 11–5.*

Wandering around up here, exploring the many nooks and crannies, the surprising secret passageways and cobbled streetlets, could easily consume the rest of your day, but head down the hill back toward the River Avon, to the great Georgian architect Robert Adam's sole contribution to Bath, **Pulteney Bridge.** There is only one other bridge in the world with shops lining either side: the Ponte Vecchio in Florence. This is, in its way, as fine.

Dining **Pierre Victoire** (Pulteney Bridge, tel. 01225/334–334; closed Sun.) is a French chain that offers an amazing bargain £5-for-three-courses lunch, with a fabulous view of the weir. **Sally Lunn's** (North Parade Passage, tel. 01225/461–634) is a tourist trap that locals love, specializing in the Sally Lunn—a sweet bread, a foot in diameter, dripping with cinnamon butter or preserves.

Cambridge

Getting There By **train** from Liverpool Street station: journey time 1 hour; trains hourly. By **National Express coach** (tel. 0171/730–0202) from Victoria Coach Station: journey time 1 hour 50 minutes; coaches hourly.

Tourist Information **Cambridge Tourist Information Centre** is in Wheeler Street, an extension of Benet Street, off King's Parade, tel. 0223/322–640.

Exploring Cambridge is one of the most beautiful cities in Britain, and the celebrated Cambridge University sits right at its heart. Students have been coming to Cambridge since the end of the 13th century, and even in a short visit you will see fine buildings from virtually every generation since then, often designed by the most distinguished architects of their day. The city center is lively and compact—one of the special pleasures of Cambridge is that in just a few yards one can pass from the bustle of the shopping streets to the cloistered seclusion of one of the colleges.

As at Oxford, the university is based on colleges, each of which is an autonomous institution with its own distinct character and traditions. Students join an individual college and receive their education from the dons attached to it, who are known as "fellows." Each college is built around a series of "courts," or quadrangles. Since students and fellows live in these courts, access is often restricted (especially during examination weeks in early summer). Visitors are not normally allowed into college buildings other than chapels and halls (dining rooms).

King's College is possibly the best known of all the colleges. Its chapel is a masterpiece of late Gothic architecture (1446), with a great fan-vaulted roof supported only by a tracery of soaring side columns. Behind the altar hangs Rubens's painting *The Adoration of the Magi*. Every Christmas Eve the college choir sings the Festival of Nine Lessons and Carols, which is broadcast all over the world.

Behind King's are the famous "Backs," the gardens that run down to the River Cam, onto which many of the colleges back. From King's, make your way along the river and through the narrow lanes past **Clare College** and **Trinity Hall** to **Trinity**, the largest college, straddling the river. It has a handsome 17th-century Great Court and a library by Christopher Wren. The massive gatehouse houses "Great Tom," a large clock that strikes each hour with high and low notes. Prince Charles was an undergraduate here in the late 1960s. Beyond Trinity lies **St. John's**, the second largest college.

Going in the other direction along the Backs from King's, you come to **Queen's College**, where Isaac Newton's **Mathematical Bridge** crosses the river. This arched wooden structure was originally held together by gravitational force; when they took it apart to see how Newton did it, they could not reconstruct it without using nails. In from the river, on Trumpington Street, stands **Pembroke College**, with some 14th-century buildings and a chapel by Wren, and **Peterhouse,** the oldest college. Beyond this is the **Fitzwilliam Museum,** which contains outstanding collections of art (including paintings by Constable) and antiquities (especially from ancient Egypt). *Trumpington St., tel. 0223/332–900. Admission free. Open Tues.– Fri., Lower galleries 10–2, Upper galleries 2–5, Sat. both galleries 10–5, Sun. both galleries 2:15–5; closed Good Friday and Christmas–Jan. 1.*

If you've time, hire a punt at **Silver Street Bridge** or at **Mill Lane.** You can go along the Backs past St. John's or upstream to **Grantchester,** the pretty village made famous by the poet Rupert Brooke. On a sunny day, there's no better way of absorbing Cambridge's unique atmosphere—somehow you will seem to have all the time in the world.

Dining **Browns** (23 Trumpington St., tel. 0223/461–655), opposite the Fitzwilliam Museum, has a menu featuring burgers and cocktails, huge salads, and daily specials, though many come for the desserts alone. It's popular, big, and bright, and the check comes in under £15. The crêperie known as **Hobb's Pavillion** (Parker's Piece, Park Terrace, tel. 0223/67480)—it's in a former cricket pavillion—serves thin pancakes with fat fillings for under £10.

Oxford

Getting There By **train** from Paddington station: journey time 1 hour; trains run hourly. By **coach** from Victoria Coach Station (several companies operate services): journey time 1 hour 40 minutes; buses every 20 minutes.

Tourist Information **Oxford Information Centre** is in St. Aldate's, opposite the Town Hall, tel. 0865/726–871.

Exploring Oxford is a place for strollers. The surest way of absorbing its unique blend of history and scholarliness is to wander around the tiny alleyways that link the honey-color stone buildings topped by "dreaming" spires, exploring the colleges where the undergraduates live and work. Like Cambridge, Oxford University is not a single body but a collection of 35 independent colleges; most are open to visitors, including many magnificent chapels and dining halls, though the times, displayed at the entrance lodges, vary. **Magdalen** (pronounced "Maudlin") **College** is one of the most impressive, with 500-year-old cloisters and lawns leading down to the River Cherwell. **St. Edmund Hall** has one of the smallest and most picturesque quadrangles, with an old well in the center. **Christ Church** has the largest, known as Tom Quad; portraits of former pupils, including John Wesley, William Penn, and no less than 14 prime ministers, hang in the impressive dining hall. The doors between the inner and outer quadrangles of **Balliol College** still bear the scorch marks from the flames that burned Archbishop Cranmer and Bishops Latimer and Ridley at the stake in 1555 for their Protestant beliefs.

The **Oxford Story** is a multimedia presentation of the university's 800-year history, in which visitors travel through depictions of college life. *Broad St., tel. 0865/728–822. Admission: £4.25 adults, £3.65 senior citizens and students, £2.95 children. Open Apr.–June, Sept., and Oct., daily 9:30–5; Jul. and Aug., daily 9:30–7; Nov.–Mar., daily 10–4.*

Two other places not to be missed are the **Sheldonian Theatre** and the **Ashmolean Museum.** The Sheldonian was Christopher Wren's first building, which he designed like a semicircular Roman amphitheater; graduation ceremonies are held here. The Ashmolean, Britain's oldest public museum, holds priceless collections of Egyptian, Greek, and Roman artifacts; Michelangelo drawings; and European silverware. *Sheldonian Theatre, Broad St., tel. 0865/277–299. Small admission charge. Open Mon.–Sat. 10–12:45, 2–4:45; closes at 3:45 Dec.–Feb. Ashmolean, Beaumont St., tel. 0865/278–000. Admission free. Open Tues.–Sat. 10–4, Sun. 2–4; closed Mon. and Jan. 1.*

For a relaxing walk, make for the banks of the Cherwell, either through the University Parks area or through Magdalen College to Addison's Walk, and watch the undergraduates idly punting a summer's afternoon away. Or hire a punt yourself—but be prepared, it's more difficult than it looks!

Dining Related to the Cambridge version, **Browns** (5–9 Woodstock Rd., tel. 0865/511–995) serves similar informal food (steak and Guiness pie, warm chicken salad) to students and tourists in a light palm-filled space. Ignore the name, and **Munchy Munchy** (6 Park End St., tel. 0865/245–710) becomes a great Oxford find for fresh Malaysian/Indonesian dishes that change daily.

Stratford-upon-Avon

Getting There The **train service** from Paddington Station (tel. 0171/262–6767 for times) is poor and involves at least one change, at Leamington Spa. There is one semifast train each morning, journey time is 2 hours 20 minutes, and there are no plans to improve matters. By **National Express coach** (tel. 0171/730–0202) from Victoria Coach Station: journey time 2 hours 20 minutes; coaches about every 2 hours.

Tourist Information
Stratford Tourist Information Centre is in Judith Shakespeare's House, on the corner of High and Bridge streets, tel. 0789/293–127.

Exploring
It goes without saying that Stratford is a must for Shakespeare enthusiasts. But even without its most famous son, the town would be worth visiting. Its timbered buildings show how prosperous it was during the 16th century, when it was a thriving craft and trading center. There are also attractive 18th-century buildings.

There are four main Shakespearean places of interest. The **Shakespeare Centre** and **Shakespeare's Birthplace** on Henley Street contain the costumes used in the BBC's dramatization of the plays and an exhibition of the Bard's life and work. **Anne Hathaway's Cottage** is the early home of the playwright's wife, in Shottery, on the edge of town; and in **Holy Trinity Church** Shakespeare, his wife, and several of their family are buried. *Shakespeare's Birthplace, Henry St., tel. 0789/204–016. Combined admission for all 4 Shakespeare Birthplace Trust properties: £7.50 adults, £3.25 children, or individual tickets £1.70–£3 adults, 70p–£1.20 children. Open Mar.–Oct., Mon.–Sat. 9–5:30, Sun. 10–5:30; Nov.–Feb., Mon.–Sat. 9:30–4, Sun. 10:30–4; closed Dec. 24–26.*

Two very different attractions reveal something of the times in which Shakespeare lived. *World of Shakespeare* is a lavish spectacle using modern multimedia techniques to describe Queen Elizabeth's royal progress from London to Kenilworth Castle in 1575. A complete contrast is **Hall's Croft**, a fine Tudor town house that was the home of Shakespeare's daughter Susanna and her doctor husband. It has contemporary furniture, and the doctor's dispensary and consulting room can also be seen. *World of Shakespeare, 13 Waterside, tel. 0789/269–190. Admission: £3 adults, £2 students, children, and senior citizens. Open daily 9:30–5; closed Dec. 25. Hall's Croft, Old Town, tel. 0789/292–107. Admission: £1.70 adults, 70p children. Open Apr.–Oct., Mon.–Sat. 9–6, Sun. 10–6; Nov.–Mar., Mon.–Sat. 9–4:30.*

The **Royal Shakespeare Theatre** (Stratford-upon-Avon, CV37 6BB, tel. 0789/295–623) occupies a perfect position on the banks of the Avon. Try to take in a performance if you can. The company (always referred to as the RSC) gives five Shakespeare plays each season, between March and January. Apart from its main auditorium, the RSC has an exciting small theater, the **Swan,** based on the original Elizabethan Globe. Its construction was funded by an anglophile American millionaire, Frederick Koch. It's best to book well in advance, but day-of-performance tickets are always available, and it is also worth asking if there are any returns. Programs are available in February from the Royal Shakespeare Theatre.

Dining
You get enormous portions from the counter at the **Vintner Wine Bar** (5 Sheep St., tel. 0789/297–259), conveniently near the theater. Big salads and good wines for under a tenner fill the place most nights. In the theater itself, the **River Terrace** (tel. 0789/293–226) offers good-value food like lasagna and shepherds pie, plus sandwiches and cakes, all for less than £10.

Windsor

Getting There
By **train** either from Waterloo direct to Windsor and Eton Riverside or from Paddington Station to Windsor Central, changing at Slough. Journey time 30 to 40 minutes from Paddington, 45 minutes from Waterloo Station; 2 trains per hour on each route. By **Green Line bus** from Eccleston Bridge, behind Victoria train station, *not* from Vic-

toria Coach Station. Make sure you catch the fast direct service, which takes 50 minutes and runs half-hourly; the stopping services take up to 1 hour 25 minutes.

Tourist Information The **Windsor Tourist Information Centre** is in Central Station, Thames Street, tel. 0753/852–010.

Exploring Windsor has been a royal citadel since the days of William the Conqueror, who built a timber stockade here on a mound overlooking the River Thames soon after his victory in 1066. Later kings added stone towers, but it was Edward III in the 1300s who transformed the old castle, building the Norman gateway, the great round tower, and new state apartments. Thereafter the castle gradually grew in complexity and grandeur as subsequent monarchs added new buildings or improved existing ones according to their tastes and their finances. Charles II restored the state apartments in the 1600s, and in the 1820s George IV, that most extravagant of kings with a mania for building, converted what was still essentially a medieval castle into the royal palace the visitor sees today.

Windsor remains a favorite spot of the royal family. The queen and Prince Philip spend most weekends here, often joined by family and friends. The state apartments are also used from time to time to entertain visiting heads of state. The entire castle is closed when the queen is in residence, but a large part—though not the royal family's private apartments—is open the rest of the time.

These are some of the highlights of the castle: **St. George's Chapel,** more than 230 feet long with two tiers of great windows and hundreds of gargoyles, buttresses, and pinnacles, is one of the noblest buildings in England. Inside, above the choir stalls, hang the banners, swords, and helmets of the Knights of the Order of the Garter, the senior order of chivalry. The many monarchs buried in the Chapel include Henry VIII and George VI, father of the present queen. The **State Apartments** indicate the magnificence of the queen's art collection; here hang paintings by Rubens, Van Dyck, and Holbein; drawings by da Vinci; and Gobelin tapestries, among many other treasures. There are magnificent views across to Windsor Great Park, the remains of a former royal hunting forest. Make time to view **Queen Mary's Dolls' House,** complete with electricity, running water, and miniature books on the library shelves. The dollhouse was designed by Sir Edward Lutyens, who planned New Delhi and many gardens (with the well-known gardener Gertrude Jekyll).

The terrible fire of November 1992, which started in the queen's private chapel, totally gutted some of the **State Apartments.** A swift rescue effort meant that, miraculously, hardly any works of art were lost. The repairs will take years to complete, probably until well into the next century. Admission charges have recently been standardized, with one charge now for all areas of the castle—a reform that saves the visitor about £1. *Windsor Castle, tel. 0753/868–286. Admission: £8 adults, £5.50 senior citizens, £4 children under 17. Call 0753/831–118 for opening times.*

After seeing the castle, stroll around the town enjoying the antiques shops. Opposite the castle, the **Royalty and Empire** exhibition in part of the Central Station re-creates in waxworks the arrival at the station of Queen Victoria to celebrate her Diamond Jubilee in 1897; the scene is incredibly lifelike. *Thames St., tel. 0753/857–837. Admission: £3.95 adults, £2.45 children under 16, £2.95 senior citizens. Open daily 9:30–5:30 (till 4:30 Nov.–Mar.).*

A short walk over the river brings you to **Eton,** Windsor's equally historic neighbor, and home of the famous public school. (In Britain, so-called "public" schools are private and charge tuition.) Classes still take place in the distinctive redbrick Tudor-style buildings; the oldest buildings are grouped around a quadrangle called School

Yard. The **Museum of Eton Life** has displays on the school's history, and a guided tour is also available. *Brewhouse Yard, tel. 0753/671–177. Admission: £2 adults, £1.30 children under 16. Open daily during term 2–4:30, 10:30–4:30 on school vacations. Guided tours daily at 2:15 and 3:15; charge £2.60 adults, £2 children under 16, including admission to museum.*

Dining Windsor's own branch of the **Dôme** (5 Thames St., tel. 0753/864–405) serves Paris bistro dishes (croque monsieur, cassoulet, ratatouille) just like the London ones, plus wine and coffee, and the check is less than £15. Close to the river, as well as the Castle, **The Courtyard** (8 King George V Pl., tel. 0753/858–388) is a pleasant setting for afternoon tea or a light lunch for under £10.

Index

NOTES

NOTES

NOTES

NOTES

NOTES

NOTES

NOTES

NOTES

NOTES

NOTES

NOTES

Fodor's Travel Publications

Available at bookstores everywhere, or call 1–800–533–6478, 24 hours a day.

Gold Guides

U.S.

Alaska

Arizona

Boston

California

Cape Cod, Martha's
Vineyard, Nantucket

The Carolinas & the
Georgia Coast

Chicago

Colorado

Florida

Hawaii

Las Vegas, Reno,
Tahoe

Los Angeles

Maine, Vermont,
New Hampshire

Maui

Miami & the Keys

New England

New Orleans

New York City

Pacific North Coast

Philadelphia & the
Pennsylvania Dutch
Country

The Rockies

San Diego

San Francisco

Santa Fe, Taos,
Albuquerque

Seattle & Vancouver

The South

U.S. & British Virgin
Islands

USA

Virginia & Maryland

Waikiki

Washington, D.C.

Foreign

Australia &
New Zealand

Austria

The Bahamas

Barbados

Bermuda

Brazil

Budapest

Canada

Cancún, Cozumel,
Yucatán Peninsula

Caribbean

China

Costa Rica, Belize,
Guatemala

The Czech Republic
& Slovakia

Eastern Europe

Egypt

Europe

Florence, Tuscany
& Umbria

France

Germany

Great Britain

Greece

Hong Kong

India

Ireland

Israel

Italy

Japan

Kenya & Tanzania

Korea

London

Madrid & Barcelona

Mexico

Montréal &
Québec City

Morocco

Moscow, St.
Petersburg, Kiev

The Netherlands,
Belgium &
Luxembourg

New Zealand

Norway

Nova Scotia, New
Brunswick, Prince
Edward Island

Paris

Portugal

Provence &
the Riviera

Scandinavia

Scotland

Singapore

South America

South Pacific

Southeast Asia

Spain

Sweden

Switzerland

Thailand

Tokyo

Toronto

Turkey

Vienna & the Danube

Fodor's Special-Interest Guides

Branson

Caribbean Ports
of Call

The Complete Guide
to America's
National Parks

Condé Nast Traveler
Caribbean Resort and
Cruise Ship Finder

Cruises and Ports
of Call

Fodor's London
Companion

France by Train

Halliday's New
England Food
Explorer

Healthy Escapes

Italy by Train

Kodak Guide to
Shooting Great
Travel Pictures

Shadow Traffic's
New York Shortcuts
and Traffic Tips

Sunday in New York

Sunday in
San Francisco

Walt Disney World,
Universal Studios
and Orlando

Walt Disney World
for Adults

Where Should We
Take the Kids?
California

Where Should We
Take the Kids?
Northeast

Special Series

Affordables
Caribbean
Europe
Florida
France
Germany
Great Britain
Italy
London
Paris

Fodor's Bed & Breakfasts and Country Inns
America's Best B&Bs
California's Best B&Bs
Canada's Great Country Inns
Cottages, B&Bs and Country Inns of England and Wales
The Mid-Atlantic's Best B&Bs
New England's Best B&Bs
The Pacific Northwest's Best B&Bs
The South's Best B&Bs
The Southwest's Best B&Bs
The Upper Great Lakes' Best B&Bs

The Berkeley Guides
California
Central America
Eastern Europe
Europe
France
Germany & Austria
Great Britain & Ireland
Italy
London
Mexico

Pacific Northwest & Alaska
Paris
San Francisco

Compass American Guides
Arizona
Canada
Chicago
Colorado
Hawaii
Hollywood
Las Vegas
Maine
Manhattan
Montana
New Mexico
New Orleans
Oregon
San Francisco
South Carolina
South Dakota
Texas
Utah
Virginia
Washington
Wine Country
Wisconsin
Wyoming

Fodor's Español
California
Caribe Occidental
Caribe Oriental
Gran Bretaña
Londres
Mexico
Nueva York
Paris

Fodor's Exploring Guides
Australia
Boston & New England

Britain
California
Caribbean
China
Florence & Tuscany
Florida
France
Germany
Ireland
Italy
London
Mexico
Moscow & St. Petersburg
New York City
Paris
Prague
Provence
Rome
San Francisco
Scotland
Singapore & Malaysia
Spain
Thailand
Turkey
Venice

Fodor's Flashmaps
Boston
New York
San Francisco
Washington, D.C.

Fodor's Pocket Guides
Acapulco
Atlanta
Barbados
Jamaica
London
New York City
Paris
Prague
Puerto Rico

Rome
San Francisco
Washington, D.C.

Rivages Guides
Bed and Breakfasts of Character and Charm in France
Hotels and Country Inns of Character and Charm in France
Hotels and Country Inns of Character and Charm in Italy

Short Escapes
Country Getaways in Britain
Country Getaways in France
Country Getaways Near New York City

Fodor's Sports
Golf Digest's Best Places to Play
Skiing USA
USA Today The Complete Four Sport Stadium Guide

Fodor's Vacation Planners
Great American Learning Vacations
Great American Sports & Adventure Vacations
Great American Vacations
National Parks and Seashores of the East
National Parks of the West